Warfare in the Age of
Gaius Julius Caesar

Caesar

Warfare in the Age of Gaius Julius Caesar
Volume 1
Arar & Bibracte to Uxellodunum
110 BC to 50 BC

Theodore Dodge

*Warfare in the Age of Gaius Julius Caesar—Volume 1:
Arar & Bibracte to Uxellodunum, 110 BC to 50 BC*
by Theodore Dodge

Leonaur is an imprint of Oakpast Ltd

Material original to this edition and presentation of the
text in this form copyright © 2013 Oakpast Ltd

ISBN: 978-1-78282-156-4 (hardcover)
ISBN: 978-1-78282-157-1 (softcover)

http://www.leonaur.com

Publisher's Notes

The views expressed in this book are not necessarily
those of the publisher.

Contents

Preface	7
Marius and the Army Changes	11
Sulla, Pompey	28
Caesar's Youth, Education and Early Services	40
Caesar's New Province—The Helvetii	50
The Battles of the Arar and Bibracte	66
Campaign Against Ariovistus	77
The Belgae	91
Battle of the Sabis	103
The Work of Caesar's Lieutenants	115
The Rhine	133
Britain	144
Cassivellaunus	154
Ambiorix	163
The Treviri and Eburones	178
Vercingetorix	192
Avaricum	202
The Siege of Gergovia	214
Labienus' Campaign	230
The Siege of Alesia	241
The Battle of Alesia	254
The Bellovaci	262
Uxellodunum	274
Caesar's Method	285
Caesar's Army	297

Preface

The present volume has been delayed nearly a year to enable the author to visit the theatre of Caesar's campaigns and his many battlefields. To do this is almost a prerequisite to writing intelligently on the subject. Familiarity with the topography gives a quite different understanding of the narrative of the ancient historians. Though Caesar's *Commentaries* are among the most exact and picturesque of historical writings, it is by patient study alone that they can be understood otherwise than superficially; without suitable maps they cannot be understood at all. From the days of ingenious but far-fetched Guischard and Turpin de Crissé, topographical descriptions and charts have habitually been copied by one author from another, to the lot of neither of whom it has fallen to personally inspect the terrain; and many errors have been thus propagated. The author hopes that this volume is reasonably free from such.

We owe a great debt to Napoleon III. for patronizing and defraying the expense of the systematic excavations and topographical and military studies which have culminated in his own and Colonel Stoffel's works on Caesar. To Colonel Stoffel we are peculiarly indebted for one of the most splendid military histories which exists. The present author has made free use of both these works; and though he has personally passed over all the ground covered by Caesar's campaigns, it would savour of impertinence to seek to better the results of Colonel Stoffel's long and accurate research or of the archaeological work of Napoleon. In all cases, however, the author has not been able to agree with these distinguished men; nor is the plan of this volume the one on which the other histories are based. The charts, while lacking the extreme accuracy of detail of the plates of Napoleon and Stoffel, will be found to answer every requirement, at a mere fraction of the cost of those works; and their insertion in the text will aid the average reader as large maps in a separate volume will not.

This history of Caesar follows the narrative of the *Commentaries*, and whenever practicable quotes from them, so as to retain the quaintness of their flavour, as far as is consistent with the space allowed. Quotations not ascribed to other sources are uniformly from the *Commentaries*. As classical names must at times be used, the author has not clung exclusively to the modern equivalents, but has interchangeably used both.

This volume pretends to be only a military history of Caesar. For clear and brilliant disquisitions on his state-craft or his personal career, or for the history of his era, the reader must go to other sources. But some of the best of the histories of Rome are full of military errors. Even the great Mommsen is by no means free from them. In all the histories which pretend to cover the complicated political and absorbing social conditions of that century, the description of military events is short and superficial. The author seeks to fill the gap.

Many pages will be found too technical to interest the general reader; but they are essential to the tracing out of the history of the art of war.

The very great array of facts which we possess with regard to the military career of Caesar makes it hard to compress all that should be said within the limits of even a large volume. But it is believed that no noteworthy fact has been omitted. The history of the art of war during the Empire has been cut down to very meagre limits; but though there were abundant wars, there was much lack of method in war during this period; and it may be said that to omit bodily the fourteen centuries from Caesar to the invention of gunpowder would not materially alter the general scope proposed for these biographies of the great captains.

Some of the comment indulged in may seem to savour of hypercriticism. But though the author may not meet the views of all in what he says, the reader will at least give him credit for qualifying himself as well as may be by careful study of all the ancient authorities, of the best recognized modern critics, and by personal inspection of the ground. With the sole exception of Colonel Stoffel, the author believes that he is the only writer on this subject who has followed Caesar entirely around the Mediterranean basin.

The principal sources of our knowledge of Caesar as a captain are the *Commentaries*, Cicero's speeches and other writings, Dion Cassius, Plutarch, Suetonius, and Velleius Paterculus; the best commentators are Guischard, Turpin de Crissé, Napoleon I., Lossau, Göler, Rustow, Napoleon III., and above all Colonel Stoffel, of whose lifework one cannot say too much.

CHAPTER 1

Marius and the Army Changes
110-86 B. C.

Caesar's legion was more like the Greek *phalanx* than like the legion of the Second Punic War. The latter had intervals between *maniples* equal to *maniple* front, and the *maniples* stood checkerwise. Each man occupied a space five feet square. The material of the legion was of the highest order—the *burgess*-soldier of the simple republic. But gradually the professional soldier came into vogue; the citizens avoided military duty; and a less reliable material filled the ranks. Marius first enlisted men solely for their physical qualifications; and foreign mercenaries were added to the army. The general, not the republic, claimed the soldier's fealty. Arms and equipment remained the same, but the trustworthiness of the soldier decreased, and the intervals in the line of battle were lessened. The *cohort* was no longer a body of citizens marshalled on a basis of property-standing, but a body of from three hundred to six hundred of any kind of men, and the legion was marshalled in two or three lines of *cohorts*. The army ceased to be a national militia, but was composed of regulars and auxiliaries. *Ballistics* and fortification were improved. Sieges grew to be more expertly managed. The fleets gained in importance. Marius' great work was the change he wrought in the army; but he was also the means of rescuing Rome from the invasion of the Teutones and Cimbri, the former of whom he defeated at Aquae Sextiae in Southern Gaul, and the latter at Vercellae in Northern Italy. Both victories redound much to his credit.

The legion with which the Romans vanquished the Grecian *phalanx*, and which gallantly took the fearful punishment inflicted on it by Hannibal, again and again facing destruction with unflinching courage, until the Carthaginians, exhausted by attrition, were forced to abandon Italy, was a very different body of men from the enthusiastic legion which Caesar led victorious to the four quarters of the then known world. Curiously enough, the formation of Caesar's legion more nearly approached that of the "simple *phalanx*" of the Greeks than that of the splendid body of *burgess*-soldiers, whose stanch front to disaster makes the Second Punic War so memorable a page in the annals of Roman courage and intelligence. Caesar's array in line of battle did not differ as greatly from Hannibal's *phalanx* in the later battles of this war, as it did from the legion of Marcellus or Nero. At Asculum, Herdonia and Zama, Hannibal's army was set up in two or three lines of legionary *phalanxes*, so to speak. Adopting the quincunx or checkerwise formation by *maniples* as the typical idea of the legion of the Second Punic War, Caesar's army, during all his campaigns, was set up more like Hannibal's *phalanx*, and at times very nearly approached it.

Let us see how the change came about.

The legion of the Second Punic War was a body composed of citizens rendering service according to the classes of Servius Tullius. This service was as much a privilege as a duty, and was jealously guarded. Only *burgesses* with a given amount of property were allowed to serve. Those who had less than twelve thousand five hundred asses were excluded from the right. They were *proletarii*, having some slight means, and *capite censi*, having nothing and reckoned merely as so many head of men.

The material of which the legion was made was thus of the very highest order; and originally the armament and place in the legion were determined by the class-rating. But later these were made to depend on length of service, so that the youngest soldiers, from seventeen to twenty-five years of age, were *velites* or light troops; those from twenty-five to thirty, *hastati* or heavy troops of the first line; those from thirty to forty, *principes* or heavy troops of the second line; those from forty to forty-five, *triarii* or reserves of the third line.

The light troops acted as skirmishers. The legionary soldier occupied a space about five feet square. The lines of *hastati* and of *principes* stood in *maniples* of one hundred and twenty men each, twelve front by ten deep, and between each two *maniples* was an interval equal to *maniple* front. The lines were some two hundred and fifty feet apart, and the *maniples* of the *principes* stood behind the intervals of the *hastati*. The *triarii maniples* had but sixty men, and stood behind the *hastati* intervals.

There were ten *maniples* in each of the three lines, so that there

LEGION OF THE SECOND PUNIC WAR

were of line troops twelve hundred *hastati*, twelve hundred *principes* and six hundred *triarii*. To these must be added twelve hundred (or more) *velites*, making forty-two hundred footmen in the legion, of whom three thousand were heavy.

There were three hundred cavalry in each legion, whose place was on the flanks. The *velites* often occupied the intervals of the *triarii*.

This body proved to have extraordinary mobility and capacity to meet unusual conditions, and with the discipline and *esprit de corps* natural to the perfect material of which it was composed made an unequalled body of troops. The wars of the third century B. C. fully proved the qualities of the legion so organized. It was at its very best.

The legion of Caesar's era was quite a different body. Changes had grown up in the state and army which affected the matter of service and thus the legion; and a number of marked alterations were brought about during the times of the civil wars. The legion descended to Caesar in a new shape, one that Marcellus and Nero and Scipio would not have recognized.

Caius Marius is a more noteworthy figure in history from his rugged, uncouth personality and his startling political success and failure than from his merit as a captain. Though unquestionably able as a leader, though Rome owed to him the victory at Aquae Sextiae, which delivered her from the Cimbri and Teutones, his position in military annals was more distinguished by the new organization of the Roman army than by any other contribution to the art of war.

When internal disquiet began to monopolize the thought and action of the citizens of the Roman republic, the army was not long in feeling its influence for the worse. The civil wars sadly marred the soldierly sentiments of the Romans, but it was Caius Marius who first gave a serious downward impetus to the character of the army. Long before his time many of the old Servian methods had got changed or distinctly modified. The minimum property which entitled a citizen to the privilege of serving had been reduced to four thousand asses. The armament of the legionary had ceased to be determined by census-rating; it had, as above stated, grown to be fixed by length of service. Wealth and luxury had supplanted the ancient habits of simplicity. The *burgesses* gradually sought to avoid service; the proletariats found in it a means of improving their condition. A certain number of campaigns were no longer essential to secure political preferment. The *burgess*-cavalry had given up serving in the field, and become a sort of guard of honour. The avoidance of military duty by the rich made it impossible to raise large forces with rapidity by the simple means of calling out the classes; and yet, as after the Battle of Arausio, contingencies occurred when large levies must be instantly made. The new barbarian territories of Rome had begun to furnish cavalry, such as the heavy horse of Thrace and the light irregulars from Numidia, as well as light infantry, such as the Ligurians and the Balearic slingers; but the heavy foot had remained Italian.

It was Marius who first gave every free-born citizen, however poor, an equal right to serve. The heavy infantry, *hastati, principes, triarii*, were all reduced to a level, and it was the officers who decided, from the qualifications of the man, where and with what arms each soldier should be allowed to serve. The armament of all the heavy foot was made the same, and gladiators were employed as masters of arms to teach the recruits the use of their weapons; while Publius Rutilius, Marius's favourite comrade and fellow legate in the African war, compiled a system of tactics for the new legion.

A son of the people, when in 107 B. C. Marius had attained consular rank, he found his advantage in raising his army, not from the self-respecting classes, but from men he could so handle as to subserve his purpose of gaining the supreme control. Later leaders, Sulla, Crassus, Pompey, followed in the steps of Marius. Under such leadership the army soon became another body, no longer representative of Roman courage, honesty and patriotism.

The right to serve in the army ceased to be a privilege,—the sole road to civic honours. The wealthy citizen would no longer consent to serve. Bodily exercises were neglected. The ranks were filled, not by representatives of every class, rich and poor, but by the *proletarii*;

and it was not long before there crept into the ranks numbers of men from peoples tributary to Rome, freedmen, strangers and slaves. Even the criminal classes were greedily recruited, and Marius once made a body-guard of slaves. Some veterans did service in exchange for grants of land, and answered the call for duty as *evocati*, having special privileges.

The legions were not now divided into simple Roman and allied. In the Social War, Roman citizenship was granted broadcast to the Italians, and the legions were composed of Romans, auxiliaries, provincial troops and mercenaries. The test of Marius was simply personal size and strength. Character went for nothing. Cavalry was raised in a manner similar to the infantry, and mostly from foreign elements. If the knights still consented to serve, it was only in posts of peculiar honour. The ancient rules for raising men were utterly disregarded. Anyone ready to pay could secure freedom from service; any one physically qualified could bear arms.

The oath of the soldier was no longer an oath to serve the republic; he swore personal fealty to the general. The growing necessity for keeping troops long under arms, which followed the extended conquests of Rome, made generals resort to every means to prevent their forces from disbanding. Gradually the honourable service of the Roman citizen to the fatherland got prostituted to the low grade of soldier of fortune. Mercenaries and standing armies took the place of voluntary service and of armies called out from necessity alone. The conquered provinces were placed under proconsuls, each with a standing army and unlimited power, and were farmed out for revenue with the inevitable result. Rome was following in the footsteps of Greece.

This change from the old method of classified personal service rendered essential corresponding changes in the marshalling of the legion. The ancient distinction of *principes*, *hastati* and *triarii* disappeared, and all troops were either heavy or light. The inherited arms and equipment were not materially altered. The old numerical force of the legion, say four thousand to six thousand heavy infantry and three hundred heavy cavalry as the normal strength, was retained; but the light troops, now all raised from the conquered provinces, were largely increased, both foot and horse, and were no longer an integral part of the legion. The horse grew in importance and effectiveness, for the Roman horseman had imitated the better models of light cavalry which his many wars in every land, from Iberia to the distant Orient, had afforded him. This improvement was traceable in the heavy cavalry in a lesser degree.

From about one tenth of the numerical force of the foot, the horse grew to the proportion of one seventh or at times more.

The number of legions in a consular army was no longer four, but ran up to any given number, even to ten, not counting the auxiliaries, horse or foot. Elephants and ballistic machines came into common use. A legion in the field had thirty small catapults and *ballistas*, each served by ten men. Still, as with Alexander, these machines were not employed in battle, but in the attack and defence of defiles, in crossing rivers, and in the attack and defence of camps and other works.

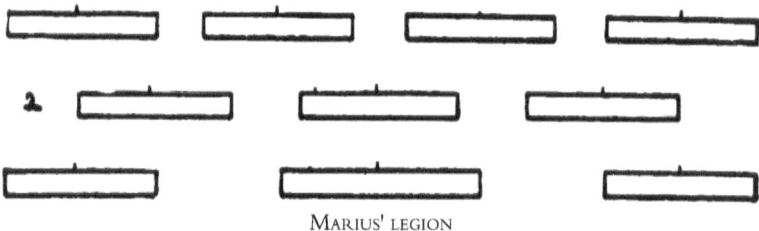

MARIUS' LEGION

Up to the time of Marius, the *quincuncial* form of the legion was retained, and the intervals still remained equal to the *maniple* front. But when the legions grew to be composed of inexpert recruits, not as in the early days of men trained to war from their youth, the individuality of the legionary could no longer be relied upon. Moreover, the Romans in their wars with Germanic barbarians and Oriental masses had found that the always present danger of the enemy forcing his way into the intervals grew more serious as the troops deteriorated in quality. This difficulty had formerly been obviated by moving the *principes* up into or close behind the intervals of the *hastati*. But Marius introduced another organization, the setting up of the legion in three lines of *cohorts*. The thirty legionary *maniples*, each of two centuries, were given up. The word *cohort* remained, but the body consisted no longer of a *maniple* each of *hastati*, *principes* and *triarii*, with *velites* and a *turma* of horse; it was a body of from four to six *maniples* of four, five or six hundred legionary soldiers. At first the intervals remained; the five feet space of each soldier, the ten deep file and the distance between lines were not altered; the *cohorts* had forty, fifty or sixty files. Shortly the intervals between *cohorts* began to diminish with the individual trustworthiness of the legionary, and the distances between lines were increased to three hundred feet. These lines were now known as first, second and third; and the first had four, the second and third each three *cohorts*. The three *cohorts* in second line stood opposite the diminished intervals of the first, the third line *cohorts* at the flanks and opposite the centre. The legionary eagle was still carried by the *primipilus* of the first *cohort* of the third line, and each *cohort* had its own special ensign (*signum*). The legionaries of first and second lines, it is thought by some, were the soldiers who were called *antesignani*; in the third line *cohorts* were the bravest and strongest soldiers; but they were no longer the *triarii*.

Upon this formation were grafted, at times not easily determined, yet other changes. The ten *cohorts* stood in two lines, five in each; or instead of ten there were fifteen *cohorts*, each of two *maniples*, and five of these were in each line. The files were now and then split and doubled, making a five deep *cohort* of double length of front, which in line would close up a full interval. Finally, by a process of steadily decreasing intervals, the *cohorts* came to all but join each other, and the legion had again become a *phalanx*. This formation without intervals was not invariable. Caesar generally set up his *cohorts* with intervals more or less wide. But a legion whose first line was nearly a solid body was not uncommon. The ancient *quincunx* had disappeared. This was the inevitable result of the loss of the old Roman patriotism, discipline and stanchness in the legionary soldier, and of his being replaced by a far inferior man who needed to be held well in hand to force him to his work. Finally, the eagle found its way into the front line, but the word *antesignani* remained, applied to a special body, of which more will be told anon.

The use of the *testudo*-formation grew into a huge rectangle, much like the modern square against cavalry, for which, indeed, in the Romans' Oriental wars it was frequently used. On open ground, marches were sometimes made in squares, like that of the *phalanx* of Brasidas—*agmen quadratum*. Marius especially excelled in his dispositions for the march. In the war against Jugurtha, he is said to have moved in a column by legions. Sulla with the cavalry and Manlius with the slingers, bowmen and Ligurians covered the column on right and left. In the van and rear, under command of military *tribunes*, were some *cohorts* in light marching order, and scouts in quantities were on the flanks.

In battle order, the Roman legions stood in the centre, the auxiliaries on the flanks, the *velites* in the spaces between bodies, on the flanks, or in front and rear as needed. Cavalry began to be more of an arm, and was hurled in masses on the enemy or employed to protect the foot. It no longer kept its old stand on both flanks. The method of fighting was not much altered, but grand tactics grew apace, until they reached their highest Roman development under Caesar.

Other changes of even more importance were made in this period. The office of dictator, that is, the supreme control, was the aim of the ambitious; it was their means of gaining possession of the state. The legates grew to greater importance and acquired more and more the command of legions and armies. They were the general officers. The military tribunes became *cohort*-commanders, and the centuries were commanded by centurions. The troops were still drilled and exercised in gymnastics, but not so the citizens. Soldiers, to keep them from idleness and turbulence, were put upon the public works, especially the great military roads.

The soldier's pay was doubled by Caesar at the opening of the Civil War. The footmen received ten *asses* a day; *centurions* twenty, cavalrymen thirty, subject to certain deductions, as of old, for rations, arms, equipments and horses.

In this era, discipline and *esprit de corps* were in a transition state from the perfect basis of the Second Punic War to the utter worthlessness of later days. Courage and good behaviour were still present, but these were maintained by the severity of the laws. Punishments were cruelly unjust at times, foolishly inadequate at others. They were inflicted no longer in accordance with the code, but to suit the moods or character of the general. The splendid victories of the Romans prove abundantly that much of the old spirit was still there. But it proceeded from a different motive. The ancient love of honour and country had disappeared, and in its place stood an avaricious grasping for booty and a greed of bloodshed and conquest. These men were no longer Roman soldiers. They belonged to the chief who led them, and he used every motive which is peculiarly suited to a low class of military recruits to bind them to his cause and use them for his own purposes. *Ubi bene ibi patria* was the accepted rule; and each general easily persuaded his troops that he represented the chief good. The civil uprisings in Rome had demonstrated how little the Roman soldier of the first century B. C. was like the Roman soldier of the war against Hannibal.

When Caesar's legions mutinied and demanded their discharge, he addressed them as *quirites*, a title which every Roman soldier in the early days viewed with pride. Just because he was a citizen, he was a soldier. But Caesar's legionaries were only soldiers. They were not citizens, nor did they care to be. The one word *quirites* shamed or frightened them into obedience.

As punishments in the army were no longer made according to

rule, so were unearned rewards distributed. Favouritism grew apace. The simple crown of leaves or grasses gave place to expensive ornaments. The officers, and later the soldiers, were freed from the duty of nightly fortification and other fatigue work. The greater triumph went to the unworthy. Luxury and pomp stepped into the place of simplicity, not only with wealthy citizens, but in the camp.

But because the soldier had degenerated, it does not follow that the ability of the leaders had gone. Rather because of the degeneracy of the rank and file, ability in the captain was enabled to push its way to the front.

The period of the Civil War shows great advance in fortification and ballistics. The form of the camp remained the same, but the walls and defences were made much more intricate. The wall was higher and thicker; the ditch was wider and usually wet; towers were more numerous and bigger, and covered ways connected them; entanglements in front of the defences were more common; the camp, especially *castra stativa,* became a fortress.

Even battlefields were fortified. Sulla erected palisades between his lines with ditches on the flanks, against the enemy's chariots at Chaeronaea. Marius entrenched himself against the Teutones at the mouth of the Isere. The Romans kept to their own method, but exceeded the Greeks in cleverness at this sort of temporary fortification.

Sieges likewise gained in skilful management. In assaults the *telenon* of the Greeks was used to swing men up on the enemy's wall. The corona consisted in surrounding a town with two lines of foot and one of horse and gradually decreasing the circumference of the lines until the walls could be reached under cover of penthouses and tortoises. The movable *testudo* of shields was commonly employed and with good results.

Lines of *contra-*and circumvallation were made more expertly than of yore. Mounds were used as formerly in Greece, but grew to enormous proportions. Sulla's at Massada was two hundred and eighty-six feet high, and upon these were other constructions and towers of one hundred and fifty-five feet, making four hundred and forty-one feet above the level.

Mines were dexterously used. Sulla's at Athens showed especial ability. Sheds, tortoises, movable towers, rams, all came into play. Catapults and *ballistas* were in constant use. The big catapult projected beams a horizontal distance of four hundred to eight hundred paces. The small catapult (*scorpio*) shot heavy lances three hundred to five hundred paces. The former was used in sieges, the latter in the field. A burning missile (*falerica*) was also hurled. The big *ballista* threw stones four hundred to six hundred paces on a curved path like that of a mortar, and was used in sieges. The small one (*onager*) was used in the field. The smallest *onager* and *scorpio* could be worked by one man.

In general, the sieges of this day were much like those of the Greeks. They had gained distinctly in skill since the days of Hannibal, but few besiegers reached the clever devices of Alexander; none approached his gallant assaults. Foreign conquest obliged the Romans to increase the power and effectiveness of their fleet. This was done with their usual push and good sense.

The government owned public forests which were devoted to ship-building, and were well managed. War vessels consisted of *biremes*, *triremes*, *quinquiremes* and up to *octoremes*; the triremes and *quinquiremes* were the ones mostly in commission. There were cruisers for light coast duty and spying out the enemy (*nives speculatoriae*), a smaller class like gunboats; transports and flat bottoms (*pontones*) for river duty. The war vessels mostly had iron rams (*rostra ferramenta*), and their sides were protected by beams and shields of various kinds to save them from the blows of the enemy's. The larger, often the smaller, vessels had decks, and missile-throwers and towers stood upon them. Each vessel was provided with grappling-irons, boarding-bridges, siege implements and machines for casting fire-pots. The use of fireships was well understood.

The fleets were manned by rowers or sailors, and by soldiers or marines. The rowers and sailors were slaves or came from the lower classes; the marines were raised like legionaries. Their oath of fealty was equally to the admiral and not to the state. A *quinquireme* had four hundred rowers, the others a corresponding number. The marines were armed like the legionaries, but had scythed lances, battleaxes and boarding-swords. The rowers were also armed.

Each vessel had a chief of rowers who gave the time of the stroke by a hammer-blow on a gong; a sort of boatswain in charge of the sails, anchors, etc.; a steersman (*gubernator*), who was also pilot; a captain (*navarchus*); and a commandant of marines (*praefectus navis*). A consul or praetor might be in command of the fleet, or a special officer (*dux praefectusque classis*) might lead it.

Harbours were natural or artificial. A favourite form of the latter was a semicircle from the shore, from which two moles ran out seaward, the entrance between which was closed by a chain. The inner harbour was

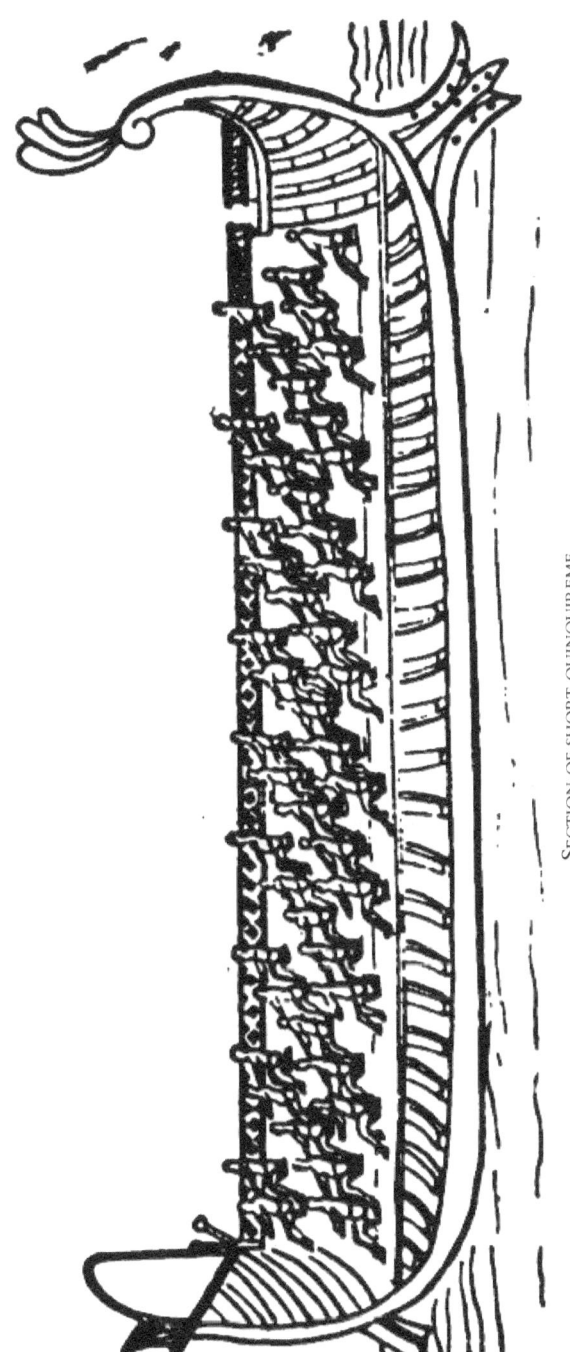

SECTION OF SHORT QUINQUIREME

in several divisions, and well provided with arsenals and wharves. These harbours were fortified both towards the sea and on the land side.

When a fleet was ready to put to sea the rowers first went aboard, then the marines. An inspection with religious ceremonies followed and the fleet set sail, the light vessels ahead, then the triremes and other war-galleys, then the transports. On landing, the vessels were drawn up on the beach, and were protected by palisades towards the sea and fieldworks towards the land. This rule, along the rocky coast of Italy, must frequently have been broken; but a fleet always passed the night ashore, when possible.

Naval battles generally took place near land, and vessels were lightened as much as possible by leaving off sails, lowering masts, and clearing decks. Ebb and flood tides were carefully watched and utilized.

The common order of battle was a parallel one in two lines (*acies duplex*), with the lighter ships in the rear line; a concave order (*acies lunata*), with the heaviest ships on the flanks to outflank the enemy; a convex order, in which the heaviest ships were in the centre; a pincer-like form (*forceps*), against a wedge (*acies cuneata*), or *vice versa*.

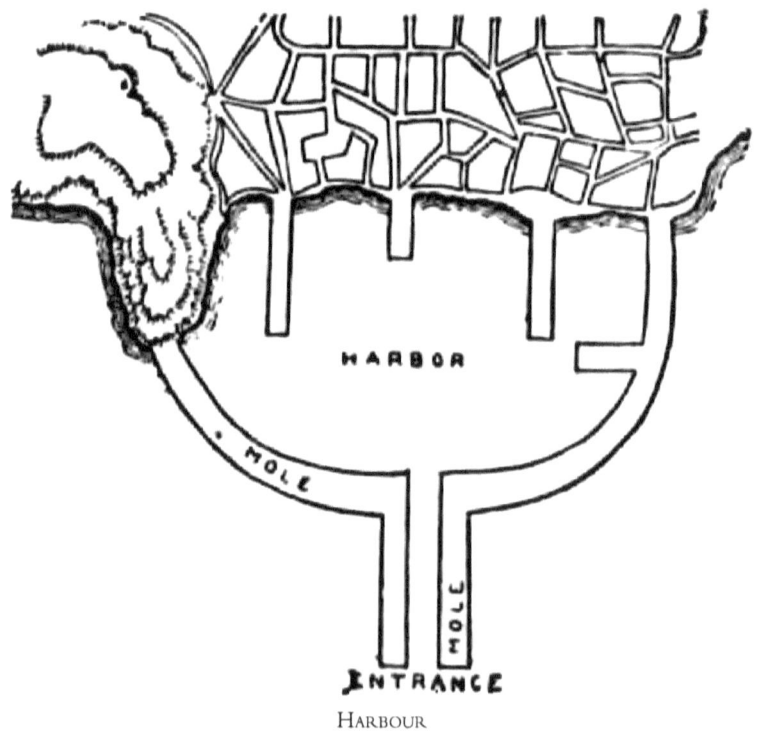

HARBOUR

The signal for battle was a red flag at the admiral's mast-head, and a trumpet-blast from each ship. Upon this all hands gave the battle-cry and intuned the battle-hymn. The missile-throwers opened the action and then the lines clashed. Each ship endeavoured to run down or ram an adversary, cut its oars, board and capture it, or set it afire.

A naval victory was celebrated by songs and music, and by decorating the prows of the vessels with laurel. The admiral was allowed a *triumphus navalis*.

To sum the matter up, the old and perfect militia-system of Rome had disappeared, the soldier had become a professional, and the forces on foot were simple mercenaries. The distinctions in the legions were exclusively military, having nothing to do with civil rank or class. And as everything now depended on the general, so there grew up about him a headquarters-guard (*praetoriani*) which was the germ of a regular army.

The wonderful campaigns and battles of this era were the work of the leaders. The condition of the army, for good or bad, reflected the spirit and character of the general. It was no longer the Roman citizen who won the victories of Rome, but the genius of great men who aimed at the control of the state.

Much of Marius' success in the Jugurthan war he owed to the skill of Sulla, his then *quaestor* and later political opponent. Metellus, Marius' chief, deserves the credit for the conquest of Numidia as far as the confines of the desert; Sulla that for the capture of Jugurtha. Marius profited by both. The great army-changes are associated with Marius; but there is little in his military feats which have other than a political significance.

To Marius is, however, due abundant praise for his conduct at Aquae Sextiae and Vercellae. Rome never ran a greater danger than from the invasion of the Teutones and Cimbri; and it was to Marius she owed her rescue. After the defeat of the Romans at Arausio (Orange) in 105 B. C, where the consuls Mallius Maximus and Servilius Caepio, with eighty thousand Roman soldiers and half as many non-combatants, paid with their lives the penalty of mismanagement,—a blow more seriously threatening than even Cannae,—Marius was sent to Gaul to repair the disaster. He had ample time, for instead of to Italy the barbarians had headed their column towards Spain. Here, forced back by the brave Iberians and the difficulties of the Pyrenees, they again marched towards the north, until they were checked by the stubborn Belgae and once more rolled in a vast flood towards the Roman province.

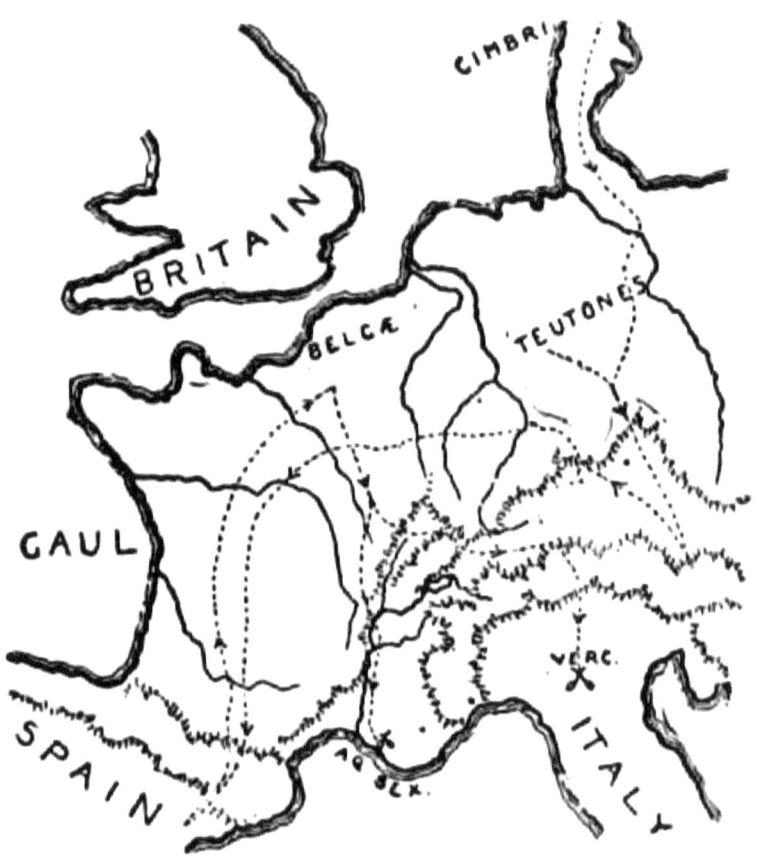

ROUTE OF CIMBRI AND TEUTONES

Marius had established himself at the confluence of the Rhone and Isere; had reduced the disaffected tribes and confirmed the fealty of others in the Province. At this point he protected the roads to the only two then available passes, over the Little St. Bernard and over the Maritime Alps. The barbarians were in two bodies. One of these essayed the Eastern Alps and in due time debouched into Italy. The other, the Teutones, aimed to pass down the Rhone and follow the coast to the Maritime Alps. These soon made their appearance before the camp of Marius, which the consul had fortified with extreme care. Though he was an excellent disciplinarian and his men were in good heart, Marius was unwilling to encounter the immense hordes of the Teutones until his men had become accustomed to the sight of their huge stature, their wild demeanour and howling battle-cry. The Romans feared these light-haired bulky barbarians as the Greeks had dreaded the Persians prior to Marathon. Not all the taunts of the enemy could make Marius budge from his secure entrenchments. Finally, tired out, the Teutones assaulted the camp for three days in succession, but were thrust back with heavy loss. They then marched for Italy, filing, say the authorities, six days and nights past the Roman camp, with their armed men and families and baggage-trains, and calling with sneers to the legionaries for messages to their wives and children in Italy.

Now came Marius' chance. Cautiously following up the enemy in the style he had learned in the Jugurthan war, daily camping nearby them on inaccessible heights and behind strong works, he finally felt that the temper of his men was equal to an attack on the enemy. Near Aquae Sextiae (Aix, *Départment des Bouches du Rhône*), even before his camp was finished, a fight was begun between the men of both armies who were getting water at the little River Arc, which lay between them. The Romans drove the barbarians—they were Ambrones—across the river and to their wagon-camp. Here took place a severe combat in which the wives of the Ambrones fought beside their husbands and the barbarians lost heavily. But though they had done good work, the day ended by the Romans falling back to their side of the river.

During the succeeding night, Marius placed Marcellus with three thousand men—some authorities say non-combatants—in ambush in some wooded ravines up the river from the barbarian camp, with orders, during the battle which he proposed to force, to debouch on

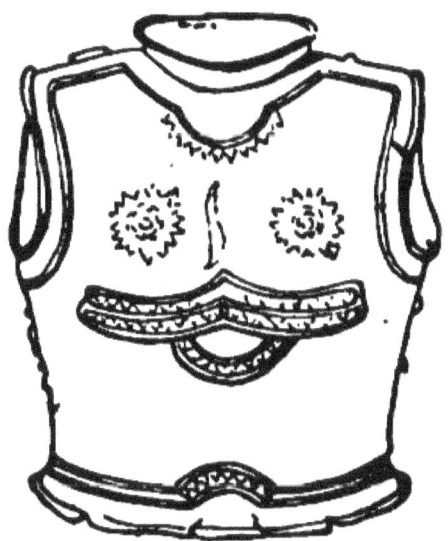

GALLIC CUIRASS. (?NARBONESE.)

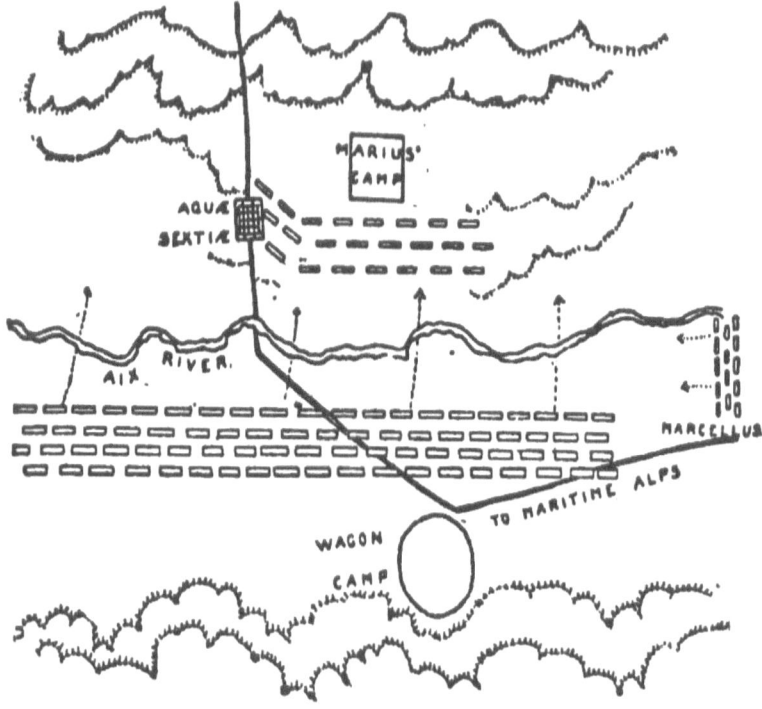

BATTLE OF AQUAE SEXTIAE

the enemy's rear. At daybreak the consul drew up the Roman army on some heights lining the river where he had established his camp, and sent his cavalry out to lure the Teutones to attack. This was cleverly accomplished. The barbarians, under the impression that the Romans would not fight, forded the stream and rushed tumultuously up the slope. They were received so stoutly by the legions that they fell into disorder and were driven back to the plain. Unused to the midday heat of the Mediterranean, the barbarians, after some hours' fighting, lost their vigour, and at the proper instant the party in ambush emerged and fell, sustained by the cavalry, upon their rear. The Teutones were as demoralized as they had formerly been eager. They fled in disorder and were cut down in their tracks, with a loss, according to Livy, of ninety thousand killed and twenty thousand captured. This was in 102 B. C.

Meanwhile the Cimbri had crossed the Rhaetian Alps, but did not at once march on Rome. Marius reached the scene in time to join his colleague Catulus. The barbarians, according to their odd but ancient custom, asked of Marius to appoint a day and place for battle, which to them was but a huge duel, governed by the same forms. This Marius did, and near Vercellae the hosts met in 101 B. C. The Cimbri were beaten and annihilated—no less than one hundred and forty thousand being killed and sixty thousand captured, as is claimed by the Latin historians. The nation disappeared from history. Rome was saved from another burning. Marius was more than a hero. He was the people's demigod.

CHAPTER 2

Sulla, Pompey
90-60 B. C.

Sulla was one of the ablest generals of his era. He learned his trade under Marius. He first used earthworks in battle to protect his lines, and at Orehomenus he used fieldworks to hem in his enemy. Sulla was bold and discreet; he was both lion and fox. Pompey was one of those captains upon whom greatness happens to be thrust. Of good but not high ability, exceptional fortune enabled him to reap the benefit of the hard work of others. He was slow and lacked initiative, but did some of his work well. His early successes in Sicily and Africa earned him the title of Great at twenty-four; but when he went to Spain and opposed Sertorius, one of the most noteworthy generals of antiquity, he more than met his match. Only the death of Sertorius enabled him to win success. The campaign in which Pompey swept the pirates from the Mediterranean was a simple piece of work excellently done; his campaign in the East had been already made easy by Lucullus, whose labours redounded to Pompey's credit. On the whole, while Pompey should not be underrated, it must be acknowledged that he earned his great repute on more than usually slender grounds.

Sulla, as a general, stands higher than any of the men immediately preceding Caesar. He got his training in the Jugurthan war under Marius, and won his first laurels by the able negotiations which mainly contributed to the capture of Jugurtha and the ending of that difficult conflict. He again served under Marius in the campaign against the Cimbri and Teutones. Later on, master and pupil marked an era in the history of Rome by their competition for the supremacy of the state.

Sulla's work in the East in the Mithridatic war was masterly. His siege of Athens, coupled to the earlier siege of Numantia by Scipio Africanus Minor, furnished the pattern on which Caesar worked and bettered, though unquestionably Caesar had studied the siege operations at Tyre and Rhodes, and had drawn his inspiration from them. All Sulla's campaigns are of marked interest. There was much in the wars of the early part of the last century B. C. which was splendid in skill and accomplishment, and which is specially noteworthy as being the school in which young Caesar learned his trade. It is hard to select any one of Sulla's numerous great deeds which shall stand alone as representative of his soldierly work. The battle of Chaeronaea, 86 B. C, on the field rendered famous by Philip's victory and the youthful daring of Alexander, is a sample of how to deal with unusual questions in war.

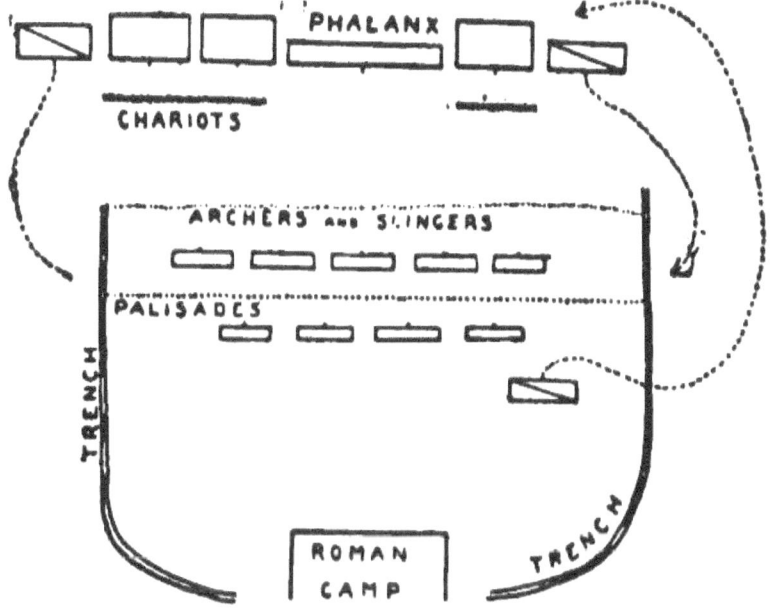

BATTLE OF CHAERONAEA

Taxiles and Archelaus, the lieutenants of Mithridates, had an army of one hundred thousand foot and ten thousand horse with ninety scythed chariots. Sulla's force, including his Greek auxiliaries, was less than a third this number, and in cavalry he was especially wanting,—on these plains a great source of weakness. His Roman troops were but sixteen thousand five hundred strong. But Sulla despised his enemy, and was confident of success. He made up for his want of strength by protecting his flanks with trenches which should save him from the charges of the enemy's horse, and by erecting a row of heavy palisades between his first and second lines, which should arrest the charge of the scythed chariots. Here was an intelligent instance of the use of fieldworks.

The battle was opened in true Oriental fashion by the charge of chariots. Sulla's first line smartly withdrew behind the palisades, which not only checked the onset of the chariots, but these, their horses being terrified by the heavy fire of Sulla's slingers and archers, turned on their own line and produced marked confusion in the Macedonian *phalanx* and in a corps of Italian auxiliaries serving in the Mithridatic Army. To repair the disaster, Archelaus ordered his horse from both flanks to charge the Roman legions. The Orientals rode down on the Romans with great *élan*, and their furious charge, despite the trenches, succeeded in breaking the Roman formation, showing clearly that without the trenches Sulla's line would have been destroyed. But the legionaries did not lose heart. They rapidly formed squares and resisted the horsemen with great determination. Sulla, meanwhile, perceiving that the enemy's *phalanx* did not readily recover from the disorder into which the chariots had thrown it, and that the moment had arrived when a blow driven home at the right spot was needed, gathered his own small force of cavalry from the right, and heading it in person charged sharply in on the exposed flank of the enemy. As was always the case with Sulla, fortune followed hard upon his boldness. The Asiatic foot offered but little resistance, and its flight unsettled the *phalanx*. The horse which was assailing the Roman legions found its task too stubborn, and turned to aid in retrieving the disorder of the foot. The legions gained breathing spell, and speedily patching up a new formation advanced sharply on the wavering foot of Archelaus. This decided the day. The entire Mithridatic army was swept from off the field.

Archelaus managed to retire to his camp, and closed the gates to save what he had got within. Immense slaughter without the walls resulted. When the gates were finally forced by the surging mass, the Romans entered with the enemy and prolonged the massacre. Archelaus saved but a twelfth part of his army. The Roman loss was trivial.

At the battle of Orchomenus, in the succeeding year, Sulla, by clever calculation in cutting ditches and more clever tactics, succeeded in penning up a new army under Archelaus in such a position as to drive him into some swamps and morasses, where he destroyed the entire force. This operation appears to have been a species of siege, by a system of gradually narrowed fieldworks, of an army camped in the open instead of protected by the walls of a fortress, and as such exhibits decided originality of conception and boldness in execution. The accounts of the operation are obscure.

Sulla was equally able as statesman and soldier. He acted, not like Marius, from impulse, but in a well-considered though rapid manner. He was tireless and active, brave and enterprising, and singularly cool in thought and deed. Carbo pronounced Sulla to have the qualities of both the lion and the fox. He won the love of his soldiers, and yet was a stern disciplinarian. He showed as marked skill in his sieges as in tactics.

The most interesting though least creditable part of the military career of Cnaeus Pompey will be dealt with at length when we find him measuring swords with Caesar. In the earlier part of his life, before he had Caesar to contend with, Pompey showed many characteristics of the great man and soldier. He must not be underrated. But Pompey was perhaps the lightest weight of all the characters who have enacted a giant's role on the stage of life. No man won the title of Great on such slender merit. No man ever wielded such vast power with so little to back it up. He compares favourably with men of a second rank; but as he stood on the same plane of power with Caesar, so must we gauge him by the same large measure. It is due to Pompey to sketch his early achievements.

Pompey had many of the virtues of the soldier. He was splendid as an athlete. He was bold in that species of war which calls not too largely on the intellect or the moral force. He could charge at the head of his horse with noble gallantry, when he was unable to plan a good campaign or assume a sudden strategic or tactical risk. He was as simple, modest and reserved in habit as he was fearless in battle. He had those qualities which endeared him to the people. Taken up by Sulla when a mere youth, he climbed into popular favour as Scipio Africanus Major had done, by belief in and assertion of his right to commands usually given to those who have long served the state. But Pompey had less than the ability of Scipio. He was clean in his private life, and his "honest countenance" was proverbial. He was upright in his family relations, but none the less divorced his wife at the nod of Sulla, while Caesar, against whom much is charged in his commerce with women, refused to do so. Pompey was retiring in civil life and lacked the graces of manner much considered at that day, though he had a fair degree of culture. In council he was slow, and to a habit of silence which came from a not over quick comprehension was referred, as it often is, a judgment he did not possess.

Pompey was but an ordinary man of good abilities. He had not the first glint of genius. Greatness was thrust upon him if it ever was upon any man. He was the very reverse of Caesar. Circumstances made Pompey; Caesar made circumstances. Pompey was cold, passionless and slow at making resolutions. In that era, when every man in power held ultra opinions of some sort, Pompey's very ordinariness sundered him from the ranks of his peers as his assertion and honest belief that he was great raised him above them. Had his conduct risen to a higher plane, other qualities might have been ascribed to him; but he must be judged by the event. In him were blended a singular modesty of bearing and extravagance in demands. He was fortunate in his beginnings; much was done for him; to what he had, more was given; he was never overtaxed, nor did luck run counter to his course. By such easy steps rose Cnaeus Pompey, the creation not of brilliant, but of steady good fortune.

Pompey possessed obstinacy to the last degree,—a quality which is often a saving clause. But it was not an intelligent obstinacy. He imagined that he was having his own way when more clever men were outwitting him. From unreadiness to assume a heavy responsibility, when thrust upon him, grew a set habit of caution which well exhibits the average plane of his character. It was not the caution of a Hannibal, who, when called on, could be bold beyond any man; it was rather a want of moral incisiveness. While not lacking good conduct and qualities he was, says Mommsen, "the most starched of artificial great men." Pompey was perhaps the best individual to hold his party together, because he did naught to disrupt it.

Pompey first came into notice in 83 B. C, when he undertook to raise an army for Sulla in Picenum. Here his personal bearing and unquestioned gallantry stood him in good stead. He raised and equipped a superior force, and when three Marian armies faced him, he had the nerve to attack them in detail before they could assemble, and the good fortune to disperse them. He led an attack on the enemy's camp—an unusual thing at that day—which did credit to the Roman name. On his joining his chief, Sulla saluted the young man of twenty-three as *Imperator*, a title which few men ever won, and those only at the end of many years of arduous and brilliant service. In 82 B. C, Pompey was sent as *propraetor* to Sicily. The island, on his approach with six legions and one hundred and twenty galleys, was at once evacuated by the enemy and afforded him an easy triumph. From Sicily he shipped to Africa, where, though with larger forces, he conducted a handsome and successful campaign against Domitius

Ahenobarbus, the Marian. His assault on the enemy's camp here, too, as well as a speedy and energetic forty days' campaign, revived the Roman name, which had fallen into disrepute. On his return, "half in irony and half in recognition," Sulla saluted him as Magnus, and he was allowed, against all precedent, the greater triumph, never granted but to those of senatorial rank.

Q. Sertorius, the Marian, had been for some years holding head against the Sullan faction in Spain. It was essential that some able soldier should go thither. Pompey as usual felt that he had a right to demand the place, and it was given him. He was not fortunate in opposing this extraordinary general, who, had his work been cast on a winning in lieu of a losing theatre, might have rivalled any Roman antedating Caesar. Sertorius was equally remarkable as a statesman and a soldier. He had practically set up an independent kingdom in Iberia. Few men have ever held a difficult people to its work, or conducted an energetic guerilla warfare so well or on so large a scale. Never coming to battle, he had wearied the Sullan general Metellus by minor operations, by cutting off his foragers and water-parties, by attacking him on the march, and by remarkable activity in small-war. Metellus had been unable to cope with him.

IBERIA

It was in the summer of 77 B.C. that Pompey went to Spain as proconsul. On his way he made the new road over the Cottian Alps (Mt. Genèvre) which Caesar later used, and settled some troubles in Gaul. He did not cross the Pyrenees till late in the fall of that year, and wintered in north-east Spain. Sertorius was on the upper Ebro; of his lieutenants, Hirtuleius was facing Metellus in Farther Spain, and Perpenna, sustained by Herennius, held the Ebro against Pompey's columns. Pompey, early in the spring, advanced to and forced the Ebro, defeated Herennius at Valentia, south of Saguntum, and captured the place. Sertorius had moved on Lauro, a town allied to Pompey, on the Sucro (Xucar), south of Valentia, and was besieging it. Pompey moved against him, and sought to shut him in. So confident was he of success that he flattered himself that he had got Sertorius where he must soon surrender. He did not know his opponent. In the struggle which Pompey forced on him, Sertorius utterly outmanoeuvred his opponent, penned him up, and under his very eyes burned Lauro and transported its inhabitants to Lusitania. Pompey was surprised enough at the turn affairs had taken.

Meanwhile Metellus had defeated Hirtuleius near Hispalis (Seville). The next year he again defeated him near Segovia when the Sertorian sought to prevent Metellus from marching to join Pompey. Foreseeing the arrival of his colleague, and lest he should be forced to divide his laurels with him, Pompey offered battle to Sertorius on the Sucro, which this general was only too glad to accept before the arrival of Metellus. On the left of the Roman line, Afranius beat back the enemy and took Sertorius' camp; on the right, however, Pompey was severely wounded and his troops badly defeated by Sertorius, Who thereupon turned on Afranius and drove him back in turn. Pompey's army was rescued by the arrival of Metellus, and Sertorius' quite unreliable forces hereupon began to disperse. The main difficulty this able man had to contend with was to keep his irregular levies together and ready for work. At times he had very large numbers, even as high as one hundred and fifty thousand men, which he had with vast labour got together; then, suddenly, on a reverse or from some unexpected discouragement, the army would dissolve to a mere handful. So now. On the junction of Metellus and Pompey, and learning of the defeat of Hirtuleius, Sertorius' army incontinently retired and dispersed to the mountains. After a period of recuperation they were again collected and Sertorius faced Pompey south of Saguntum. Meanwhile his galleys interfered with the Roman victualling fleets along the coast.

After some manoeuvring another battle was fought on the River

Turia (Guadalaviar). It was a long and stanch struggle for mastery. Finally Sertorius defeated Pompey and his cavalry, while Metellus broke Perpenna's array. The result was favourable to the Sullans, and Sertorius' army again dispersed. Sertorius betook himself to Clunia, a fortress on the upper Durius (Douro), where he was besieged. But the Spanish Army was once more got together, and Sertorius cleverly escaped from Clunia and joined it. The end of the year 75 B. C. saw him again facing the Sullans, with equal chances.

On the whole, however, Metellus and Pompey had done well. Southern and Central Spain had been recovered, and Sertorius had made no gain. This was Metellus' work rather than Pompey's. The colleagues went into winter-quarters, Metellus in Gaul, Pompey between the Durius and Iberus, near modern Valladolid.

In the spring of 74 B. C. Sertorius began a small-war against Pompey. The latter was besieging Pallantia (Pallencia), when Sertorius drove him from it. At Calagurris, though joined by Metellus, he was likewise defeated, and then driven out of the upper Ebro region. Whenever Pompey met Sertorius, he succumbed. The succeeding year was characterized by much the same fortune, though Pompey made some headway in getting allies among the Spanish cities. The war had been going on eight years. It was a serious drain on Italy, and Spain itself by stress of war was lapsing into barbarism. Pompey and Metellus had found their master. The legions were heartily sick of their ill-rewarded labours. Many people in Rome began to fear Sertorius as a second Hannibal, though indeed there was no such danger. It was Sertorius' peculiar abilities, so well suited to the people and mountains of Spain, which enabled him to do such brilliant work. Able as he was, the gigantic conception of a Hannibal was beyond him,—as beyond all others.

Finally, as a piece of good fortune for Pompey, Sertorius was assassinated in 72 B. C. Perpenna, his second in command, was no such opponent, and him Pompey and Metellus speedily put down within the next year. Then regulating the affairs of the two Spanish provinces, they returned to Rome, and together triumphed. This campaign cannot be said to have added to the laurels of Pompey the Great.

In the war against the pirates, Pompey showed considerable skill. Not that the task was one to tax the resources of a great soldier. The Mediterranean pirates were to the Roman legions and fleets much what a gang of *desperadoes* is to a well-organized police. But the pirates had long been a scourge to Roman commerce, and their suppression

THE MEDITERANEAN

became necessary. In 67 B. C. Pompey was given absolute power in the premises. He began in a business-like way. He divided the entire field into thirteen districts and placed a lieutenant and a sufficient force in each, with instructions to raise and equip men and galleys, search the coasts and hunt down the pirates. Pompey himself undertook the western Mediterranean, and cleared the coast of Sardinia, Sicily and Africa, so as to re-establish the grain traffic with Rome. Part of his force did the like on the shores of Gaul and Spain. In forty days Pompey had cleared the western half of the Mediterranean, and proceeded to Syria and Cilicia. The resistance offered was slight. There was no general organization. But Pompey was shrewd. He chose to be indulgent to many and moderate to most, rather than to crucify every pirate caught, as it had been the rule to do. This conduct of itself helped break up an already lost cause. The Cilicians alone offered any serious resistance; and these the Roman superior force and well-equipped galleys completely overwhelmed. The land resorts of the pirates were next broken up. Pardon brought many to terms. In three months from the first blow the entire war was finished. Some four hundred vessels, including ninety war-galleys, were taken; thirteen hundred in all were destroyed; ten thousand pirates perished and twenty thousand were captured. Many Roman prisoners were rescued.

The pirates had threatened Rome with starvation. Pompey's victories brought abundance. Everyone had feared to go to sea; the. Mediterranean was henceforth open to all. No wonder Pompey was heralded as the saviour of Rome. Yet he had done only a good piece of work, scarcely a great one.

The consul Lucullus had been ably conducting war in the East against the great Mithridates, who had overrun all Asia Minor (74 B. C). His colleague, Cotta, having been defeated in the Propontis (Sea of Marmora), Lucullus hastened to his relief and forced the king back with heavy loss. Setting matters to rights at sea, he followed up his advantage with a sharp offensive, crossed the Halys, marched across Pontus, won a fierce battle at Cabira, and fairly drove the great king out of his own kingdom. Capturing many cities by siege, Lucullus advanced into Armenia Minor, while Mithridates took refuge with Tigranes, king of Armenia. In order to forfeit no present advantages, Lucullus, unauthorised by the Senate, crossed the Euphrates into Armenia, and defeated Tigranes in the great Battle of Tigranocerta near the Tigris. The kings joined forces, but Lucullus beat them again and marched on Artaxata, the capital of Tigranes. A mutiny among his legions prevented his reaching his objective, and forced him to retire across the Tigris into Mesopotamia. While Lucullus was taking Nisibis by storm, Mithridates returned to Pontus, and defeated the Roman army left there, at Zela. Though handicapped by fresh mutinies and recalled by the Senate, Lucullus still made a handsome retreat to Asia Minor.

While Lucullus had ended unsuccessfully, he had in eight years of hard campaigning done much to weaken the resources of both Mithridates and Tigranes. In 66 B. C. Pompey went to Galatia to supplant Lucullus, purposing to advance into Pontus, whither his Cilician legions were to follow him. He had nearly fifty thousand men. Mithridates opposed him with thirty thousand foot, mostly archers, and three thousand horse. He no longer had his ancient ally and son-in law, Tigranes, to rely upon, and would have gladly made peace; but he would not unconditionally surrender, as Pompey demanded that he should do. Mithridates led Pompey some distance into his territory, harassing him severely with his superior horse. Pompey properly ceased to follow, and marching to the upper Euphrates crossed and entered Mithridates' eastern provinces. The king followed Pompey along the Euphrates and finally arrested his progress at the castle of Dasteira, from which secure position he scoured the lowlands with his cavalry and light troops. Pompey was forced to retire to Armenia Minor until his Cilician legions came up. Then he invested Mithridates in his eyrie and ravaged the land. After six weeks' blockade Mithridates put his sick and wounded to death to save them from falling into the hands of Pompey, and made his escape, marching by a circuit towards Armenia, Tigranes' territory. Pompey followed, but again perceiving Mithridates' intention of luring him away from Pontus, he resorted to a clever stratagem. In front of Mithridates, on the route he was pursuing south of the Lycus, near where Nicopolis was later built, was a narrow valley. Pompey, in lieu of following in Mithridates' rear, by a secret forced march got beyond him and occupied the heights surrounding the valley. Mithridates, unaware of this fact, marched next day as usual, and camped at nightfall in the very spot which placed his army in the trap ably laid for him by Pompey. In the middle of the night Pompey attacked. The army of Mithridates was wrapped in sleep and unable to resist. It was cut to pieces where it stood. Mithridates fled. Unable to go to Tigranes, he made his way along the east and north shores of the Euxine (Black Sea) to the Chersonesus (Crimea). Tigranes was at the mercy of Pompey. He gave up his recent conquests, and paid six thousand talents into the Roman war chest. Pompey had dictated peace.

In one easy campaign Pompey had thus overcome the two great Oriental kings,—of Pontus and Armenia. The territory of Rome had been indefinitely extended. No wonder that his name was in every mouth.

Asia Minor

Pompey for a while pursued Mithridates, which brought about a campaign against the tribes of the Caucasus. The king he could not overtake; the Caucasians he forced into a peace. Mithridates, from his refuge in Panticapaeum in the Crimea, harboured extravagant ideas of attacking Rome from the north by enlisting the Scythians and Danubian Celts in his favour as Hannibal had enlisted the Gauls. But this wild plan was ended by his death in 63 B. C. He had waged war against Rome for twenty-six years.

Pompey finished his work by reducing the new provinces, Pontus, Syria, Cilicia, to order, by subduing disorders in Syria, and settling affairs with the Parthians. He then returned to Rome for the reward which was his by right.

Lucullus had made much headway with the conquest of the East, for which his ability and enterprise were well suited. Pompey with his large forces, lack of initiative, and extreme caution, had completed what Lucullus had begun. Had he launched out as boldly as his predecessor he would not have accomplished so much. He had on all hands opportunities for brilliant strokes. He did nothing that was not safe. He kept his superiority of force at all times. His course was the very best to reap what Lucullus had sown, but it would never have conquered the East without such preparation as Lucullus had made. The campaigns of the latter compare favourably with those of Pompey, who was heralded as the representative of all that was most splendid in Roman annals, while Lucullus was forgotten. We shall be better able to gauge Pompey's real abilities when we try him in the same balance with Caesar.

ANCIENT HELMET

CHAPTER 3

Caesar's Youth, Education and Early Services
100-58 B. C.

Caesar was born 100 B. C. of an old Roman family. He owed much to the care given him by his mother. His education was carefully conducted and well bestowed. He was not strong as a lad, but gymnastics and a settled regimen improved his physique, which had a tendency to epilepsy. He was somewhat of a dandy, and a leader of the young society of Rome. He early developed talent as an orator and held many minor offices. His party—the Marian—was out of power, and the young man was wise in keeping out of the whirlpool of politics. Caesar had less to do with military affairs than most of those who rose to distinction in Rome. His work was in the line of statesmanship. He saw much of the world and at twenty-three made a reputation in his oration against Dolabella. He was well known as an able man, but not as a soldier. At thirty-nine he became praetor and received Spain as province. He was of middle age and had as yet done nothing but accumulate immense debts. In Spain he showed energy and ability, reduced Lusitania, and so managed its finances as to discharge all his debts. When he returned to Rome, Pompey, Caesar and Crassus became *triumvirs*; Caesar was made consul and allotted Gaul. In 58 B. C, at the age of forty-two, he entered upon that part of his career which has made him so great a part of the world's history.

Gaius Julius Caesar was born in 100 B. C. (some authorities hold 102 B. C), of an old patrician family which had come from Alba under the reign of Tullus Hostilius, and which had enjoyed many public trusts. His father had been praetor and had died when Caesar was about sixteen years old. His mother, Aurelia, was of good stock of plebeian origin, and was a woman of exceptionally fine character. Caesar was proud of his forbears. In pronouncing the funeral oration of his Aunt Julia, who had married Marius, Suetonius tells us that he thus spoke of his descent:

"My aunt Julia, on the maternal side, is of the issue of kings; on the paternal side, she descends from the immortal gods; for her mother was a Marcia, and the family Marcius Rex are the descendants of Ancus Marcius. The Julia family, to which I belong, descends from Venus herself. Thus our house unites to the sacred character of kings, who are the most powerful among men, the venerated holiness of the gods, who keep kings themselves in subjection."

Aurelia devoted her life to her son's education, and by this his natural mental and moral nature enabled him to profit as few youths can. He grew to manhood with many of the best qualities of head and heart stamped upon him. As pedagogue he had a Gaul, M. Antonius Gnipho, who had received all the benefits of an education in Alexandria. His body grew strong,—though originally delicate and having a tendency to epilepsy,—his carriage was erect, his manner open and kindly, and his countenance singularly engaging and expressive, if not handsome. He had black, piercing eyes, pale face, straight aquiline nose, small handsome mouth, with finely curled lips which bore a look of kindliness; large brow showing great intellectual activity and power. In his youth his face was well-rounded. He was moderate in his diet and temperate; his health, harmed by neither excess of labour or of pleasure, was uniformly good, though at Corduba and later at Thapsus he had serious nervous attacks. He exposed himself to all weathers, was an excellent gymnast, and noted as a rider. "From his first youth he was much used to horseback, and had even acquired the facility of riding with dropped reins and his hands joined behind his back." (Plutarch).

By judicious exercise he gradually became able to endure great fatigue. His dress was careful, and his person neat and tasteful to the extreme. Like the youth of every age he was over fond of outward adornment. Suetonius speaks of his key-pattern ornamented *toga* and loose girdle. Sulla once remarked that it would be well to look out for yonder dandy—and dandies in every age have notably made among the best of soldiers and men. This habit of personal nicety—not to say vanity—clung to him through life. "And when," says Cicero, "I look at his hair, so artistically arranged, and when I see him scratch his head with one finger," lest perchance he should disarrange it, "I cannot believe that such a man could conceive so black a design as to overthrow the Roman Republic" (Plutarch).

Caesar was fond of art as of books. He spoke Greek and Latin with equal ease and fluency, as was common to the cultured classes. He wrote several works which earned him a reputation for clear and forcible style, but he was not equally happy as a poet. Tacitus says:

"For Caesar and Brutus have also made verses, and have placed them in the public libraries. They are poets as feeble as Cicero, but happier in that fewer people know of them."

His life up to manhood was that of a city youth of good family and breeding, perhaps according to our notions lax, but within the bounds set by the age in which he lived; in later years he was a thorough man of the world. He was fond of female society, and cultivated it throughout his life. He possessed a marked taste for pictures, jewels, statues; and, as we are told by Dio Cassius, habitually wore a ring with a very beautiful seal of an armed Venus. He joined excellent physical endurance to very exceptional mental and nervous strength. "He was liberal to prodigality, and of a courage above human nature and even imagination," says Velleius Paterculus. Plutarch calls him the second orator in Rome. Pliny speaks of his extraordinary memory. Seneca gives him credit for great calmness in anger, and Plutarch says he was affable, courteous and gracious to a degree which won him the affection of the people. "In voice, gesture, a grand and noble personality, he had a certain brilliancy in speaking, without a trace of artifice," testifies Cicero. To the external advantages which distinguished him from all other citizens, Caesar joined an impetuous and powerful soul, says Velleius. One could scarcely add a single qualification to his equipment for the profession of arms. Such was Gaius Julius Caesar in the estimation of his contemporaries.

At fourteen years of age, Marius procured for him the appointment of priest of Jupiter. At sixteen he was betrothed to Cossutia, the daughter of a wealthy knight, but broke the engagement a year later. At eighteen he married Cornelia, daughter of Cinna. He is said to have been already well known for his personal and intellectual characteristics; but this was doubtless as the promising young scion of a well-known family, rather than from any services actually accomplished.

When Sulla rode into power on the wreck of the Marian party, he would have liked to bring over this brilliant young man to his cause, but he found Caesar immovable. He ordered him to put away Cornelia, whose father had belonged to the Marian faction, but this Caesar bluntly refused, though he forfeited his priesthood and his wife's fortune, was declared incapable of inheriting in his own family, and ran danger of his life. This was at a time when such men as Piso and Pompey divorced their wives to suit the politics of the day, and scores a high mark to Caesar's credit. Finally, after a period of concealment in the Sabine country, through the influence of friends, Caesar was forgiven by Sulla. But Sulla prophesied truly, says Suetonius, that there was more than one Marius lurking in the personality of Caesar.

ÆGEAN

Caesar deemed it wise, under the circumstances, to keep away from Rome. He could not remain without being thrust actively into the political turmoil, which he could see was but an interlude. Such discretion he manifested all through his political career. He spent some time in Bithynia, where he was guest of King Nicomedes.

Here, under the *praetor* M. Thermus, he served as *contubernalis* (*aide de camp*) against Mithridates, and was (81 B. C.) actively employed both in war and diplomacy. At the siege of Mitylene he received a civic crown for saving the life of a Roman soldier. His reputation for morality of demeanour was rudely compromised by his conduct at the court of Nicomedes; but such facts do not concern the soldier. The morals of each age and clime must stand by themselves. Caesar in no wise differed from his compeers. He then served at sea under Servilius in the campaign of 78 B. C. against the Cilician pirates. On Sulla's death he returned to Rome.

Here his conduct was marked by great moral courage and independence coupled with common sense and a liberal policy; and in some civil proceedings his powers of oratory, which he studied with great care, raised him high in the estimation of the people. It was an usual means of introducing one's self to the public to pose as advocate in some great political prosecution. Such was Caesar's part in the prosecution of Dolabella. He was twenty-one years old, and his oration, "which we still read with admiration," says Tacitus, in a moment made him famous. He later attacked Antonius Hybrida, and was engaged in other celebrated causes. These attacks were really aimed at Sulla's party, though still in power, rather than at individuals.

Preferring not to join for the present in the profitless political struggles of Rome, Caesar set sail for Rhodes, which at that time was a marked centre of learning, intending to devote some time to study. On the way thither he was captured by pirates of Pharmacusa (Fermaco), a small island of the Sporades. The pirates demanded twenty talents ransom, but Caesar contemptuously volunteered to pay them fifty, a piece of originality which insured him good treatment. While waiting some forty days for the receipt of the ransom-money, Caesar gained such influence with these men, that he was treated rather as a king than as a prisoner. He disarmed all their suspicions and entertained them by his eloquence and wit. He is said to have told them—which they treated as a jest—that he would return, capture and crucify them all. He was as good as his word. Collecting vessels and men so soon as he was released, he fell unawares upon the pirates, recovered his money, took much booty, and punished them as he had threatened to do. Suetonius states that from motives of pity he had them all strangled first and only nailed their corpses to the cross.

After a short stay in Rhodes, where he studied under Apollonius Molo, the most celebrated of the masters of eloquence, he undertook on his own authority and cost a campaign against Mithridates in Cyzicus, in which he was measurably successful. He now learned from Rome that he had been nominated *pontifex*, in place of his uncle, L. Aurelius Cotta. He returned, and shortly after was also elected military tribune. He declined service in armies under the command of the Sullan generals, at the time of the campaigns against Sertorius in Spain. He would gladly have gone to the front to learn his duties in the field, but did not care to take a part against one who represented the old Marian party. He as usual cleverly avoided useless complications. Still he was ambitious of power, and set to work to form a party for himself in the state; and by employing fortune, friends, energy and ability, he succeeded in doing this. Being made *quaestor*, he accompanied the proconsul Antistius Vetus to Spain. Returned to Rome, he was in 68 B. C. made curator of the Appian Way and *aedile curulis*, and largely increased his popularity by the splendour of the public games he gave.

His next office was that of *judex quaestionis*, or judge of the criminal court, in 64 B. C, and in the succeeding year he was made *pontifex maximus*. After still another year he became praetor. During all this time he had been earning the hate of the aristocrats and the favour of the people. He was assigned the charge of the province of Hispania Ulterior, in 61 B. C, but could not leave Rome till someone had become bondsman for his debts, amounting, it is said, to over four thousand *talents*, or, according to Plutarch, to eight hundred and thirty *talents*, from one to five million dollars, as the sum. Caesar's recklessness in money matters was a characteristic which pursued him through life.

Crassus was prevailed on to be his security. He relied for repayment on Caesar's future successes. He was not deceived. Political preferment in Rome was coupled with opportunities of making money indefinitely great. The control of a province opened endless avenues of gain. And though no one was more careful to observe the forms of law, though no one was more law-abiding in the technical sense, Caesar was in larger matters as unscrupulous as Napoleon. It was the habit of his day.

Caesar's province as *praetor*—Farther Spain, or Boetica,—possibly included some adjoining territories. He left Rome so soon as his money matters were arranged, without waiting for the instructions of the Senate, whose action was delayed by some political trials. The lowlanders of his province had been long subject to forays by the mountaineers of Lusitania, a section of country only half subject to the Roman power, if at all. Caesar found two legions, or twenty *cohorts*, under the colours. These he at once increased by a third legion, or ten additional *cohorts*, giving him some ten thousand men. The tribes of Mons Herminium (Sierra di Estrella) in Lusitania (Portugal) were constantly troubling the province. Unable to control them by the command of the Roman people, whose authority the hardy uplanders laughed to scorn, Caesar promptly undertook a campaign against them, and by vigorous measures reduced them to submission. Much of the detail of this campaign is not known. The other tribes of the mountains, lest they should suffer a like harsh fate, migrated beyond the Douro. This enabled Caesar to possess himself of the strong places of the country in the valley of the Munda (Mondego), basing on which, he set out to pursue the fugitives, whom he soon reached. The barbarians turned upon him, and to unsettle his *cohorts* by making the *legionaries* eager for booty, they drove their herds before them. But Caesar's men always felt the influence of the strong hand, and these *cohorts*, though new to him, had already learned to obey. An army is the mirror of its captain, reflecting his force and character as well as his intelligence. So now. Not a soldier left the ranks, and the Lusitanians were quickly routed. In this campaign Caesar scoured the country on both banks of the Durius.

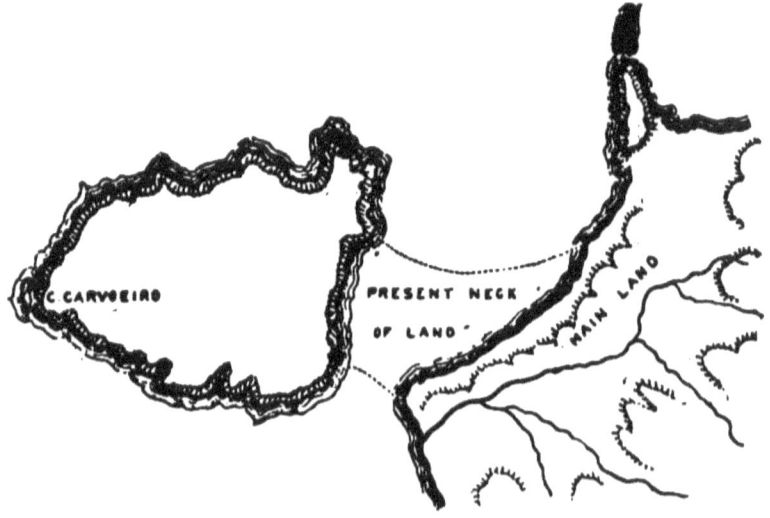

CAPE CARVOEIRO

Meanwhile the Mt. Herminianites had again revolted, hoping that Caesar would be defeated by the migrating tribes, and that they could close the road against his retreat and have him at their mercy. Caesar had advanced towards the Durius on the eastern slope of one of the minor ranges. Finding that the barbarians had closed this way, and not caring to encounter a guerilla warfare when he could operate to better advantage, he sought an outlet on the slope which descends towards the sea; but this, too, the barbarians closed by occupying the country from the foothills of the mountains to the shore. Caesar had to fight his way through; but this his legions found no difficulty in doing on the easier terrain near the sea. In attacking the enemy, Caesar operated by his left and managed to cut them off from the interior so as to drive them towards the sea, where he could more readily handle them. They took refuge on an island, which some critics have identified with the headland of Carvoeiro, now joined to the mainland, some forty-five miles north of Lisbon. The strait could be crossed in places at low tide on foot, but with difficulty. Having cooped up his enemy, Caesar proposed to destroy him. It was impracticable to cross the strait under the fire of the barbarians. Caesar built some rafts, and put over a portion of his troops. Part of the rest, over eager, attempted to ford the strait, but, sharply attacked by the barbarians, they were driven back into the rising tide and engulfed. The first attack thus failed, the small part for which the rafts sufficed being unable to effect a landing.

But Caesar never gave up what was possible of accomplishment. Camping opposite the island, where he could hold the Lusitanians, he dispatched messengers to Gades for ships. On the arrival of these, he was able to put a suitable force over to the island, which done, he had no difficulty in subduing the enemy's force. This matter ended, he sailed to Brigantium (Corunna), whose inhabitants, terrified at the novel sight of such mighty vessels, voluntarily gave up the contest.

This campaign resulted in the submission of all Lusitania, and added much territory to the Roman holding in Spain. Caesar was saluted Imperator by his soldiers and allowed a triumph by the Senate, which also decreed a holiday in honour of his success. So little is given us by the historians beyond the bare outline of the campaign, that we can say of it only that it was Caesar's first lesson in war. When he attacked the Gallic question, he showed that he was familiar with war, but not with the management of its greater problems. Gaul was his school in the grand operations of war. It is to be regretted that we do not know how he had learned what unquestionably he knew of the art previous to his first campaign in Gaul. He had manifestly covered an immense territory, but we know naught of his method.

With the civil administration of his province after this war we have no concern. Caesar accumulated great wealth; as Suetonius says, by the begging of subsidies; as Napoleon III. phrases it, "by contributions of war, a good administration, and even by the gratitude of those whom he governed." The fact remains, but Caesar did no more than every governor of a Roman province felt it his right to do.

Caesar unquestionably cared for money, but not from miserly motives. Hannibal was accused of avarice; but every coin he accumulated went to fan the flame of war against his country's oppressors. Caesar used his gold to create an army, to win to himself the love of his legions. Such an amount of booty was taken in Spain as not only to reward his soldiers with exceptional liberality, but to pay off his own debts. His ambition was satisfied in every way.

That Caesar was ambitious is no reproach. No man lacking ambition ever rose out of mediocrity, ever accomplished anything in the world's economy. At a small village in crossing the Alps, Caesar is said to have exclaimed: "I would rather be first here than second in Rome!" Every great man is ambitious. It is the purpose of his ambition and the means he takes to satisfy it which are the test of its being a virtue or a vice. Caesar's ambition was more personal than Hannibal's. It was akin to that of Alexander and Napoleon. In the temple of Hercules at Gades, standing before the statue of Alexander, Caesar exclaimed that he had yet done nothing, when long before his age Alexander had conquered the world. Such was not the ambition of Hannibal nor Gustavus.

For his victories in Spain, Caesar was entitled to a triumph, but he denied himself this glory in order to run for the consulship.

The Roman Senate had demonstrated its inability to control the rival factions which were shaking the foundations of the state. Finally a breach between the Senate and Pompey, who was the strongest man in Rome, was brought about by its refusal to grant an allotment of lands for his Eastern veterans. As a result, Pompey, Caesar and Crassus formed a secret compact to act together to divide the power and offices of Rome. They and their friends, with the easy methods of the day, could readily control both the Senate and the people.

Caesar was unanimously elected consul, and with him was chosen Calpurnius Bibulus. The latter was to all purposes, and easily, shelved as a nonentity. Caesar's first year was passed in law-making. He was able, by Pompey's aid, to procure the passage of a law by which he received for five years control of Illyria and Cisalpine Gaul, with four legions. This was his first great step upward. The governorship would enable him to win renown and to create an army devoted to his own person, a stepping-stone to almost any greatness. Among his other

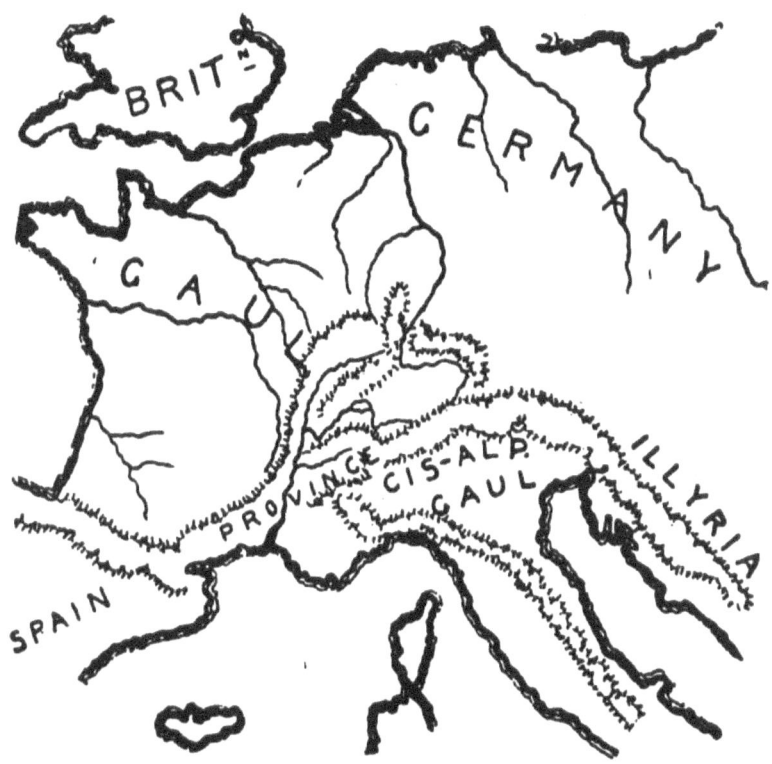

CAESAR'S PROVINCES

measures he caused Ariovistus, king of the Suevi, one of his later great antagonists, to be declared a friend and ally of Rome.

Before leaving for Gaul he married his daughter Julia to Pompey, as a bond during his absence, and himself—his wife Cornelia having died some years before—married Calpurnia, daughter of Piso, the ex-consul. Cicero and Cato, Caesar's rich and powerful opponents, it was agreed should be exiled. The foundation was well laid for permanence.

Caesar had reached the goal of his political ambition by years of persistent effort and by means of every kind, not always such as were most to his credit. But now began a new life. He was forty-two years old, and politics ceded to arms. We shall hereafter view him in a new and far more worthy role,—a role which has made one of the great chapters in the history of the art of war.

Chapter 4

Caesar's New Province— The Helvetii
60-58 B. C.

The Gauls had always been the most dreaded foes of Rome. Whoever put an end to the danger would be the national hero. This fact Caesar recognized. The Gauls were a fine, hearty people. They had many fortified towns, but the population lived mostly in open villages. There was good agricultural development, much pastoral and some mining industry. The men were warlike and brave, but fickle in temper. Their cavalry was excellent; the foot unreliable, though gallant. The common people were downtrodden by the knights and Druids; the powerful princes, and cantons had the weaker population and tribes as clients, exacting service and affording protection. Just before Caesar's arrival the Helvetii had prepared a descent from their Alpine home to the lowlands. Caesar saw that this migration would complicate his problem, and refused them the passage they requested across the Roman Province, fortifying the Rhone below Geneva against them. The Helvetii made their way down the north bank of the Rhone. The Gallic tribes, some of whom were under Roman protection, appealed to Caesar for help. The Helvetii were three hundred and sixty-eight thousand strong, and had begun to ravage the Gallic lands as they marched towards the Saône.

Many months before Caesar left for Gaul, reports reached Rome that the Gallic allies on the Arar (Saône) had been defeated by the Germans, and that the Helvetii were in arms. The news created great consternation. All feared a fresh invasion of barbarians such as had been barely averted by Marius. A general levy was ordered. Caesar had asked as his province only for Cisalpine Gaul and Illyria. Under the pressure of danger the Senate added Transalpine Gaul to his charge.

The Gauls had a memorable record in Roman annals, but the greater part of their warlike feats lie buried in obscurity. We know that late in the seventh century B. C., an expedition of Celtic Gauls moved through southern Germany to Illyria, while another crossed the Alps and seized on the valley of the Po. It was the descendants of these latter Gauls who burned Rome. In the fourth century, other tribes moved down the Danube to Thrace and ravaged northern Greece. Some of them pursued their way to Byzantium and passed into Asia, where they overran and held a large territory—Gallo-Grecia or Galatia. Rome was constantly fighting the Gauls during the third and fourth centuries, but her knowledge of them was confined to such as lived south of the Alps or in Mediterranean Gaul. She had spilled much blood and spent much treasure to bring the Padane Gauls to terms, but these tribes were no sooner subdued than they again rose when Hannibal crossed the Alps. They were not finally reduced for a generation after the Second Punic war.

The foothold of the Romans in Gaul had been acquired in the usual way, by taking the old Greek colony of Massilia under its protection and subduing the neighbouring tribes for its benefit, about the middle of the second century B. C. Next Aquae Sextiae was settled as an outpost to Massilia. Between the Rhone and the mountains lay the Vocontii as far as the Isère; from this river to the Rhone lay the Allobroges with Vienna as their capital; from the Rhone to the Saône and Jura mountains the Sequani, with Vesontio; between the Saône and Loire the Ædui, with Bibracte; on both sides of the Allier the Arverni. The Ædui and Arverni had long disputed for the hegemony of Gaul; the Allobroges favoured the latter. Rome stepped in and helped the Ædui. In 121 B. C., Domitius Ahenobarbus and Fabius Maximus put down the Allobroges in two great battles. Thus was founded the Roman Province in Gaul. To it was later added Narbo. The irruption of the Teutones and Cimbri about the date of the birth of Caesar threatened to destroy the structure so carefully

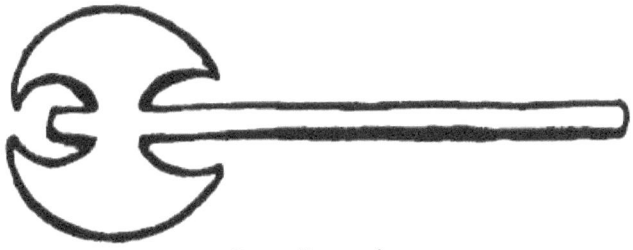

GALLIC BATTLE-AXE

reared. The barbarians successively beat five Roman armies. But the victory of Marius at Aquae Sextiae forestalled the danger and reestablished the Roman influence.

The boundaries of the Province had been established from Tolosa and Narbo, south and east of the Cebenna mountains, up to Vienna, thence along the Rhone to the Alps, and thence southerly to the ocean. They were such when Caesar took it in charge.

There was constant friction among the Gallic tribes in and adjoining the Province, and many of their representatives visited Rome. Among these were Ariovistus the German and Divitiacus the Gaul. From these men, both able and well-informed, Caesar learned much about the conditions governing the land as well as its geography and topography. It was, except in the remote regions, by no means *terra incognita* which Caesar was to take in charge. He found a good base for his operations in the Province when Gaul was assigned to him as his share of the triumvirate spoils.

Gaul was in a turbulent state. War had never ceased within its borders. There were ceaseless insurrections; and a Roman army passing through southern Gaul to Spain was sure to have to fight its way. Despite the constant turmoil, the Province was, however, a favourite resort. Its endless wealth of trade with the interior, already begun by the early Greek settlers, was attractive, and its climate was balmy and agreeable. The land still bore traces of Hellenism, but it had gained the practical Roman imprint. Much money was made in trade. Still a residence in the Province had its drawbacks, and was always subject to danger.

Cicero says:

"Until the time of Caesar, our generals were satisfied with repelling the Gauls, thinking more of putting a period to their aggressions than of carrying war among them. Marius himself did not penetrate to their towns and homes, but confined himself to opposing a barrier to these torrents of peoples which were overflowing Italy. . . . Caesar alone determined to subject Gaul to our dominion."

The Romans looked to conquer other peoples, but only to protect themselves from the Gauls. To resist a Gallic invasion there was always a levy *en masse*, and there was a special treasure in the Capitol to furnish means for only this occasion.

This never-ending terror of the Gauls—equalled only by that of Hannibal, which lasted but eighteen years—explains why the Roman people, after the conquest of these enemies, felt so beholden to Caesar. The meed due all other conquerors was small compared to his. Other victories had meant aggrandizement; that over the Gauls meant safety. It was a knowledge of all this, of the reputation and power he could thus win, which inspired Caesar in his task.

Cisalpine Gaul we already know from the campaigns of Hannibal. Transalpine Gaul was bounded by the Rhine, the Alps, the Mediterranean, the Pyrenees and the ocean. It comprised France, the Low Countries, the Rhenish provinces and Switzerland. This huge country had an irregular mountain-backbone running through its centre from north to south,—a watershed on the east of which the streams flowed into the Rhone and the Rhine, and on the west into the Garonne, the Loire and the Seine, or into their affluents. All these rivers flowed in basins well-defined, and furnished excellent means of communication throughout the country. A glance at the course of the rivers shows how excellent the lines of advance or retreat of an army might be. The central mountain chain was readily crossed in many places.

In climate there were the same distinctions in Gaul as today. The province was mild; the north, still covered by dense forests, was colder than today. The forest of Arduenna (Ardennes) extended over an area of two hundred miles wide, from the Rhine to the Scheldt and the frontier of the Remi. The country had a wooded character, and deep forests covered territory which today is under close cultivation. It is difficult to gauge the population; but to take a reasonable percentage of arms-bearing men, the troops raised on various occasions would argue something over seven million souls. Gaul was divided into numerous tribes, which Tacitus states as sixty-four, but which others place at three or four hundred. This latter number may be accurate, if it be held to comprise the many client-tribes, or small tribes relying upon some powerful neighbour for protection, and bound to send its contingent to its patron's wars. This sort of feudalism existed throughout the country. Powerful individuals had large forces of clients; powerful cantons had numbers of client-cantons. In central Gaul the Arverni and the Ædui strove for the hegemony. Such competition for control created a very loose national tie, and made Gaul all the more ripe for conquest.

To the north of the Sequana (Seine) and Matrona (Marne) and west of the Rhine lived the Belgians, to whom Caesar accords the palm as the bravest of the barbarians. They remembered with pride that they had defended their borders against the Cimbri and Teutones. Being farthest removed from the province, and least accessible to merchants, these people had nothing to render them effeminate; while a constant war with the Germans across the Rhine, though they claimed kindred with them, tended to make them bold and hardy. In the southwest of Gaul, back of the Garumna (Garonne) lived the Aquitani. Between these and the Belgians, the land was occupied by various tribes of Celts or Gauls. The province was in every sense a part of Gaul. Its peoples had the same origin; they had merely felt the influence of the Greek colony at Massilia, as they now did that of Rome. The Belgae comprised several notable tribes. The Bellovaci, who abutted on the sea, could put one hundred thousand men into line. The Nervii placed Caesar in the most desperate strait he ever faced. The Treviri and the Remi were bold and hardy. Central Gaul, or Celtica, counted the Arverni, the Ædui, the Sequani and the Helvetii as principal nations. The latter stood proudly aloof in their mountain homes; the three former warred much for the supremacy of Gaul. Aquitania, in the era of Caesar, had less importance to the Romans.

These large cantons were divided into tribes, and further into clans. They had many towns or *oppida*—Caesar mentions twenty-one—which were mostly well placed and fortified. The bulk of the people lived in open villages. Roads practicable for wheels existed in every section, and there were bridges over many rivers. Navigation on the rivers and sailing vessels at sea were common.

The Gauls were tall in stature, and of light complexion. They dyed their hair; the commoners wore beards, the nobles only a moustache. They were dressed in trowsers and a sleeved shirt, with a mantle among the rich, a skin among the poor. Gold was plentiful among them, and bred the habit of wearing collars, earrings, bracelets and rings. They were fairly expert in agriculture, though some tribes preferred pastoral pursuits, and manufactured linen cloths and felts. Much grain, and cattle and horses, were raised. Their houses were built of wood and wicker-work. Copper was mined and worked. Some tribes wrought in iron and plated it with tin and silver. They ate beef, pork, and other domestic meats, drank milk and brewed ale and mead, in which they frequently overindulged. Italian wine was highly considered; a jar of it was deemed at times worth a slave. They were pleasant and kindly, but vain and quick-tempered, fickle and restless. Brave in battle, they wilted under defeat. They spoke in precise hyperbole and wrote with Greek letters. The women were strong and beautiful, and often as brave and hardy as the men. The husband had the right of life or death over his wife or child. A free man might not legally be put to the torture; a free woman was not exempt. In Caesar's day, as in Han-

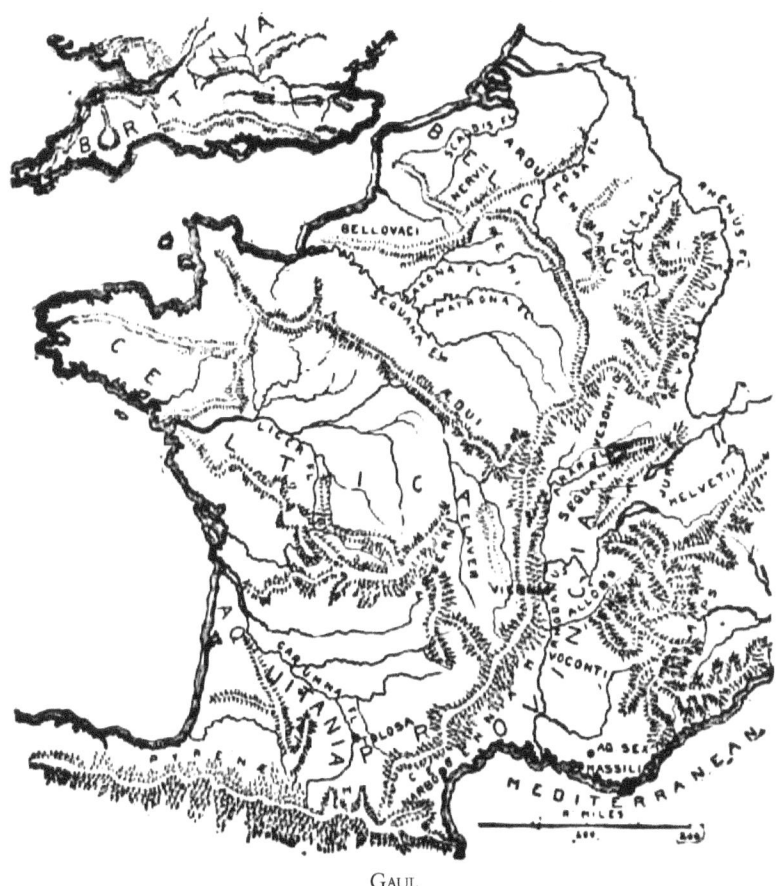

GAUL

nibal's, the Gauls wielded the long two-edged cutting sword. Some tribes preferred long pikes with wavy blades; all cast darts, and bore both bows and slings. Their metal helmets were ornamented with the horns of animals or with a bird or beast, and were surmounted with a high tuft of feathers. They carried big shields and wore a breastplate or coat of mail, which they manufactured themselves. The Gallic cavalry was superior to the foot, as it contained the nobles. This arm was their delight. They took pride in their horses and sought noble breeds. Tilting was a frequent sport, and at banquets duels to the death were not unknown.

The Gauls imitated well what they saw of value among others. Their armies were followed by a long array of wagons, and at night they fortified their camps with a circle of them. They challenged to single combat any champion of the enemy before battle, killed their prisoners, and preserved their heads as trophies. Levies *en masse* were common, at which the last arrival forfeited his life. This put every man on the alert. They transmitted news with great rapidity by signals and relays of men, and by peculiar shouts from place to place. The Gauls were superstitious, and part of their religious observances consisted of human sacrifices. The Druids, who originated in Britain, kept them well under control. Their gods approximated to those of all antiquity, there being deities with the attributes of Jupiter, Mars, Apollo and Neptune.

The two classes of distinction were the knights and the Druids. The commonalty was ground between these as between the upper and nether millstone. Each knight or noble had a following of clients, who were devoted to him to the death. The government of each nation lay in a king or an assembly.

Among the Gallic cantons, someone or other was always in the ascendant, and exercised for a time the control of all the land. At the period of Caesar's receiving Gaul as a province, the Sequani had the upper hand, and had severely oppressed the Ædui, ancient allies of the Romans.

The Helvetii, in modern Switzerland, were then, as history has always shown them to be, a stout-hearted, big-fisted, self-reliant people. They waged a never-ceasing warfare with the Germans, whose tribes constantly invaded their borders or were invaded by them. Orgetorix was a bold, ambitious and wealthy chief of the Helvetii. He had persuaded his people, three years before the beginning of Caesar's governorship, that their valour would easily conquer for them the more fertile plains of Gaul, and thus enable them to extend their empire beyond the narrow limits of their unproductive hills, all too confined for their numbers, their pride, and their repute in war. Wrought up by the promises of gain and fame which Orgetorix thus held out to them, the Helvetii proceeded to gather together as many beasts of burden and wagons as possible, proposing to move with all their possessions and an abundance of corn, to serve for sowing as well as victual. Orgetorix was appointed to make arrangements with neigh-boring potentates for passage over their territories. But Orgetorix proved faithless to the trust reposed in him, and instead of serving his fellow-citizens, laid plans for obtaining sovereignty over the Helvetii for himself and his descendants. Being brought to trial, his adherents rose in arms, but Orgetorix died,—it was supposed by suicide,—and this put an end to the matter.

The Helvetian mind, however, excited by the allurements of the fertile plains towards the great sea, still clung to the plan of emigration. In the third year, 60-59 B. C., having made all their preparations, and each one carrying three months' supply of meal, they fired their twelve towns, four hundred villages and numberless farms, burned all the corn which they were unable to carry with them, and in order to leave no inclination to return, destroyed every vestige of their homes and habitations. Several neighbouring tribes—the Rauraci, the Tulingi, the Latobriges, and some of the Boii—cast in their fortunes with the Helvetii.

The Helvetii had to choose between two routes. They could find an exit from their valleys into Gaul through the land of the Sequani, across the pass between the Rhone and the Jura mountains, now the Pas de l'Ecluse, just below Geneva. This was a rugged road, difficult to march over, "by which scarcely one wagon at a time could be led," and which could be easily held and their progress intercepted by a mere handful of enemies skilfully disposed. Or they could cross to the south side of the Rhone and pass through the land of the Allobroges, where the river—the boundary between themselves and this

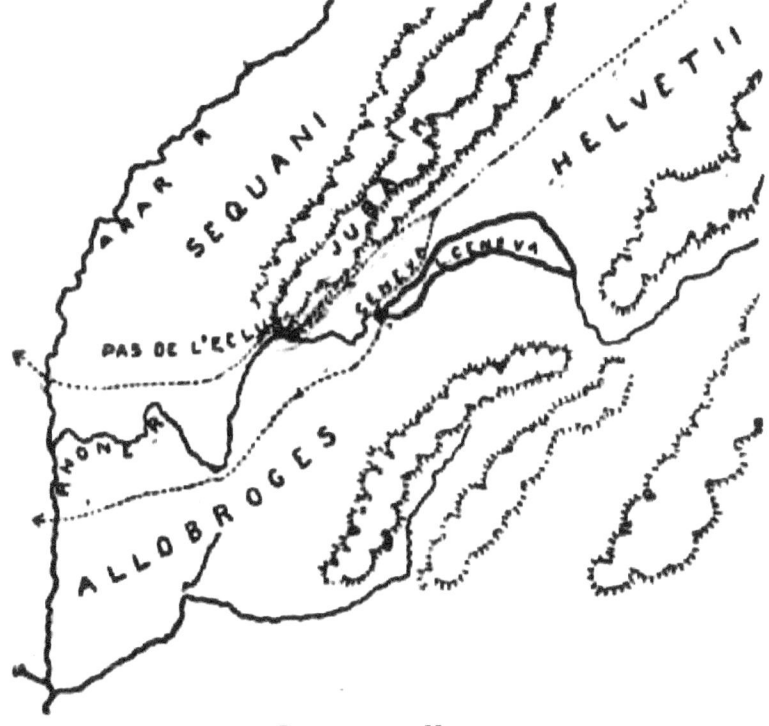

ROUTES OF THE HELVETII

people—was then, it is said, though it is not now, fordable in many places. The river has somewhat altered its width and course. Genava (Geneva), then built only on the left bank of the Rhone, was the town of the Allobroges nearest to the Helvetii, and here was also a bridge. This latter route was easy. The Helvetii felt confident of their ability to persuade or compel the Allobroges to allow them to pass, for this people had been recently conquered by the Romans and were bitter accordingly. They made a rendezvous upon the banks of the Rhone for their whole people, three hundred and sixty-eight thousand souls, for the spring equinox of 58 B. C.

All these facts must have come to the ears of Caesar long before the time of which we are to write, for the Helvetii had been openly preparing their expedition for two years, and one of Caesar's strong points was his ability to gather news. Caesar had not got ready to leave Rome, where political complications and the advocacy of new laws retained him. But he was carefully watching events. War was what he anticipated. In the division of spoils by the triumvirate, Caesar had advisedly chosen Gaul for his consular province. His purpose was to subdue the country, not only to save Rome from future incursions, but, equally important to him personally, to create for himself an army, in those troublous times an essential for the great, the possession of which was to be his key to abiding success. Caesar's motives must not be impugned; neither must they be overrated. He was neither a Gustavus nor a Washington. He worked for Rome; but Rome was Caesar. *L'empire, c'est moi!* was his motive if not his motto.

In March, 58 B. C., the time was rife; events would no longer wait his leisure. Caesar hastened from Rome to Geneva, which journey he accomplished, says Plutarch, in eight days. There was at the time in Transalpine Gaul but a single legion, the Tenth. This he at once headed for Geneva, and ordering the province to raise and equip with utmost speed as many more men as could be done, he took the only possible step momentarily to arrest the advance of the barbarians by causing the bridge at that city to be broken down.

So soon as the Helvetii heard of Caesar's arrival, they sent an embassy to him composed of their most illustrious men, requesting the privilege of crossing the province peacefully, there being no other available route, and promising good behaviour on the march. But remembering that L. Cassius, when consul with Marius in 107 B. C., had been defeated and slain and his army passed under the yoke by the Helvetii, and far from believing in their pacific intention, Caesar

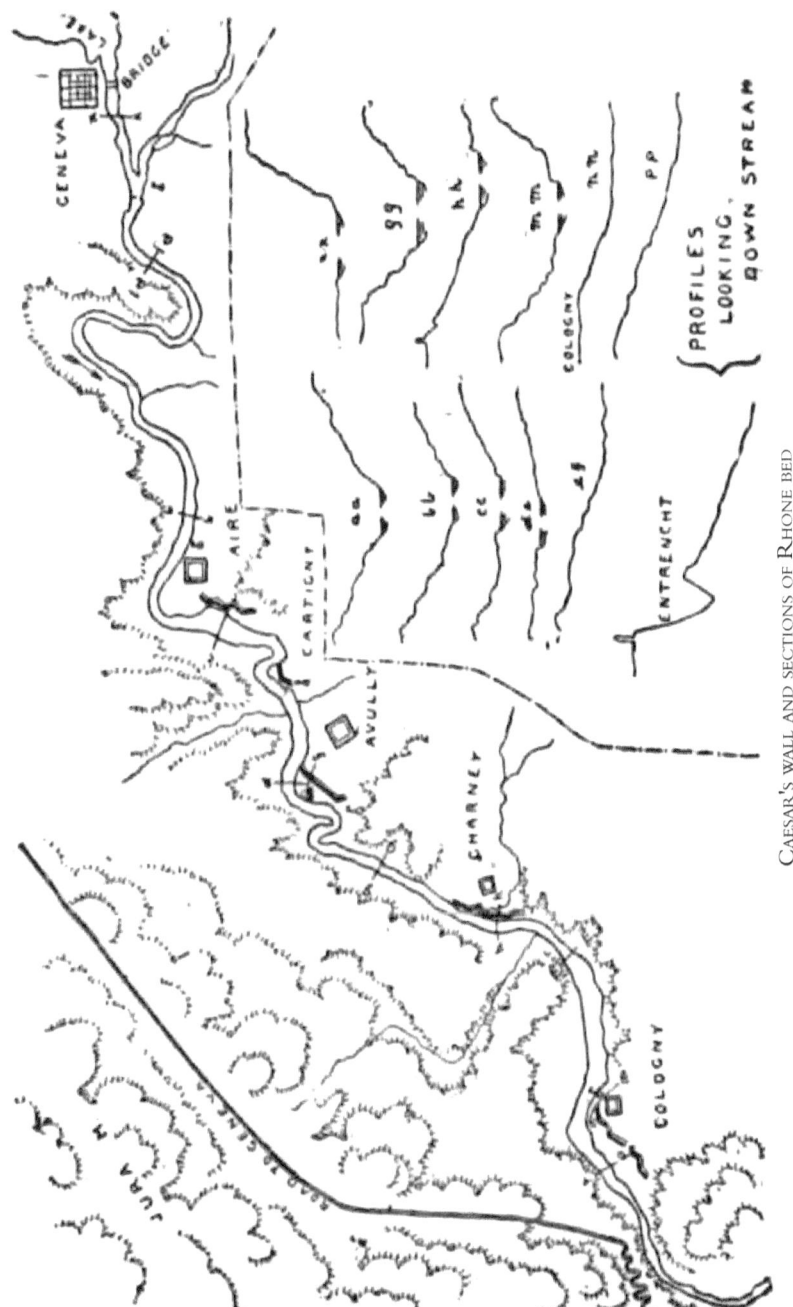

Caesar's wall and sections of Rhone bed

decided to decline the request. Moreover, he recognized that it was impossible for a body of nearly four hundred thousand souls to pass through the province without devastating it like a plague of grasshoppers. And once in Gaul, the Helvetii would but add one more tribe to conquer, while their territory would almost certainly be speedily filled by the Germans whom the Helvetii now held in check. Still, desiring to gain time to raise troops and complete his preparations, Caesar listened courteously to the ambassadors and declared his willingness to consider the matter; inviting them to return two weeks later, on the ides of April, when he would have his answer ready to give them. It is evident that the Helvetii believed that Caesar was sincere. He had conveyed to them the impression that he would grant their request. The proceeding is a fair sample of Caesar's political management. He was a very Talleyrand in statecraft.

Meanwhile, with wonderful expedition and skill, he built entrenchments at intervals along the left bank of the Rhone from the lake of Geneva to the Jura range at the Pas de l'Ecluse. This has been supposed to be continuous fortification; but it can scarcely have been such; many critics, however, think that the several redoubts may have been joined by a simple line of works. A continuous defence was unnecessary. Caesar had not men enough to man such a line. The Rhone itself is an enormous ditch with scarp and counterscarp, which takes the place of entrenchments. Caesar had the Tenth legion, say five thousand men, and perhaps an equal number of new levies, and could have well built in the period mentioned a wall sixteen feet high and eighteen miles long, as given in the *Commentaries*. Colonel Stoffel estimates that the work assumed to have been actually done could be performed by three thousand men in three days. Dion Cassius says that Caesar fortified the most important points, and much of the course of the Rhone here is so well fortified by nature that there is no need of art. Caesar had too much to do to undertake what was not necessary. The assumption that *murus fossaque* was a continuous line is untenable.

Only opposite the modern villages of Aire, Cartigny, Avully, Chancy, Cologny, were fortifications needed, because at these places the slope of the left bank was gradual. It was here that Caesar cut the trenches sixteen feet deep. With the natural scarp of the river bank the line was complete and continuous. The words cannot be held to mean a built wall for the entire distance, and the topography clearly tells the story. The whole line was fortified with well-manned redoubts at suitable intervals, as at all possible fords or crossing places, and the fortifications were held with a strong garrison. Caesar unquestionably distributed his forces at the five named points. From there they could easily concentrate on any threatened point in a few hours; and we may presume that he posted observation parties at the several places where the Helvetii could best be seen.

It is strange that the Helvetii, who must have clearly perceived what Caesar was intending to do by thus fortifying the valley against them, should have kept quiet two weeks while waiting for his answer, instead of either attacking his half-finished works, or of moving by the other route. Probably the glib tongue of Caesar had been employed to such good purpose in his intercourse with them that they gave credit to the words which his acts belied.

When the ambassadors returned on the ides of April to receive their answer, Caesar, being now well prepared, bluntly informed them that the Roman customs would not allow him to comply with their wishes. He intimated at the same time that he should be compelled to use force if they attempted to pass, and as they could see, was justified in considering himself master of the situation. Some slight efforts were made by the disgusted Helvetii to try the strength of Caesar's works or to steal a march by night across the fords, but these proved signal failures, and they found that they must turn to the other route, having lost two weeks and been completely outwitted by the Roman.

For this purpose, they endeavoured to procure from the Sequani, who occupied substantially the territory covered by the Jura and its foothills, the necessary permission to pass over their land, and, as they could not themselves prevail in this request, they enlisted the services of Dumnorix, the Æduan, who had married the daughter of Orgetorix and who stood in high consideration among the Sequani, to intercede for them. This Dumnorix did, and shortly obtained the desired right. Hostages were given by each party, the Sequani to allow the passage, the Helvetii to refrain from pillaging on the way.

The rumour of this action reaching Caesar, and hearing, moreover, that the Helvetii were heading for the land of the Santones, on the coast, northwest from the Tolosates, about modern Toulouse, he determined to prevent this movement also; for a wandering tribe of warlike barbarians could not fail to be a danger to the Roman supremacy, and the Tolosates had become Roman clients. What was more, the Helvetii would probably take possession of the best corn-bearing region of the province, which he himself might need, and would keep within no distinct boundaries.

CAESAR'S ROUTE ACROSS THE ALPS

Caesar estimated correctly that the Helvetii would need some weeks in completing their preparations for the march; and leaving Titus Labienus, his most trusted legate, in command of his works, he himself hastened to Cisalpine Gaul, raised two new legions (the Eleventh and Twelfth), called in three old ones (the Seventh, Eighth and Ninth) which were wintering at Aquileia, and with these five crossed the Alps by forced marches into Gaul. His route lay through Ocelum over Mont Genèvre, and by Grenoble to Lyon, the road opened by Pompey when he was in command of Spain. He experienced some difficulty on the road from the opposition of the mountain tribes, who, despite the reduction of Cisalpine Gaul, were still their own masters; but, though they held the commanding points of the passes, he defeated these barbarians in several smart encounters, safely reached the land of the Allobroges with his five legions, and crossed the Rhone near modern Lyon, to the territory of the Segusiani. All this he had accomplished in an incredibly short time. From Ocelum to the land of the Vocontii, about modern Grenoble, he took but seven days, thus making about sixteen miles a day over a rough mountain mule-road. It had taken two months from the refusal of the demand of the Helvetii to raise and place his troops upon the Rhone.

The Helvetii had, indeed, consumed much time in negotiations to secure their passage over the Pas de l'Ecluse, and in their actual march, loaded as they were, still more. But once across this natural obstacle they had made better speed, and, passing through the land of the Sequani, had reached that of the Ædui, which they were ravaging in the most cruel manner in revenge for Caesar's evident perfidy to them. These people and the Ambarri, their kinsmen, both tribes located north of the Rhone, appealed to Caesar for help, alleging their ancient friendship for Rome and present distress. The Allobroges also appealed, assuring Caesar that they had nothing remaining. All were clients of Rome. The Helvetii, to judge by the lay of the land, must have followed the Rhone to modern Culoz and then struck across country to the River Arar, which they reached near modern Trévoux. Their slowness is natural when we consider that some three hundred and sixty-eight thousand men, women and children, followed by a train of ten thousand wagons (for it would take at least so many to carry three months' victual for this number), had to pass through a single defile. Caesar had relied on this essential slowness to get his troops from Italy. He lost no time in deciding to attack and punish the

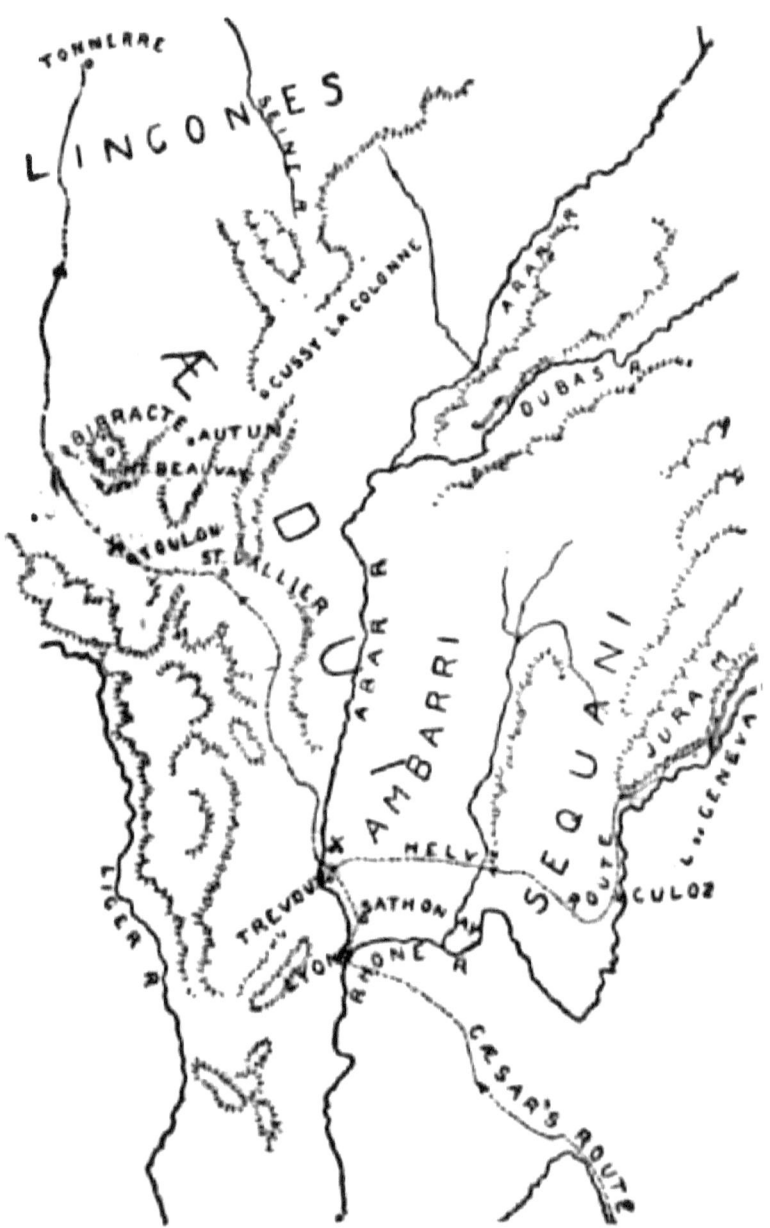

Theatre of Helvetian Campaign

Helvetii, and told the supplicants that they might rely on his protection. He required from them, however, a number of troops, especially a body of cavalry, of which arm he had none.

It is rather strange that Caesar, throughout his campaigns in Gaul, relied all but exclusively, on native horse; and stranger still, that he left the command of this horse to native leaders. His reasons for the last were probably mainly political; but the plan was not always followed by good results, and was constantly attended by danger. The Gallic horse, however, proved for his purposes much better than the Roman. They were an exceptional body of men.

CHAPTER 5

The Battles of the Arar and Bibracte
June, 58 B. C.

Caesar had six legions. He came up with the Helvetii on the Saône above Lyon. Three quarters of the enemy's force had crossed the river. Caesar by skilful dispositions surprised and destroyed the quarter remaining on the left bank. He then crossed and cautiously followed the rest, who, somewhat abashed, retreated. The Helvetii still had seventy thousand warriors, and were heading down the Loire. At one place Caesar sought to attack them, but his well-conceived tactical combinations failed to work. Finding that his rations were growing short, Caesar then ceased from pursuit and moved towards Bibracte, where was much corn. The enemy turned upon him, deeming him to have acted from fear, and offered battle. Caesar drew up his legions expertly, and awaited their attack. The battle was hotly contested. At one period, having advanced too far, Caesar was attacked in rear and forced to form two fronts. But Roman discipline finally prevailed; the victory was complete and overwhelming. A bare third of the Helvetians remained. These Caesar compelled to return to their ancient homes. He had exhibited intelligent decision, coupled to a marked caution, in this first campaign.

After crossing the Rhone, Caesar had established a camp, not unlikely on the heights of Sathonay, south of where the Helvetii were lying while they effected a passage of the Arar. It was here that Labienus probably joined him, from the Geneva works, which it was now useless to hold. This gave Caesar six legions,—thirty thousand men; and the Ædui and the province raised for him some four thousand horse. He was now ready to act with vigour.

Caesar's reconnoitring parties, of which he had already learned to keep a more than usual number out, soon brought him word that the Helvetii were leisurely crossing the Arar by means of boats and rafts. The Saône flowed then as now so slowly in places that one could scarcely distinguish the direction of its current. At one of these places, north of Trévoux, the Helvetii were ferrying over in boats, for they were not sufficiently clever to bridge the stream. Caesar at once set out for that vicinity. He dispatched spies to ascertain the enemy's movements, and shortly learned that three quarters of their force—three cantons—had been got over, leaving one canton on the left bank where he himself still was. Here was his opportunity. Breaking up at midnight with the Seventh, Eighth and Ninth legions, he marched between that hour and six a. m. about twelve miles, up the left bank to the place where the enemy was crossing, and sharply pushing in upon the unsuspecting Helvetii, he surprised them, cut a large number to pieces, and dispersed the rest, who fled in terror into the neighbouring forests. It was early in June.

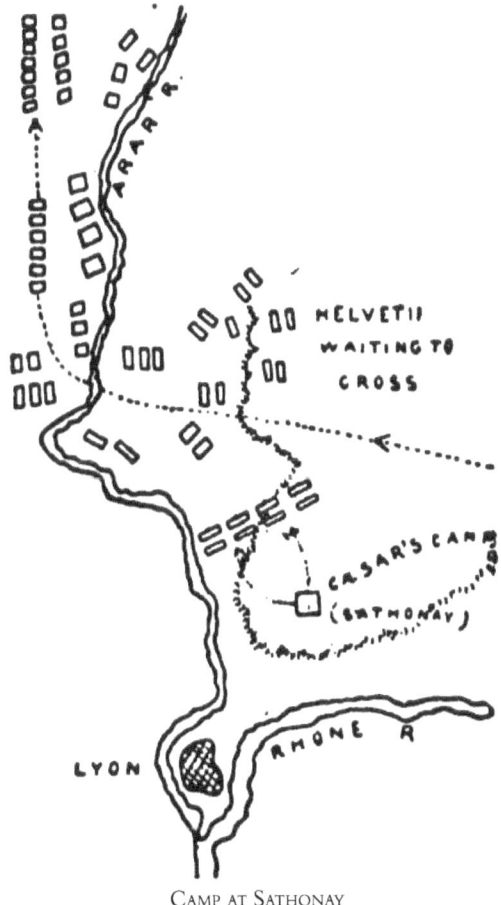

CAMP AT SATHONAY

As a curious fortune would have it, this happened to be the particular canton—the Tigorini, whose home was near modern Zürich—that had defeated and slain Cassius, in which disaster had perished Piso, of the family into which Caesar had lately married. This defeat crippled the forces of the Helvetii, but left something like two hundred and eighty thousand people still to be dealt with, of whom seventy thousand were warriors; and they had plenty of rations. The locality of the battle is well proven by excavations which have revealed immense numbers of skeletons of men, women and children, some cremated, but all hastily interred, and of broken arms and ornaments.

Caesar at once bridged the Arar near the battlefield, and crossed. It seems surprising that the Helvetii, under whose very nose this operation took place, should have made no effort to interfere with it, but nothing is said in the *Commentaries* of an attack. All they did was to observe him closely. Caesar no doubt had vessels on the river which were transporting rations in his wake, and these aided in the passage. The other three legions soon rejoined him from camp at Sathonay. Astonished to see Caesar do in one day what they had taken twenty to accomplish, the Helvetii again sent ambassadors to him, to represent that they were desirous of peace and would go and settle wherever Caesar would allow; but that, if opposed, Caesar must remember that the Helvetii were brave and numerous and feared no one, as the Romans well knew from experience. Caesar replied that if they would give him hostages to do as they agreed, he would treat with them; but the ambassadors haughtily answered that they were in the habit of receiving, not giving hostages, and left in high dudgeon.

Still the Helvetii were anxious not to fight. They preferred to carry out their original project, though they must have keenly felt Caesar's blow in the destruction of a full quarter of their number. They marched away on the succeeding day, intending still to head for the land of the Santones. To do this they could not advance directly west, on account of the intervening mountainous region, which placed two distinct ranges between them and their objective. They headed northwest, so as to strike the lowest part of the watershed between the Saône and Loire, which they could cross and thence move west.

Caesar was not placed so as readily to bring them to battle, as their column and his own were more or less confined in the narrow space between the Arar and the mountains. A slow, dogged pursuit was his only immediate resource, but he threw out his Gallic cavalry under command of Dumnorix the Æduan, to reconnoitre their movements. A day or two afterwards a body of five hundred Helvetian horse attacked this force, and under unequal conditions inflicted on it a defeat and some considerable loss, though Dumnorix outnumbered them eight to one. Emboldened by this easy success, the Helvetii began to indulge in constant rearguard fighting. Caesar was cautious. War on so large a scale was still a novelty to him. The teaching of the art in that day did not embrace what we now call the grand operations of war. What he knew of them he had assimilated, as no one else had possessed the intelligence to do, from the history of his predecessors, from the splendid deeds of Alexander and Hannibal. But this was theory merely. Caesar still felt a lack of confidence in his own ability; he knew that his grasp was not yet as large as his problem, and wisely kept without the limits of a general engagement. But he did his best to prevent the Helvetii from plundering and foraging; and thus, at a distance of about five miles, he followed them closely for fifteen days.

Caesar was being led from the vicinity of the Arar, and the question of supplies was becoming grave. The corn brought up the river to him proved bad, and the crops were not yet ripe. The supply of forage at this season was limited, and was consumed by the immense column of the enemy. The Ædui had agreed to furnish Caesar with corn, but it was not forthcoming, though he had made a number of demands for it. It seems that the Æduan population, seduced by the representations of Dumnorix, who was, as before stated, serving in Caesar's army, were neglecting to furnish it, lest Caesar, having by their help overcome the Helvetii, should in turn deprive them of their liberties. Dumnorix was anxious to see Caesar thwarted, for the Romans interfered with his own plans of aggrandizement. He had, in fact, played the traitor in the late cavalry conflict with the Helvetii, and had been the cause of the loss of the field by retiring at the first attack. Caesar suspected that all was not right. He called some of the leading Æduans together, and discovered where the difficulty lay. He was much tempted to make an example of Dumnorix; but, probably from motives of policy, lest the latter's fellow-citizens should feel aggrieved and turn definitely from his alliance, he feigned to forgive him at the intercession of Divitiacus, his brother, who was a great friend of Caesar's and a faithful ally of the Romans. Caesar, however, caused Dumnorix to be watched, determined not to allow him to push matters too far.

The Helvetii, at modern St. Vallier, had borne to the west to advance towards the valley of the Liger (Loire), down which they proposed to march, and to cross at Decize. Caesar's scouts reported that on their march they had encamped at the foot of a hill some seven miles distant (not far from modern Toulon), and he saw at last his opportunity of attacking them to advantage. He reconnoitred the approaches to the hill with care, and sent Labienus after midnight, with two legions and guides, to ascend to the summit by a circuit and get into the Helvetian rear, while he himself, with the other four legions, preceded by cavalry, broke camp long before daylight to approach closer to the enemy's front. The plan, well conceived and ordered, all but succeeded. Labienus actually reached his goal unknown to the Helvetii. The victory of Caesar, who advanced to within fifteen hundred paces of the enemy, seemed secure. But Considius, an excellent officer and experienced, one of Sulla's old staff, whom Caesar sent out with the vanguard scouts, in some way lost his head and gave his chief quite erroneous information to the effect that the Helvetii and not the Romans had occupied the summit. He imagined that he had recognized their weapons and standards. This report led Caesar to believe that Labienus had not reached his post, and he was unwilling to attack without the aid of the ambush. Thus lieutenant and captain failed to work in unison, and the chance of an immediate success was lost. Caesar withdrew to an adjoining height, where he went into line, to invite an attack by the enemy. Labienus, whose orders on reaching the summit were to wait for Caesar's attack, refrained from an advance. It was not till the close of the day that Caesar learned the actual facts. The enemy had meanwhile moved away.

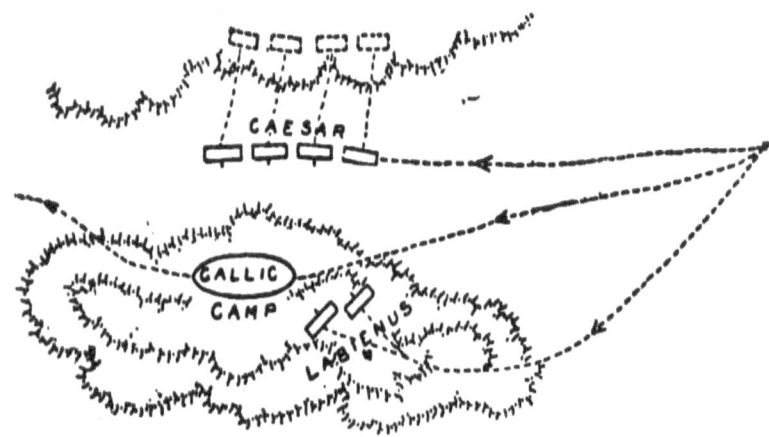

OPERATION NEAR TOULON

Caesar was not in the habit of doing his own reconnoitring, even in important cases, if we may judge, from a number of such instances as this. He was constant and careful and intelligent in procuring information; but of all the great captains he seems to have relied most upon the eyes of others. In this case, and in others to be narrated, his own observation would have been more fruitful. The Helvetii, having thus escaped from the ambuscade, were much elated that Caesar had not attacked,—as they deemed from fear; but they had no idea of assaulting Caesar's strong position.

From passing the Arar, the Helvetii had marched two weeks at the rate of about seven miles a day. It was the end of June. Finding that he was running short of corn, and that the Ædui were still slow in furnishing it, Caesar decided next day to make a push past the Helvetii for Bibracte (Mt. Beuvray, near Autun).

Bibracte is apt to be located at Autun, but that it was Mt. Beuvray is much more probable. The Gauls were wont to place their towns on hills, like Gergovia or Alesia; or if on a plain, it was surrounded by a stream or marsh, as Avaricum. They would scarcely have located their capital and largest city, Bibracte, at the foot of the mountains where lies Autun. Several ancient roads centre on Mt. Beuvray, and the hilltop is full of the ruins of a town. There is every indication that this was the Bibracte of the Ædui.

From where Caesar lay the place was about eighteen miles, and here he was sure to find food in plenty. The time for issuing rations, which was usually done every fifteen days, when each man received twenty-five pounds of wheat, was two days hence, and the soldiers were near the end of their supply.

The Helvetii were told of Caesar's movements by a deserter from the Gallic cavalry, and construed his manoeuvre as a retreat. Their assumption that Caesar was afraid to attack them was strengthened by his thus giving up pursuit, and instead of keeping on towards the Loire valley, they turned back to attack Caesar and cut him off from retreat. They began to harass the rear of the Romans by more daring though isolated attacks.

Their action accorded well with Caesar's mood. He determined to afford them an opportunity for battle. He occupied the first available eminence which he reached in his march on Bibracte. The battlefield appears to have been identified by Colonel Stoffel as near Toulon. Here he drew up his forces, sending the cavalry forward to arrest the too speedy approach of the enemy, who had some seventy thousand warriors, while himself had from thirty thousand to thirty-six thousand *legionaries*, perhaps twenty thousand auxiliaries (Appian says Gallic mountaineers), and four thousand horse. He drew up his four old legions (Seventh, Eighth, Ninth and Tenth), in three lines halfway up the slope, the two legions (Eleventh and Twelfth) recently raised

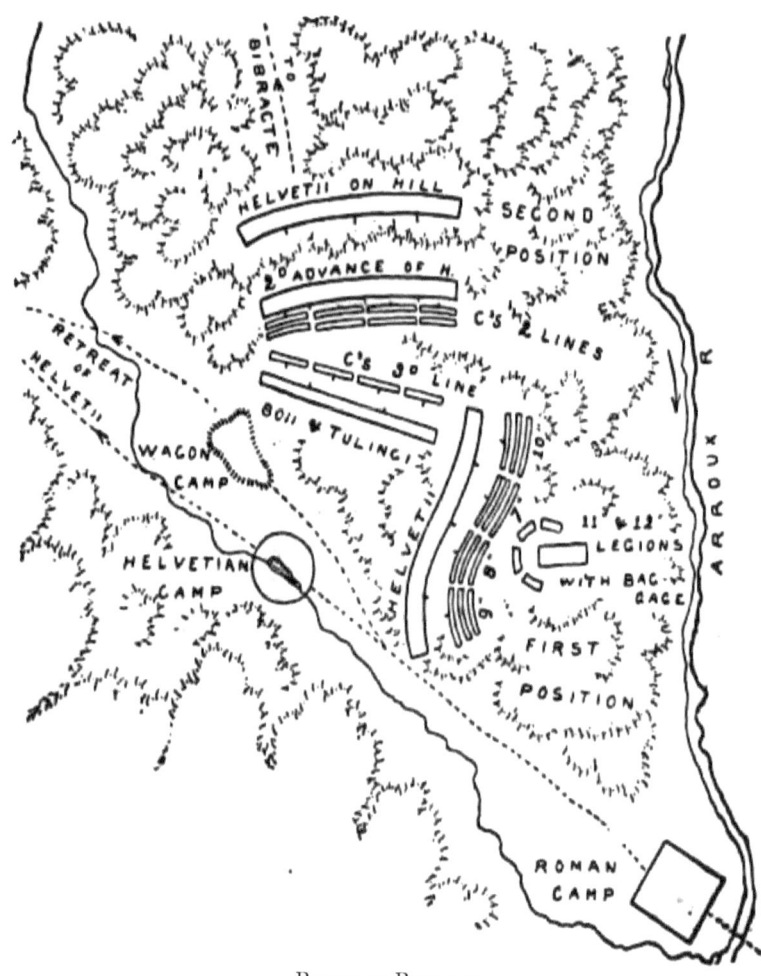

BATTLE OF BIBRACTE

in Cisalpine Gaul and all the auxiliaries on the plateau in the rear, with the baggage parked and entrenched and committed to their care. Here, as on other occasions, Caesar declined to use his new legions in the fighting lines, but kept them in the background. The baggage referred to is *sarcinae*, that which the soldiers themselves carried. The legions thus went into action in light order. The location of the train baggage (*impedimenta*) is not given.

These three lines must not be confounded with the old three line formation of the Punic wars, of *hastati*, *principes* and *triarii*. The *cohort* was now formed in one line, as has been already explained. The two or three lines which Caesar used were separate and distinct, each legion being drawn up in three lines of *cohorts*. The Helvetii parked their wagons in an irregular circle on some low ground opposite Caesar's position, and having repulsed the Roman allied cavalry, drew up in *phalangial* order,—a formation in which all barbarians are wont to fight pitched battles,—and advanced on the Roman army with closed ranks. They joined their shields together in *testudinal* fashion, in front, on the flanks and aloft, so as to ward off the first shower of *pila*, and came on with an impetus which promised hot work.

Caesar had prepared his men by the usual *allocutio*, or battle-speech, and in order once for all to encourage his men to feel that he proposed to share their danger, whatever it might be, he dismounted from his own horse and obliged the other mounted officers to do the like. He may have been distrustful of the stanchness of some of his new officers. He did not yet know them. This act with the *legionaries* meant: "I will stay here and fight with you, for I have given up my means of flight." It was an act the direct reverse of officers dismounting in action, as is sometimes done in these modern days of musketry. The Roman first line, awaiting the Helvetian onset and hurling their javelins from the height on which they stood, succeeded after a while in breaking gaps in the Helvetian *phalanx*, and immediately charged down upon the barbarians with the sword. A most obstinate combat ensued. Many of the Helvetian shields had been pierced by the Roman *pila*, whose iron points being turned, the spear could not readily be plucked out, thus making the shields so cumbersome that the barbarians threw them away. The *pilum* of this era was a little short of two metres, half of which consisted of a long flexible blade with a barbed point, or some equivalent. They could be hurled from sixty to eighty feet; and when cast at a *testudo*, would often pin two shields together and render them useless. Despite this initial check the barbarians exposed their persons recklessly, as the hardy mountaineers of Helvetia have always done. But robbed of their bucklers, the Romans were enabled to do the greater execution, and after long-sustained effort forced the enemy slowly but surely from the field. In no wise broken or demoralized, the Helvetii retired in good order to an eminence three quarters of a mile away. Here they halted and once again made a stand.

The two new legions and auxiliaries still remained with the wagons. As the old *legionaries* followed up the retiring foe, they advanced beyond where the Helvetian rearguard, consisting of some fifteen thousand allied Boii and Tulingi, had filed into position which enabled them to protect the Gallic wagon-park. These troops, now on the

Roman rear, charged down upon the legions with the utmost fury, perceiving which diversion the Helvetian main line again advanced, giving vent to exultant shouts, and resumed the battle with yet greater vigour. Caesar states that they fell upon his exposed flank. This does not appear from the topography, and the phrase "exposed flank" may perhaps be the equivalent of the phrase "masked batteries" of 1861. It will be remembered that the right side with the ancients was always weak, as the shield was carried on the left arm, and the right flank of a body of troops was shieldless. It is constantly referred to as *latus apertum*, and the legions were always nervous about this flank. A convenient way of explaining a defeat or suggesting a tactical danger would be to speak of an attack on the exposed flank. Caesar thus refers to the *triarii* long after their disappearance from the legions.

Caesar was thus compelled to form two fronts to receive this double attack. He faced the standards of the third line to the rear to meet the Boii and Tulingi, holding back the new onslaught of the Helvetii with his first two. The danger was grave, but there was still a reserve of two legions, and Caesar pushed the fighting home. For a long while the combat wavered; the Helvetii would not give up the contest, however unequal, but after a long and obstinate combat the legions drove the enemy back to the hill they had first retired to, and forced the rearguard party of allies to the wagons. The Helvetii had fought like heroes. During the entire action, from noon to eventide, not a man had shown his back. Bitter fighting was now resumed for the possession of the wagon-park and continued till late at night. The enemy threw their weapons from the wagons and entrenched themselves between the wheels, whence they used their long pikes. The women and children took part in the battle. It was only after supreme efforts that the wagon-park was finally captured. The victory was complete. The Helvetii fled after sustaining losses which reduced their number to one hundred and thirty thousand souls. Caesar did not pursue. His cavalry could not effect much in this hilly country, says Napoleon. But the indisposition to pursue came of the caution of inexperience rather than because Caesar judged it to be useless.

Caesar's dispositions for the battle and the vigour of the fighting had been in the highest degree commendable, but he may perhaps be criticised for advancing so far from his reserves as to be liable to be taken in flank and rear. Less than the two legions and the auxiliaries could have guarded the entrenched baggage-park, and the presence of one of them in a supplemental line as at Pharsalus would have rendered victory more speedy and less costly. The loss of the Helvetii was very heavy; but a large part of the entire people escaped from the massacre. These, marching four days and nights without a halt, reached the territory of the Lingones (near Tonnerre), where they hoped to find corn as well as safety. This tribe, however, under Caesar's declaration sent by couriers that he would treat them in the same manner as the Helvetii if they harboured or traded with these enemies of the Roman people, refused to have any communication with the footsore and famished barbarians. The Helvetii, in the severest distress, at once sent messengers soliciting peace.

Caesar had remained three days at Bibracte, or near the battle-field, to bury the dead and care for the severely wounded. His loss is not given, but it must have been very large. On the fourth day he followed up the Helvetii, and having gone into camp nearby, he received their embassy, which we can imagine couched in less arrogant language than the last. To the Helvetian petition he assented upon their delivering up hostages, their arms, and a number of slaves who had deserted to them from the Roman camp. Having complied with Caesar's demands, they were treated with liberality, and furnished with food; but they were obliged to march back to their own country and to rebuild their towns and villages, and until they were able to accomplish this, the Allobroges were instructed to supply them with corn. Caesar "drove this people back into their country as it were a shepherd driving his flock back into the fold," says Florus. A party of six thousand of the Helvetii (Verbigeni) attempted to escape towards Germany; but they were at Caesar's order stopped on the way by the tribes through whose territory they tried to pass, brought back and "treated like enemies," which no doubt means that they were sold as slaves or massacred,—one of those cases of unnecessary cruelty which blot the pages of Caesar's glorious campaigns.

The location of the battle has by some been placed at Cussy la Colonne, but that place does not suit the topography of the Commentaries. Napoleon III. places it nearer Bibracte, but Stoffel's researches are the latest and most reliable.

Lists were found in the Helvetian camp, written in the Greek character, showing that three hundred and sixty-eight thousand in all, men, women and children, Helvetii and allies, had left their homes, to wit: Helvetii, two hundred and sixty-three thousand; Tulingi, thirty-six thousand, Latobrigi, fourteen thousand; Rauraci, twenty-three thousand; Boii, thirty-two thousand. Of these, ninety-two thousand were fighting men. There returned home, according to Caesar's census, but one hundred and ten thousand; the rest had perished in the migration, the battles or the massacres, or had dispersed. Of the latter it is probable that very many eventually returned to Helvetia. The gallant Boii were allowed to settle among the Ædui, who desired to receive them.

This first campaign of Caesar's in command of a large army is characterized by great dash and ability coupled to a certain caution apparently bred of self-distrust. He was greatly aided by the want of unity and prompt action among the Helvetii, who, had they been more alive to their advantages, might have greatly hampered Caesar's movements. For a first campaign the conduct and results were certainly brilliant.

Caesar entrenched his camp near Tonnerre, and here he remained until midsummer.

CAESAR, THE CITIZEN

CHAPTER 6
Campaign Against Ariovistus
August and September, 58 B. C.

The Ædui, Seqnani and Arverni now invoked Caesar's aid against the German Ariovistus, who had crossed the Rhine and taken land and hostages from them. Caesar saw the danger of permitting German invasions. He sent word to Ariovistus that he must restore the hostages and return across the Rhine. The German retorted, haughtily and with truth, that he was doing no more than Caesar was and with equal right. Caesar determined to march against him, and moved to Vesontio. Here arose a dissension among the legions, having its origin in a dread of the Germans and of the unknown lands they were about to invade. Caesar suppressed it by his persuasiveness, and the army marched against Ariovistus. A conference with him led to no results. The German then cleverly marched around Caesar's flank and cut him from his base—a remarkable manoeuvre for a barbarian; but by an equally skilful march Caesar recovered his communications. Then, learning that Ariovistus was, under advice of his soothsayers, waiting for the new moon before coming to an engagement, he forced battle upon him and signally defeated him. In the two campaigns of this first year, Caesar had shown much caution, bred probably of inexperience, but he had also shown boldness and skill in abundant measure. The numbers against him had not greatly exceeded his own; and he had not been called on to show the decision of Alexander in Thrace or Hannibal in Iberia.

After the brilliant Helvetian campaign, the Gauls with Caesar's consent convoked a general assembly of tribes, and the whole of the country sent ambassadors to sue for the victor's good-will. They saw that they now had a Roman consul of a different stamp in their midst. Among the supplicants came embassies from the Ædui, Sequani and

Arverni led by the Æduan Divitiacus, who particularly begged Caesar's assistance against Ariovistus, a king of the Germans (the people dwelling beyond the Rhine), "a savage, passionate and reckless man." This chief, it seemed, having been called in to aid the Sequani and Arverni against their domestic enemies, the Ædui, had as a reward for this help forcibly taken one third of all their land, and was now driving them from another third to accommodate fresh arrivals of his own subjects, of whom one hundred and twenty thousand had already come across the Rhine to settle on the more fertile Gallic lands. Nor was this their only grievance, for Ariovistus had taken all the children of their nobles as hostages, and had treated these tribes with consummate cruelty. Particularly the Ædui had been oppressed and compelled to swear that they would not even complain of their torments, or invite aid from Rome, or ask back their hostages.

The Suevi were the largest of the German nations and the most powerful. They were divided into one hundred cantons, each of which furnished yearly one thousand men for war, and one thousand for tillage, and these alternated, the tillers being bound to maintain the warriors. They were big-framed and hardy in the extreme, strong and savage, and disdained all other peoples. Their land was said to be surrounded by desert wastes, they having devastated the lands of all their neighbours. Two immense forests, the Hercynian and that called Bacenis, began at the Rhine and ran eastward. The former covered the territory between the Danube and the Main, the other was substantially the Thüringerwald of today. South of this latter dwelt the Suevi.

Caesar was of course alive to the danger of allowing tribes of Germans to migrate at will in large bodies across the Rhine, for, emboldened by success, they might soon spread over Gaul, reach the province, and from thence move to Italy, like the Cimbri and Teutones. The Rhone alone separated the province from the Sequani, on whose land they were already trenching. Moreover, the Ædui had long been "kinsmen" of Rome and deserved protection. Caesar had proposed to himself to conquer Gaul. A less conception of his problem is unlikely. As a preliminary, the ejection of the Germans from the land was essential. His method of thought stopped at no halfway measures. He had not come into Gaul merely to protect Roman territory or interests in the old way. He came for conquest, which as a soldier he saw was the only true way to cut the knot of the Gallic difficulty, and which as a statesman he saw might be a stepping-stone to future greatness. Caesar was equipped in authority,

men and purpose for war, and it was war he desired. The sooner it
came, the sooner he would be able to subdue Gaul. One reason was
as good as another to serve as a *casus belli*. To examine such questions
as these is scarcely within our present purpose. Let us keep as closely
as may be to the current of military events.

THE RHINE AND THE GERMANS

Caesar sent messengers to Ariovistus, who was probably on the
Rhine somewhere about modern Strasburg, collecting an army
among the Tribocci, proposing an interview. Ariovistus returned word
that when he desired to see Caesar, he would come to him; if Caesar wished to see Ariovistus, he might himself come; that he saw no
reason why Caesar had any business in that part of Gaul which he,
Ariovistus, had conquered, as he should not venture into those parts
which Caesar held. This was bold language, but it has the ring of honest bravery in it. Caesar, who looked at the reply from the stand-point
of true Roman arrogance, answered that he was surprised that Ari-

ovistus, a man who had been styled "king and friend" by the Roman Senate, should refuse his proposal for a conference; he required this chief to bring no more men from across the Rhine into Gaul, nor seize upon land; at once to cause to be restored the hostages of the Ædui, and to cease from war in Gaul. Should he do so, Caesar and the Senate and people of Rome would still regard him as a friend; if not, Caesar, under his instructions to protect the Ædui and other allies of the Roman Republic, would take the case in hand without delay. To this ultimatum, Ariovistus made answer, that he had conquered the Ædui in battle, and had rightfully made them pay tribute in exactly the same fashion as the Romans did by those whom they had subdued; that he should not restore the Æduan hostages; that if the Ædui did not pay tribute, he would compel them to do so, and that their title of "kinsmen" of Rome would avail them naught. He ended his message with a challenge, averring that none had ever entered the lists against him but to be exterminated. Caesar had certainly met his match in aggressiveness.

It is not quite clear how broad was the authority Caesar possessed by law. The governors of Roman provinces were usually prohibited from leaving their limits without the express permission of the Senate. But the governor of Gaul had been given, or had assumed, a wider authority, and was expected to protect the allies of the Roman people. As a matter of fact, there was no control whatever over Caesar, except that exerted by his colleagues in the *triumvirate*. And this related only to affairs in Rome.

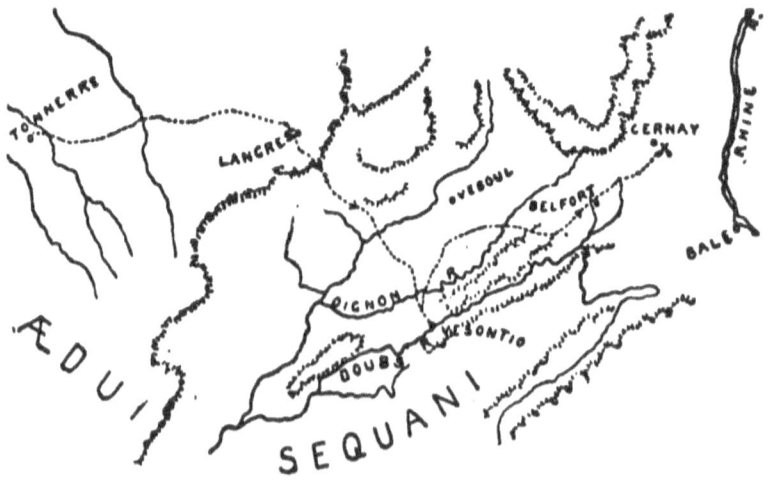

MARCH AGAINST ARIOVISTUS

Learning at the same time that the Germans were ravaging the Æduan lands, and that other large bands of Suevi were on the right bank of the Rhine opposite the Treviran district, making preparations to cross the river, Caesar determined to strike Ariovistus before any reinforcements could come over to his assistance. Accordingly, after rationing his men and accumulating a supply of corn, he set out early in August from the neighbourhood of Tonnerre, and by forced marches moved towards the upper Arar, where lay Ariovistus. There was subsequently a Roman road which led from Tonnerre to Langres, so that we may fairly assume that there was a previous Gallic path or road, and it was this Caesar took. Being informed on the way, perhaps near modern Langres, that Ariovistus was on the march to seize Vesontio (Besançon) on the Dubas (Doubs), capital city of the Sequani, a depot containing large supplies and an admirable position for strength, of very considerable importance to whomsoever held it, and fearing that Ariovistus might be nearer to the place than he actually was, Caesar turned from his straight road to the Rhine, which ran by way of Vesoul and Belfort, and forcing his marching day and night, made such speed that he reached Vesontio and threw a garrison into it before Ariovistus could arrive. The *Commentaries* describe Vesontio so clearly that there can be no mistake in its location.

"It was so well fortified by nature that it offered every facility for sustaining war. The Dubas, forming a circle, surrounds it almost entirely, and the space of sixteen hundred feet which is not bathed by the water is occupied by a high mountain, the base of which reaches on each side to the edge of the river."

No military narrative exceeds the *Commentaries* in lucidity; few equal it in its keen descriptions and clear-cut style.

It is evident that Caesar was active in the pursuit of information, though the Romans as a rule were lax in this particular. Like Alexander and Hannibal—like all great commanders—he had antennae out in front of the army which felt its way. He was at all times abundantly supplied with knowledge about the countries and peoples he was to invade and contend with. This he procured by spies, deserters and reconnoissances, the latter conducted mostly by native cavalry. The Roman horse could by no means vie with the Gallic in doing such work, and Caesar had a way of insuring the almost uniform fidelity of the latter.

Ariovistus, learning that Caesar was moving towards him, arrested his advance on Vesontio, deeming it wiser to remain near the reinforcements which he could draw from across the Rhine. Moreover,

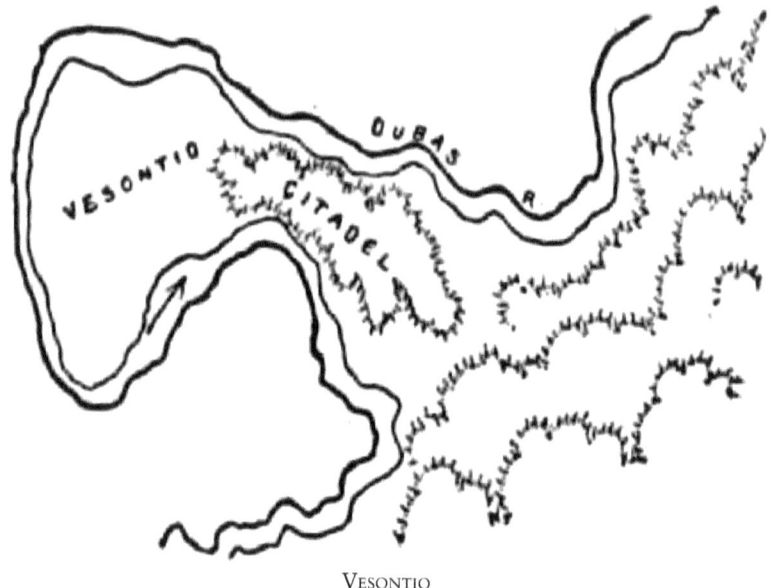

Vesontio

the proximity of the Rhine, near modern upper Alsace, afforded a *terrain* which was better suited to the operations of his cavalry.

At Vesontio Caesar remained some days. A grave danger here beset him,—one which well shows how deep was the decay of the *morale* of the Roman army. There were in the army a number of *tribunes* and *praefects*, one might call them volunteer line officers, men who had accompanied Caesar for friendship or excitement or profit, having been given their commissions for political or personal motives, but who were inexperienced soldiers and lacking in that stanchness which few men in an army possess unless they have taken up arms as a business. Many of these holiday-soldiers, frightened by the tales they heard of the stature and fierceness of the Germans and of the dangerous route before them,—which tales were well borne out by the daring courage of the Helvetii, who themselves feared these Teutons,—besought Caesar to allow them to return to Italy, each one alleging some peculiar personal pretext. Even those who were willing to remain strike one as little enough like what we are apt to dub Romans.

"These could neither compose their countenance nor even sometimes check their tears; but hidden in their tents, either bewailed their fate, or deplored with their comrades the general danger. Wills were sealed universally throughout the whole camp. By the expressions and cowardice of these men, even those who possessed great experience in the camp, both soldiers and *centurions*, and those (the *decurions*) who were in command of the cavalry, were gradually disconcerted. Such of them as wished to be considered less alarmed, said that they did not dread the enemy, but feared the narrowness of the roads and the vastness of the forests which lay between them and Ariovistus, or else that the supplies could not be brought up readily enough. Some even declared to Caesar that when he gave orders for the camp to be moved and the troops to advance, the soldiers would not be obedient to the command, nor advance in consequence of their fear."

This disaffection was spreading to the ranks and threatening the most serious results. Caesar grasped the grave nature of the matter, and his strong will at once rose to the occasion. He called a council of war to which all the *centurions* were invited, and with his customary skill and reasonableness, but without weakening his powers as commander to compel, he presented to them the matter of roads, rations, the skill and courage of the enemy and their own, alleging in conclusion that he should march on the enemy immediately, and if the other legions would not follow, he would march himself, with his favourite Tenth legion, alone. But he did not believe, said he, that the rest were afraid to go, having Marius as an example, who, with their ancestors, had defeated these same Germans. His self-reliant persuasiveness—and we know from abundant sources how persuasive Caesar could be—at once changed the tide of feeling. Dismay gave place to cheerfulness, good heart resumed its sway. The legions expressed their devotion and obedience, the Tenth particularly and instantly, and loudly proclaimed their willingness to follow Caesar to the end of the world, alleging that they had never thought of usurping the right of the chief to decide on the movements of the army.

This and other similar facts not only show that Roman human nature was pretty much the same as human nature has been all over the world and in all ages, but they show that the most essential quality of an army is discipline. These troops, not yet hardened to service, were acting as militia or unseasoned volunteers will sometimes act. It is probable that Caesar, himself yet inexperienced in the duties of commanding officer, had not kept his troops sufficiently occupied with drill and camp-duties to prevent their wasting their idle time in foolish gossip. How much the disaffection is overdrawn in the *Commentaries*, to show Caesar's eloquence and moral power, cannot be said, but the bald facts must be as stated. Caesar's management was wise in not having re-course to rigorous measures.

From Vesontio towards the Rhine, if he would go the straight road, Caesar must cross the northern part of the Jura foothills. That part of the route which lay along the valley of the Dubas was extremely rough, in parts a continuous defile, and much more wooded and difficult then than now. But Divitiacus pointed out to him that by a northerly circuit, of which the Dubas would be the chord, he could move in a comparatively open country and reach the undulating plains of the Rhine valley without danger of ambush. Divitiacus, always intelligent and useful, had been reconnoitring the region in front of the army, and found that the circuit would not exceed fifty miles. Proceeding, towards the end of the third week in August, along this route in the direction of the enemy, in seven days Caesar reached the vicinity of Ariovistus, who was reported some twenty-four miles off. Unless Caesar's marches were far below the usual rate, and he would not loiter under the circumstances, he must in seven days have marched at least eighty-five or ninety miles. This would carry him beyond Belfort, usually chosen as the scene of the battle against Ariovistus, to near Cernay. This is Göler's opinion. Rüstow is in error in selecting the upper Saar as the theatre of the approaching campaign.

Not anticipating Caesar's speedy coming, Ariovistus himself requested a conference, in a way which made Caesar believe that the German had grown more reasonable, and it was agreed that the two generals should meet on a naked eminence in a large plain between both camps, with an escort only of horse. No large plain exists near Belfort, another reason for placing the scene farther to the east. Caesar, scarcely trusting his Gallic cavalry under such exceptional circumstances, had "taken away all their horses," and had mounted his trusted Tenth *legionaries*, so that they might accompany him. They seemed to be ready and expert horsemen. Reaching the place of conference, they were drawn up in line two hundred paces from the mound, the cavalry of Ariovistus taking a similar station on the other side. Each commander was accompanied to the meeting by ten mounted men.

So far from the conference accomplishing any good end, Ariovistus, according to what Caesar wishes us to infer from the *Commentaries*, behaved in a most haughty and provoking manner. But even the *Commentaries* show Ariovistus to have talked in a reasonable way. He claimed only the same right to conquer a province in Gaul that the Romans had exerted, and to collect tribute in the same way; he denied his intention of invading Gaul further, and agreed to a "hands-off" policy, if Caesar would accept it. But the *Commentaries* allege that

Ariovistus' cavalry showed the bad faith of the transaction by commencing an attack on Caesar's escort, "hurling stones and weapons at them." Caesar, forbidding his men to retaliate, lest the blame should be cast upon him, withdrew from the conference. The eagerness of the legions to engage was greatly increased by Ariovistus' treachery. Two days after, Ariovistus again requested a meeting or an embassy, and on Caesar's sending to him two of his officers, he seized these and cast them into chains, though one was a Gaul and the other bound to him by the sacred ties of hospitality.

At the same time Ariovistus moved to within six miles of the Romans, and encamped at the foot of the Vosegus (Vosges) mountains; and next day, by a bold and skilful manoeuvre, he marched around Caesar's flank and within his immediate reach, and camped two miles off, west of modern Reinigen, in a position which actually cut the Romans off from their base and the convoys of corn furnished by the

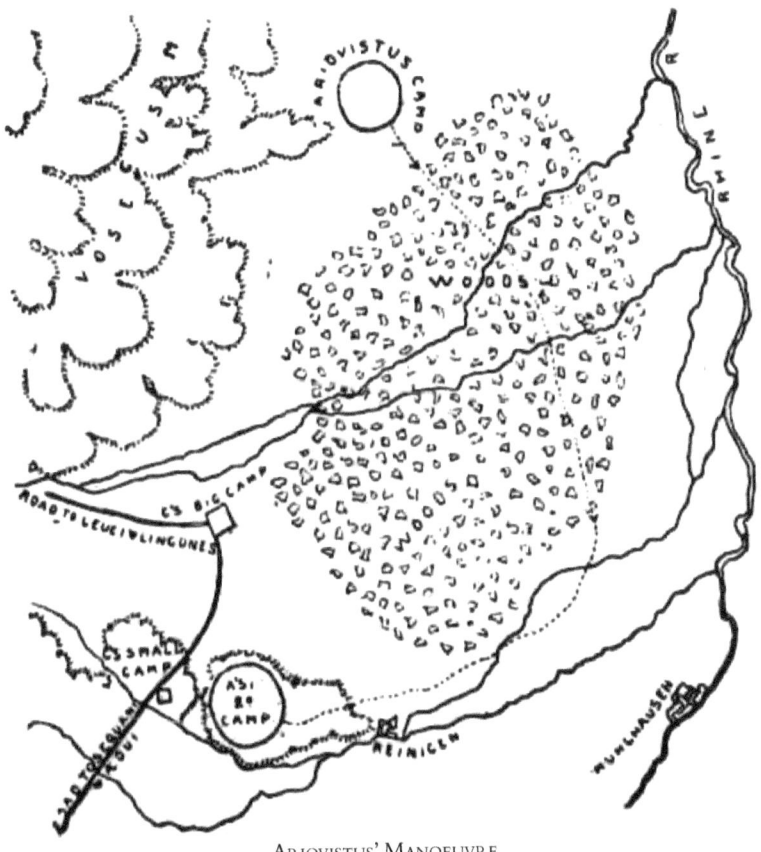

Ariovistus' Manoeuvre

Sequani and Ædui. But it fortunately left open the communications with the Leuci and Lingones farther north, on whom in part Caesar depended, though theirs was a scant province from which to draw his supplies for so large a force.

From the slight description of this manoeuvre of Ariovistus in the *Commentaries*, it would at first blush seem that Caesar had lost an excellent opportunity of striking his enemy on the flank while thus marching near to and around the Roman camp, and this criticism has been frequently made. During such a manoeuvre, any column, especially with baggage, is wont to be more or less out of order, and there can be no better time to attack. The march of Ariovistus was, in this case, protected by the forest, of which a portion still remains at the present time; and Caesar had not yet learned that power of summary action for which he later grew so noted, and did not attempt to interfere with the march of the enemy. In fact, it is probable that Caesar did not at the moment know of the manoeuvre. Nor was it usual with the ancients to take advantage for attack of a flank march by the enemy.

Caesar, however, did the next best thing. For five successive days he emerged from his camp and drew up in battle array, inviting action; but Ariovistus, satisfied with his position, the effect of which he perfectly comprehended, kept to his camp, merely throwing out his cavalry, which was six thousand strong, to skirmish with the Roman allied horse. The German horseman at this period was accompanied by a foot soldier, who was practised to run alongside, holding to the horse's mane, and to fight in connection with the cavalry. By these peculiar tactics the Germans puzzled the Gallic squadrons, though it was really nothing new, but an ancient device to be found among many peoples.

Caesar was unable to provoke Ariovistus to battle. The real reason for this was that the female soothsayers of the Germans had decided by divination that their army could not conquer if it fought before the new moon. This Caesar did not at the moment know. Fearing to be definitely cut off from his base, which Ariovistus might attempt to accomplish by a further advance, he himself resorted to a similar manoeuvre. He was not above taking a lesson from this skilful barbarian. Forming his army in three lines, he marched out as if ready to give battle, and moving by the right, placed his line on the west of the German camp in such a manner as to regain the road along which lay his communications. Halting at a distance of not more than two thirds of a mile from Ariovistus' camp and two miles and a half from his own, Caesar held the first two lines in readiness to resist the enemy's attack if made, and set the third to entrench a new camp and, as usual, surround it with a rampart. Ariovistus sent some sixteen thousand light troops and all his cavalry to interfere with the Romans in this operation, but this body was driven off. In the new camp, when completed, Caesar left two legions and some auxiliaries. With the other four legions he marched back and reoccupied the old camp. Though divided, Caesar was now in better position. He had re-established himself upon his own communications, and had placed Ariovistus where he could not undertake the offensive to advantage. In attacking either Roman camp, the troops from the other would be able to fall upon his flank.

Next day Caesar marshalled his forces from both camps for battle, taking up a position in advance of the larger one, but as Ariovistus did not accept the gage, the Romans retired to their entrenchments about noon. Then Ariovistus sent part of his forces to attack the lesser camp, and a vigorous combat with some loss ensued, which lasted till night, when Ariovistus retired. From some prisoners captured on this occasion Caesar finally ascertained why it was Ariovistus was unwilling to fight: "that it was not the will of heaven that the Germans should conquer if they engaged in battle before the new moon," and deemed it wiser to force a general engagement at once, so as to let the moral effect of fighting against fate do its demoralizing work among the German troops.

On the following day, probably September 10, Caesar secretly drew the two legions from the small camp and joined them to the four of the larger camp. He drew up all his auxiliaries before the lesser camp to impose on the enemy by the number of their array, and to simulate the continued presence of the two legions. This must have been cleverly done to have escaped detection. With all his legionaries, in three lines, Caesar advanced on Ariovistus' camp. A suffiient force had been left in each of the camps to defend the ramparts. At last Ariovistus saw from Caesar's pronounced action that it was imperative to fight. He had no entrenched camp, and could probably not resist a determined assault should Caesar make one. He accordingly drew up his forces by tribes with an interval between each two,—Harudes, Marcomanni, Tribocci, Vangiones, Nemetes, Sedusii, Suevi,—and surrounded the whole rear and flanks with his wagons so "that no hope might be left in flight." The women remained in the wagon-train as witnesses of the battle, and conjured with frantic cries and gestures their husbands, fathers and sons to fight so as not to deliver them to the sword or to slavery, as had been the fate of the women of the Cimbri and Teutones at Aix.

It is probable that Ariovistus much exceeded Caesar in force, but by how much it is impossible to say. Caesar's total, after his losses at Bibracte, cannot have been much more than fifty thousand men, allowing a full complement to each legion.

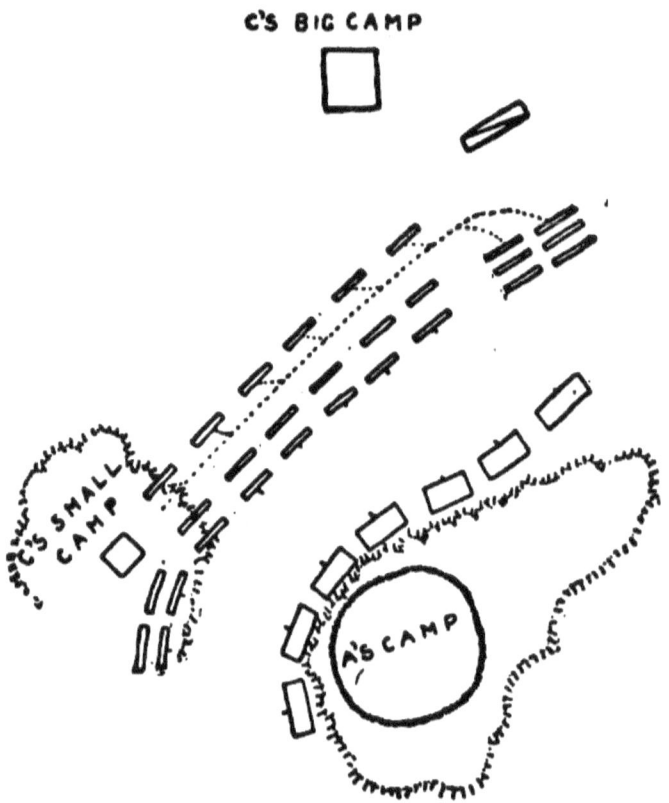

BATTLE AGAINST ARIOVISTUS

The Romans faced east, Ariovistus west. Caesar placed his *quaestor* in command of one of the legions and a legate over each of the others, with instructions to force the fighting. He himself opened the action with the Roman right wing as was his wont, and "because he had observed that part of the enemy (opposite to him) to be the least strong." The Germans were drawn up in a species of *phalangial* order. The Roman soldiers attacked the foe with their usual vigorous onslaught, but the Germans met them by a rush given with such impetuosity that the *legionaries* did not have time to shift ranks so as to cast all their javelins; they were almost immediately constrained to resort to their swords. They were for the moment put on the defensive. But they quickly resumed their ancient habit of offense, and to resist their onset the

Germans grouped themselves in bodies of three or four hundred, who made a tortoise, covering themselves with their interlocked shields. The Roman soldiers held to the attack with consummate courage, advancing boldly into the intervals and ranks of the enemy, and tearing away their shields by main force. Some leaped upon the roof of shields so interlocked, forced them apart, and hewed at the Germans from above. The left wing of the barbarians was thus routed, but the enemy still held firmly upon the right, where he was by far stronger. The Roman line was unable to make the least impression, and finally wavered. Perceiving this danger, young P. Crassus, who commanded the cavalry, not being at the moment engaged, but placed where he could see what was going on, took command of the third line which had lain in reserve, ployed it into column, and led it quickly to the support of the Roman left. The shock of these fresh troops broke the enemy's resistance. No doubt the divination of their soothsayers had produced its due effect, and they saw in the Roman success the hand of fate. They turned from the Roman line, ceased resistance, and soon melted into utter rout and flight, nor stopped till they reached the Rhine, a matter of fifty miles distant. Their flight was presumably down the valley of the Ill, up which they had advanced. Some, it is said, swam across the Rhine, near Rheinau. Some others, among them Ariovistus, managed to find boats in which to cross, and thus escaped. The rest were cut down by Caesar's Gallic cavalry. The two Roman ambassadors who had been cast into chains were recovered.

The Suevi, who had come down to the right bank of the Rhine with intention to cross, hearing of the terrible defeat of Ariovistus, at once decamped. But their enemies, the Ubii, from lower down the river, hung upon their rear and inflicted severe loss upon them. This victory ended, for the time being, any fear of the Germans.

Caesar, having thus conducted two successful campaigns in one season, early put his army into winter-quarters in the land of the Sequani, likely enough near Vesontio, under command of Labienus. He himself returned to Cisalpine Gaul to hold the assizes, as well as to be nearer the political turmoils of Rome and to watch for his own interests.

In this initial year of his command of an army, Caesar showed plainly those qualities of rapid decision and action, courage and intelligent grasp of the situation, which always yielded such vast results. But he was at times more markedly cautious than later in his military life, as if he had not yet learned to trust to his good fortune, nor acquired wide experience in arms. One can notice mistakes and a certain indecision in these campaigns, to which Caesar was not later so much subject; though the same quality crops up all through his military career. He has been criticised because he did not attack Ariovistus on his dangerous flank march past his camp, but this has already received comment. It has also been observed that the sixteen thousand men sent by Ariovistus against the working-party on the new camp might have been destroyed instead of merely driven back by his protecting lines of *legionaries*, who much outnumbered them. But Caesar accomplished his purpose and completed his second camp, which was all he needed to do. Chief criticism of all, Caesar should apparently have been in command of his left wing opposed to the stronger part of the German line, instead of on the right, where the enemy was weaker. It was the common habit for the commander to open the attack with his right in person; but in this instance it was distinctly unwise, as the bulk of the work had to be done on the left. If young Crassus had not acted with unusual intelligence and promptness, Caesar might have forfeited the victory, for his success on the right in no wise demoralized the enemy's other flank. His presence on the right was a tactical lapse.

Though indeed the fact does not detract from Caesar's merit, it cannot be said that the balance of numbers of the untrained barbarians opposed to his army during this year was so excessive as to make his triumph over them a remarkable thing for Roman legionaries. His army had been trained to war in the best manner then known. He himself was able to command it and manoeuvre it by a perfect method. His enemy, while somewhat larger, had no such preponderance as to make the victory of the Romans an extraordinary achievement. One rather admires the Helvetii and Germans, with their comparatively poor discipline, art and equipment, for their noble courage in defence of what they undoubtedly believed to be their rights. In this campaign the odds of the barbarians against Caesar was in no sense as great as that against Alexander in his Eastern campaigns; while the opposition to Hannibal was many-fold as great. But no general, ancient or modern, ever encountered such overwhelming odds and stood his enemies off so successfully as the great Carthaginian; no general ever attacked with the fury of Alexander.

CHAPTER 7

The Belgae
Spring of 57 B. C.

The redoubtable Belgae had raised a coalition against Caesar during the winter, and so soon as forage grew he set out with sixty thousand men—legions and allies—against them. Arriving opportunely among the Remi, he anticipated their defection, and by politic treatment transformed them into allies who thereafter remained constant. The Belgae and allies had nearly three hundred thousand men, but as all were not yet assembled, Caesar was able to attack them in detail. He sent a detachment to invade the land of the Bellovaci, one of the most powerful of the coalition, crossed the Aisne, and camped beyond the then existing bridge in the land of the Remi. He went cautiously to work, showing none of Alexander's self-confident dash, and sought to induce the enemy to assault his entrenched camp. This they declined, and made a clever diversion around Caesar's left flank, hoping to capture the bridge in his rear and cut him off. But Caesar caught them while crossing the fords, and in a partial engagement routed them with his light troops alone. Easily disheartened, the coalition dissolved, and the Belgian tribes left, each for its own territory. Caesar then attacked Noviodunum, but being repulsed, resorted to a siege with success. Having done this, he could deal with the tribes separately.

During the succeeding winter of 58-57 B. C., Caesar, in Cisalpine Gaul, received news from Labienus that the Belgae were threatening trouble, and had roused their neighbours to resistance in the fear that Roman success should also overwhelm them, so soon as Gaul south of them was subdued. They made a coalition and exchanged hostages to insure mutual action. Thus far, the result of Caesar's work had been to save Rome from a possible danger; but it had roused the Belgae, perhaps a more redoubtable enemy than the Helvetii or the Germans.

This rising was not altogether regretted by Caesar. He saw in it the opportunity and excuse for pushing his conquests beyond their present limits. The boundary of conquered Gaul must be the Rhine on the north and east, or there could be no permanent rest. He had his six old legions, the Seventh, Eighth, Ninth, Tenth, Eleventh and Twelfth. Raising two new ones in Italy, the Thirteenth and Fourteenth, he sent them under his nephew and lieutenant, Q. Pedius, into Transalpine Gaul, probably by the Great St. Bernard, to the land of the Sequani. This made eight legions, each probably with not much less than its full complement. If we assume five thousand men to each, he had forty thousand heavy foot. To these we may add Gallic auxiliaries, Cretan archers, slingers and Numidians which, from certain allusions in the Commentaries, we may place at thirteen thousand, or a total of fifty-three thousand foot. Add again five thousand cavalry and some Æduan foot under Divitiacus, and we have an army of over sixty thousand men. The non-combatants (servants and camp-followers) were numerous. His lieutenants were M. Crassus, *quaestor*, and T. Labienus, C. Fabius, Q. Cicero, L. Roscius, L. Munatius Plancus, C. Trebonius, Q. Titurius Sabinus, and L. Arunculeius Cotta, legates, all good men and tried. We later find some others placed in responsible command. Caesar had authority from the Senate to appoint ten lieutenants of *propraetorian* rank. But his legates are not, as a rule, mentioned as such.

When the season had advanced so that there was an abundance of forage, Caesar joined the army, probably at Vesontio. Learning by scouts and by spies of the Senones and other tribes, neighbours to the Belgae, whom he sent out as less suspicious than other Gauls, that the Belgae had raised an army, and that it was encamped in a certain region north of the Axona (Aisne), but apparently not ready to move, Caesar, after properly providing for rations, broke up and headed towards their boundaries, some fifteen days distant. It was late in May. From Vesontio he marched back over the route he had taken when he moved against Ariovistus, to Langres, and thence by Bar-sur-Aube, to

GALLIC BUCKLER FOUND IN NORMANDY

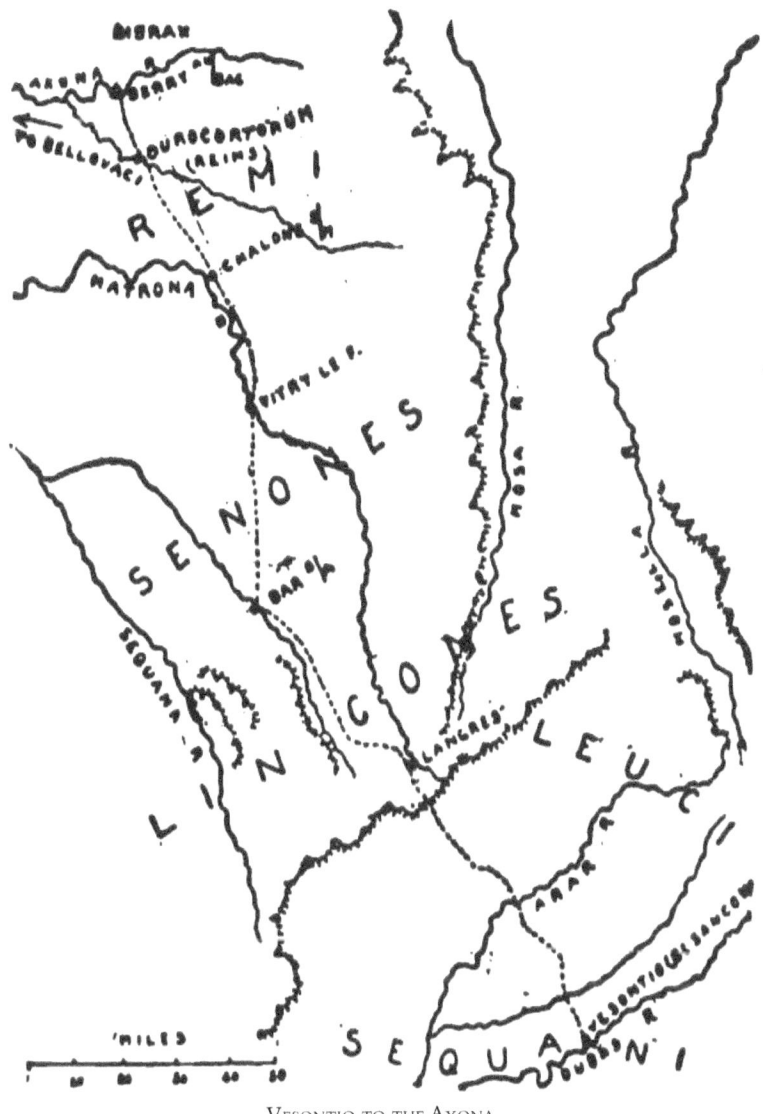

VESONTIO TO THE AXONA

Vitry le François,—one hundred and forty-five miles in fifteen days. This route is laid down on the assumption that there was an ancient Gallic road between these points.

This march on the enemy's army as objective was in accordance with Caesar's energetic mood, as well as in strict conformity with the best rules of warfare. A summary attack on the enemy before his plans are completely developed into action is uniformly the surest means of disconcerting him, and of providing for his discomfiture. It was always Napoleon's plan, and whenever energetically employed is apt to succeed even beyond expectation. Having determined on this course, Caesar's speed in carrying out his purpose was characteristic of the man, and a first step towards victory.

The result justified Caesar's anticipations. The nearest tribe of Belgae, the Remi, at once submitted, awed by the unexpected arrival of Caesar in their very midst. They had not yet committed themselves to the coalition, but, familiar with its details, their submission put Caesar into possession of all the facts. They were not unwilling to play in northern Gaul the role which was assumed by the Ædui in the centre of the country. It was the safest, and they proved constant to their pledges.

The Belgae were of German origin. Their distant ancestors had come from beyond the Rhine, and they were equally haughty and warlike. They, alone and unsupported, had thrown back the wave of the Cimbri and Teutones which had come so near to wrecking Rome. The Commentaries open with the statement that the Belgae were the bravest of the barbarians. They were very numerous. It seemed that the Bellovaci had promised to the common cause one hundred thousand fighting men, of whom sixty thousand picked troops should go into the field; the Suessiones and Nervii, fifty thousand each; and twelve other tribes a total of one hundred and thirty-six thousand more. The actual forces under the colours were as follows:

Bellovaci,	around modern		Beauvais	.	.	60,000 men.
Suessiones,	"	"	Soissons	.	.	50,000 "
Nervii,	"	"	Hainault	.	.	50,000 "
Atrebates,	"	"	St. Quentin	.	.	15,000 "
Ambiani,	"	"	Amiens	.	.	10,000 "
Morini,	"	"	Artois	.	.	25,000 "
Menapii,	around modern		Flanders / Brabant	.	.	7,000 men.
Caletes,	"	"	Havre	.	.	10,000 "
Viliocasses,	"	"	lower Seine / Arras	.	.	10,000 "
Veromandui,	"	"				
Aduatuci,	"	"	Namur	.	.	19,000 "
Four German Tribes			.	.	.	40,000 "
						296,000 "

As the Germans of the left bank of the Rhine had joined the coalition, it was not improbable that additional help would likewise come

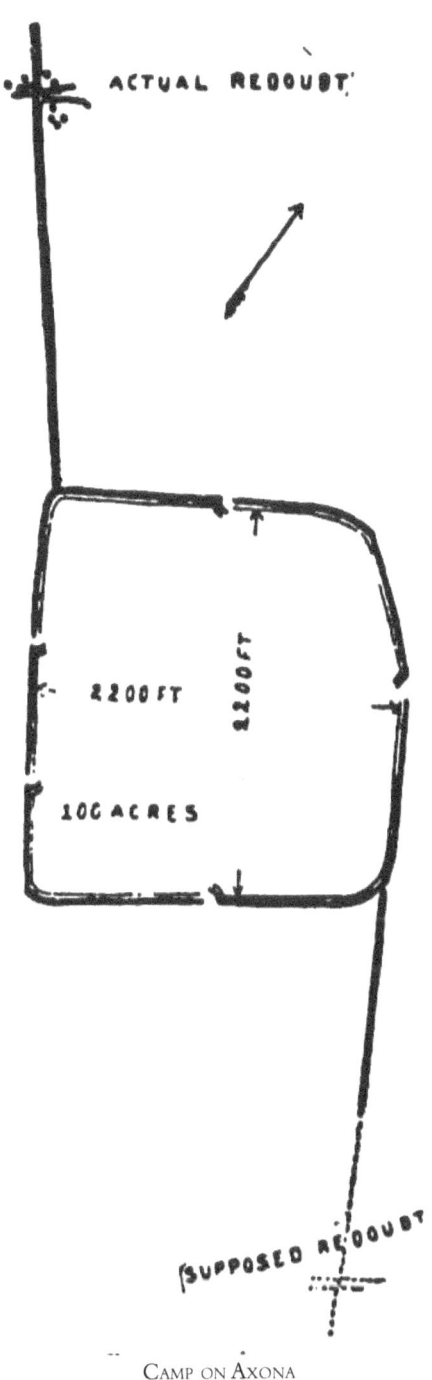

CAMP ON AXONA

from across the river. Galba, king of the Suessiones, which tribe Divitiacus had once ruled, was to be commander-in-chief.

This coalition covered the whole of what is now northern France and Belgium. Caesar plainly saw that he must not allow this gigantic force to assemble, but must speedily attack it in detail if he would not be overwhelmed by it as a whole. He therefore, as a diversion, sent Divitiacus with the contingents of the Ædui, Remi and Senones into the territory of the Bellovaci on a ravaging expedition. This was an excellent thrust, even if Divitiacus should prove unable to accomplish much, for his presence alone was apt to produce present dissension in the ranks of the Belgian cantons. Divitiacus, though allied by friendship to the Bellovaci, did his work in a handsome manner. Caesar himself, learning that the enemy was near at hand, advanced across the Matrona (Marne) through Durocortorum (Reims), and to the Axona at modern Berry au Bac. Here was a bridge. Caesar took possession of it, crossed the river and went into camp.

His army was in good spirits and able. His legions were vastly superior to the barbari-

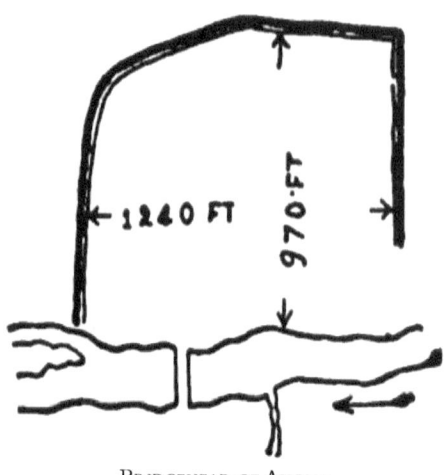

BRIDGEHEAD OF AXONA

ans; his Gallic allies probably as good, and Caesar could of course handle them to better advantage than the enemy his own troops. In his camp there was but one head, one purpose.

The River Axona protected a large part of the territory of his new allies, the Remi, and formed an excellent defensive line. His camp lay north of the Axona, on the hill between the river and a low, marshy brook now called the Miette. There are substantial remains of the camp extant. The hill was eighty feet above the Axona, and the slopes were such as to allow a convenient deployment of the legions. The bridge, if he continued to hold it, made certain that his rations could be securely delivered to him by the contributory tribes in the rear. This bridge he at once fortified on the north side by a bridgehead, with a rampart and palisades twelve feet high and a trench eighteen feet wide; and he placed Q. Titurius Sabinus in command of the south bank with six *cohorts*, or about three thousand men. Caesar was, to be sure, astride the river, but the bulk of his force was on the offensive bank, he had good communications with the province, and his camp formed an excellent intermediate base for action against the Belgae.

The enemy was near at hand. They had invaded that part of the territory of the Remi which lay north of the Axona. They had laid siege to Bibrax (Vieux Laon), some eight miles north of Caesar's camp. Their method of siege was to drive the defenders from the ram-parts by showers of stones and arrows, and then to advance against the wall a *testudo* (or tortoise made by the soldiers holding their shields close together over their heads) to cover workmen who should undermine it. At the close of the first day the besieged managed to smuggle some messengers through the lines, never carefully held at night, and sent word to Caesar that they must be aided or speedily surrender. Caesar at once sent them a force of his best Numidian and Cretan archers and Balacrean slingers. This reinforce-

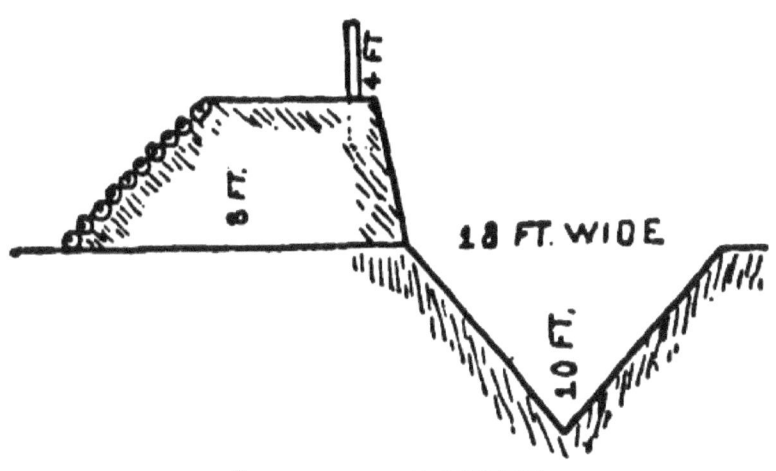

SKETCH PROFILE OF CAMP DEFENCES

ment probably penetrated the town by the south, where impregnable escarpments made the besiegers lax in their watch. They were active only on the other three sides.

The easily discouraged Belgae drew off from the siege, and giving up hope of taking the place, devastated the region. They then advanced and took up a position within two miles of the Romans. Their camp appeared from the fires to have a front some eight miles long.

Caesar was cautious about engaging this enormous army until he had made essay of their valour and discipline as well as of that of his Æduan horse, and he made daily cavalry reconnoissances by which the Romans could gauge the value of the enemy in action. They soon ascertained that the allied horse was quite equal to the Belgian; and the Roman soldier was by far his superior. The legionary's ambition rose accordingly. This caution on Caesar's part was as much an outcome of his own inexperience as it was the desire of teaching his troops that they were safe in despising numbers. He could not afford to have one bad check now, as its effect might be so far-reaching as to prejudice the results of his whole plan of action in Gaul. But having satisfied himself and his soldiers of their superiority, he concluded to bring on a battle. We admire the method and skill of Caesar, but we look in vain for that *élan* which characterized even the first campaigns of Alexander—that mettle which made no tale of the enemy. Caesar's caution was advisable, but it does not appeal to us like the Macedonian's brilliant gallantry.

The ground on the north slope in front of the bridgehead was not only available for ranging the Roman battle-lines, but its left

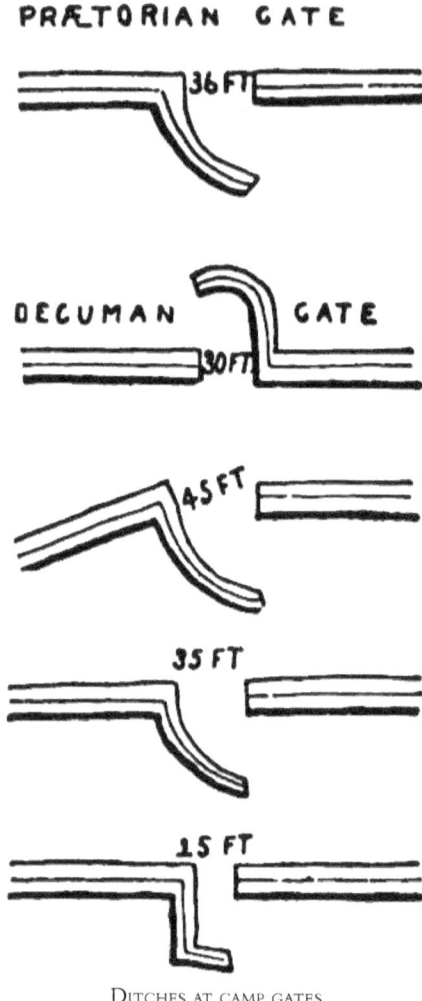

Ditches at camp gates

was protected by the Miette and Aisne; the right could lean on the camp. But between the camp and both the Axona and the brook were gaps through which the barbarians with their vast numbers might penetrate, and take the legions in reverse. These gaps Caesar fortified with a wall and trench four hundred paces long, at right angles to the front of the camp, and built a redoubt at each outer end, where he placed some of his military engines to support his right flank in case the enemy should overlap him. He left the two new legions in camp as a reserve. The other six he drew up in line on the north slope of the hill. The enemy did the same in front of their own camp. Between the two armies was the marshy bit of land made by the brook. Neither army appeared willing to cross this strip, lest the disorder into which it might fall during the crossing should enable the other to take it at a disadvantage.

The action was opened by some cavalry exchanges between the two armies, in which the Roman allies again proved their superiority after a hot contest. Caesar, not caring himself to attack, but wishing to lure the Belgians on to begin the engagement, after some hours thus spent in line, led back his forces to camp. The barbarians, who were really anxious to fight, for their victual was not overabundant, but unwilling to assault Caesar's entrenchments, now tried another, scheme. They marched round the Roman left to the river, where they

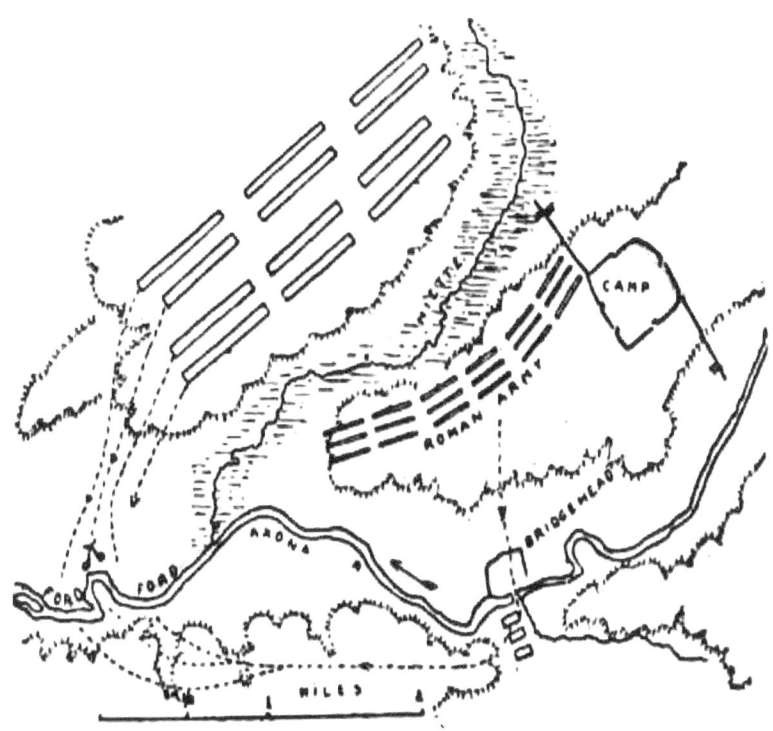

BATTLE OF THE AXONA

had discovered a passable and strangely enough to Caesar unknown ford below the camp; and here they began to make their way across in small parties, purposing to cut off the bridge or the command of Titurius; or failing this, to devastate the region of the Remi on which the Romans relied for much of their corn. It is probable that the country was heavily wooded. Caesar at all events did not discover the turning manoeuvre until informed of it by Titurius. Leaving his legions still in camp, Caesar himself, with his cavalry and light troops, moved rapidly to the rear, crossed by the bridge and advanced to meet this serious threat. His force consisted of his Gallic cavalry, and of Numidian and Cretan archers and Balacrean slingers, the best of their kind, and of great value and utility. He arrived at the ford not a moment too soon, for the barbarians were already swarming across the river in considerable numbers. The light troops attacked them with vigour. As they were in disorder from the difficulties of the ford, which they were crossing without any preparation or support, Caesar had them at his mercy, and inflicted enormous losses upon them. The cavalry cut those who had reached the south bank to pieces, and drove back the other warriors who were gallantly seeking to force their way over the river on the bodies of the slain, which all but filled up the ford. The victory was won with small effort. The fact that the legions were not brought on to the field is a fair gauge to the battle of the Axona.

The barbarians, disappointed at not taking Bibrax, nor drawing Caesar into battle on their own ground, nor being able to cut him off by crossing the river, lost heart and determined to retire. To this they were especially constrained, when on hearing that the Ædui had invaded the land of the Bellovaci, this latter tribe at once decamped to protect its own territory. It was agreed, however, among all the tribes before dispersing, that they should again assemble to resist the Roman army whenever it might invade the country, on the territory of whatever tribe was first attacked.

They accordingly broke camp that night about ten p. m., and began their rearward movement. As the column of each tribe naturally strove to be first in order of march, the army as a whole set out on their retreat in much confusion. This was increased by the darkness. Perceiving the disorder, but fearing an. ambush, Caesar, with Fabian caution, remained in camp till daybreak. Having then satisfied himself that there was no such danger, he sent his cavalry under Pedius and Cotta, and three legions under Labienus, to harass the rear of the retreating enemy. This was effectually done, and without loss. The Roman troops cut down many thousands of the barbarians, who had no further idea of resistance, and allowed themselves to be slaughtered like so many brute beasts. The pursuit was checked at night, and the party returned to camp. Judging from the account in the *Commentaries*, the pursuit was not over vigorous. The remorseless energy with which Alexander followed up his broken and flying enemy was entirely lacking here.

Next day, Caesar made a forced march of twenty-eight miles down the Axona to a city of the Suessiones which had joined the Belgae. It was called Noviodunum (Soissons). He hoped to take the place by storm, as it had but a scanty garrison, the tribe being absent in the general expedition. The wall and ditch were, however, so high and wide that the town could not be captured out of hand. The *Commentaries* simply state that Caesar attempted the assault. It appears probable that he did so without proper precautions, and being driven back with loss, made no second assault. Hannibal, it seems, was not the only general who was balked by walls and ditches; and the towns he assaulted were fortified by Roman skill and garrisoned by Roman soldiers. The *Commentaries* are our only source of information for the details of this war, and as these were written with a purpose, and are as eminently plausible as they are remarkable as a narrative of events, it is often difficult to read between the lines so as to guess at the exact truth. But in this case it is evident that Caesar was beaten back by the garrison of Noviodunum. Finding that the assault was a failure, Caesar camped nearby and sent back for the *vineae* and other engines of siege. *Vineae*, it will be remembered, were portable, strongly constructed huts, open at both ends, which could be placed together so as to make galleries to approach the walls of towns for undermining. They served the same purpose as parallels in modern war.

AZONA TO SABIS

The army of the Suessiones meanwhile returned, and a reinforcement to the garrison was thrown into the place during the following night. The *Commentaries* lead one to infer that the entire body of Suessiones filed in. It would seem as if this should have been prevented by Caesar. The tribe could be more easily fought outside than inside the place, and if he had enough men to besiege it in the presence of the relieving army, he certainly had enough to prevent their entering the town. It is probable that the barbarians outwitted Caesar in this matter also. But Caesar started to make a terrace; and when the siege apparatus arrived, the barbarians, astonished at the enormous preparations made by the Roman engineers, and their speed in the work of the siege, concluded that they had better sue for peace. By intercession of the Remi, whose allies they had always been, their suit was granted, the people were disarmed, and the usual hostages taken. In the town was found a large supply of arms.

Caesar then marched across the Axona against the Bellovaci,—the most dangerous of the allies,—who retired into their capital town called Bratuspantium (Breteuil, or possibly Beauvais). But when the Roman army came near the place, a deputation of old men was met who sued for peace; and so soon as Caesar had arrived within sight of its walls, the women and boys made supplication from the ramparts. Divitiacus, who had returned after disbanding his Æduan army, also pleaded for this people, which had been misled by its chiefs, and out of respect to him and to the Æduans, Caesar took the Bellovaci under his protection, requiring, however, six hundred hostages from them as well as the surrender of their arms. Such hostages were, as a rule, the children of the king, if any, and of important citizens, or else were illustrious men, needful to the state and influential in its councils. The Bellovaci declared that the promoters of the Belgic war had fled to Britain, with which country there was considerable intercourse.

The neighbouring people, the Ambiani, on being approached, also brought in their submission, and now Caesar concluded to turn northeasterly towards the land of the Nervii.

Chapter 8
Battle of the Sabis
July-September, 57 B. C.

Many of the Belgian tribes had sued for peace. Not so the Nervii and their allies. Caesar marched against them. At the River Sabis he was surprised by the barbarians, owing purely to insufficient scouting. While the legions were preparing to camp, the enemy fell violently upon them. They were caught unprepared, and came close to being overwhelmed. Caesar was never, except at Munda, in so grave a danger. Finally, by superhuman exertions on his own part, and by cheerful gallantry on the part of his men, the tide of battle turned, and the barbarians were defeated with terrible slaughter. Out of sixty thousand Nervii, but five hundred remained fit for duty; of six hundred senators, but three returned from the battle. Caesar then marched down the Sabis to a city of the Aduatuci (Namur), which after some trouble he took. The campaign had been successful and glorious. Caesar had made serious but natural mistakes, of which happily the Gauls were not able enough to take advantage.

The Nervii were the most warlike of the Belgians, and they not only absolutely refused to make terms, but reproached the other Belgians for submission. This people kept themselves entirely aloof from commerce or intercourse with other nations, and in this manner had preserved their native strength and hardihood. The Nervii had got the Atrebates and Veromandui to pool issues with them, and the Aduatuci were on the way to join the coalition. The women and children had been sent to a spot defended by a marsh, perhaps Mons, whose hill is now surrounded by low meadows once marshes. In three days' march Caesar reached a point near modern Bavay, not far from the Sabis (Sambre), on which river, ten miles away, he learned from some prisoners that the Nervii and the adjoining allied tribes were awaiting the Roman army, at a place near modern Maubeuge. Caesar kept up his advance and struck the Sabis on the left or north bank. The Nervii were on the right or south bank. He sent forward his light troops to reconnoitre, and the usual number of centurions to choose a place for camp. The common formation for the march of the Roman army (*i. e.* each legion being followed by its own baggage) had been carefully noted by the neighbouring tribes, and its manner reported to the Nervii; some native deserters had also joined them with similar information from the Roman camp; and the Nervian chiefs were advised to promptly attack the leading legion as it approached its new camping ground encumbered with its *impedimenta*, because, hampered by the baggage-train following it, they would probably be able to destroy it before the other legions could arrive to its support. This would in the opinion of the Gallic advisers quite demoralize the rest of the army and result in Caesar's complete overthrow. Orders were accordingly issued by the Nervian chiefs to attack as soon as the baggage-train came in view. Such action was all the more promising as the locality was rough and wooded, and suitable for the Nervii to fight in, they having little horse but most excellent infantry.

It was towards the end of July. Caesar's officers had chosen for camping a place where an uncovered hill sloped gently down to the left bank of the Sabis, at Neuf-Mesnil. On the other side of the river was a like hill (Haumont), the upper slope of which, beginning some two hundred paces away from the river, was heavily wooded. In these woods the Nervii hid their camp. Having no cavalry, they resorted to a clever means to stop the enemy's. They bent down saplings and interlaced their branches with brambles and brushwork, thus making the stiffest kind of hedge. The people of this section still do the same thing today to fence in fields. By this means the Nervii intercepted the advance of the Roman allied horse which was reconnoitring, and effectually prevented the discovery of their position. Every warrior was kept out of sight, excepting only a few *videttes* near the flats along the river, which was here but about three feet deep; and these served to attract the Romans' attention and prevent their scouting beyond the river. Their skilful dispositions exceeded Caesar's.

Knowing that he was approaching the enemy, Caesar, instead of the usual column, adopted an order of march proper to the occasion. First came the cavalry; then the six old legions; then the baggage all in

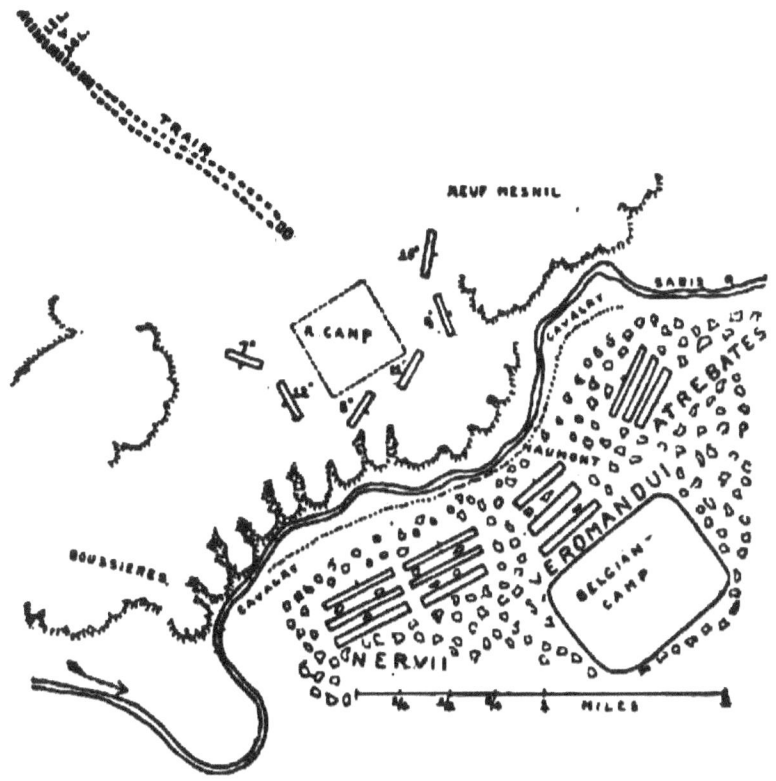

BATTLE ON THE SABIS

one train; last the rear and baggage guard, consisting of the two new legions. But Caesar was far from imagining that the whole force of the enemy was close at hand. His scouting was not effective.

On approaching the camping-ground, the cavalry sent a detachment across the river with slingers and archers to drive away the Nervian *videttes*, while the six leading legions set about fortifying the camp. The Nervian horsemen skirmished well, holding the edge of the wood in such a way that the Romans did not discover the Gallic line of battle.

The Ninth and Tenth legions, meanwhile, began work on the left front of the proposed camp; the Eighth and Eleventh on the front facing the river, the Seventh and Twelfth on the right front. The legionaries, unsuspicious of danger, dispersed to collect palisades and other stuff, with but the slender cordon of horse out as pickets. While all this was passing, and so soon as the wagon-train had come in sight, this being the preconcerted signal, the Nervii and their allies, the

Atrebates and Veromandui, rushed impetuously from their ambush, brushed away the Roman skirmish-line of horse like a cobweb, forded the river and fell, as it were an avalanche, upon the Romans, who were entirely unconscious of their presence and unprepared for an assault. It was evident that Caesar had not yet grown expert in reconnoitring his ground in the presence of the enemy, nor careful in his method of camping. Here was an unwarranted breach of the usual Roman method, which always put out a line of battle to protect a camping party. The surprise was complete. It was all but certain that Caesar's army would be wiped from existence. In the onslaught the Atrebates were so placed on the enemy's right as to attack the Ninth and Tenth legions; the Veromandui in the centre, the Eighth and Eleventh; the Nervii on their left, the Seventh and Twelfth. The Nervii were opposite the rugged left bank of the Sabis at Boussières.

But for the discipline of the legions, which was in every sense commendable, the Roman army would have been destroyed. Many of the soldiers were at a distance seeking material for the rampart; the rest were busy at work with what they had already brought. Lucky it was that the men had become hardened in their past year's campaigns. Better still, they had gained confidence in their leader. There was not a sign of demoralization. The stanch qualities which later enabled Caesar with them to complete the overthrow of all his enemies had already taken root. So soon as the enemy was seen to emerge from the woods, every legionary caught the alarm. The trumpet was quickly sounded, and the standards displayed; the officers were happily all at hand, it being one of Caesar's explicit orders that none such should, under any pretence, leave his legion till the camp was fully fortified; and the Roman soldiers had already learned how to fall quickly into the ranks.

The attack of the barbarians had been so well-timed and sudden that the officers, many of them, had not even time to put on their badges, such as were usual to distinguish the several ranks, or the men to take off the leather covers with which, during the march, they were wont to protect their often beautifully ornamented shields. Nor could they by any means seek each man his own *cohort*. They fell in under whatever standard was nearest, while Caesar and his lieutenants rushed to and fro, encouraging the patchwork lines and striving to call order from confusion.

The line was barely formed in this irregular manner, when the enemy reached the ground. They had crossed an open stretch of nearly three quarters of a mile and forded a river, which may have occupied twenty minutes. The surface was considerably cut up by the artificial hedges before referred to, which might be described as a sort of abatis. This circumstance operated to prevent all manoeuvring. The line thus thrown together was an irregular convex formation, standing in so confused a manner that the legionaries had no notion whatsoever of what was going on around them. Each small body fought where it stood, as it were, for its own sole safety. There was no possibility of mutually assisting each other. Aid could not be sent from one to another part of the line. There was, for the nonce, no head, no purpose. A worse surprise can scarcely be imagined. Still there was no manifestation of fear; the legionaries set their teeth and proposed to fight it out as best they might.

The Ninth and Tenth legions were, as stated, on the left. These men behaved with all the gallantry for which Caesar so loved the Tenth, cast the *pilum*, fell to with the *gladius*, and after a hearty tussle drove back the Atrebates in their front; for these barbarians had become tired and out of breath with their sharp rush across the river and their hurried attack. They were pushed, with great loss, across the ford, followed up and cut down by thousands. The Atrebates rallied for a moment, but were again broken and hustled back until the Ninth and Tenth finally reached the Gallic camp.

The Eleventh and Eighth legions in the centre likewise behaved with praiseworthy fortitude. After a wavering combat, in which both sides lost heavily, the success of the Ninth and Tenth on their left so emboldened these two bodies that, with a shout of triumph, they made a common charge on the foe and pushed the Veromandui in their front sharply down to the river, on whose bank they kept up the combat.

But this very success was the cause of the gravest danger. The advance of the four legions of the left and centre absolutely exposed the front and left of the camp works just begun, and left naked the flank and rear of the Seventh and Twelfth legions on the right. While all this was going on, a heavy force of sixty thousand Nervii, under Boduognatus, the chief in command, had been fording the Sabis and climbing the heights of Boussières. Perceiving the opening, this entire force fell on the two legions, which numbered some ten thousand men, striking them on the right flank (*aperto latere*) with a fierceness which the Romans had never yet encountered. The cavalry and light troops, who, after being driven in, had just rallied and placed themselves in reserve, were again utterly disorganized by this overwhelming onset; while

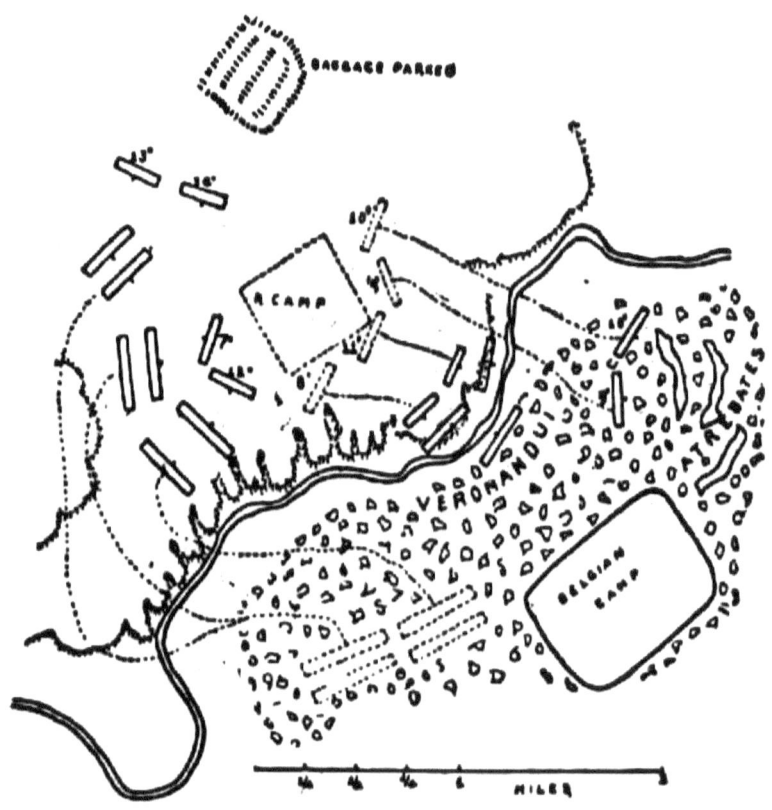

BATTLE ON THE SABIS (SECOND PHASE)

the host of non-combatants,—drivers, servants and sutlers,—penned up in the camp, seeing a column of the barbarians penetrating into its very midst, made a hasty exit from the half finished rear-gate in the wildest confusion, and made for the woods. So apparently fatal was the disaster and rout, that some auxiliary cavalry, reputed to be the best in Gaul, took to its heels, and conveyed to the tribes along the route by which Caesar had advanced, and at home, the news that the Romans had been surprised and utterly destroyed.

Caesar, at the earliest onset of the enemy, had rushed to the left, where the line was first threatened, and encouraged the Ninth and Tenth legions, who under his cheerful words and bearing had gone to work with a will which accomplished wonders. Thence he galloped to the centre, where his presence exerted a like happy effect. On his reaching the right, he found matters in the worst possible condition. On this front had fallen the attack of the Nervii themselves, the bravest of the brave. The standards of the Twelfth legion had been planted so closely together that the troops were huddled in masses, and unable to fight to any advantage. The files were pressed too close to use the sword. There had been a terrible loss of officers, the missiles falling on the close ranks with awful fatality. In some *cohorts* every *centurion* was killed or wounded. If Caesar had not yet been hard pressed by the Gauls, he had his fill of fighting now. The efforts of the troops were apparently slackening. The enemy, in vast numbers, was pushing in front and overlapping the flanks, and more and more were coming. There was no reserve. The other legions had not yet worked out their problem. The matter was at its climax. Defeat stared Caesar in the face,—massacre was its result. Snatching a buckler from a soldier in the rear, with the inspiration of dire necessity,—as he later did at Munda, where, as he said, he fought for his life,—Caesar rushed on foot to the front to re-establish order. Seeing their chief performing the part of the common soldier, the courage of the men nearby at once revived, and the good feeling spread. They opened ranks so as to wield the *gladius*. Their battle-cry resumed its normal resonance, and the resistance to the enemy became more resolute. Rushing thence to the Seventh legion, Caesar reanimated that body in like manner, and brought it sharply up to the support of the Twelfth, and, as some critics read the *Commentaries*, got the two legions back to back, so as to prevent being surrounded. The benefit of Caesar's gallantry was immediate. It struck the same key-note as Napoleon's heading the grenadiers at the bridge of Lodi. Such is the effect of a great man's divine fury upon other men. It was the burning genius of the heart within, which could thus in a moment transform disaster into victory, could revive the ardour of courage fast ebbing away.

Meanwhile the two legions of the rearguard, having notice of the battle, hastened up, and being seen approaching by the enemy spread a disheartening effect among their ranks. Labienus, who with the Tenth legion had gained possession of the enemy's camp beyond the ford, also perceived from the hill opposite the distress of the Twelfth and Seventh, and speedily sent the Tenth to their succour. This admirable body of men came up at a *pas de charge*, and took the Nervii in the rear with a shock which instantly re-established the fighting on the right; and, seeing the change of tide, the camp-followers and cavalry regained their courage, and turning upon the foe drove the flanking column of the barbarians from the camp.

The tide had turned; the battle was won, but so tenacious of their ground were the Nervii that the survivors stood and fought on the bodies of the slain, and even piled them up as breastworks. It was by brute pressure alone that these obstinately gallant barbarians could be forced to cease from fighting. The little remainder Caesar drove into flight. They had fought with a doggedness exhibited by no foes Caesar ever encountered. The Roman army was exhausted as it had rarely been, and its losses had been heavy. Camp was at once fortified; the men buried the dead, and took their rest.

The old men from the Nervian retreat shortly sent and sued for peace. They stated that of six hundred senators but three had returned from the battle; that of the sixty thousand men who had been engaged, a bare five hundred could now bear arms. Such had been the splendid valour of the vanquished. Caesar accepted their plea, arrested further butchery, and commanded the neighbouring tribes not to assail them in their utter present weakness.

The Aduatuci had been on the march to the assistance of the Nervii, but frightened at the reports of the battle of the Sabis, they turned back, deserted their other towns, and conveyed all their people and goods into one, peculiarly adapted for defence. This town, whose name is not given, was situated upon a precipitous hill well-nigh inaccessible on every side but one, where a gentle slope not over two hundred feet in width descended to the plain. This slope they had fortified with a very high double wall. These people were descendants of some six thousand of the Cimbri and Teutones, who had been left behind in charge of the baggage, while the bulk of the tribes had marched south and been destroyed by Marius two generations before. This site was doubtless in the angle made by the Sabis and Mosa (Meuse) opposite Namur. Mt. Falhize is suggested as the location, but it does not as well correspond with the text or with the distances marched as the other.

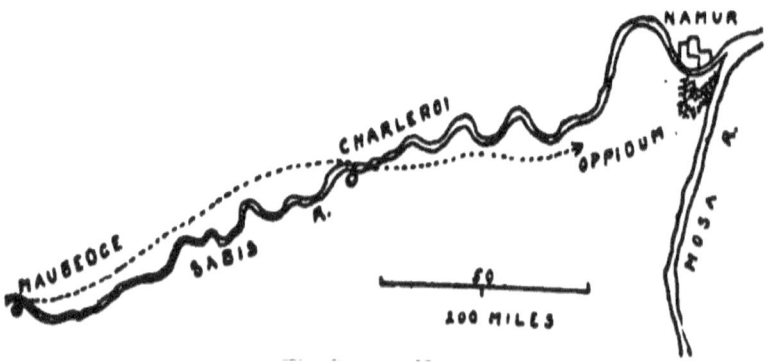

THE SABIS TO NAMUR

Against this town of the Aduatuci, Caesar, with seven of the legions—one was detached under Crassus—at once directed his march down the Sabis. Reaching the place, he found its location impregnable, and, seeing that he could not otherwise capture it, he began a siege by the construction of a rampart or line of contravallation. This work was twelve feet high and fifteen thousand feet long, with redoubts at intervals. The length of the works is often given as fifteen miles, but this is a manifest error, as the topography plainly shows. After the *quindecim millia* of the text, the word *pedum* must be understood. The barbarians endeavoured to interrupt this work by repeated petty attacks, but to no effect. When they saw the construction of a tower and *vineae* at a distance, they taunted the Romans for their small stature, which, indeed, then as now, was in marked contrast to the bulky bodies of the Germans, and of the Gauls who were of German lineage, and asked who would bring the tower to their walls. But when this same tower began to move towards them, and actually did approach their walls, they at once sent ambassadors to treat for peace, alleging their belief that the Romans were aided by the gods. They begged that they might retain their arms as a defence against their local enemies. Caesar demanded unconditional surrender and disarmament, but told them that he would command their neighbours to abstain from attack. The Aduatuci were fain to submit. Their manner of surrendering their arms was to throw them from the town rampart into the trench, and the supply was so great that it filled the trench and made a pile nearly up to the height of the rampart for a considerable distance along its circuit. Despite their surrender, the chiefs had acted treacherously, and had yet concealed a third part of their arms. After this apparent disarmament the gates were opened, and the Roman legions marched in and took possession.

When night came on, the Romans were all ordered from the town to their camps. Caesar feared the violence and rapacity of his legionaries, and the ill results which might flow therefrom. Still this was a lesser danger than to retire from a town just captured. The Aduatuci naturally believed that the Romans would be less careful now that they had received the surrender of the town, and planned an attack that very night upon what appeared to be the least strong part of Caesar's contravallation wall. They had the arms not surrendered, and they made new bucklers of bark and wicker-work. They delivered the assault shortly after midnight and with considerable vigour. Caesar, suspecting possible treachery, had provided for just such an occurrence.

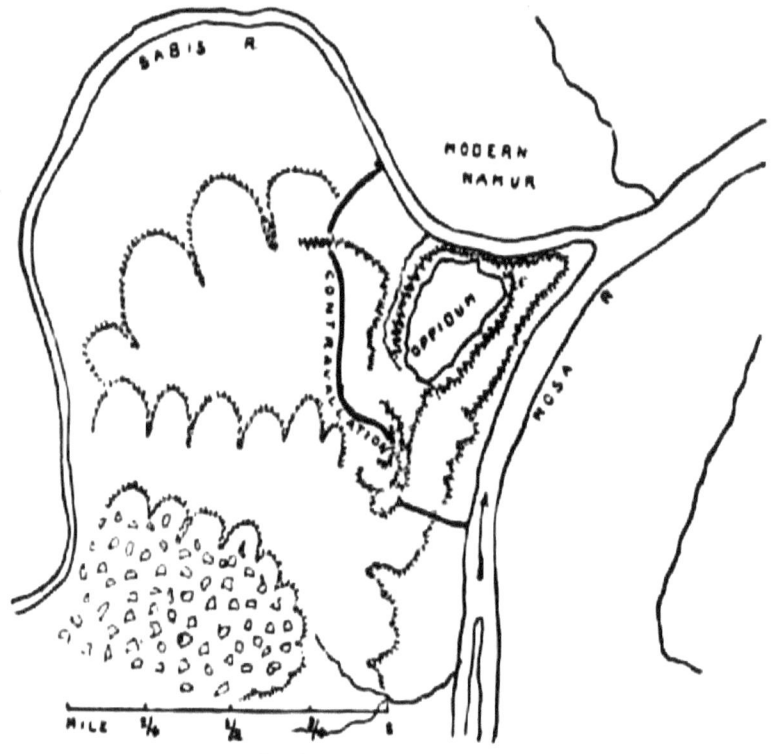

THE TOWN OF THE ADUATUCI

The usual signal-fire was lighted at the point of attack, and the *legionaries* at once rushed from all points to the defence of their threatened rampart. The Aduatuci fought like brave men, but, with a loss of some four thousand killed, they were driven back into the town and penned in. Caesar retaliated for this treachery by marketing the whole spoil of the town. There were fifty-three thousand people sold as slaves. This was early in September.

During this time, Crassus, who had been detached with the Seventh legion against the maritime tribes living on the northwest coast of Belgium, had done his work well, and reported that these peoples had all been brought under the Roman sway. His method of operation is not known.

So great had the fame of Caesar's conquests become that many of the nations from beyond the Rhine, the Ubii in particular, sent ambassadors to tender their submission to the Romans. But desirous of returning to Italy, and as the cold season was now approaching, Caesar put his troops into winter-quarters along the River Liger (Loire), among the Carnutes, Andes and Turones, echeloned between Orleans and Angers; and, inviting these ambassadors to return early the next summer, himself set out for the south. Reaching Rome, a thanksgiving (*supplicatio*) of fifteen days was decreed,—a longer period than had ever before been granted a Roman general.

The best praise of this splendid campaign is its own success. The energy, rapidity, clear-sightedness and skill with which Caesar divided, attacked and overcame the Belgian tribes is a model for study. The fact that he had next to no fighting to do is all the more to the credit of his strategy. But in this his second campaign, he still committed errors. Many of these are more or less frankly acknowledged in the *Commentaries*. His miscalculation in his unprepared and therefore unsuccessful assault on Noviodunum was a natural enough mistake, one to which all, even the greatest, commanders are liable. His being surprised, as

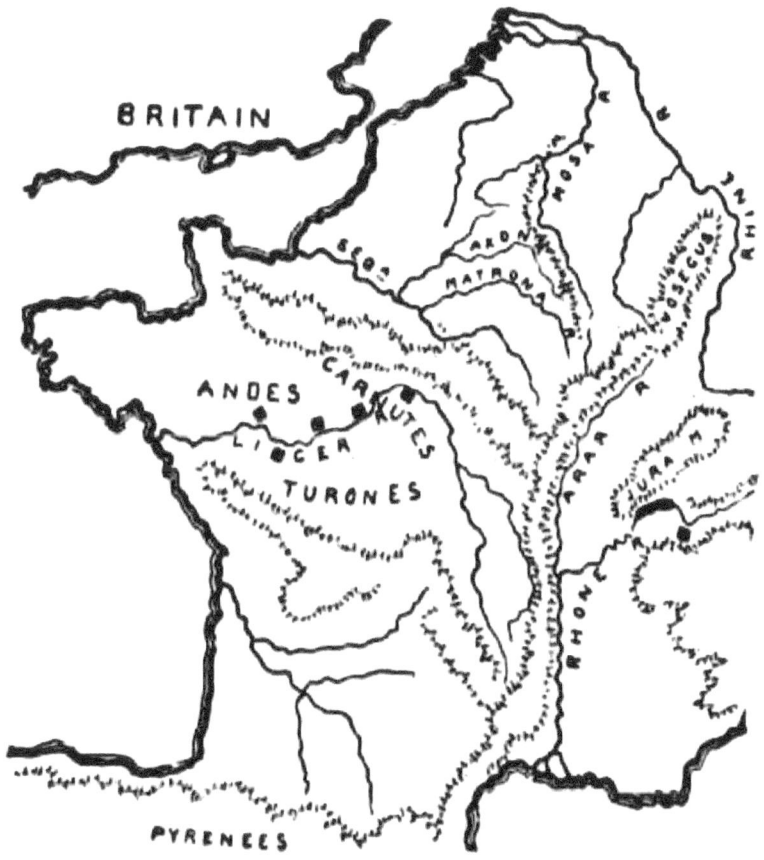

Winter-Quarters, B. C. 57-56

he was at the river Sabis, by the Nervii was due to a piece of carelessness which came near being, and but for the stanchness of the Roman character would have proved, fatal. He should have placed a garrison at once in the town of the Aduatuci, to forestall the night attack which he suspected might occur, and but for good luck would have proved much more disastrous to him. He should not have allowed his political desire to visit Rome to prevent his receiving the embassies tendering submission by the German tribes. The surprise at the Sabis is the most grave of these errors. Caesar appears to have had, contrary to all Roman precedent, no troops out to protect the camping-parties, except a small cavalry detachment, which plainly had been checked by the enemy close to the river and was unable to penetrate the woods. This fact should at once have excited Caesar's curiosity and have led to greater caution. That he was not absolutely destroyed on this occasion he owed to the excellence of his troops, and by no means to his own skill or care. The *Commentaries* on this subject show an uphill effort to palliate his error. But it was too glaring to cover. The truth can be easily read between the lines.

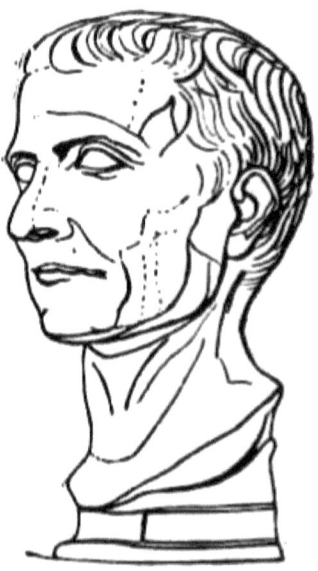

CAESAR, EARLY IN GALLIC WAR

CHAPTER 9

The Work of Caesar's Lieutenants
57-56 B. C.

Caesar usually spent his winters in Cisalpine Gaul, to be near events in Italy. During this winter, he sent Galba, one of his legates, to open the road from Italy over the Simplon and down the modern Rhone. At Martigny, Galba had a serious battle with the natives, but defeated them. Crassus, another legate, wintered among the Veneti on the coast, and sent ambassadors to gather corn. These officers were seized by the Veneti and held so as to compel the return of their hostages. On learning of this, Caesar at once made preparations to avenge the act. He must protect his envoys; and to subdue the Veneti would more-over give him easier access to Britain. In order to cover more ground, Caesar decided to divide his forces. Labienus went to the Rhine region; Crassus to Aquitania, Sabinus to the coast of modern Normandy. Brutus was put in command of the fleet. After a tedious campaign against the Veneti, they were utterly overthrown by Brutus in a naval battle. Meanwhile Sabinus conducted a successful campaign against the Unelli, and Crassus a brilliant one in Aquitania. The year was finished by a partial campaign against the Morini on the Channel, by Caesar. The work of the year had mostly been done by Caesar's lieutenants.

On leaving for Italy for the winter of B. C. 57-56, Caesar had sent Servius Galba, with the Twelfth legion and some horse, against the tribes south of the lake of Geneva, the Nantuates, Veragri and Seduni, to open one of the most available roads over the Alps between Cis and Transalpine Gaul, which ran from Milan *via* the Simplon or the Great St. Bernard to the Rhone valley. The merchants and settlers, in passing through-this valley, had generally experienced a good deal of trouble from the native tribes, who subjected them to heavy imposts, if they did not rob them outright. It was essential for military security that

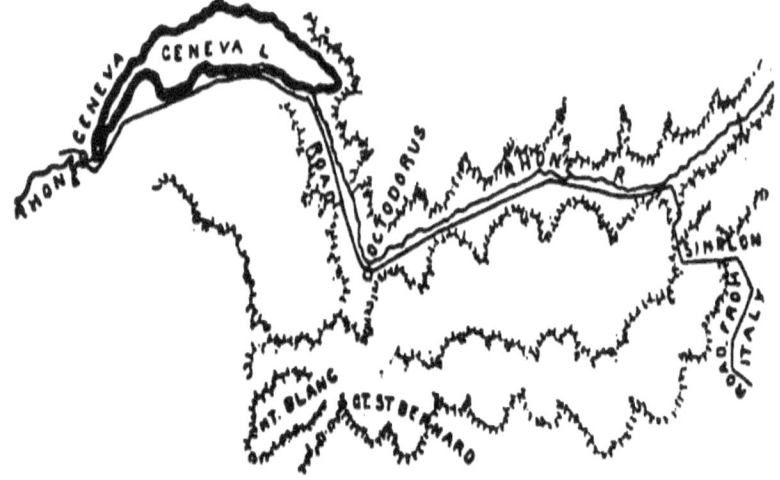

OCTODORUS VALLEY

this road should be made free to passage. Galba was given permission to winter in the Alps, if he deemed it essential. This Galba did, and having defeated the barbarians in several combats, he received their submission and hostages, and camped in the Rhone valley, where lay the town called Octodorus (Martigny), detailing two *cohorts* to occupy the land of the Nantuates farther down the river.

The valley is cut in two by the Rhone. The Roman camp lay on one side, the Gallic on the other. The Gauls formed the plan of cutting off this solitary legion, which by reason of its small number they thought could easily be done. They were indignant at the holding of so many of their children as hostages by the Romans, and they feared annexation to Rome,—the fate of all the tribes of Gaul.

These local clans had accordingly occupied all the surrounding heights and passes, so as to cut Galba off from victual and assistance. This action, taking Galba entirely by surprise, placed him in a most difficult situation. Calling a council of war, it was determined to hold the camp and abide the attack which the barbarians were sure to make. This was the only present resource, though, for some unaccountable reason, the fortifications of the winter-quarters' camp had not yet been completed. Even Roman orders and regulations were not invariably obeyed.

The assault of the Gauls came in due time and was sudden and severe. The defence was obstinate and the legionaries moved from place to place to resist the constantly repeated attacks on the wall. But the number of the defenders was small, and the enemy, whose force was considerable, were able constantly to bring fresh troops to supplant the weary. So vigorously was the fighting pushed that even the Roman wounded could not retire from the trenches. For six long hours the barbarians continued to press on in continual waves, until the Romans had discharged all their darts, and Galba saw that their only hope lay in cutting their way out with the sword. The sortie was suggested by *primipilus* P. Sextius Baculus, who had distinguished himself at the Sabis, and C. Volusenus, a military *tribune*. To carry out the idea, Galba gave orders to collect as many weapons as could be got from those which had fallen into the camp, and then to make a sally from all the gates at once. This desperate venture resulted in unexpected success. Surprised beyond measure at the sudden appearance of the Romans and their vigorous onslaught—for they were momentarily expecting a surrender—the barbarians, disconcerted, turned and fled. This is a fair sample of the inconstancy of the Gaul of that day. Brave to a noteworthy degree, when surprised or once defeated, he could not rally. The bulk of the fighting done by the legions was far from taxing their stanchness.

The legionaries pursued and slaughtered above a third of the enemy, who could not have fallen much short of thirty thousand men. After this victory, having devastated the valley as a punishment for the treachery, and being unwilling to trust to the bad roads and worse population for his supply of corn, Galba passed through the Nantuates, picked up his two *cohorts* and returned to the province to winter, pitching his quarters among the Allobroges. His conduct had been brave and sensible.

Caesar, while in Hither Gaul, believed that he was safe in setting out to Illyricum, as the Belgae had been subdued, the Germans expelled, the tribes along the most important road over the Alps defeated, and Gaul appeared to be quiet. But peace was not of long duration. Crassus, with one of the legions, had taken up winter-quarters among the Andes, a tribe near the Atlantic on the north shore of the Bay of Biscay. Of the neighbouring tribes the Veneti were the strongest. They owned all important harbours on the coast, drove a thriving commerce with Britain and Spain, and possessed great numbers of vessels and considerable wealth. Crassus, running short of victuals during the winter, had sent out some prefects and tribunes among the tribes to negotiate for a supply of corn. T. Terrasidius had gone to the Unelli, M. Trebius to the Curiosolitae, and Q. Velanius and T. Silius to the Veneti. These tribes, led by the Veneti, having determined among themselves on protecting their territories and made a compact to act together, seized these officers, hoping thereby to be able to compel the return of their own hostages. They sent, in fact, to demand such surrender as the price of the return of Crassus' ambassadors.

Caesar, being informed of these things by Crassus, but unable to take action during the winter, sent back orders to build a fleet in the Liger, provided rowers, sailors and pilots from the Mediterranean coast of the Province, and commanded everything to be prepared for a marine expedition. So soon as the season of B. C. 56 opened, he hurried to Gaul. The revolted tribes, knowing that they had, by seizing ambassadors, committed the most inexpiable of all offenses, prepared for the worst. They fortified their towns, collected in them all the breadstuffs which they could bring together, and brought their fleet to Venetia, their principal seaport, situated probably in the estuary of the Auray River, which discharges into the Bay of Quiberon. They knew that ignorance of their tides and inlets and harbours would place the Romans at a great disadvantage. Allies, according to Caesar, were even sent for to Britain. All the cantons on the coast from the Loire to the Scheldt gave aid, material or moral.

There was not a moment's hesitation in Caesar's mind as to the ne-

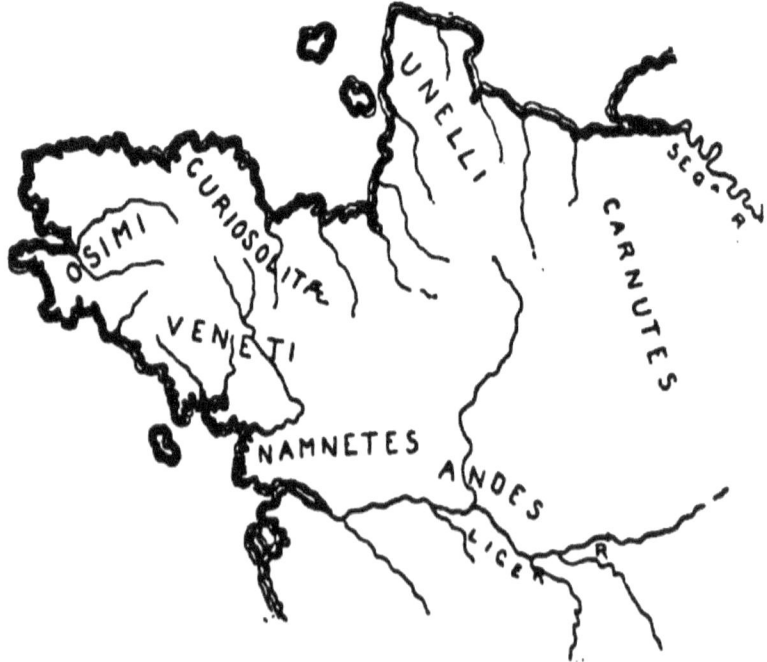

THE VENETAN COUNTRY

cessity of subduing this insurrection. The term insurrection is used, inasmuch as these tribes had once handed in their submission to Crassus, and now again rose in defence of their liberties. But it seems a harsh word to apply to these gallant peoples resisting the encroachments of an invader with no right but that of might to back him. The difficulties Caesar by no means underrated, but they were as nothing compared to the necessity of punishing the Veneti. If any tribe could, after giving hostages in token of submission, be allowed to transgress, without speedy retribution, the most universally accepted of the laws of nations, observed even among distant barbarians, then all his conquests in Gaul were but a house of cards. This is the motive Caesar would have us believe he acted on. It is a valid one as far as it goes.

But there was another reason for Caesar's determination to subdue the Veneti. This people practically owned all the commerce with Britain. They were loath to have Caesar seize it, as they feared he would do. Strabo tells us that Caesar had already planned to invade Britain, and to reduce the Veneti was a necessary first step, for they controlled the sea, and while he might push his way between their fleets, they could seriously threaten his rear during his absence.

It must be acknowledged in Caesar's behalf that the necessity existed of subduing the whole of Gaul, if Rome was to extend her dominion in this direction, if indeed Italy was to be safe; and if Alexander was justified in avenging the attacks of Persia on Greece, so was Caesar justified in avenging those of the Gauls on Rome. It is hard to criticise the universally claimed right of simple conquest among the ancients; and once we accept so much, nothing remains to blame except unnecessary harshness in the exercise of conquest. Caesar was justified from his standpoint.

As to the method to be pursued in this campaign, Caesar decided that it was essential to divide his forces, to occupy the country in a military sense, in order to impose on other tribes who might be tempted to imitate the example of the Veneti. He therefore sent Labienus with part of the cavalry to the Treviri near the Rhine, with orders to sustain the Remi and keep quiet among the Belgae, and to resist possible inroads of the Germans from across the river; for they had been invited to make another incursion by the Belgae. Crassus, with twelve legionary *cohorts* and a stout body of cavalry, he sent to Aquitania, to preserve quiet, and prevent Aquitanian support to the Venetan insurrection. Triturius Sabinus he stationed among the Unelli, and other tribes along the coast of modern Normandy, for a simi-

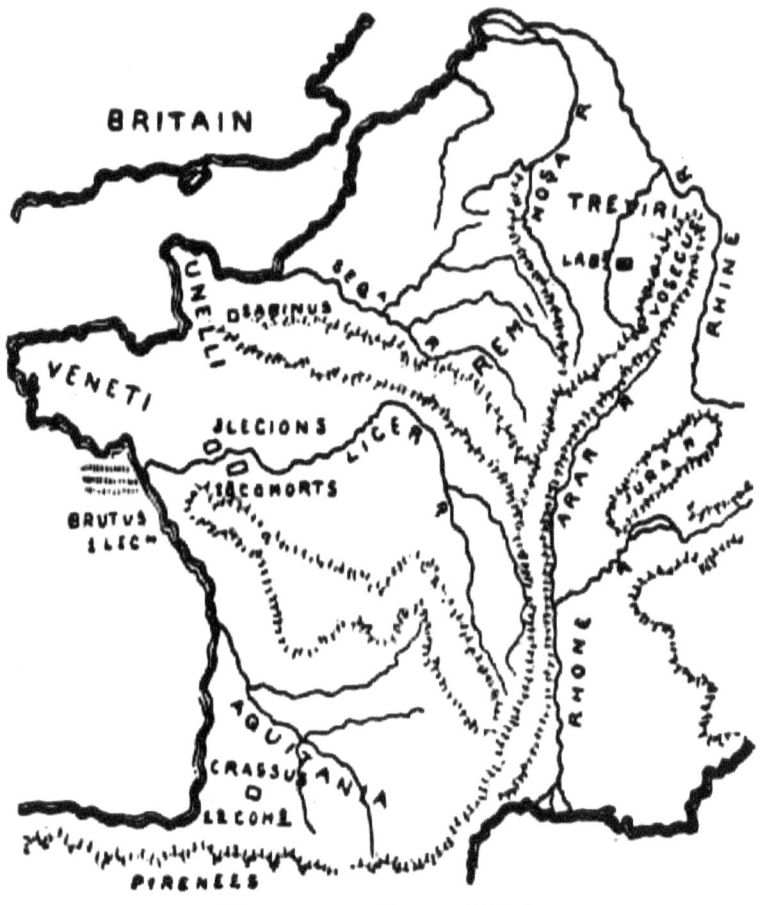

DISTRIBUTION OF LEGIONS, 56 B. C.

lar purpose. Decimus Brutus was given command of the fleet. He had brought some galleys from the Mediterranean, and vessels were borrowed from the Pictones, Santones and others.

Caesar's eight legions at the opening of the campaign were thus distributed: north of the Liger, three legions; in Aquitania one legion and two *cohorts*; a legion on the fleet; two legions and eight *cohorts* with Caesar. Galba had no doubt rejoined from his winter among the Allobroges. Caesar probably rendezvoused in the vicinity of Nantes, not far from the mouth of the Loire, and thence crossed the Vilaine.

The towns of the Veneti were exceptionally difficult of access. Generally on points of land, they were at high tide inaccessible except by boats; and the retiring tide, while it gave access to land forces, was apt to leave the boats stranded and defenceless. Again, whenever, after great exertions, any town had been cut off from the sea or been put into a desperate strait, the barbarians would simply embark their goods on their own boats, of which they had a vast number, and escape through the creeks and bays, with which the Romans were not familiar. This shifting from place to place they carried on all through the summer of 56 B. C. Their ships were flat-bottomed so as to be the more readily used in inland navigation, but with high bows and stern to resist the waves and the shock of rams. The wood was seasoned oak, the parts of which were held together by heavy iron spikes an inch thick, and their anchors had iron chains. Their bows, made much higher and stronger than those of the Roman galleys, rendered them all the more difficult to attack or to grapple to. Their sails were of soft and thin but tough skins. These boats were in all respects seaworthy, and far better adapted to shoal water warfare than those which the Romans had built on their usual pattern. Only in speed, and this by rowing, did the Roman galley excel that of the Veneti; the latter was impelled by sails alone.

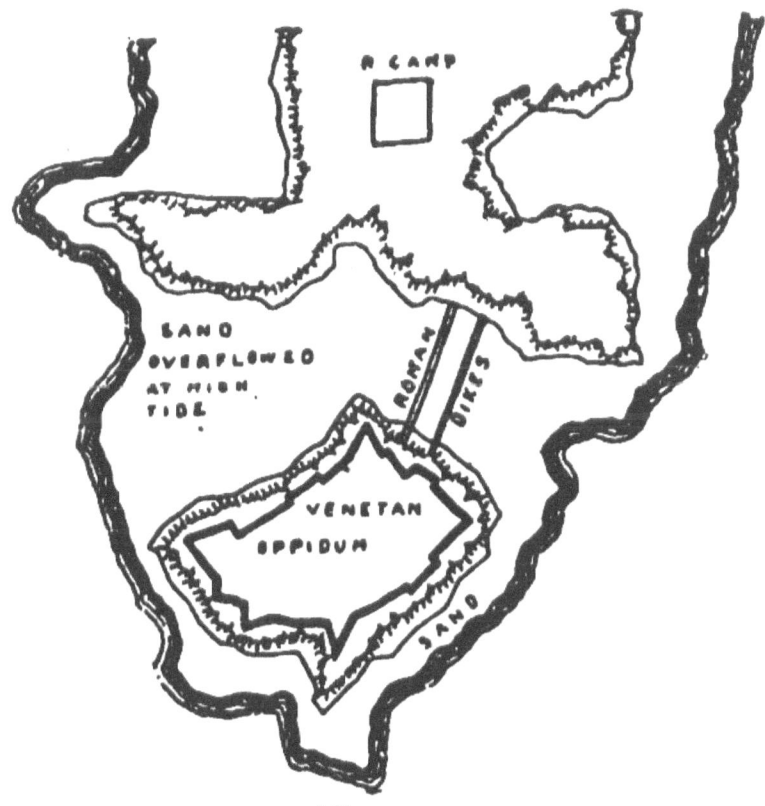

A Venetan town

The Roman method of taking the Venetan towns was to build out from the main land two parallel dikes, sometimes as high as the town walls, which when completed excluded tides and gave an excellent approach for engines and men—a place of arms, in fact. It was a vast labour and the operation was rendered nugatory in most cases by the escape of the barbarians as above explained.

The bulk of the season thus passed without success. Caesar saw that he could accomplish nothing without a fleet, and this was not yet assembled, though it had been ordered many months before and rendezvous given at the mouth of the Liger. The tides, an unknown element to the Romans, the lack of harbours, the inexperience of Roman sailors in these waters, and many other causes had operated to delay the preparations. But there is still something which the *Commentaries* do not explain. Roman galleys were very speedily constructed. Scipio Africanus, *e. g.*, built and launched twenty *quinquiremes* and ten *quadriremes* in forty-five days; Caesar had been at work nine months, and his fleet was not yet equipped. The delay was not a reasonable one. We know but half the truth.

After taking a number of the Venetan towns, it was plainly brought home to Caesar that he was making no practical headway. He accordingly determined to risk the event on the result of a naval battle. He camped on the heights of St. Gildas, on the east of the Bay of Quiberon, and waited for his fleet. This was shortly after assembled. So soon as matters were made ready, the Roman fleet moved against the Veneti into the bay. When it hove in sight, about two hundred and twenty of the vessels of the Veneti sailed out and confidently made ready for battle. The Roman line formed near modern Point St. Jaques, with its right not far from shore.

The Roman ships were lower; even their turrets were not as high as the stern of the barbarian ships, so that the marines could not effectively cast their darts, while fully exposed to those of the enemy. It was a question what tactics could be advantageously employed. The Romans were superior only in courage and discipline, and their vessels in speed, but this was offset by their being unused to and apprehensive of the ocean, to which they ascribed qualities different from their native Mediterranean. But they luckily had on board a great number of grappling hooks (*falces*), not unlike those used in sieges to pull stones from the tops of walls, or, as some construe it, had provided sickles tied to the end of long poles. These Brutus, by a stroke of genius, divined how he could put to use. A *falx* was slung

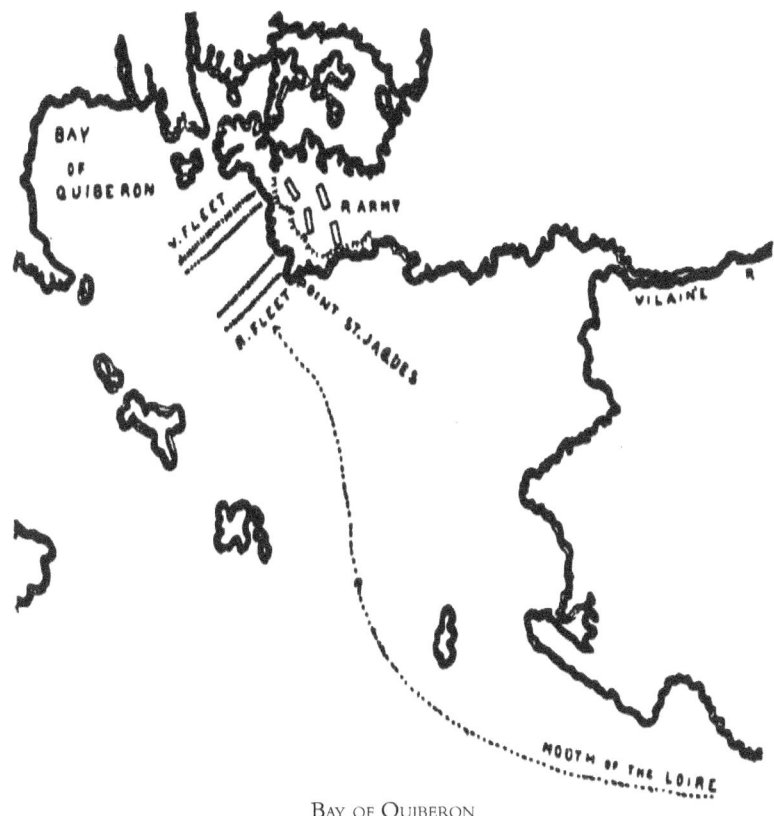

BAY OF QUIBERON

to the mast; the Romans rowed alongside the enemy and grappled on to the main cable which held up the yard and sail of a Venetan ship; after doing which the oarsmen would pull vigorously away, thus cutting the cable and letting fall the yard and sail. The vessels thus disabled,—for they had no oars,—were then at the mercy of the waves and ready to be boarded by the much superior Roman soldiers. Each one boarded succumbed.

This naval fight, the first of which we have any record on the Atlantic ocean, was witnessed from the hills by Caesar and the entire Roman army,—a vast encouragement to deeds of valour. It must have been a splendid spectacle. Though the ships of the enemy outnumbered the Romans two or more to one, after many of them had been disabled and boarded, Roman valour prevailed, and the uncaptured ones soon attempted to take refuge in flight. But a dead calm suddenly arose so that they could not move,—Caesar's fortune always came to his aid at opportune moments. The wind in this bay today blows at this season east or northeast till midday, then almost invariably a calm sets in. The attempt at flight was unfortunate. It dispersed the Venetan ships so that when the calm came, the Roman galleys could attack them one by one, without their being able to assist each other. From about ten o'clock till sundown the contest raged, and so effectual were the tactics and discipline of the Romans that very few of the Venetan galleys got to land,—and these under cover of night.

All the valour, youth and strength of the Veneti had been assembled in this one fleet. After its utter destruction there remained to them no means of defence. They had neither men nor vessels. They were fain, therefore, to throw themselves on Caesar's mercy. But, deeming, as he says in the *Commentaries*, that he could not forgive their infringement of the sacred rights of ambassadors, Caesar determined to make an example of this tribe. He put all the senate to death and sold the rest of the people into slavery. It would be hard to decide whether this act was more unpardonable for its mistaken policy or for its ruthless cruelty. Caesar never considered this latter point. He did not often err in the former; but one or two of his acts of extermination appear to be grave mistakes. While one hardly palliates a similar policy on the part of Alexander, the cruelties of Caesar appear more monstrous on account of the intervening centuries of growth in civilization and international law. Not only was the military necessity which often constrained Alexander to his acts absent in Caesar's case, but the latter's destruction of human life far exceeds anything of which Alexander was ever guilty. Almost all critics—including Napoleon—are particularly severe upon Caesar's unnecessary cruelty to the Veneti. Caesar had less excuse than precedent for his action. It is strange that Alexander and Hannibal have been so constantly upbraided for what is termed their cruelty, while this quality is rarely imputed to Caesar.

During the early part of this campaign against the Veneti, Titurius Sabinus had been engaged with the affairs of the Unelli, a canton south of modern Cherbourg, in Normandy, whose king was Viridovix. This chief had collected a large army from all the adjoining tribes, principally the Lexovii and Aulerci-Eburovices, added to which were numbers of robbers and soldiers of fortune from all parts of Gaul. Sabinus started from the vicinity of Angers on the Loire, marched north, and camped among the Unelli. The remains of a camp some four miles east of modern Avranches, known as Camp du Chastellier, indicate his probable location; and though the remains may be those

THEATRE OF SABINUS' CAMPAIGN

of a later camp, it was not uncommon to pitch new camps on the old locations of predecessors. This camp shows an interesting variation from the usual shape, dictated by the ground.

Sabinus was a cautious officer, with a bent to stratagem. He kept to his camp, which he had established so that his breadstuffs could not be cut off. Viridovix camped over against him some two miles away on the other side of the little river now called the See, daily drawing up in battle array, and taunting the Romans for cowardice in not accepting the gage. Even his own men grew dissatisfied and ashamed; but Sabinus had his purpose in thus acting. He wished to bring about a habit of carelessness on the enemy's part by inducing him to underrate his opponents. Having succeeded In so doing, he selected a crafty Gaul, and by promises of valuable gifts, persuaded him to pretend desertion to the enemy, where suitable representations to Viridovix might convince that chief that the Romans were actually cowed by the situation. This spy was directed to state to the chief that the Romans were compelled during the following night to decamp and march towards Caesar, whose campaign against the Veneti was rumoured to be going wrong; and he was to seek to persuade him

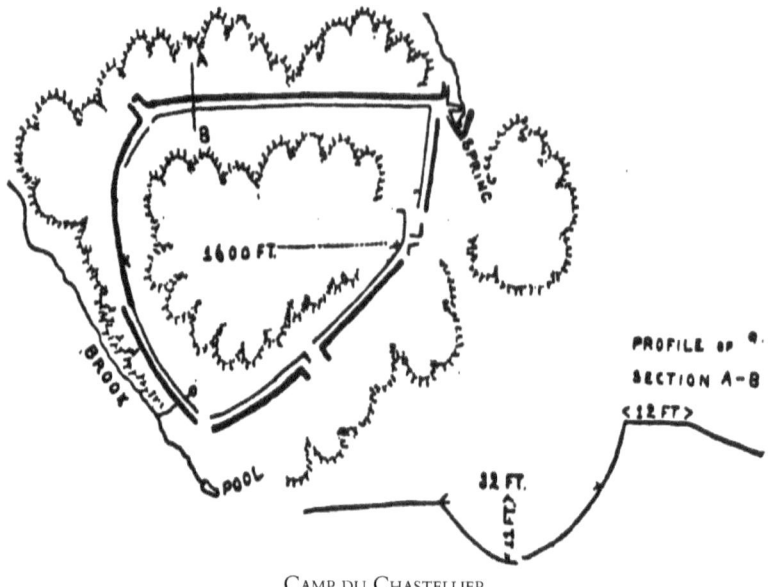

CAMP DU CHASTELLIER

that the Roman army could be easily attacked and destroyed before its retreat. The spy proved to be a clever one. Viridovix, in effect, lent a willing ear to his story, and determined on assaulting the Roman camp without loss of time.

This camp was situated on a hill, rocky and steep on the west, less so on the other sides. Towards the north it sloped gradually down a mile or so to the River Sée. In pursuance of their project the Gauls not only armed themselves fully, but carried large quantities of fagots and brushwood to fill up the Roman trench. They were over-eager to reach the camp before the Roman army should get away; and, loaded down as the warriors were, in toiling up the ascent, they arrived in its front wearied and out of breath. Sabinus had been watching for just this chance. The signal was given, and the Romans, fresh and ready for the combat, rushed out upon the Unelli from the two corner gates at once. Surprised and overwhelmed, the barbarians offered no resistance worthy the name; but, turning, sought safety in flight. The legionaries and horse followed hard at their heels, and slaughtered the greater part of them. This victory and the shortly arriving news of Caesar's triumph over the Veneti—for Caesar and Sabinus each heard of the victory of the other about the same time—so entirely broke up the coalition of these peoples that tribe now vied with tribe in their anxiety to bring in their submission and be assured of its acceptance.

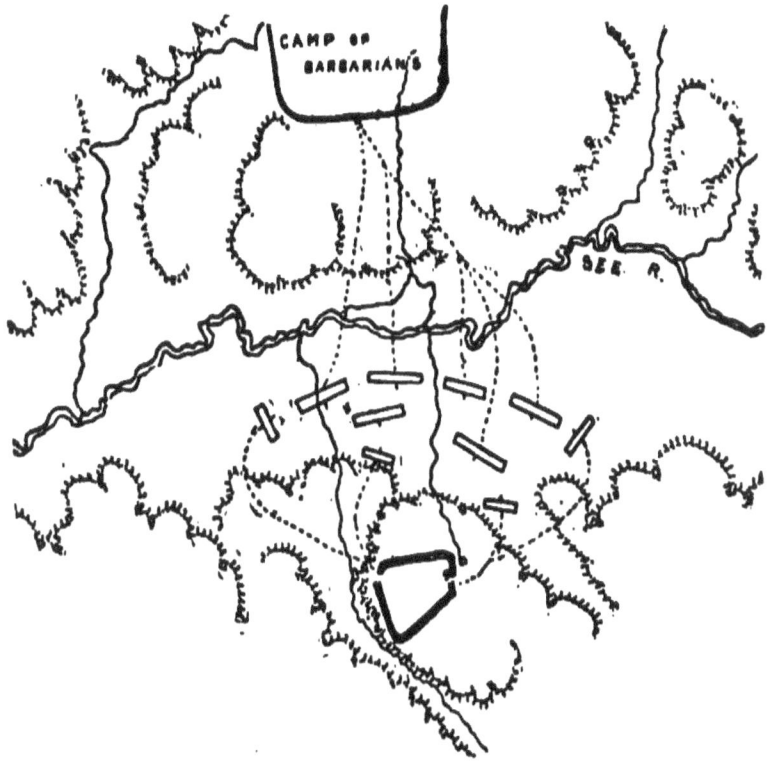

SABINUS' BATTLE

This battle is another fair index to the hasty and impetuous, but frail character of the Gauls. Generous, courageous, patriotic, they were dangerous opponents at the inception of a campaign. But they became easily discouraged, and were never long of one mind. Their treaties for mutual support were wont to be short-lived. They were unable to bear disaster. Polybius and Caesar gauge the Gauls alike.

P. Crassus, meanwhile, had a large task set him in Aquitania, the territory which is comprised between the Loire and the Pyrenees, where the Romans, a few years before, under Valerius and Manlius, had suffered two galling defeats. Moving south and collecting corn in plenty, summoning to his aid the best men of Tolosa, Carcaso and Narbo, in the southwest province, and enlisting auxiliaries, both foot and horse, among the best material to be had in the cantons under Roman sway, Crassus crossed the Garumna (Garonne) and marched into the land of the Sotiates on the left bank.

These barbarians, having brought together a large force and much cavalry, attempted to attack the Romans on the march. They opened the action by a diversion with the horse, meanwhile placing their infantry in ambush. The horse was speedily routed, and the Roman infantry, somewhat in disorder with the fray, was resuming its march and passing a defile, when it was suddenly assaulted by this force, which debouched from hiding, with exceptional vigour. The combat at once waxed hot. The barbarians were fighting for their soil; the legionaries to show what they could do without their general-in-chief, and under a very young commander, and no doubt also with the clear appreciation which every Roman must have always had of the slender chance to be found in flight. And again Roman discipline prevailed. The Sotiates were defeated with great slaughter.

Crassus then laid siege to their capital, placed variously at modern Lectoure or Sos, the principal of their towns on his line of march. The resistance was so effective that he was obliged to build *vineae* and turrets. The Sotiates, many of whom were copper-miners, developed great skill in resisting these means of siege, undermining the Roman ramparts, and themselves building *vineae*, but without eventual success. The Romans were so bold and persistent that they were obliged to surrender. During the capitulation the chief, Adcantuannus, with six hundred chosen men bound to him by a special oath, essayed to cut his way out, but was headed off. Despite this fact, he was not denied equal terms, out of regard to his gallantry. Crassus then marched upon the Vocates, also on the left bank of the Garumna, and the Tarusates on the Aturis (Adour).

These peoples were intelligent enough to send for auxiliaries into

Theatre of Crassus' Campaign

Hither Spain, where war had been a long time waged with the Romans, and obtained from there not only men, but officers of rank familiar with the Roman method of warfare, many of whom, indeed, had served under Sertorius, the great partisan-chief. These officers, whose training had been of the very best, began to fortify suitable positions, to occupy available defiles, and to harass Crassus to such an extent and in so able a way, that he found that unless he soon came to battle, he would be cut off from his bread and driven to a retreat beset by danger. He therefore called a council, as was usual. These Roman assemblies belie the saying that a council of war never fights,—the Romans held them and remained combative. They now decided to fight.

Next day Crassus drew up in two lines with the auxiliaries in the centre, and offered battle. But the enemy, though greatly superior in numbers, preferred their Fabian tactics, intending not to attack the Romans until they could force them into retreat for want of corn, and thus have them at a disadvantage, loaded down, as they would be, with their baggage. Crassus saw that there was nothing left but for himself

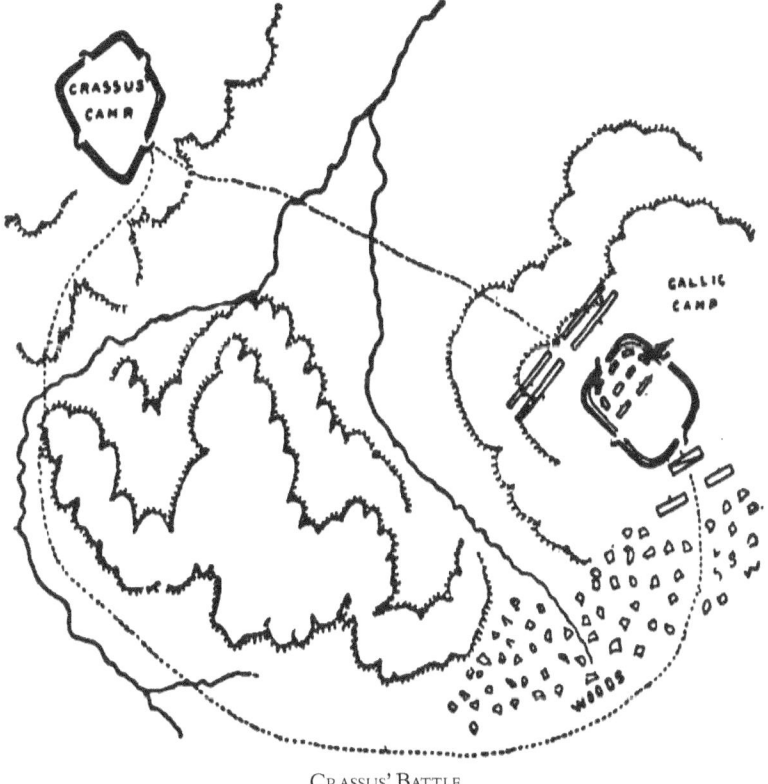

CRASSUS' BATTLE

to attack, though to assault fortifications was much against the rule. This he did, relying greatly on the eagerness of his troops, who loudly demanded battle, and deemed the barbarians to be afraid.

The enemy had occupied and entrenched a formidable camp, in the Roman fashion. The attack was boldly made on the front and flanks of the enemy's works. By a heavy fire of missiles the Romans sought to drive the defenders from the ramparts, so that an assault might be made with success, if undertaken. The auxiliaries served to supply the legionaries and light troops with stones and weapons, to bring turf and material to fill the trench. While the battle was at its height, Crassus was informed that the Decuman, or rear gate of the enemy's camp, was not well guarded. Moreover, as a rule, the rear of every camp was less well entrenched than the front and flanks. Selecting the horse and such of the *cohorts* as had been left to guard his own camp, and were therefore fresh, Crassus sent this force, with promises of great reward in case of success, by a long circuit and out of sight, around to the rear. The barbarians had so little anticipated this, that the Roman soldiers demolished the fortifications of the rear gate and filed into the enemy's camp, before the bulk of the foe were aware of their being at hand. The manoeuvre was crowned with success. The Romans fell upon the enemy's rear with loud shouts and blare of trumpets, encouraged by which the legionaries in front redoubled the ardour of their fighting. No assault appears to have been needed. The barbarians were unable to resist this double onset. Terrified, they turned from the battle, cast themselves from the ramparts, and fled into the plains. Out of their entire number of fifty thousand men, barely a fourth escaped the sword of the Roman horse, which pursued them across the open. This battle, fought in the fall of B. C. 56, resulted in the submission of substantially all Aquitania.

The whole of Gaul had now been reduced, save only the land of the Morini and Menapii, which extended along the coast southerly from the mouth of the Rhine to modern Boulogne, the land which the Dutch have since so laboriously rescued from the ocean. These peoples had never sent ambassadors to Caesar, and when he approached their territory, taught by defeat of other Gauls, they retired into the forests and morasses of the coast and bade him defiance. Having no towns, but dwelling in tents or in caverns, this was to them no great hardship. Caesar in person undertook to drive them from their lairs. Arrived at the edge of the forests bordering on the lowlands of the sea, the vicinity of St. Omer, inland from Calais, to which locality

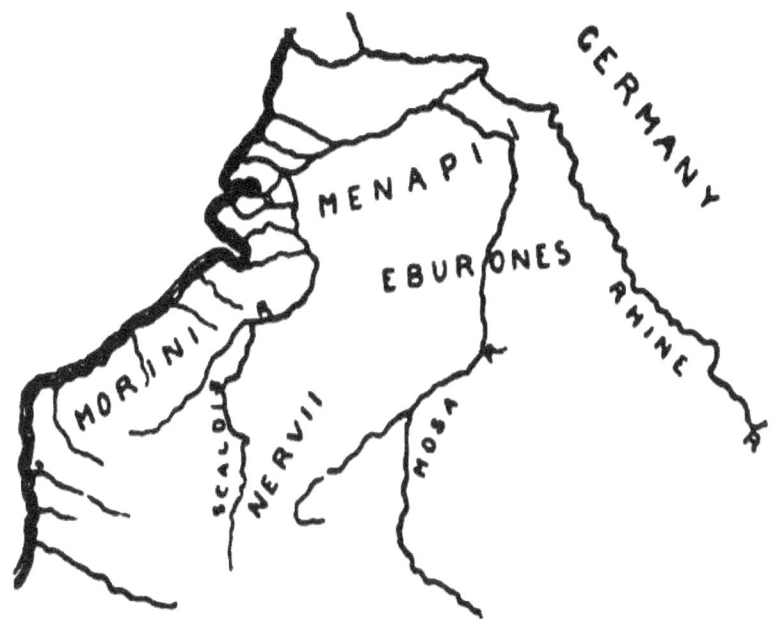

THE MORINI AND MENAPII

these tribes had removed all their possessions, some slight interchange of hostilities took place, the barbarians attacking the Romans while preparing to camp. Seeing that there was grave danger of ambuscades while advancing through the forests, Caesar began to cut a wide swath for his line of operations and astonished the enemy beyond measure by the rapidity with which he laid the forest low. For their own poor tools enabled them to work but slowly. The cut timber Caesar piled on either side of his path as a rampart. He had particularly good engineers (*praefecti fabrum*). Especially L. Cornelius Balbus and the knight Mamurra were noted for cleverness in enginery and sieges. This apparently vast undertaking testifies to the ability of these officers.

The Roman army, say the *Commentaries*, had already reached the rear of the retreating barbarian forces and had cut out a number of cattle and wagons from their train; but owing to the lateness of the season and the setting in of severe storms, Caesar was obliged to defer his operations against the Morini and Menapii and to go into winter-quarters. After ravaging the country and burning such dwellings as there were, the troops were camped among the Aulerci and Lexovii on the coast between the Sequana and Liger (Normandy).

Caesar gives the best complexion to this as to his other campaigns; but the truth is that he never entirely subjugated the northwest of

Gaul. The Morini and Menapii were but prevented from spreading mischief. They remained independent.

To Caesar belongs the credit of the intelligent cutting out of the work of this campaign. But the success of Sabinus and Crassus must remain their own. Their execution of Caesar's plans came fully up to expectation, and redounds much to their credit. The outcome of Caesar's fourth campaign, against the Veneti, must be set down in no small measure to the able conduct of Brutus with a quantum of good fortune added. No criticism can belittle the splendid achievements of Caesar; neither must they be overestimated. With the best troops in the then world, perfect in discipline, commanded by officers trained in all the minutiae of war, he was contending with peoples all but savage, unapt at regular war, disunited in counsel, and unable to put into the field forces much superior to the Romans in numbers, and in view of all conditions far inferior to them.

The fifth campaign, against the Morini, has been called one of pure ambition, quite unnecessary for the conquest of Gaul. But this does not so readily appear. The Rhine, the ocean and the Pyrenees were the only boundaries which Caesar could set to his conquest of Gaul, if he was to make it at all; and without entering into the question of Caesar's right to conquer a square rood of the country, it may be assumed that everything within those boundaries must be counted under the same head. As usual, Caesar personally returned to Cisalpine Gaul for the winter months of B. C. 56-55.

LIGHT-ARMED SOLDIER

Chapter 10

The Rhine
Spring of 55 B. C.

Some German tribes, the Usipetes and Tenchtheri, had crossed the Rhine not far above its mouth, crowded from their homes by the Suevi, the most powerful of the Teutonic nations. Once in Gaul, they had advanced into the Vosegus country. Caesar's plan necessitated a check to these barbarians, who had over one hundred thousand warriors. From his winter-quarters near Amiens, he marched to the Meuse in May. In the ensuing negotiations, the enemy acted, Caesar claims, with duplicity. So, confessedly, did he. And when their ambassadors next came to his camp, he detained them, put his legions in order of battle, marched upon the unsuspecting Germans, surprised and put the entire body—four hundred and thirty thousand men, women and children—to the sword. A very few escaped across the Rhine. This is unquestionably the most atrocious act of which any civilized man has ever been guilty. It accomplished its end, but this fact does not palliate its enormity. Caesar then built his celebrated bridge, and crossed the Rhine, probably near Bonn. The Suevi retired into the forests beyond their domain. After eighteen days he returned and broke down the bridge. The foray had no useful results.

At the beginning of the next year, B. C. 55, there was an incursion across the Rhine, not far above its mouth, by some German tribes which three years before had been harassed and driven from their lands by the Suevi. They had wandered about in Germany during the three years and finally, as a last resort, had crossed the Rhine and devastated the land of the Menapii with great slaughter. The preceding winter (B. C. 56-55) had been spent there, and no one knew what their next movements might be.

The Suevi have been already mentioned. They had sent over the troops which Caesar had defeated two years before under Ariovistus.

They were a fierce and warlike people. They subsisted on meat and milk rather than corn, were great hunters, and celebrated for their strength and stature. In the coldest weather they wore nothing but skins which scantily covered their bodies, and constantly bathed in the open rivers. Their cavalry was drilled to dismount and fight on foot, the horses being trained to remain where left, until the riders could again rejoin them. They used no housings upon their horses, and presumably, like the Numidians, no bridle, despised luxury and forbade wine. On the east side of this people the territory was said to be devastated for six hundred miles; on the west they bordered, among other peoples, on the Ubii, whom they had reduced to the payment of tribute. It was some of these Ubian tribes, the Usipetes and Tenchtheri, which had now forced a passage of the Rhine to the number of four hundred and thirty thousand souls, and had advanced some distance inland. It was thought, and truly, that this advance had been made with the consent of some of the Gauls, who hoped by this immigration to be able to increase their power of opposing the Romans. The place of crossing was probably near modern Cleves and Xanten, which were opposite their territory. On the left bank, from Xanten down, is a chain of heights some thirty miles long, at the foot of which the river used to flow. Two gaps pierce these heights, at Xanten and near Cleves. That these passes were used by the Germans in their incursions is shown by their having been fortified by the Romans after the conquest. The Usipetes and Tenchtheri had moved forward nearly to the Mosa (Meuse).

Caesar joined his legions in Normandy in April, B. C. 55, earlier than usual. He determined to make immediate war upon these Germans, who, justified by the invitation of sun-dry Gallic tribes, had already made incursions as far as the Eburones and Condrusi, the latter clients of the Treviri. He mobilized his army in the early spring, from his winter-quarters between the Sequana and Liger. Calling together the tribes of the vicinity at Samarobriva (Amiens), he wisely refrained from accusing them of complicity with this incursion, but used his powers of persuasion to such effect as to secure from them victual, a goodly number of auxiliary troops, and especially a fine body of five thousand horse. From the winter-quarters of his legions, Caesar probably rendezvoused, early in May, at Amiens, and thence marched to Cambrai, Charleroi, Tongres and Maestricht, where he crossed the Mosa towards the end of the month. This would have been his most natural route. There was need of prompt measures.

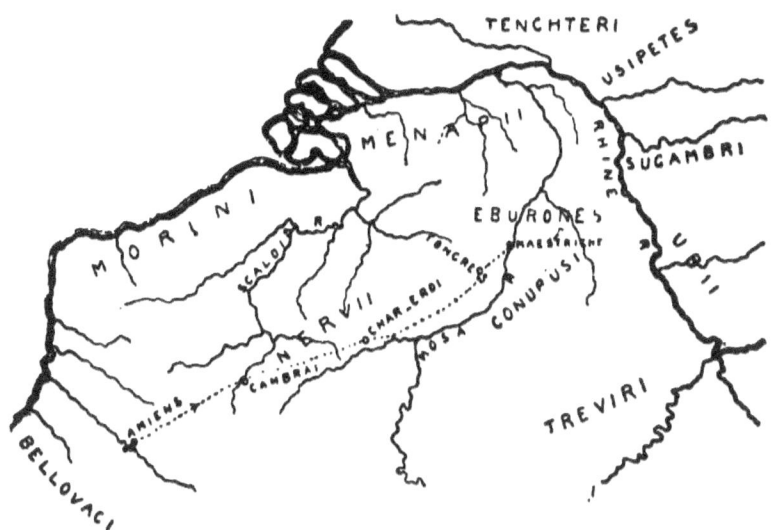

NORMANDY TO THE RHINE

The danger was imminent. There must have been over one hundred thousand warriors among these migrating peoples.

Before he reached the Mosa, Caesar met ambassadors sent by the Germans, who were authorized to treat, provided Caesar would consent to their keeping the lands they had already conquered. But this Caesar would by no means permit, informing them that they must go back across the Rhine, where, he suggested, the Ubii, who dwelt near modern Cologne, would now grant them territory willingly; for this tribe had begged his aid against the Suevi, and stood ready to perform his behests. The German ambassadors pretended to assent to these terms, but asked Caesar to delay his advance for a short space until they could report to their senate and return. This delay Caesar would not grant, as, according to the *Commentaries*, he believed that they desired only to gain time until their horse, which had gone on a distant raid among the Ambivariti beyond the Mosa for provision, could return. Crossing the Mosa and continuing his advance to within some twelve miles of the enemy, Caesar, perhaps near Straelen, again met the ambassadors, who made similar excuses, and prayed for a delay of at least three days, when the tribes would cross the Rhine if the Ubii bound themselves by oath to receive them.

It was early in June. Caesar had left the vicinity of the Mosa, and had probably advanced beyond modern Venloo. The Usipetes and Tenchtheri were on the levels near Goch on the Niers River. He agreed to advance but four miles, to the nearest place where he could get water for the army. If our topographical assumption is so far correct, this was the Niers. No sooner had his cavalry moved forward to its vicinity than the Germans attacked this body with some eight hundred horse and threw it back in disorder, killing seventy-four of their number. Their tactics were peculiar.

"They made an onset on our men and soon threw them into disorder. When our men in their turn made a stand, they according to their practice leaped from their horses to their feet, and, stabbing our horses in the belly and overturning a great many of our men, put the rest to flight, and drove them forward so much alarmed that they did not desist from their retreat till they had come in sight of our army."

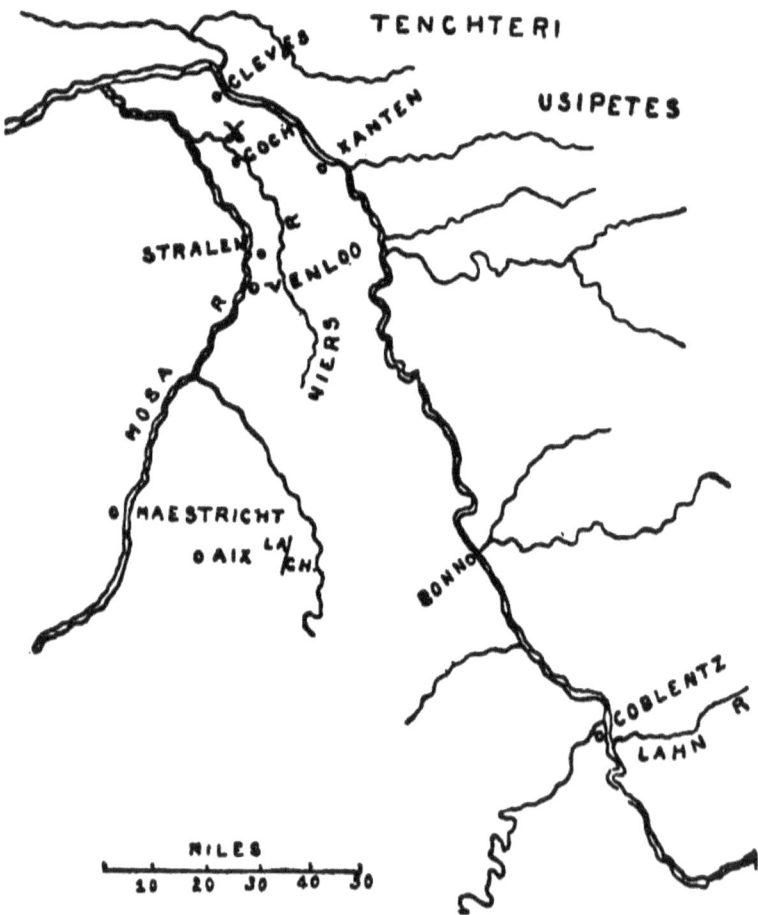

Rhine and Meuse Region

This looks like a serious case of fright. The attack appears to have been caused by some misunderstanding. It seems curious that five thousand of the Roman allied horse should have been thus driven back by so small a force. The attack must have been vigorously made and weakly met. This German horse was always a fighting arm. Irritated at the defeat, Caesar determined to avenge it as an act of treachery, for, as he explains, the attack had been made while the ambassadors were still treating, and a truce existed; "after having sued for peace by way of stratagem and treachery, they had made war without provocation." He at once proceeded to do the same act he so heartily condemns, paying no heed to explanations or apologies.

The next day the Germans again sent a large embassy to apologize for the yesterday's misadventure; but Caesar construed the act to be for the original purpose of obtaining a further truce till their still absent horse could arrive. The ambassadors Caesar detained, and putting his army in three lines, probably in columns by *cohorts*, with the cavalry beaten the previous day in the rear, moved forward the intervening eight miles at a double-quick, and reaching their camp in an incredibly short time, took the Germans entirely by surprise, and fell on them with fury. Such was their consternation that, after a short resistance by a few who were not panic-stricken, the Germans threw away their arms and fled in all directions. The cavalry was sent in pursuit and drove the fugitives into the *cul de sac* formed by the confluence of the Mosa and Rhine. Here those who did not perish by the sword threw themselves into the river and were mostly drowned. Few succeeded in getting across. All, including women and children, were indiscriminately butchered, to the number of four hundred and thirty thousand souls. The whole nation was exterminated, save only the absent cavalry, and but a few Romans were wounded.

This whole campaign lacks clearness in the Commentaries. Florus confuses it still more by placing the defeat of the Usipetes and Tenchtheri in the confluence of the Moselle and Rhine, and Dion Cassius by stating that Caesar reached them among the Treviri. This latter has been the theory of many, who, in compiling their data, stray unwarranted from the *Commentaries*. The country in the Moselle-Rhine angle is much cut up, has no traces of ancient roads, and could scarcely have supported these tribes. To conduct his march on the theory that he reached the enemy there, Caesar would have been led through the Forest of Ardennes, a fact which he does not mention, as he most likely would have done. It looks more probable that the situation was as described, and that, on learning of Caesar's approach, the Usipetes and Tenchtheri withdrew their foragers and retired towards their base among the Menapii. To cross the Rhine near the Moselle would have led them to their enemies, the Ubii; and to make them head that way is an improbable assumption.

This awful act in the Gallic drama has uniformly received the severest condemnation of thinking men. None of the extensive acts of retaliation of Alexander, not all the deeds of Punic cruelty charged upon Hannibal by his bitterest enemies during his fifteen years in Italy put together, can equal the sum of destruction of human life here wantonly exhibited. Unlike some of the holocausts of Alexander,—which were required for his own and his army's safety at the distance from his base at which he found himself,—this slaughter appears to have been absolutely uncalled for. If the barbarians broke the laws of international intercourse, Caesar had done the like. So indignant were

THE RHINE

his political enemies in Rome, that Cato openly proposed that Caesar's head should be sent to the surviving Usipetes and Tenchtheri in expiation of his attack while their ambassadors were in his camp. Perhaps no more inexcusable act was ever perpetrated. Even the plausible tone of the *Commentaries* quite fails to convey an extenuation.

The unnecessarily harsh measures of Caesar would not be thus insisted on were it not that of all the great soldiers of antiquity, the one least deserving the accusation, Hannibal, has come down to us bearing the reproach of cruelty. That the charge is unjust has been abundantly proven. It may be that none of these captains can be properly taxed with inhumanity; that the trait belongs to the age and not to the men. But if cruelty is to be imputed to any of them, it is certain that, of the three great captains of antiquity, Caesar was by far the most reprehensible, Hannibal the least.

Having accomplished this "brilliant success," as Napoleon III. phrases it, Caesar determined, as a means of imposing on the Germans, to cross the Rhine, so that those tribes which were still unconvinced of his power might feel that they were not safe from Caesar's reach even in their own territory. He deemed it wise to show the Germans that no obstacle, natural or national, could arrest the Roman arms, and to make them see that, however distant, they could be reached and punished if they indulged in any more incursions into Gaul.

The occasion was good. The party of cavalry which had been on a raid at the time of the destruction of the Usipetes and Tenchtheri had retired across the Rhine and joined the Sugambri, which was one of the most powerful tribes between where the modern Ruhr and Sieg join the Rhine. Caesar sent and demanded their surrender by the Sugambri, as belonging to those who had treacherously attacked the Romans. This demand was refused, and at the same time the Ubii sent again to beg for aid against the Suevi, who were grievously oppressing them. They offered all their ships for transportation across the river, but this means Caesar neither deemed safe, nor, says he, was it consistent with the dignity of the Roman republic to depend on others.

This invasion of German soil was dictated solely by ambition. It was beyond Caesar's province. Without an unprecedented construction of the rule of the Roman Senate, he had indeed no authority to go beyond Gaul. Under the then well-understood laws of nations, he had no right to attack a tribe which had committed no covert or overt act of hostility against himself or Rome, other than the right of conquest. This it is not desired to deny to him. So much is said of his rights and motives only to brush away the often made assertion that Caesar was actuated by no motive save the patriotic one of defending the Roman republic.

The refusal of the ships and the project of building a bridge was probably the result of a desire to have a perfectly secure means of returning to Gaul in case of any reverse. This was wise. But it is a question whether the invasion itself was wise. In Gaul, Caesar had of course maintained the offensive, as he must, if he was to subdue the whole country. But it is scarcely doubtful that the best military policy beyond the borders of Gaul was a strict defensive, especially at so distinct a natural barrier as the Rhine. He had made an example of all who had crossed it into Gaul, and this was sufficient.

The location of the bridge has been much disputed. It cannot be absolutely proven. The confluence of the Rhine and Moselle below modern Coblentz has many advocates. Those who place the slaughter of the Usipetes and Tenchtheri at this place naturally favour it as the crossing point. Some authorities put the passage as far down the river as Cologne.

There is reason for selecting Bonn as the crossing point. The fact given in the *Commentaries*, that Caesar passed from the land of the Treviri to that of the Ubii, would suit many localities. But he was at no great distance from the Sugambri, and the confluence of the Moselle and Rhine is far above the territory of this people. The next year but one, having crossed "a little above" the present bridge, Caesar started from the Rhine and marched to Aduatuca (Tongres) through the forest of Arduenna, from east to west, near by the Segni and Condrusi. From Cologne he would have marched north of these peoples; from Coblentz, south. The bed of the Rhine about Bonn is well suited for piles; south of Bonn it is more rocky, and the mountainous banks would make the location less desirable for a bridge. Fifty years later, as we are told by Floras, Drusus crossed at this place to attack the Sugambri; and Drusus would likely have profited by Caesar's experience. The probabilities run strongly in favour of Bonn.

To rapidly build a bridge at this point over the Rhine, without previous preparation or a bridge train, is today no contemptible engineering feat. The river is over a quarter of a mile wide. Caesar accomplished the task in ten days from the time when he began to cut the timber. It was mid-June. The bridge was supported on piles driven into the bed of the river and held firmly in place by cross pieces and braces. His own description is clear:

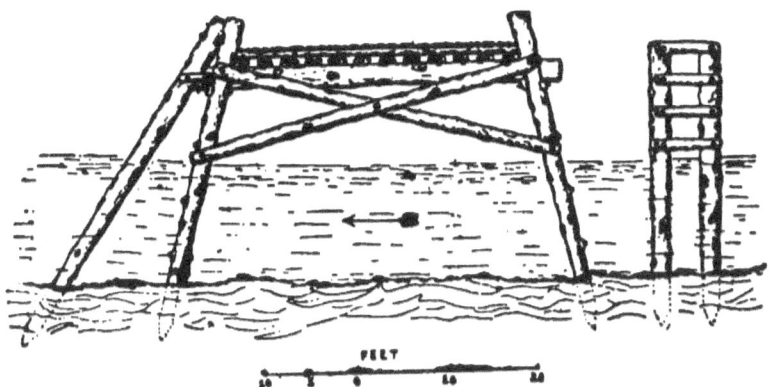

The Rhine Bridge (cross section)

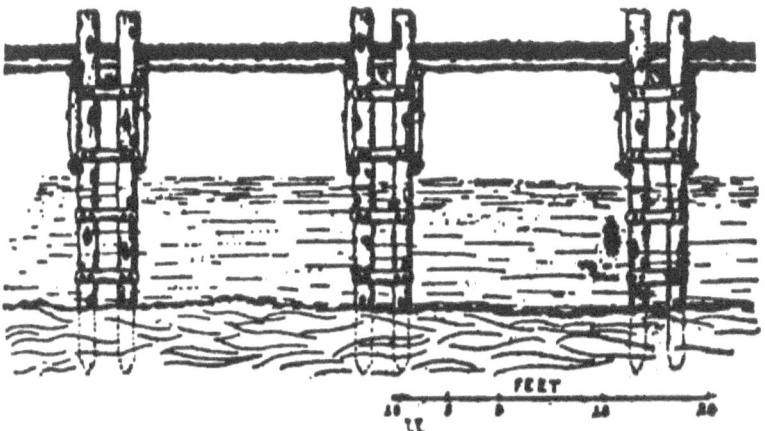

The Rhine Bridge (elevation)

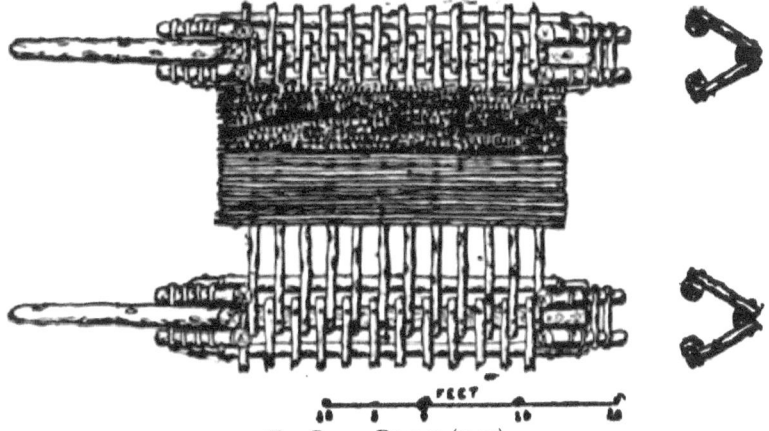

The Rhine Bridge (plan)

"He devised this plan of a bridge. He joined together at the distance of two feet, two piles, each a foot and a half thick, sharpened a little at the lower end, and proportioned in length to the depth of the river. After he had, by means of engines, sunk these into the river, and fixed them at the bottom and then driven them in with rammers, not quite perpendicularly, like a stake, but bending forward and sloping, so as to incline in the direction of the current of the river; he also placed two (other piles) opposite to these, at the distance of forty feet lower down, fastened together in the same manner, but directed against the force and current of the river. Both these, moreover, were kept firmly apart by beams two feet thick (the space which the binding of the piles occupied), laid in at their extremities between two braces on each side; and in consequence of these being in different directions and fastened on sides the one opposite to the other, so great was the strength of the work, and such the arrangement of the materials, that in proportion as the greater body of water dashed against the bridge, so much the closer were its parts held fastened together. These beams were bound together by timber laid over them in the direction of the length of the, bridge, and were (then) covered over with laths and hurdles; and, in addition to this, piles were driven into the water obliquely, at the lower side of the bridge, and these serving as buttresses, and being connected with every portion of the work, sustained the force of the stream; and there were others also above the bridge at a moderate distance, that if trunks of trees or vessels were floated down the river by the barbarians for the purpose of destroying the work, the violence of such things might be diminished by these defences, and might not injure the bridge."

Engineering feats are measured largely by the amount of available material and labour. As Caesar had all the men he could use and more, as the material was close at hand, and as the form of bridge was one well-known to the Romans, the construction is noted chiefly for its great size and the remarkable speed with which it was accomplished. And it has already been stated that Caesar had exceptionally good engineers. He did not have to contend with opposition to his passage.

Having completed the structure and posting a strong guard at either end in a suitable bridgehead, Caesar led his army across and moved up the Sieg and Agger. Several nations at once offered submission; the Sugambri retired from their territory with all their wealth, "and concealed themselves in deserts and woods." Caesar devastated their country, and marched into the land of the Ubii. This fact also points to the vicinity of Bonn as the crossing-place. Had it been at Coblentz, he would have been in Ubian territory on reaching the right bank.

Among the Ubii, Caesar learned that the Suevi had also sent away all their possessions and wives and children; had collected all their fighting men at a spot about the centre of their land, a number of days' march to the east, and were awaiting the arrival of the Romans. But having, as the *Commentaries* state, accomplished all he intended, and having spent eighteen days beyond the Rhine, Caesar returned to Gaul and broke down the bridge.

He had really accomplished nothing. He had not recovered the cavalry demanded of the Sugambri; he had done no more than promise help to the Ubii; he had failed to attack the Suevi. The question arises whether he would not have stood better in the eyes of the Germans if he had not crossed at all, except, indeed, for their wonder at the bridge. In a military sense, he would, perhaps, have acted more wisely if he had remained in Gaul. This land had been sufficiently defended by twice driving the Germans back across the Rhine with so savage a punishment; his invasion of the German territory had brought absolutely no result. In fact, it may be said, that his failure to accomplish anything on the east shore of the Rhine must have tended to lower his standing among the Germans. But his reputation in Rome and his self-esteem had been greatly raised by the performance, to which his letters, as well as the *Commentaries*, lent great lustre. And his friends in Rome had something to offset against the avalanche of reproach with which his enemies sought to overwhelm him for his slaughter of the Usipetes and Tenchtheri. The passage of the Rhine was as splendid a subject to enlarge on as it was, in a certain sense, a brilliant achievement.

GALLIC HORSEMAN. (FROM A SARCOPHAGUS.)

Chapter 11
Britain
Fall of 55 B. C.

Caesar had the traveller's instinct. To invade Britain was even less a part of his Gallic problem than to cross the Rhine. But he determined to see that island, and a pretext—that they had given help to resisting Gallic tribes—was readily conjured up. He sought information from merchants and leading Gauls and sent a subordinate over to Britain to prospect; but he learned little. He shipped two legions and some cavalry in transports and crossed in August. He reached the Dover cliffs and actually landed at Deal, though with difficulty, owing to the warlike opposition of the Britons. After a few days, a storm damaged the fleet; the Britons attacked Caesar, but were defeated; a peace was patched up; hostages were promised, who were never delivered; and having accomplished nothing whatever except as a discoverer, Caesar returned to Gaul. He had run great risk of being cut off, and had illy provided against probable contingencies. There is little commendable in a military sense in the first invasion of Britain. It had no connection with the Gallic theatre of war.

Though the season was well advanced—it was late in the summer—Caesar determined to move over to Britain, as he says:

"Because he discovered that in almost all the wars with the Gauls succours had been furnished to our enemy from that country; and even if the time of year should be insufficient for carrying on the war, yet he thought it would be of great service to him if he only entered the island and saw into the character of the people, and got knowledge of their localities, harbours and landing-places, all which were, for the most part, unknown to the Gauls."

This explanation has the look of an afterthought. The fact of British aid to the Gauls seems doubtful, and rests almost entirely on this statement and another that the Suessiones, under Divitiacus, had extended their control to Britain.

It is probable that Caesar had a good deal of the traveller's instinct in addition to his ambition, and desired to know something about the island and its people, its harbours, resources and accessibility. Plutarch and Dion Cassius agree that the expedition against Britain was of no use to Rome. Suetonius says Caesar was in search for pearls, a rather weak motive. Any reason, good or bad, which could plausibly be used, sufficed for a *casus belli* when Caesar wished to invade a country. And so it was with Britain. Returning to the coast in July, and calling to him all the merchants he could find, he interrogated them, and ascertained that these people knew only that part of the British coast which was immediately opposite to Gaul, and little indeed of that, inasmuch as they had never been able to go inland, and had traded only in one or two places.

Caesar's description of Britain is vague, but good considering the difficulties of obtaining information. He thought the climate of Britain more temperate than that of Gaul. The same products of the soil were known, but ripened more slowly. The population was considerable, and the east and south coasts had been peopled by the Belgae, who had crossed the Channel for spoil and ended by settling in Britain. Cantium (Kent) had thus been settled. Each tribe had its king. Caesar mentions the Trinobantes, in modern Essex and Middlesex, whose *oppidum* was no doubt London; the Cenimagni in Suffolk; the Segontiaci in Hampshire and Berkshire; the Bibroci in Sussex and Surrey; the Ancalites and the Cassii farther north. The Britons were, on the whole, less advanced in civilization than the Gauls. Their habitations were huts of wood and rough thatch. They buried their corn in underground vaults. Their towns were mere places of refuge in forests, defended by a ditch and rampart. They had the same bodily structure as the Gauls, but the Britons were taller and bolder, with long blond, rather than red hair. They wore skins and lived on flesh and milk, with little vegetable food. They painted their bodies blue with woad. Polyandry was common. They sold tin to the Phoenicians at a very early age, but relied on foreign nations for bronze. They had no ships. Their religion was Druidical. They fought with long swords and small bucklers, and skirmished, rather than fought in masses, as the Gauls did. Their chariots were numerous and able.

As Caesar could ascertain little about Britain, he sent Gaius Volusenus with a ship of war to make a rapid examination of the coast, to ascertain what harbours there might be for a large fleet, and something about the peoples, their sys-tem of war and customs. He ordered the fleet to assemble in one of the harbours of the Morini,—later Portus Itius, not improbably Boulogne, though it cannot be taken as settled,— whither he himself, by steady marches from the Rhine, repaired with all his forces, and commanded to be brought many ships from all directions, including those with which he had fought the Veneti. While this was going on, several tribes from Britain, who had, no doubt, heard through merchants of Caesar's victories, and of his preparations to invade their land, sent in their offers of submission. These ambassadors he received with courtesy, and sent back with them Commius, a Gallic chief, whom Caesar had made king of the Atrebates, and in whom he reposed great confidence. This man,. Caesar says, stood high in the sight of many leading Britons. Commius was to visit as many of the British tribes as he could; make them familiar with

GAUL TO BRITAIN

Caesar's exploits; tell them what manner of people the Romans were; satisfy them that the newcomers would be friends and not foes; and say that Caesar in person would shortly arrive. Volusenus brought back his report in five days. He had not even landed. He had seen and could tell but little. This brief time, and apparent lack of push, had enabled him to catch but a glimpse of the coast.

The Morini had luckily given in their submission and surrendered numerous hostages, excusing their late resistance on the score of want of knowledge of the Romans. This had been done without a further' campaign, which Caesar had anticipated; there was now no enemy left to prejudice his rear. He had, during August, provided eighty transports, which sufficed for the two legions, the Seventh and Tenth, presumably under Galba and Labienus, which he proposed to take with him, to be escorted by a suitable number of war galleys. The two legions must have been less than ten thousand strong. The horse, four hundred and fifty effective, was marched to and embarked on eighteen transports from another harbour some eight miles up the coast, Portus Ulterior (Ambleteuse), where, in addition to some tardiness, they had been held by contrary winds. The *quaestor*, the *legates* and *praefects* were divided up among the men of war, in such a manner that each had a certain number under his charge. The rest of the army Caesar left with Titurius Sabinus and Arunculeius Cotta to hold head against those coast-tribes of the Menapii and Morini which had not yet so frankly submitted as to make him feel confident he could trust them unwatched. A garrison under Sulpicius Rufus was also left in camp in the harbour of departure.

Caesar set sail with the first favourable wind, towards the end of August, B. C. 55, and in a few hours (one to ten a. m.) arrived on the British shore opposite the chalk cliffs of Dover. In Caesar's day the sea came so close to the cliffs that a dart thrown from the top would reach the tide-covered beach; but by about 950 A. D., the old port had been quite blocked up by alluvium. As this spot did not appear to be a good place for landing, after cautioning his officers to act promptly in their orders, he sailed—at about three p. m.—some seven miles farther up the coast, doubling, according to Dion Cassius, a lofty promontory, no doubt South Foreland, and stopped at Deal.

The Britons, who had assembled in great numbers on the shore to oppose his landing, guessed his intention and followed up his movement, sending cavalry and chariots on ahead. Their opposition to the landing of the Romans was very spirited. This they conducted by advancing into the water and casting their javelins at the Roman *legionaries* as they attempted to land. The men thus found it difficult to get out of the boats, because these drew too much water to get close to shore, and they themselves were heavy-armed and laden with camp-gear. Caesar, to escape from this dilemma, sent some ships of war to a cove close by, where, with sling-stones, arrows and engines he could attack the Britons in flank. This diversion surprised them and obliged them to retire somewhat up the beach. Perceiving that the soldiers were still slow to land, the standard-bearer of the Tenth legion leaped into the waves with the *legionary* eagle, and called on the men to follow him if they would not see their sacred emblem captured by the enemy under their very eyes. The soldiers of the Tenth at once swarmed to the shore, which example so encouraged the whole body of the Romans that they speedily leaped into the water to drive away the enemy.

"The battle was maintained vigorously on both sides. Our men, however, as they could neither keep their ranks, nor get firm footing, nor follow their standards, and as one from one ship and another from another assembled around whatever standard they met, were thrown into great confusion. But the enemy, who were acquainted with all the shallows, when from the shore they saw any coming from a ship one by one, spurred on their horses and attacked them while embarrassed; many surrounded a few, others threw their weapons upon our collected forces on their exposed flank. When Caesar observed this, he ordered the boats of the ships of war and the spysloops to be filled with soldiers and sent them up to the succour of those whom he had ob-served in distress. Our men, as soon as they made good their footing on dry ground, and all their comrades had joined them, made an attack upon the enemy, and put them to flight, but could not pursue them very far, because the horse had not been able to maintain their course at sea and reach the island. This alone was wanting to Caesar's accustomed success."

It is little items like these which enable one to draw a comparison between the ancient and modern soldier. To read of a disembarkation of troops today, under heavy fire, conducted in such a haphazard way, where each man appeared to consult his own ideas of prudence or courage instead of acting under the orders of his officers, would savour of absurdity. Discipline of old was good, but even under Caesar it did not seem to reach the grade of the best discipline of today; that is, what they called discipline was a different thing from ours.

The particular tribe of Britons which had been thus beaten concluded to sue for peace, and there came back with the British ambassadors Commius, whom Caesar had sent into Britain with the messengers that had been dispatched to him into Gaul. This man the Britons had seized and thrown into chains, a fact which seems to deny the influence the *Commentaries* claim that Commius had in Britain. The Britons now returned Commius with pretended excuses for their con-duct, saying that the multitude had overwhelmed them. The apparent complete submission of these coast-tribes constrained Caesar to forgive this breach of the law of nations. He felt that he was not strong enough to do less. He took some hostages and required more. These were promised, but not presently delivered. Thus in four days after the legions had landed, a peace was patched up with the peoples who inhabited the shore line on which he had landed, to wit, Kent.

The cavalry, which had sailed in eighteen transports from another port, reached the coast, but met with a serious storm nearby. They were unable to land, though they tried to do so, and returned to Gaul. At the same time a very high tide destroyed and damaged a large number of the vessels in which the legions had crossed the Channel. This was the season of full moon and high tides, at the end of August, 55 B. C. The Romans had not drawn their ships far enough up on the shore. The war-galleys had been beached; the transports were riding at anchor. The heavy seas filled the galleys and dashed the transports one against the other. Those that were not crushed lost their anchors, tackling and sails. The inability to repair this loss, and the fact that the Romans had not corn enough to winter in Britain, not only caused a certain feeling of insecurity among the soldiery, but afforded the Britons an opportunity to reconsider their action in submitting to Caesar. Therefore, instead of bringing in their promised hostages, they conferred together, and agreed to attack Caesar's camp, in the belief that if they could destroy this army, none other would ever cross to Britain. Caesar's camp was small. The *legionaries* had come without much baggage. Caesar, we hear, had but three servants with him, though this does not give one much of an idea of the general *impedimenta*. The barbarians saw he had no cavalry and had lost many ships. The opportunity looked favourable to expel him.

Suspecting, though not informed of their designs, Caesar made provision against every probable contingency, and saw personally to it that the discipline of the camp was stringently enforced. Peace was not ruptured, and the barbarians went to and fro in the Roman quarters. The ships were duly repaired—for there were numberless shipwrights in the expedition—by using the seasoned timber and the brass of the worst damaged ones to repair the rest. Such materials as had been lost in the wreckage were sent for to the continent. Only twelve remained unfit for further use.

Not long after, the Seventh legion, having gone out as usual to forage at the only place left nearby where the wheat had not been cut, was attacked by the enemy from an ambush while the men were scattered filling their sacks. This legion, surrounded by a host of cavalry and chariots, was on the point of succumbing, for the novelty of the dashing chariots and the strange shouts given by the Britons had greatly demoralized the men. They had huddled together in a mass, and the barbarians were casting weapons on them from all sides. Even the Gallic wars had not yet made them proof to panic.

"Their mode of fighting with their chariots is this: firstly, they drive about in all directions and throw their weapons, and generally break the ranks of the enemy with the very dread of their horses and the noise of their wheels; and when they have worked themselves in between the troops of horse, leap from their chariots and engage on foot. The charioteers in the meantime withdraw some little distance from the battle, and so place themselves with the chariots that, if their masters are overpowered by the number of the enemy, they may have a ready retreat to their own troops. Thus they display in battle the speed of horse, together with the firmness of infantry; and by daily practice and exercise attain to such expertness that they are accustomed, even on a declining and steep place, to check their horses at full speed, and manage and turn them in an instant, and run along the pole and stand on the yoke, and thence betake themselves, with the greatest celerity, to their chariots again."

Caesar, perceiving that something was wrong from the great clouds of dust which could be seen from the camp, had speeded to the assistance of the legion attacked, with those *cohorts* of the Tenth which happened to be on duty. Disengaging it by a vigorous assault on the Britons, who promptly retreated, he deemed it wise to retire at once to the shelter of the camp. The Seventh legion had lost heavily. For several days no further action was taken on account of the rainy weather; Caesar was kept close to the limits of his works preparing for a further attack; while the Britons collected troops from all the neighbouring tribes, urging that now was their opportunity to redeem their cause. Caesar had no cavalry save about thirty horsemen brought over by Commius, but he determined nevertheless to engage the enemy so soon as his troops were again in proper condition. He thought he could accomplish something with even thirty horsemen. After the lapse of a few days, the Britons made a demonstration on the camp. Caesar drew up his legions in its front with the purpose of accepting battle. But the Britons, though they made a smart assault, were unable long to withstand the well-drilled ranks of the legions, and being routed and pursued, lost many men; whereupon the Romans devastated the vicinity and returned to camp.

The Britons now again sued for peace, which Caesar deemed it wise to grant after doubling the number of hostages they were to furnish. And, no doubt fearing that he could not enforce their present delivery, he ordered these to be brought over to the continent by a given time. Then, the autumnal equinox being near at hand, which Caesar desired not to encounter at sea, he embarked and safely reached the shores of Gaul. He had been less than three weeks in Britain.

Two ships were, however, carried farther down the coast. The three hundred soldiers in these, after safely landing, were on the march to rejoin the main army, when they were surrounded and attacked by some warriors belonging to the Morini, who were shortly reinforced up to six thousand men. The legionaries defended themselves manfully, drawn up in a circle for nearly four hours, until Caesar's cavalry, which he had sent out in quest of them, happened at the eleventh hour to come to the rescue. The Morini were penned in by the cavalry and large numbers were killed.

For this act of the Morini speedy vengeance was taken. Labienus, with the Seventh and Tenth legions, just back from Britain, marched into their land, and, as the morasses were almost dry at this season, was able to reach and capture all the tribes which had taken part in the attack. These were no doubt summarily dealt with.

The legions under Sabinus and Cotta, which had been sent out among the Menapii, had been unable to hunt up the natives in their forest retreats. Having, therefore, mowed down all the crops and burned the habitations, they returned to camp.

The limited effect of Caesar's invasion of Britain is well shown by the fact that out of all the tribes who handed in their submission, only two sent over the hostages demanded. The peace and its security had been a mere farce.

Caesar now took up winter-quarters among the Belgae, and, returning himself to Rome, was decreed a thanksgiving of twenty days. This decree was, however, violently opposed by his enemies under leadership of Cato, who depreciated or laughed at his performances as much as his friends extolled and overrated them.

It cannot be claimed that the campaigns of this year had been brilliant. The crossing of both the Rhine and the Channel had been without result. In the former case this has already been pointed out. The campaign into Britain is subject to equal criticism. Caesar's preparations for crossing were lamentably wanting. He had too few ships; he sailed without his cavalry, absolutely essential among tribes which had chariots and horses in plenty. The expedition may be said to have been undertaken in a happy-go-lucky way.

The invasion of Britain was no part of Caesar's military scheme so far as concerned the mere protection of Rome by the conquest of Gaul. But Caesar was looking to his own interests quite as much as to those of Rome. To him his own success was Rome's. Each conquered land enhanced his reputation and might add to his riches; fame and wealth furthered his political aspirations. This ambition was proper enough. It is what has inspired some of the greatest of men and soldiers. But it was the ambition of a Napoleon, not of a Gustavus. It led to over-rapid operations, not carefully planned, the results, or rather the lack of failure of which are largely due to good fortune. The most necessary elements of the work of a great captain are: a distinct conception of his plan; scrupulous preparation for what he undertakes; and courage tempered with caution in its execution. He should not undertake operations without full consideration of what every step may mean. These elements scarcely appeared in either the German or British campaign of this year. Caesar's right to go to Britain he based upon an unproven, perhaps quite improbable assertion, that the Britons had aided the Gauls during his campaign against them. He made no pretence of examining the ground. Volusenus, sailing alone along the coast, could at best bring him but little information—quite insufficient to warrant him in risking his two legions. His preparations and conduct were deficient in that he left no force whose special duty it was to protect his return should he be driven back; that he carried along no victuals or baggage; that he left his cavalry to come behind in a haphazard way; that he had no vessels in reserve; that he apparently knew nothing about the ebb and flow of the tide on the shores of Britain, or had not thought of it; that he inflicted harm on the enemy rather than gained an advantage himself; and that he showed an unnecessary cruelty against the Britons as he had against the Gauls and Germans. Some of the best critics go so far as to say that both campaigns of this year were awkward and deficient in conception and execution, and were as far from useful as from glorious. Had Alexander planned his steps after this fashion, he would never have penetrated beyond the edge of the Persian empire; had Hannibal contrived his work in Italy as carelessly, he would not have held his own for one campaign. Indeed, it may be said that Caesar's good star was at the bottom of his coming out whole.

And yet, if viewed in the light of reconnoissances in force, to ascertain, in unknown lands, what he might be able to do with a stronger expedition thereafter, perhaps both these campaigns may be absolved from such criticism. On no other ground, however, are they even tenable. But is the commander-in-chief, whose death would mean the destruction of his army, warranted in leading such a reconnoissance in person?

GALLIC SWORDS

CHAPTER 12

Cassivellaunus
Spring and Summer, 54 B. C.

Not satisfied with his first trip to Britain, Caesar prepared to cross again. This time he took better precautions, though there is little to justify either invasion from a military point of view. In all he had eight hundred craft, carrying eight legions and four thousand horse. The balance of his force he left on the Gallic coast under Labienus, to protect his base. He set sail in July, landed safely, and marched inland to attack the Britons. Once more a storm damaged the fleet. Caesar returned, hauled up the fleet on the beach, entrenched it, and again set out. After several engagements with the Britons, he forced a passage of the Thames near Kingston. Cassivellaunus, who commanded the Britons, opposed him ably, but Caesar marched as far as St. Albans, for many tribes deserted the national standard, and Cassivellaunus was unable to do much to check him. When Caesar was at a distance, the tribes in the rear attacked the fleet camp and compelled his retreat. Caesar recognized that there was nothing for him to gain by subduing the island. He had seen what manner of land and people there were in Britain. He retired, having accomplished much as a traveller, nothing as a soldier, and returned to Gaul in two embarkations without accident.

Caesar had not yet satisfied his curiosity with regard to Britain. When leaving for Italy to attend to political affairs after the campaign of the preceding year, he commanded his lieutenants to construct as many new vessels as possible during the winter, and to have the old ones well repaired, purposing to cross the Channel a second time. He planned the new ships himself, making them somewhat broader, so as better to accommodate the cavalry and other burden, and with lower sides, so as to be more easily loaded and unloaded. They could also be more readily drawn up on the beach. These, as described by Caesar, were for a similar purpose substantially imitated by Napoleon, in 1804, showing the conditions to have remained practically the same for the intervening centuries. They were fitted to row or to sail. The equipments were brought from Spain. No doubt Caesar recognized the failure and faults in his first invasion of Britain. No man was more ready to profit by his own or his opponent's errors than he. This is really one of Caesar's strong points, though in writing the *Commentaries* he is unapt to acknowledge as much. He determined that he would do the work over again in a more business-like manner, so that it might not only add to the dominion of Rome, but to his own reputation in such a fashion as to silence those wordy and troublesome adversaries who had laughed at his first expedition.

During Caesar's winter absence from his Gallic legions, he was called on to settle what promised to prove a warlike question in Illyricum. The Pirustae had been laying waste the boundaries of that province. To meet the emergency Caesar at once began to raise troops. But seeing his promptness and having heard of his Gallic exploits, the Pirustae sent ambassadors to make their peace, praying humbly for pardon, and offering to make compensation for all damage committed. These terms were accepted, for Caesar did not wish to turn from the Gallic problem, and hostages were given for their performance.

On returning to his Gallic army in June, Caesar found that about six hundred transports and twenty-eight ships of war had been constructed or repaired and made ready to launch. Strabo says he had established a naval arsenal at the mouth of the Sequana. Ordering the fleet, when ready, to rendezvous and await his arrival at Portus Itius, which was the nearest harbour, as he supposed, to Britain, he himself took four legions without baggage and eight hundred horse, and marched against the Treviri, who were threatening trouble, and it was said had again invited the Germans across the Rhine. There is no clue to which legions he took. The Treviri, we remember, were very numerous and strong in cavalry, and occupied territory bordering on the great river. Two chiefs, Indutiomarus and Cingetorix, his son-in-law, were contending among the Treviri for the upper hand in the government. Indutiomarus placed in the Ardennes forest all the people incapable of bearing arms, raised an army and prepared to fight. But when many chiefs deserted him to make submission to Caesar, he concluded to do the like. Caesar gave the power to Cingetorix, who had been singularly attached to him. This made of Indutiomarus an implacable enemy. Both having brought in their submission and delivered up two hundred hostages, including Indutiomarus' relatives,

Caesar, being anxious to go to Britain, settled the matter for the time being, though leaving the two chieftains unreconciled, and returned to Portus Itius. His trip had consumed the month of June.

Here he found that all the ships, save forty, which had not been able to reach this port from the Matrona, where they were built, stood ready for sailing. He had six hundred transports and twenty-eight galleys, plus a number of private barks, eight hundred in all. In order to leave less chance of trouble in the rear during his coming absence, he proposed to carry with him nearly all the Gallic horse, numbering four thousand men. They would be in the nature of hostages for the good behaviour of the tribes to which they belonged. With them he also insisted upon taking Dumnorix, the chief of the Ædui, a man "fond of change, fond of power, possessing great resolution and great influence among the Gauls," with whom he had heretofore had difficulty, for Dumnorix was aiming at the chieftaincy of the Ædui, and the autocracy of Gaul. This man used every artifice to persuade Caesar to leave him behind, and finally, unable to accomplish his purpose, he broke out into open revolt and rode away with the whole cavalry force of the Ædui. Though Caesar had been detained twenty-five days waiting for a favourable wind, and one had just begun to blow, he saw that he could not for a moment temporize with so grave a matter. He sent the bulk of his horse in pursuit. The fugitives were caught up with, and the mutiny came to a speedy termination by the killing of Dumnorix; for the commanders of the pursuing troops had been ordered to bring him back, dead or alive.

Caesar made much more careful preparations for his present descent on Britain, and for the protection of his rear. There were assembled at Boulogne eight legions and four thousand cavalry. His legate, Labienus, was placed in command of the detachment left in Gaul, which consisted of three legions and two thousand horse,—seventeen thousand men, at normal strength,—a force amply large to provide temporarily for the safety of the land. Labienus was also to take steps to insure Caesar a steady supply of corn. His orders were general, to act for the best interests of Caesar under any circumstances which might arise. Labienus was, to all appearances, a faithful, and was unquestionably a clever lieutenant. One can but wonder how he could prove so treacherous as he later did, or sink so low in ability. Caesar took with him the other five legions and two thousand horse,—some twenty-seven thousand men, if we assume the legions to be full. There is no means of telling how strong the legions at this time were. Later they were greatly depleted, and it is probable that at this date they fell below the numbers given.

Caesar embarked and set sail, with over eight hundred craft, one day at sunset, thought to have been the twentieth of July. The fleet sailed with a southwest wind till midnight, when the wind fell; but, by dint of hard rowing and continuous, the British coast was made in the morning, and next midday, after having been carried somewhat too far north, probably to Goodwin Sands, from whence the vessels were rowed back, made good the landing at several points, at a place which the preceding year Caesar had discovered to be a suitable spot. The Britons had been frightened by the appearance of this enormous fleet,—the like of which they had never imagined,—and in lieu of opposing the landing, had, as Caesar learned from some prisoners, concealed themselves some distance back of the coast on the high land.

The operation of this year stands out in marked contrast to that of the last. Caesar had brought victuals, baggage, a sufficient fleet, his cavalry, and enough troops to enable him to accomplish some result. For quite a season he could subsist on what he had, and he had perfected arrangements for future supplies. Caesar probably chose his camp in a safer place, taught by the experience of the last year.

Leaving Q. Atrius in charge of the ships, with a strong guard of ten *cohorts*—two from each legion—and three hundred horse, Caesar marched by night towards the place, some twelve miles distant, where prisoners had told him the enemy lay encamped. Here he was met by an advanced party of warriors, who, with chariots and horsemen, essayed to dispute his passage of a small river, very probably the Little Stour, near Kingston or Littlebourne. The Gallic cavalry, however, easily threw this force back, and following it up, Caesar found the main army strongly entrenched in a fort well protected by felled trees, "which the Britons had before prepared on account of a civil war." The locality cannot be identified, nor indeed are most of the places settled beyond dispute. But some of them may be considered as practically determined. The Britons, not content with having harassed the marching column very materially, offered in a desultory way quite a stubborn defence of their fort; but the Seventh legionaries, having thrown up a temporary terrace and forming a *testudo*, overwhelmed the barbarians with missiles, captured the fort, and drove the Britons out of the woods. The loss of the Romans was small. Caesar forbade their pursuing to any distance, lest they should fall into an ambuscade. He desired, moreover, to entrench his camp more carefully than usual.

On the morrow, when Caesar was about to pursue the Britons, and had already given marching orders to several detachments of foot and horse, three of which had proceeded some distance, had caught up with the barbarian rear, and were pushing them to a fight in retreat, he received by mounted messengers word from Atrius that a storm had destroyed and damaged a number of the ships. These had been left at anchor, and had been violently dashed against each other by the heavy sea. The experience of the last year had not been heeded, and the same danger had been incurred. Recalling the *cohorts* already in pursuit, Caesar marched back to the fleet. Here he found that forty of the vessels had been seriously broken, but that the damage to the rest could be repaired with time and labour. He detailed skilled workmen from the legions for this purpose. He also deemed it wise to send to Labienus in Gaul to have additional ships built. And he now took the precaution, though at great labour, to haul the ships up on the beach out of the reach of the waves, and strongly fortified the position. This work consumed ten days and nights of unremitting toil, for eight hundred ships would take up much space and were not easily handled. If each was eighty feet long by twenty wide, and they were put six feet apart and in four lines ten feet apart, they would occupy a mile of beach three hundred and fifty feet wide. To add the space required for the crews and room to receive the legions as well would make a camp covering much ground. This was, however, no unusual feat for the Romans. The time occupied was mainly used in putting the fortifications beyond fear of capture. August had come, and Caesar had made small headway.

The same *cohorts* were left to protect the new camp, and Caesar marched back to the place where he had last met the enemy. Here he found the Britons assembled under command of Cassivellaunus, a noble chieftain whose territories were separated from the maritime states by the Tamesis (Thames) about eighty miles up from the sea, above London. The several tribes, who were constantly at war, had laid aside their own feuds in order to meet the common enemy, and though Cassivellaunus was universally disliked, he had been recognized as the best commander.

The British foot was useless against the legions. Cassivellaunus recognized this fact, and appears to have discharged it. But the cavalry and chariots proved useful. They hovered about Caesar's column on the march, made frequent attacks, and gave unceasing trouble to the Romans, who, at first, daunted by the fierce looks of these barbarians, their woad-stained skins, and their courageous demeanour ended by finding discipline more than a match for their wild tactics. After camping, a constant skirmish was kept up with the outposts. The Britons at one time appeared suddenly from the woods and drove in a Roman guard with serious loss. But Caesar sent forward two *cohorts* as reinforcement, and the action after some time resulted in greater loss, by far, to the Britons, who were driven back to the forest. The method of fighting of the Britons was novel to the Romans. The charioteers did not act in large bodies, nor indeed the cavalry, but in small squads, relying upon their individual prowess. They would often purposely retreat and then turn furiously upon the pursuers, and as often as necessary they relieved the fighting men with fresh ones. The drill and heavy masses of the Roman legions were by no means suited to this method of warfare. The Roman allied horse was subjected to the same difficulty, for the Britons, seeing that they could not meet the squadrons on equal terms, merely skirmished in loose order and cut out an occasional horseman whenever chance offered.

Caesar does not give us details of just what means he adopted to meet these novel tactics. One is led to believe that Caesar's *legionaries* in this their fifth year of campaigning were not as apt at coping with the unusual as Alexander's *phalangites*, who could and did skirmish as well as they fought in line or column, against any and all comers. Still, Caesar's legionary was an adaptable fellow, able to turn his hand to almost anything. He had already had considerable experience in dealing with new methods of warfare, and to rank him as he was at this period after the Macedonians, who had been trained by Philip, is no disgrace. Later, he came well up to their standard. Probably without altering anything of the regular formation or manoeuvring of the legion, Caesar was able to meet the Britons at their own tactics.

Next day the enemy assembled "with less spirit than the day before," on the hills surrounding the camp, and challenged the Romans to battle by advancing cavalry skirmishers, who galloped tauntingly around the Roman horse without venturing to make a serious attack. This challenge being refused, when towards noon Caesar sent out the legate Trebonius with three legions and all the cavalry on a foraging expedition, the Britons, who lay in ambush, suddenly and from all sides, fell upon them. The barbarians fought with uncommon vigour and daring. They pressed on so sharply that the legionaries were compelled to close in round their standards. But, as always, Roman discipline under able leadership prevailed; the Britons were driven back and broken, and in the pursuit, a vast number of them were killed. The cavalry, finding itself sustained by the foot, kept so close to their heels that they were unable to display their peculiar tactics. Reinforcements which came up to their aid were likewise dispersed. The punishment was severe, and thereafter no attack in force was made on the Roman columns.

After these preliminary combats, Caesar advanced on Cassivellaunus *via* Maidstone and Westerham. He saw that the enemy proposed to draw the war out to a great length and believed that he had better force the fighting. In order to reach Cassivellaunus, he must cross the Thames. Several places were fordable, and at each of these localities the enemy-had erected defences. Caesar chose a spot between Kingston and Brentford. Here he found that Cassivellaunus had driven sharp stakes into the farther bank and into the river bed nearby, with the points below the surface of the water, and expected to be able to overwhelm the Romans when they should get into disorder in forcing the ford. These stakes were probably driven both above and below. Caesar had got wind of this device from prisoners, and was able to avoid the snare. Sending his cavalry to points up or down the river so as to cross and take the Britons in flank, and, following up its manoeuvre with the legions, who, though the water was up to their necks, dashed into the ford with courage, the combined onset was so sharp and vigorous that Cassivellaunus' men sought safety in flight. Polyaenus says Caesar had an elephant, the sight of which greatly disturbed the Britons. This is not elsewhere mentioned, and is doubtful.

It was the middle of August. Many of the auxiliaries of Cassivellaunus now deserted him, and he was reduced to defend himself with his own forces, amounting to four thousand men in chariots, perhaps seven or eight hundred chariots, with their auxiliary fighters. He showed himself an adept in a small system of warfare. Knowing all the paths of the country, he was able adequately to hide his people, cattle and goods, and to fall upon the Roman foragers wherever they went, from one ambush after another. So clever were his devices, that he succeeded in almost entirely preventing foraging at a distance from the main body of the legions; and so effectively did he interfere with their obtaining corn, that one is tempted to make the same criticism upon Caesar's passing over to the north side of the Thames which was applied as a whole to his first invasion of Britain.

At this time, the Trinobantes, who lived in modern Essex and Middlesex, came in and surrendered, they being one of the most powerful tribes and inimical to Cassivellaunus. No doubt Caesar had exerted all his diplomacy to bring about this result. The Trinobantes were secured from plundering by the Roman soldiers, and on giving forty hostages, and furnishing corn for the troops, Caesar reinstated their chief, Mandubratius, who had been to Gaul to see Caesar, and was still with him. The old king, his father, Cassivellaunus had killed. Other tribes, the Cenimagni, Segontiaci, Ancalites, Bibroci and Cassi, soon followed this example. These tribes covered substantially the entire southeast section of Britain. Learning from the new allies to what place Cassivellaunus had retired, that he had fortified his capital,—at modern St. Albans, probably,—though it could have been little more than a camp, and had collected in it a large force and much cattle, Caesar took up his march thither. After reconnoitring the camp,—it had a rampart and ditch, "admirably fortified by nature and by art," and lay in a thickly wooded district,—he determined upon attacking it from two directions. The storming columns made short work. The Britons did not long resist the assault, but hurriedly retreated by the gate on one of the sides which had not been attacked, leaving behind corn and cattle, and losing many people in the flight and pursuit. This was not a very flattering victory, nor a decisive, but it furnished a pretext to declare the advance a success, and enabled Caesar to withdraw from a campaign which promised no eventual gain.

While Caesar was thus engaged, Cassivellaunus sent messengers to the tribes in Kent whose kings were Cingetorix, Carvilius, Taximagulus, and Segonax, and persuaded them to make a sudden attack on the Roman fleet and camp. This they did with a large force, but the Romans, expertly sallying out upon them, routed them, killed a vast number, and captured Lugotorix, a celebrated leader. This was, indeed, fortunate. A disaster at the rear would have meant destruction of all Caesar's forces.

After this defeat Cassivellaunus, thoroughly alarmed by his want of success, by the wasting of the country, and by the desertion of many tribes, concluded to treat for peace. He employed Commius to make advances for him. Caesar, as the summer was far spent,—it was now the end of August, and he felt that he must return to Gaul, where some tribes had revolted and others were threatening to follow suit,— after taking great numbers of hostages and prescribing a tribute to be paid the Roman people, and forbidding Cassivellaunus, moreover, to attack the Trinobantes or Mandubratius, concluded peace. By no means all of the vessels which had been sent back to Gaul for supplies had returned to Britain. Many had gone astray. Caesar had fewer ships by far than he had brought over. He was compelled to convey his army back to Gaul in two trips, for his numbers were swelled by an array of hostages and prisoners. There were many disasters to vessels returning empty from the first crossing, but the transfer was managed without loss of a skip containing soldiers, and Caesar reached Gaul after an absence of two months. Having housed his ships, he called a great congress of the Gallic tribes at Samarobriva (Amiens) in the land of the Ambiani.

The operations of this year in Britain were practically as resultless as those of the previous one, though the care and skill with which the invasion was conducted were in this case commendable. Caesar had accomplished nothing substantial. As Tacitus remarks, he had made rather a survey than a reduction of Britain. He had not added a new province to Rome, nor indeed paved the way for so doing. He had not left a force to hold what he had conquered. He had brought back hostages, to be sure, but their possession was unable to assure him any control over the island. We are constrained to look upon the expeditions to Britain in the light of invasions made without proper warranty, consideration or effect. They had no influence upon the military problem in Gaul. However valuable as giving historians their earliest bird's-eye view of Britain, from a military point of view they were unnecessary and ineffective.

WOUNDED GAUL. (FROM A SARCOPHAGUS.)

CHAPTER 13

Ambiorix
Winter, 54-53 B. C.

The crops had been poor. Caesar spread his legions in winter-quarters over a large area, so as more readily to subsist. The camps were three hundred miles apart between extremes. Of this fact the Gauls took advantage. Ambiorix attacked Sabinus at Aduatuca. Instead of fighting it out, Sabinus relied upon Ambiorix's promise of free exit, and sought to march to Cicero's camp, the nearest to his own. But he did this carelessly, was attacked, and entirely cut up. Ambiorix then marched to Cicero's camp and tried the same artifice of promising free exit. Cicero acted the soldier's part and held to his camp. Caesar heard of these events. He had but seven thousand men whom on the spur of the moment he could concentrate. With these he set out to rescue Cicero. So soon as he reached the vicinity, Ambiorix quitted the siege of Cicero's camp and advanced to meet him. It was nine to one. Caesar, with admirable ruse, led on Ambiorix, who despised his meagre numbers, to attack him in careless order; and falling suddenly on him, defeated his army and dispersed it. He thus released Cicero from his bad case. Few of Cicero's men had escaped wounds or death. Labienus meanwhile had been attacked by the Treviri, but had won a brilliant victory.

Owing to an exceptionally dry season the corn-crop had not been good in Gaul during the year 54 B. C.; so that Caesar, as he says, was obliged to disperse his legions to provide them food in winter-quarters during the succeeding winter. Fabius, with one legion, was sent to the Morini, and established himself at modern St. Pol; Q. Cicero, brother of the orator, went with one to the Nervii, between the Scaldis and Sabis, and camped probably at Charleroi; Roscius, with one, was placed among the Esuvii, in southern Normandy, near Séez;

Labienus, with one, was among the Remi, near the Treviri, very likely at Lavacherie; Crassus, Plancus and Trebonius, with three legions, occupied Belgium, between the Scaldis and Isara,—Trebonius at Amiens, Crassus among the Bellovaci at Montdidier, twenty-five miles from Amiens, Plancus near the confluence of the Oise and Aisne; and the new legion last raised on the Po, and five *cohorts*, under Sabinus and Cotta, were placed near the Meuse, among the Eburones, the country governed by Ambiorix and Cativolcus, at Aduatuca (Tongres). The bulk of the legions were thus in the northwest section of Gaul. The exact locations are, of course, not certain. The only ones which are determined are Samarobriva and Aduatuca. The others are set down according as topographical features or the subsequent establishment of Roman oppida, or camps, suggest the probable earlier locations, and are approximately correct.

These forces made up a grand total of eight legions and five *cohorts*. This was the same number Caesar had had for a year. No new ones were raised till later,—though some authorities claim that there was, at this time, one extra one, or nine legions and a half.

Caesar determined to remain with the army until the camps were all fortified. One legion (Plancus') was later hastily sent to the Car-

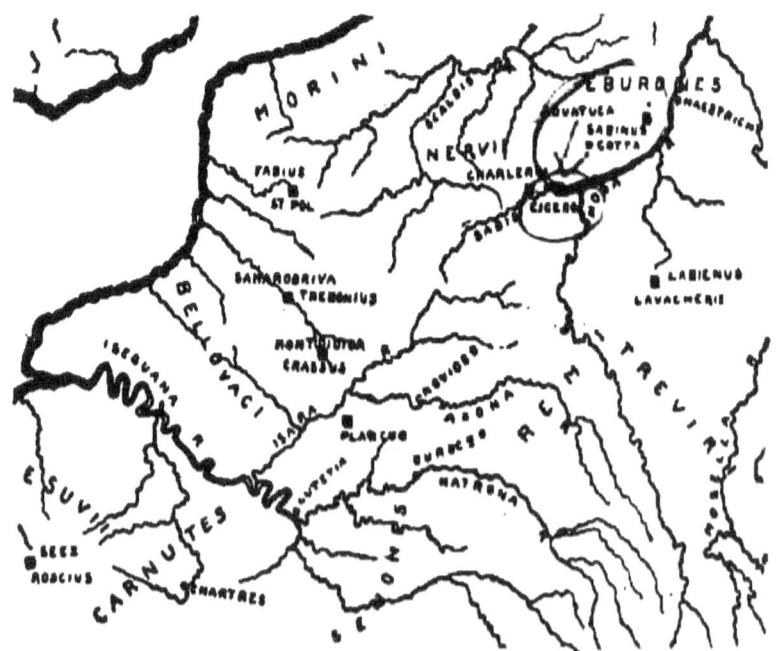

Winter-Quarters, B. C. 54-53

nutes in the neighbourhood of modern Chartres, where Tasgetius, who was one of Caesar's firm allies,—for Caesar had replaced him on the throne of his forefathers from which he had been driven,—had been murdered by his subjects. Plancus' orders were to hunt up the murderers, and send them to Caesar for trial.

It proved in the event that these several camps were unable to support each other in case of need. They were, as the crow flies, over three hundred miles distant between extremes; or if the camp of Roscius be left out, the other camps could not be contained in a circle of a diameter less than one hundred and sixty miles. Why Caesar chose to so divide his forces can be explained only on the score of extreme stress of victual. Even this scarcely suffices. Corn he had or must procure, despite the bad harvests, and he could in some fashion have brought the supplies into magazines. His method was clearly a miscalculation, natural enough, but not Caesarian. Having, not far from the end of October, received word from his *quaestor* that the camps were all entrenched,—it appears that he did not personally inspect the camps,—Caesar prepared to leave for Cisalpine Gaul.

Gaul was only outwardly quiet. The Roman legions were really camping on a volcano. The Gallic tribes had been fearfully maltreated, and the mistaken policy was now bearing fruit. The people were poor, their chiefs had lost all power and influence, large districts had been devastated, and starvation promised to be the lot of thousands. The Romans were always careless in providing for conquered peoples. Caesar had been particularly so in Gaul. He imagined that this very fact would prevent insurrection; but it produced the reverse effect. Fury and despair outweighed calculation or common sense.

It does not appear that a general rendezvous had been given the legions, in case it became essential for them to concentrate. To do this was, in fact, not the method of Caesar, who had not yet taught himself some of the most necessary lessons of the military art, which even among barbarians require to be observed. In the African campaign, we shall see a still more glaring instance of this, the outcome of a certain habit of carelessness on Caesar's part. Caesar's theory was that each isolated body, as was possible in a well entrenched and victualed Roman camp, should defend itself, and take the most available means of procuring succour from neighbouring legions. When he was absent, he did not, in fact, leave any one in command. Each legate was independent. With his enormous grasp of the requisites of any military situation, this is somewhat curious.

Two weeks after all the legions had been settled, a sudden insurrection arose among the Eburones (a tribe south of the confluence of the Meuse and the Rhine), under leadership of Ambiorix and Cativolcus. These chiefs had apparently been friendly. They had at least brought in provisions to Sabinus and Cotta. Though these chiefs struck the first blow, Indutiomarus of the Treviri is thought to have been the prime mover of the rising.

The insurgents began by making an assault on the Roman soldiers who were gathering forage and wood for the camp under Sabinus at Aduatuca. That this was Tongres is not doubtful. No other place satisfies all the requirements of distances and topography made by the *Commentaries*. These parties rallied, held together and reached camp, whose defences had just been completed. The Spanish cavalry made a successful sortie, which, coupled to the stanch front of the legionaries, broke up the attack. Then, after their usual treacherous manner, the barbarians asked for a conference. This was unwisely granted. C. Arpineius, a Roman knight, and Q. Junius, a Spaniard, who personally knew Ambiorix, being sent on the parley, the Gallic chief informed the messengers, with every show of truth, that he had been compelled by his people to make the attack on the camp; that he himself was Caesar's constant friend; that this day had been selected throughout Gaul for an attack on the isolated legions; that a large force of Germans was within two days' march; that for their own safety, Sabinus and Cotta had best retire; and he promised under oath that he would give them a safe-conduct.

Upon these statements being reported, a council of war was held, at which the most opposite opinions were stormily expressed. Cotta, backed by many of the *tribunes* and *centurions*, was for holding on. They had rations; he believed that Caesar would come to their relief, and that untold forces of the Germans could be encountered in their fortified winter-quarters; why, then, should they, on the advice of the enemy, cast aside these advantages? But finally, late at night, Sabinus succeeded in imposing his opinion on the others. This was to the effect that though the information did come from an enemy, they would do well to regard it and not wait till the Germans arrived; that Caesar had probably started for Italy; that they had the choice of quick retreat or a prolonged siege; that they could easily join the nearest Roman winter-quarters, which were but sixty miles away; that the statement of Ambiorix bore the stamp of probability, though he was an enemy. It was determined to retreat towards Cicero at early dawn.

The soldiers spent the night without sleep, making preparations for the march. At daybreak the column started on its way, not in close order and with due precautions, but strung out and hampered by an immense amount of baggage, as if relying solely on Ambiorix's promise of safe-conduct, and not in the least on their own resources. This utterly un-Roman conduct shows how much more the safety of an army depends upon the commander than upon the men.

Camp at Aduatuca

The enemy, from the stir of the camp, quickly perceived that the Romans had decided on retreat. They accordingly placed an ambuscade in the woods about two miles from the camp, on the road the Romans must pursue on the march towards Cicero's camp. This was in the defile of Lowaige, on the heights north and south of the village, where the Geer flows between two hills. The Gauls occupied both exits and the adjoining eminences.

The Roman army started on its ill-fated march. No sooner had it descended into the valley where the Gallic troops lay hid, than the barbarians emerged from cover and attacked the head and rear of the Roman column. Sabinus, who had been for retreat, quite lost his head; Cotta, who had yielded to his views only after long persuasion, was active and full of vigour. The discipline of the soldiers was lax, and each one, instead of rallying on the standards, sought rather to save some of his goods from the baggage-train. The column was much extended. It was hard to convey orders. The march had been begun without the precautions essential to such an operation. The men were not kept closed up; no method of defence was apparent; every one worked on an independent basis. The train soon had to be abandoned. Danger crowded the *legionaries* together, and the army was drawn up in a square (*orbis*) for defence.

The Gauls behaved wisely. They did not seek plunder, but first victory. They began a system of tiring out the Roman legions. Out of the square, from time to time, certain *cohorts* would charge on the enemy and uniformly defeat him; then retire again to their place in the line. The barbarians soon ceased to offer resistance to these charges. Whenever one was made, they would retire; but so soon as the Roman *cohorts* turned back, being lighter armed, they would rush forward and beset their flanks, and the flanks of the *cohorts* exposed by their advance. Though, in the square, the Roman lost his initiative, the impetus which made him strong, yet from early morning till near nightfall the legionaries held their ground without disgrace, but at a serious loss in men and officers. Sabinus, still weakly relying on Ambiorix's word, sent Cnaeus Pompeius, during a lull in the fighting, to ask a conference with him. To this being granted and protection again promised under oath, he himself and a number of tribunes went; but during the conference they were surrounded and slain; whereupon the Gauls again attacked the circle, and, owing to the demoralization of the men, speedily forced their way into it. Cotta was slain; a few of the *cohorts* cut their way out of the *mêlée* and managed to get back to the camp, where the survivors all committed suicide during the night. A handful of fugitives found their way to the camp of Labienus, nearly seventy miles distant.

Ambiorix, elated at his victory, made forced marches with his cavalry,—the infantry following as rapidly as possible,—to the westerly clans of the Aduatuci and the Nervii, to rouse them to embrace this opportunity of revenge and freedom. These tribes, elated by his exaggerated promises, willingly joined him, and all the neighboring and dependent tribes were sent for. Having assembled a large force with the utmost dispatch, they attacked some foraging parties, and then the camp of Cicero at Charleroi, who had heard not a word of the disaster to Sabinus and Cotta, and who was expecting nothing so little as an insurrection. The *legionaries* rushed to arms and manned the *vallum*, and the Gauls were foiled in their hope of seizing the place out of hand. Cicero at once dispatched messengers to Caesar, but of these—despite great promises of reward—none made their way through the enemy's lines. The roads and passes had been all beset by the Gauls. Ambiorix had taken his precautions well.

The Romans had got together a great deal of timber for winter-quarter fortifications. During the night after the attack they worked hard at the defences of the camp, shortly building one hundred and twenty towers (the towers were built as they still build scaffolds in Italy, by lashing together upright and cross poles), weaving hurdles and preparing burned stakes and mural spikes for use from the battlements. Not even the wounded could cease from labour. The enemy attacked next day, and thanks to the preparations were beaten back. Desultory attempts to take the camp continued for some days. Cicero, though sick, would give himself no rest until obliged to do so by his men. The *legionaries* defended the camp well, though with difficulty. A winter camp was more extended than the daily camp and gave a much longer rampart to defend. Unable to make sensible progress, the Gallic chiefs signified their desire to confer with Cicero. On this being granted, Ambiorix plausibly stated the same things with which he had persuaded Sabinus, refraining however, from promises, and told of the destruction of that legion. He claimed that the cause of war was the burden laid on the Gauls by the Romans in wintering regularly in the country and consuming the corn which was needed to keep their own people in life. To all this Cicero made the soldier's answer that the Romans never treated with foes in arms, but that if the enemy would lay down their arms and state their case as supplicants, no doubt Caesar would do them ample justice. Ambiorix retired baffled.

The Nervii then set about to besiege the Roman camp, and built around it a rampart eleven feet high and a ditch thirteen feet deep. They had learned these methods from Roman prisoners and former wars. Though they had few tools to work with, but were "forced to cut the turf with their swords and to empty out the earth with their hands and cloaks," so vast was their number that in three hours they had made a rampart fifteen thousand feet long. The text here says *passuum*, but it is probably meant for *pedum*. The former would make the length of the rampart ten miles; it was in effect less than three, for they had to surround only the camp of a legion. Next day they built towers, *mantelets* and galleries, and made mural hooks. They had attained some skill in the *minutiae* of sieges.

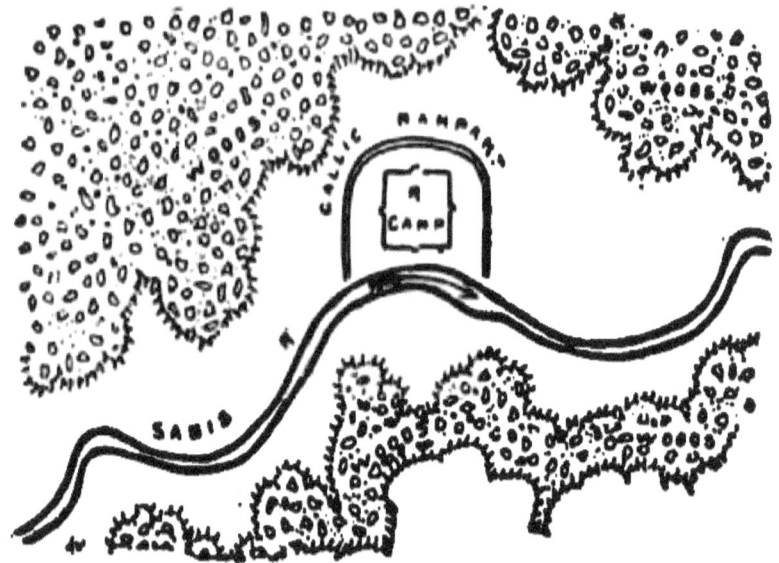

CICERO'S CAMP

Cicero was now entirely shut in. On the seventh day there was a high wind, and the barbarians, by means of hot clay balls and heated javelins, set on fire the camp-huts which were thatched after the Gallic fashion, and under cover of the confusion of the flames made a vehement assault. The legionaries stood manfully to their work, despite the fact that their baggage was being consumed, and utterly worsted the enemy. The *Commentaries* give prominence to some acts of personal gallantry.

"In that legion there were two very brave men, centurions, who were now approaching the first ranks, T. Pulfio and L. Varenus. These used to have continual disputes between them which of them should be preferred, and every year used to contend for promotion with the utmost animosity. When the fight was going on most vigorously before the fortifications, Pulfio, one of them, says: 'Why do you hesitate Varenus? or what better opportunity of signalizing your valour do you seek? This very day shall decide our disputes.' When he had uttered these words, he proceeds beyond the fortifications, and rushes on that part of the enemy which appeared the thickest. Nor does Varenus remain within the rampart, but respecting the high opinion of all, follows close after. Then, when an inconsiderable space intervened, Pulfio throws his javelin at the enemy, and pierces one of the multitude who was running up, and while the latter was wounded and slain, the enemy cover him with their shields and all throw their weapons at the other and afford him no opportunity of retreating. The shield of Pulfio is pierced and a javelin is fastened in his belt. This circumstance turns aside his scabbard and obstructs his right hand when attempting to draw his sword; the enemy crowd around him when thus embarrassed. His rival runs up to him and succours him in this emergency. Immediately, the whole host turn from Pulfio to him, supposing the other to be pierced through by the javelin. Varenus rushes on briskly with his sword and carries on the combat hand to hand, and having slain one man, for a short time drove back the rest; while he urges on too eagerly, slipping into a hollow, he fell. To him, in his turn, when surrounded, Pulfio brings relief; and both having slain a great number, retreat into the fortifications amidst the highest applause. Fortune so dealt with both in this rivalry and conflict, that the one competitor was a succour and a safeguard to the other, nor could it be determined which of the two appeared worthy of being preferred to the other."

This story lends local colour to the rivalries of the Roman soldier's life. The number of defenders of the Roman camp was daily becoming smaller, and these were weakened by exertion. Of the messengers dispatched to Caesar, none reached him. Some were captured and tortured in sight of the camp. Finally, a Nervian who had deserted to the Romans undertook to carry a message and succeeded in reaching the chief.

Caesar was at Samarobriva. He had not left for Italy so soon as he expected. He at once headed Trebonius' legion for the scene of danger, and ordered Crassus, who was at Montdidier, to march to headquarters with his legion to replace Trebonius. Fabius, with his legion, was directed to march from St. Pol toward the Nervian frontiers, and join Caesar among the Atrebates.

Caesar received notice of Cicero's peril about four p. m. So rapid was his message and so alert was Crassus that this officer reached Caesar at ten a. m. next day, a march of fully twenty-five miles. The camp at Samarobriva was protected by the rearguard of Trebonius' legion until Crassus' arrival, when it set out to rejoin the column. Crassus was left behind at the main camp to protect the baggage, treasure, prisoners, archives and the vast amount of corn there collected. At the same moment Caesar had sent word to Labienus to march to meet him in the vicinity of Cicero's camp; but Labienus replied, explaining the state of revolt of the Eburones and the imminent danger from the Treviri. He knew the confidence Caesar reposed in his judgment and relied on his properly gauging the reason of his failure to obey orders. He was right.

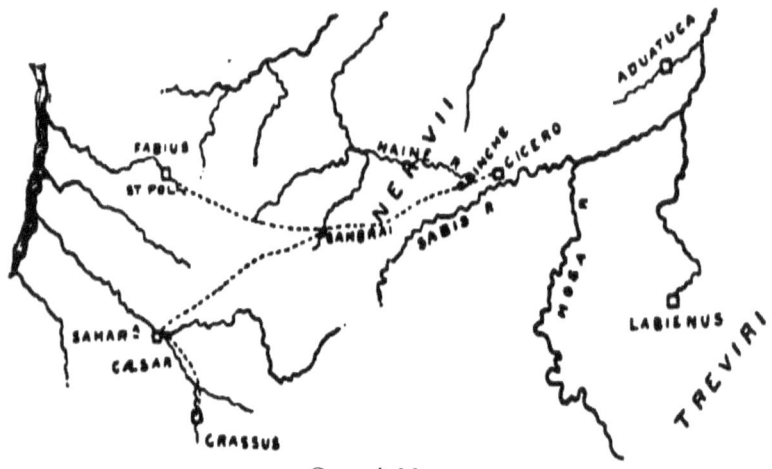

CAESAR'S MARCH

Caesar instantly followed Trebonius' legion. He had, in addition to that body, but four hundred horse available at headquarters, or a total of only two small legions, perhaps seven thousand to eight thousand men. One of the most singular facts in the military history of Caesar is the manner in which he was repeatedly caught in dilemmas with but a handful of troops at his disposal. We shall see him at Alexandria, Zela and Hadrumetum in a desperate strait from lack of foresight. It required luck superior to Alexander's, as well as his own splendid resources, to save him from destruction in these false positions. Caesar's fortune will ever remain proverbial, and indeed, had not the fickle goddess laid aside her wonted character to favour him, Caesar would have ended his career before he had made himself an enduring name. No great captain was ever rescued from the results of his own neglect so often as was Caesar.

Caesar now had but a handful, but he felt that dispatch was of more moment than larger forces. On the first day he covered twenty miles in the direction of modern Cambrai, and was joined on the road by Fabius, not far from that place. Pushing on, he reached the borders of the Nervii, and learned from prisoners what the conditions were. He managed to send word to Cicero that he was coming, by a Gallic horseman, who shot an arrow, or threw a javelin with the message tied to the thong into his camp, and urged him to hold out to the last. The message was in Greek. Polyaenus says it was brief: "Courage! Expect succour!"

In five days Caesar marched from Samarobriva to near the winter-quarters of Cicero, not far from one hundred and ten miles, twenty-two miles a day, over winter roads, a good but not wonderful performance. He camped in the vicinity of Binche. So soon as the Nervii discovered Caesar's approach, they raised the blockade and marched towards him, some sixty thousand strong. Cicero sent Caesar word that the enemy had turned against him. He had no men left to send as a reinforcement to his chief. Caesar had but about seven thousand men, and saw the necessity for caution. His having but one man to nine of the enemy was due to his miscalculated system of winter-quarters. He broke camp at Binche, advanced, and soon ran across the enemy. He first caught sight of them across the valley of the Haine. He camped on Mount St. Aldegonde in a very contracted space, to make the Nervii underestimate even the paltry force he had with him. He then sent forward his horse to skirmish with the enemy, and by simulating retreat, draw them on to attack the camp. He and his legion lay west of the Haine; the barbarians were on its east bank; Caesar manoeuvred so as to get them to cross the stream to the attack. He also began fortifying and gave orders to the soldiers to act with apparent confusion, as if in fear, so as still more to lure the Nervii on.

The ruse succeeded, and the barbarians advanced, took up a disadvantageous and careless position, and sent out a proclamation that they would receive and spare any deserters from the Roman legions. They believed that they had bagged their game. They then began the

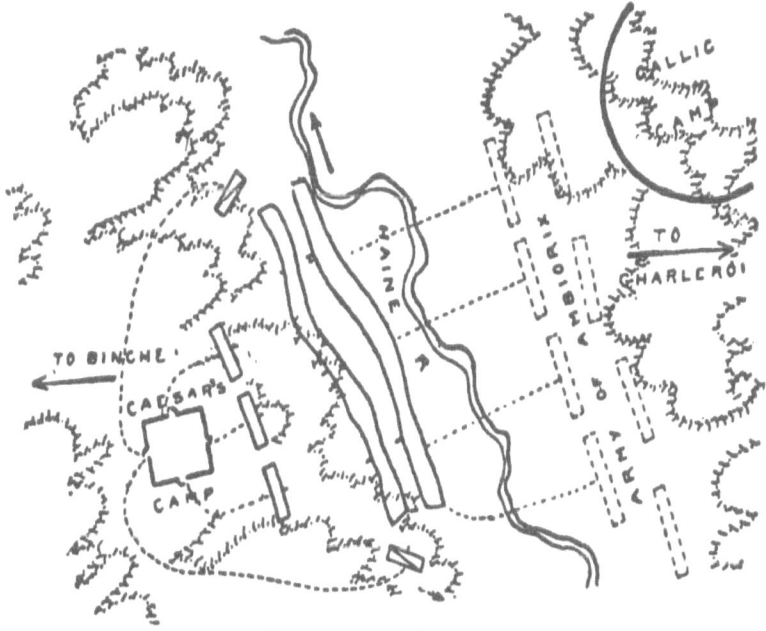

BATTLE AGAINST AMBIORIX

fight as if nothing were so sure as victory, advancing to the gates and ramparts in enthusiastic disorder. Caesar still simulated fear, to render them yet more careless, and held his men sharply in hand, intending to take them unawares. At the proper moment he gave the signal. The legionaries rushed from all the gates at once; and the cavalry sallied out with unexpected dash. So entirely surprised were the barbarians by the vigour and courage of their opponents that they fled in dismay. They were pursued with great loss, but the pursuit was not kept up to any distance, owing to the wooded and cut-up nature of the country. In pursuit, Caesar was never equal to the great Macedonian. No one but Napoleon was.

Having thus opened the way, Caesar marched to Cicero's camp, where he found the garrison in sad case, but still full of courage.

"The legion having been drawn out he finds that even every tenth soldier had not escaped without wounds."

This was a heavy loss, which might be estimated at seven *per cent*, killed, and eighty-three *per cent*, wounded; or, out of a legion of five thousand men, three hundred and fifty killed and four thousand one hundred wounded. Caesar highly commended the legions and officers for their valour, and distributed rewards among the bravest. Both praise and gifts had been gallantly won.

News of this victory was speedily conveyed to the Treviri. This determined Indutiomarus, who had been on the point of attacking Labienus, to withdraw from his front,—at least for the time being. The news had travelled sixty miles between the ninth hour and midnight. Caesar had reached Cicero's camp at three p. m.; before midnight some of the Remi raised a shout of joy which announced the victory to Labienus. This is not so wonderful a performance as it sounds. A single courier might have done it; three or four, relieving each other, very handily. Fifty miles have been run in less than seven hours, in these so-called degenerate days.

No sooner was the campaign thus happily decided than Fabius was sent back to his winter-quarters. Caesar determined to remain in Gaul. Profiting by his bitter experience, he concentrated his forces; established his own headquarters at Samarobriva, with three legions, Crassus', Cicero's, Trebonius', in three several camps. Of these there are some relics still: a camp at the citadel of Amiens; the Camp de l'Etoile; and one near modern Tirancourt. Labienus, Plancus and Roscius remained *in situ*.

The defeat of Sabinus and Cotta had bred a feeling of uncertainty

NEW CAMPS

all through the land; nocturnal meetings were held, and insurrections were threatened and expected on every hand. An attack on Roscius had all but occurred. Among the Senones, on the Upper Sequana, there was a political upheaval, and a refusal to comply with Caesar's demands, which he does not appear to have felt in a position to enforce. This badly affected the tribes. The Remi and Ædui alone remained quite true. By calling together the principal citizens and alternately using threats and courtesies, most troubles were for the moment averted, though a constant turmoil went on.

Indutiomarus, chief of the Treviri, was, it appears, the head and front of this entire movement. He tried to get the Germans across the Rhine, but they had conceived a hearty dread of Caesar. Still Indutiomarus ceased not his work, and finally his efforts induced some isolated tribes of the Senones and Carnutes to join him; and the Aduatuci and Nervii seemed ready to help. But his army was largely composed of outlaws and criminals. He called an armed assembly of chiefs, and under its inspiration advanced and camped again before Labienus. This officer kept to his ramparts, simulating fear,—a trick whose repetition never seemed to make it stale,—but watching keenly for a good chance for attack. Growing more careless day by day, Indutiomarus finally laid himself open.

Labienus had a good body of native horse which he had quietly as-

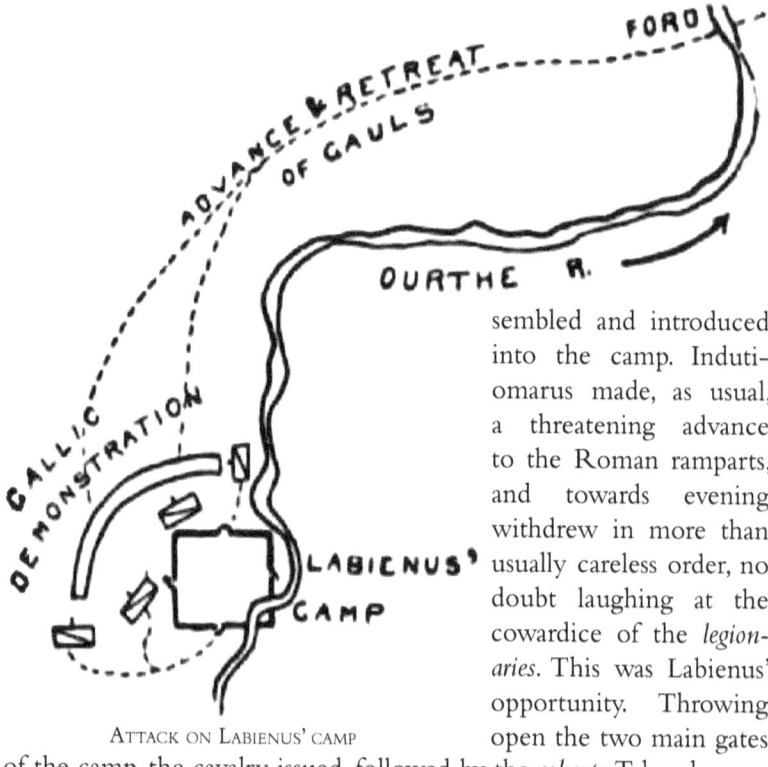

ATTACK ON LABIENUS' CAMP

sembled and introduced into the camp. Indutiomarus made, as usual, a threatening advance to the Roman ramparts, and towards evening withdrew in more than usually careless order, no doubt laughing at the cowardice of the *legionaries*. This was Labienus' opportunity. Throwing open the two main gates of the camp, the cavalry issued, followed by the *cohorts*. Taken by surprise the enemy fled. Indutiomarus himself was slain, and much loss was inflicted on the barbarians. This victory and the death of the chief plotter allayed the turmoil greatly; but though the Nervii and Eburones dispersed to their homes, it was far from quieting Caesar's apprehensions of further trouble.

These operations show the immense role the Roman fortified camp played in the days of short-carry weapons. Gunpowder first nullified the importance of the camp. A modern field battery would with a few rounds demolish a Roman *vallum*. Today, anything like a camp would be subject to irresistible concentric fire. Well chosen natural positions had to be sought as a defence against artillery.

Cicero's defence at Charleroi leads Napoleon to contrast ancient war with modern very skilfully:

"*Si l'on disait aujourd'hui à un général: 'Vous aurez, comme Cicéron, sous vos ordres, 5,000 hommes, 16 pièces de canon, 5,000 outils de pionniers, 5,000 sacs à terre; vous serez a portée d'une forêt, dans un terrain ordinaire; dans quinze jours vous serez attaqué par une armée de 60,000 hommes ayant*

120 pièces de canon; vous ne serez secouru que quatre-vingts ou quatre-vingt-seize heures après avoir été attaqué.' Quels sont les ouvrages, quels sont les tracés, quels sont les profils que l'art lui préscrit? L'art de l'ingénieur a-t-il des secrets qui puissent satisf aire à ce problème?"

The quartering of the legions in such widely separated localities was certainly a grave error, severely punished in the event. But the rapid, able and decisive measures adopted by Caesar to retrieve the disaster are quite beyond praise. The superb courage with which he set out with a mere handful of men to relieve his beleaguered lieutenant, and the skill he showed in dealing with the barbarians when he met them, cannot but excite the highest admiration. It is this sort of conduct on Caesar's part which makes one forget the carelessness which lay at the root of so many of his brilliant strokes. Criticism seems to be almost out of order.

Sabinus had given proofs of ability. How he contrived to allow himself, against the advice of Cotta and his other fellow officers, to enter into negotiations with the crafty Ambiorix is an enigma. And having left his camp to make a junction with Cicero, why he should have marched in loose order and without proper precautions is still more of a puzzle. His only real chance was to stick to his camp and defend it as Cicero did, and as he had Caesar's orders as well as all precedent to do. There can be no excuse for the shiftlessness of his order of march. This disaster is one more instance of the folly of divided command, for Sabinus and Cotta were equal. Caesar should have given absolute command to one or the other legate. That the system of rotation and division of authority did not wreck the Roman army, is referable solely to the wonderful character of the people of Rome. No other army has ever had such a system and survived it. The conduct of Cicero stands out in marked contrast to that of Sabinus.

The incisive conduct of Caesar in remedying the disaster did not fail of effect among the Gallic tribes, and produced its full influence, political and military. The Nervii, Menapii and Aduatuci, who had been in arms, returned home; the maritime cantons followed suit; the Treviri, and their clients, the Eburones, retired from before Labienus. In Rome Caesar's reputation stood higher than ever.

CHAPTER 14

The Treviri and Eburones
Spring, 53 B. C.

During the winter another uprising was planned, headed by the Treviri. Caesar determined to take the rebels unawares. He set out, despite the winter season, and successively surprised and punished the Nervii, Senones and Carnutes. He then reduced the Menapii on the lower Meuse, while Labienus a second time defeated the Treviri. Caesar again crossed the Rhine, to impose on the Germans, having done which he begun his pursuit of Ambiorix, who was now isolated. He sent his cavalry ahead to surprise and capture this chief, if possible, but without success. The Eburones were now hunted down without mercy. Caesar divided his force into three columns, which advanced on three several lines throughout northern Gaul. His baggage he left at Aduatuca. During his absence, some German tribes, who had crossed on a foray, attacked the camp at that place and came close to capturing it. Though Caesar thoroughly suppressed the rising of this year, he was unable to catch Ambiorix. He went into winter-quarters near Sens.

It had become necessary to raise and have on hand a greater number of men, as well as to fill large gaps occasioned by the last campaigns. Caesar deemed it essential to show the Gauls that the resources of Rome were ample; that to destroy one legion meant to have two others spring ready equipped from the earth. By negotiation with Pompey, whom business retained in Rome, he was able to obtain a legion which the latter had raised in Gaul when he was proconsul in Spain. The men had been furloughed to their homes, but they were recalled to the eagles and the legion took its place in line. Two additional legions were enlisted in Gaul by Caesar's lieutenants, Silanus, Reginus and Sextius. The three new legions were

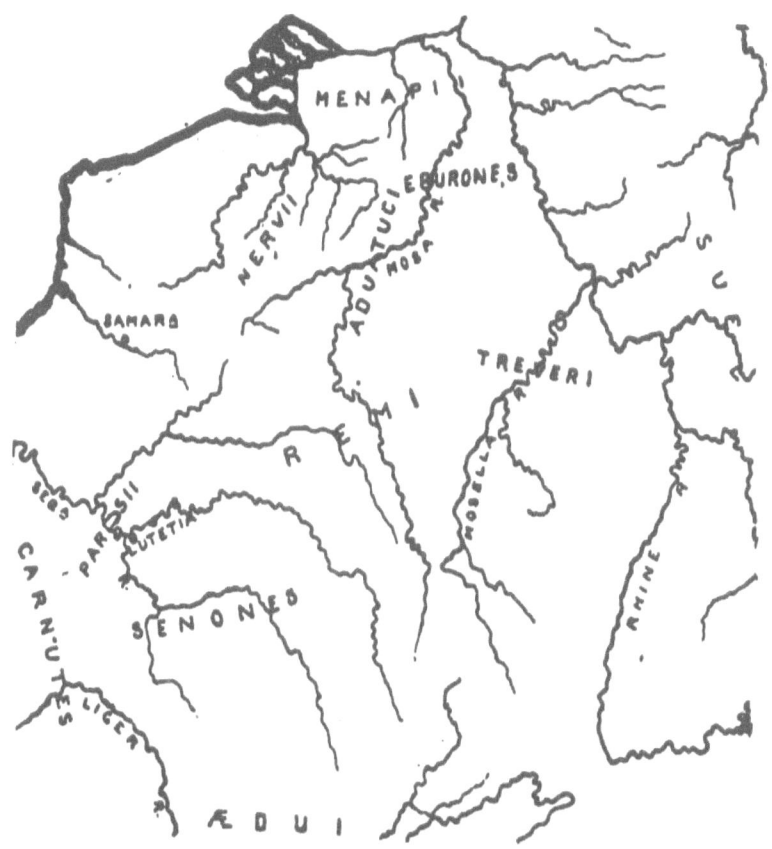
CAMPAIGN AGAINST NERVII AND OTHER TRIBES

the First, the Fourteenth (it took the number of the one destroyed at
Aduatuca), and the Fifteenth. Thus thirty *cohorts* replaced the fifteen
lost by Sabinus. Caesar now commanded ten legions.

After Indutiomarus' death, the Treviri elected new chiefs from his
family. They were unable to induce the nearby Germans to join their
cause, but persuaded some of the Suevi to do so. Ambiorix joined
them. Rumours of war were far spread. The Senones were still an-
tagonistic, and the Carnutes abetted them. The Nervii, despite their
fearful punishment, the Aduatuci and Menapii were under arms. Anticipating trouble with the tribes which had placed themselves under
the leadership of the Nervii, and knowing that they were constantly
striving to induce the Germans to undertake another invasion, Caesar
determined to strike them unawares. Suddenly and before the season
for campaigning opened, perhaps in March, he concentrated the four
legions nearest headquarters at Samarobriva (under Fabius, Crassus,

Cicero, Trebonius), marched upon the Nervii, rushed like a hurricane over their territory, captured great booty, devastated the land and carried off victual. By taking them off their guard, he had them at his mercy. Having cowed them, he compelled them to give him hostages for good behaviour, and returned to his winter-quarters.

Here he called an assembly of the Gauls. All sent representatives except the Senones, the Carnutes and the Treviri. Caesar transferred the congress to Lutetia (modern Paris), so as to do both his political and military scheme justice at the same time. From here, he made a demonstration against the Senones and Carnutes, whose territory adjoined the Parisii. These tribes, under Acco, retired into their *oppida*; but they were unable to resist Caesar's prompt measures. They respectively begged the Ædui and Remi to intercede for them; and on giving the hitherto refused hostages, Caesar overlooked their defection. He had no time to split hairs. He was content to check a growing disposition to revolt. The hostages given were confided to the Ædui for security. Caesar then closed the congress. His rapid and well-considered action had tranquillized central Gaul, and he could devote himself to the war with Ambiorix, chief of the Eburones. It was of the highest importance, Caesar thought, in a military as well as a political sense, that the disgrace of Aduatuca should be wiped out.

As a part of his scheme, Caesar had imposed a fresh levy of horse on the Gallic tribes. The Senonian cavalry under Cavarinus he ordered to accompany him. He was distrustful of its fidelity, as it contained many of the chief men of the tribe, unless he had it under his eye.

The Menapii, north of and next to the Eburones, were the only tribe which had never sent ambassadors to Caesar. They were allies of Ambiorix, and Caesar desired first to detach this people from his alliance. So long as they were unsubdued, Ambiorix retained an inaccessible place of refuge in their woods and morasses. Next to the fear that Ambiorix would persuade the Germans to a fresh war, was the safety this chief possessed in this alliance. The two things to be accomplished were the reduction of the Treviri and the detaching from Ambiorix of the Menapii. The last task he undertook himself, the first he left to the management of Labienus, who knew the problem well, as he had wintered on the borders of the Treviri, and had already tried issues with them.

Sending all his baggage and two legions to Labienus, Caesar moved with five legions, in light marching order and in three columns, against the Menapii, who at once took refuge in their natural fastnesses. They had assembled no forces. Caesar divided his five legions into three columns, under Fabius, Crassus and himself. By the aid of the Senonian cavalry, and by bridging the marshes and streams, he advanced on three lines into their land. These lines were probably down both banks of the Meuse and down the Aa or Dommel, affluents of the Meuse, running from south to north through the Menapian territory. Caesar began by relentlessly devastating their country, capturing their cattle, and taking prisoners all the prominent men he could reach. Shortly the Menapii sued for peace. Though independent from their isolation, they were not wont to act in unison, and were quite unable to resist organized invasion. Caesar granted their petition on their undertaking by no means to harbour Ambiorix; and leaving some of the cavalry, under Commius the Atrebatian, among them, he marched towards Labienus and the Treviri. His route was probably up the Rhine, for we next find him at Bonn.

Labienus had wintered in his old camp at modern Lavacherie. The Treviri had harboured certain designs against him, and even since the victory over Indutiomarus made sundry demonstrations against his

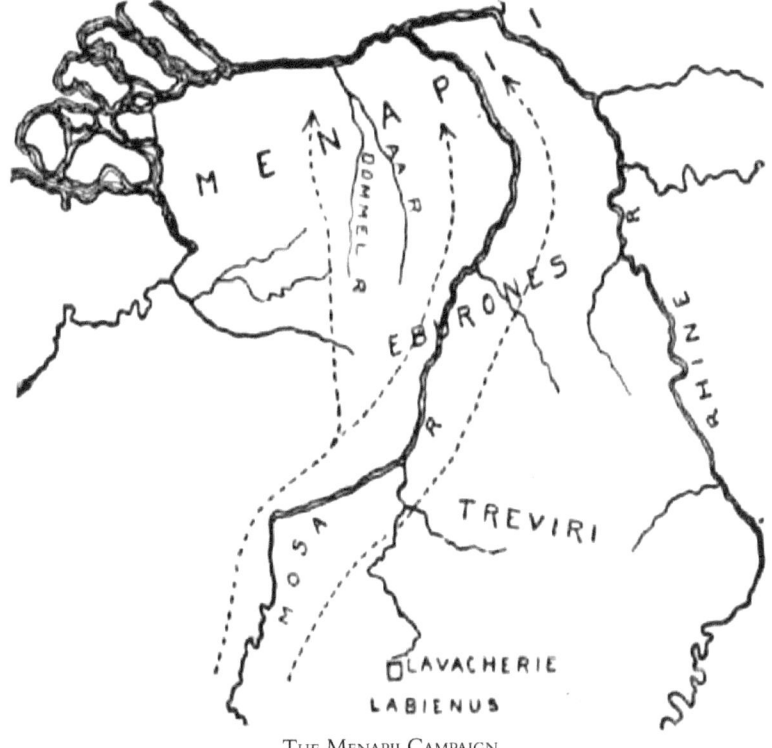

The Menapii Campaign

camp; but hearing that he had received two fresh legions from Caesar, they determined to await the Germans, whom they had now some reason to expect. They established themselves on the right bank of the Ourthe. Labienus did not await the barbarians. Taking twenty-five of his thirty *cohorts* and his cavalry, five remaining to guard the baggage, he anticipated their advance by marching against them, and camping on the other side of the Ourthe, a mile distant from their station.

The enemy were evidently anxious to wait for German succour. Labienus desired to bring them to speedy battle. He stated in public, in such a manner that the rumour might be carried to them, that, not de-

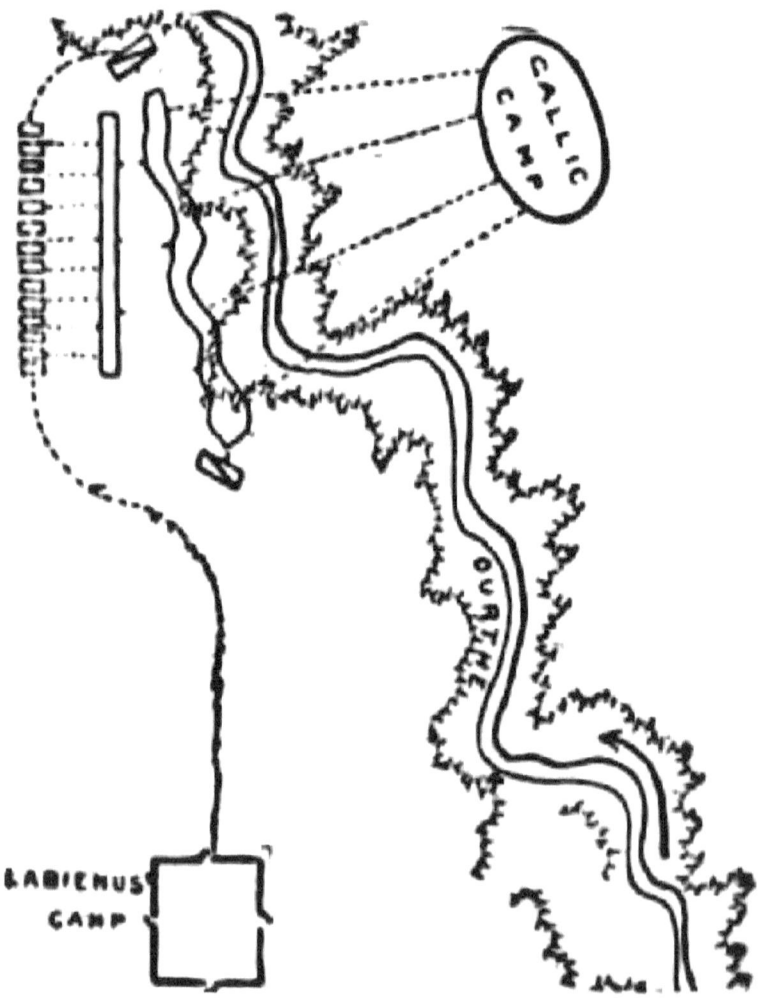

The Treviri Campaign

siring to measure swords with both Treviri and Germans, he proposed to retreat the next day, and made certain preparations which looked like hurried and confused withdrawal, actually leaving his entrenchments. This fact the enemy's scouts soon saw, and some deserters carried to them the statement of Labienus. Fearing that they might lose the booty of the Roman camp, and encouraged by the apparent flight, the barbarians crossed the river and attacked the Roman rear so soon as it had filed out of camp, with the expectation of an easy victory. They had placed themselves in a dangerous position, with the river at their back, and, the river banks being precipitous, had lost all semblance of order in the crossing. Labienus had explained the whole purpose to his lieutenants and *centurions*, and had placed his baggage under its guard on a secure eminence. Exhorting his legions to fight as they should, Labienus, whose troops were well in hand and whose simulated retreat was but a well-drilled manoeuvre, speedily gave the order to face the eagles to the enemy, and deploy into line. The command was executed with clockwork precision. The horse was thrown in on the enemy's flanks. The battle-shout was clear and crisp. The Treviri, taken utterly at a disadvantage, showed little fight. Falling upon them with the utmost fury, the legions and cavalry cut most of them to pieces. The rest fled to the forests. Labienus had ably used his knowledge of the impetuosity and lack of cool calculation in the Gauls. This sharp lesson forestalled the threatened irruption of the Germans, who returned home. The state was turned over to Cingetorix, who had always been an ally of Rome, in the place of Indutiomarus.

It will be noticed that whenever the Roman troops fought with steady discipline, the Gauls, whatever their numbers, were inevitably beaten. There were no open-field pitched battles in the Gallic war, in the sense we understand the words. At the River Sabis, Caesar had to fight, because he had allowed himself to be surprised. The Gauls were always ready to fight; they clung strenuously to their struggle against the Roman conquest, and deserve credit for heroic efforts. But in line of battle they could never face the legions. Ambiorix was now isolated. The Menapii on one hand and the Treviri on the other were subdued, and the Germans could no longer be counted on.

Caesar, from the land of the Menapii, had marched up the Rhine, and hearing of Labienus' victory, remained at Bonn, near the place where he had crossed two years before. He determined again to cross the river, principally, as he states, to impose upon the Germans by a show of force, because they had assisted the Treviri, but also in order to prevent their receiving Ambiorix. He built again a similar bridge at a place a little above where he had built the first one. This bridge was completed yet more quickly; still "by great exertion of the soldiers." Leaving a large and suitable guard at the west bridgehead, he crossed with the legions and cavalry and advanced into the German territory. The Ubii at once approached and easily proved to him that they had been faithful to their alliance, and that it was the Suevi who had sent auxiliaries to Ambiorix. The Suevi had gone so far as to make drafts on their clients and assemble a large army ready for invasion. Caesar employed the Ubii as scouts to discover the movements of the Suevi, and through them ascertained that, on learning of Caesar's approach, they had retreated to the Bacenis forest (Hartz mountains) on the boundary of their territory. Caesar did not deem it wise to march against them, on account of the impossibility of rationing his men in a land whose inhabitants had paid no heed to agriculture, and which would therefore be little better than a desert after the Suevi had driven off their flocks and herds. The barbarians had calculated shrewdly. But in order to leave them convinced that he would return and thereby prevent their undertaking immediate operations, after recrossing his army to the west bank, he broke down two hundred feet of the farther end

PURSUIT OF AMBIORIX

of the bridge and "at the extremity of the bridge raised towers of four storeys," and "strengthening the place with considerable fortifications" on the left bank, left therein a strong guard of twelve *cohorts* under Volcatius Tullus. He himself with the bulk of his ten legions, so soon as corn began to ripen, set out across the Forest of Arduenna against Ambiorix, determined to punish him for his treachery to Sabinus.

Caesar marched from the bridge *via* Zulpich and Eupen. He sent forward all the cavalry force, under L. Minucius Basilus, to endeavour to surprise Ambiorix, promising to follow rapidly with the legions. He instructed Basilus to march secretly and refrain from lighting campfires. This officer performed his duty with excellent discretion and skill, directing his course by information got from prisoners taken on the way to a place where Ambiorix was said to be hiding with a small body of cavalry. So speedily did he march that he reached the retreat of Ambiorix before any rumour of his being on the road had come to the ears of this chief; surprised and almost succeeded in capturing him. But "Fortune accomplishes much," says Caesar, "not only in other matters, but also in the chances of war." And Ambiorix, by a rare stroke of luck, made good his escape. His escort proved loyal, made a smart fight, and under cover of it he mounted a horse and fled.

It seems that this chieftain had begun to see the folly of continuing the struggle against Caesar, for he sent notice to his allies that each one must now provide for his own security,—an act of desertion which roused up fury against him. Cativolcus, king of the Eburones, committed suicide. Many of the tribes which had risen in arms fled with their , possessions from the anger of Caesar into the forests and morasses. The Segni and Condrusi threw themselves on his mercy and were forgiven, having proven that they had not abetted Ambiorix. But they were cautioned to secure and surrender to Caesar all Eburones who took refuge among them.

Caesar's task was now vastly easier. He could deal with the barbarians in detail, and needed much fewer men under his own command. Having reached the ancient ford on the Mosa (at Visé), he divided his army into three parts. His baggage he sent to the camp at Aduatuca, among the Eburones, where Sabinus' legion had been destroyed, and where many of the fortifications still stood, which would relieve the soldiers from much of the work incident to preparing a fresh camp. He left the Fourteenth legion and two hundred cavalry to guard it, under command of Cicero. Labienus with three legions he sent toward the ocean, near the boundary between the Eburones and Me-

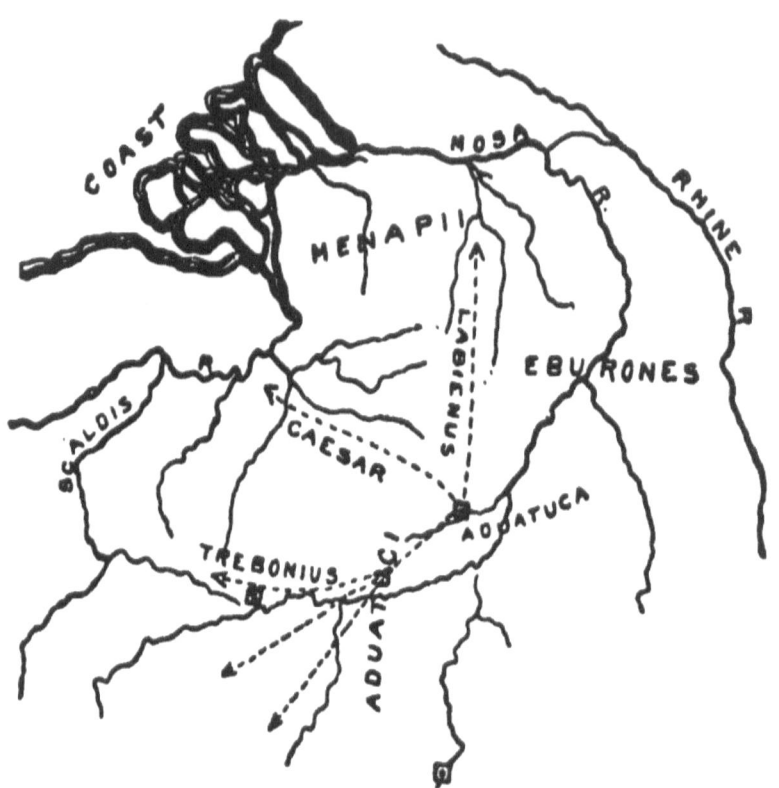

THE THREE COLUMNS

napii, on a reconnoissance to ascertain the standing of this part of Gaul, and to take measures accordingly. Trebonius he sent southwest with three to lay waste the region contiguous to the Aduatuci; he himself, with three legions, marched towards the Scaldis (Scheldt), intending to pursue Ambiorix to the confines of the Forest of Arduenna, between modern Brussels and Antwerp, whither he had retired with a few mounted companions.

By some authorities the River Sabis is read instead of the Scheldt, because the latter does not flow into the Mosa, as is stated by the *Commentaries*. The phrase is, "the River Scaldis which flows into the Mosa." But Caesar could readily be in error geographically, and the Scheldt does empty into the sea not far from the mouth of the Meuse; the Scheldt was more likely to be the objective of one of the columns than the Sabis. A column which marched only so far as the Sabis could accomplish nothing, and this, moreover, was Trebonius' direction.

A rendezvous was given to both Labienus and Trebonius if possible to again rejoin Caesar at Aduatuca on the seventh day, when, from their several reports, Caesar would be able to determine the situation and decide upon future operations. On this day rations were due to the troops remaining in garrison. The amount of work thus cut out for the short space of a se'nnight reminds one forcibly of some of Alexander's campaigns against mountain barbarians. The three columns were really more like three forced reconnoissances. Little could be accomplished in so short a time.

The tribes which had scattered from their allegiance to Ambiorix had so effectually done this, that there was neither town nor camp nor army to attack. They had retreated in small parties to the woods, and the only warfare they could wage was to attack isolated soldiers who were foraging or straggling for booty.

"There was, as we have observed, no regular army, nor a town, nor a garrison which could defend itself by arms; but the people were scattered in all directions. Where either a hidden valley, or a woody spot, or a difficult morass furnished any hope of protection or of security to any one, there he had fixed himself. These places were known to those that dwell in the neighbourhood, and the matter demanded great attention, not so much in protecting the main body of the army (for no peril could occur to them all together from those alarmed and scattered troops), as in preserving individual soldiers, which in some measure tended to the safety of the army. For both the desire of booty was leading many too far, and the woods with their unknown and hidden routes would not allow them to go in large bodies. If he desired the business to be completed and the race of those infamous people to be cut off, more bodies of men must be sent in several directions, and the soldiers must be detached on all sides; if he were disposed to keep the companies at their standards, as the established discipline and practice of the Roman army required, the situation itself was a safeguard to the barbarians, nor was there wanting to individuals the daring to lay secret ambuscades and beset scattered soldiers. But amidst difficulties of this nature, as far as precautions could be taken by vigilance, such precautions were taken; so that some opportunities of injuring the enemy were neglected, though the minds of all were burning to take revenge, rather than that injury should be effected with any loss to our soldiers."

Caesar found that his time would not admit of his dealing single-handed with the question as it stood; and he desired to spare his *legionaries*. He invited the neighbouring tribes, by promise of abundant booty, to come and aid in exterminating these tribes, which were chiefly Eburones. This he had made up his mind to do, as a punishment for their destruction of the legion of Sabinus and Cotta, under circumstances which, according to his view, were treacherous in the extreme. Caesar could not forgive the tribes the bad faith of their leader. He visited them with punishment the more terrible as it ended only with their extinction.

Rumour of this invitation reached the Germans across the Rhine, who deemed that it also applied to them, and gave them a rare chance of plunder. A certain tribe, the Sugambri, abutting on the Rhine, crossed a force of two thousand horsemen in boats thirty miles below Caesar's bridge, and began collecting and driving off cattle, "of which the barbarians are extremely covetous." Learning at the same time that the camp at Aduatuca had been left without much of a garrison, and drawing small distinction between friend and foe, their greed of gain tempted them to try their fortunes there. They concealed their booty and marched on Aduatuca, crossing the Mosa at Maestricht.

Caesar and his lieutenants were unable to return to the camp at Aduatuca by the seventh day,—by no means a remarkable circumstance,—and the garrison, which had been left with but seven days' rations, began to clamour to go foraging. Cicero had so far kept them closely within the ramparts. To collect victuals soon became a matter of necessity, and Cicero determined to send out some parties for food, not imagining that there could be any grave danger, as all the tribes had been scattered and there must be nine legions at no great distance. He erred in sending out too large a force,—five *cohorts*, and these probably the best,—leaving the camp by no means safely garrisoned. As ill-luck would have it, not long after these foraging parties had left camp, the two thousand German horse put in an appearance and found the camp insufficiently defended. Though his position had indeed been a trying one, the condition of affairs showed lack of care on the part of Cicero. A soldier must assume that the improbable will happen.

The Germans had so suddenly approached by the Decuman gate, that a number of sutlers had been surprised with their booths outside, and the *cohort* there on guard was unable to do aught but retire in confusion and close the entrance behind them. Inside the camp everything was in disorder, and the forces all but lost their power to act. It was even surmised that Caesar must have been defeated, and that this was the van of the victorious army of Gauls. But for the presence of mind of Sextius Baculus, who was invalided by wounds, but who

CICERO AT ADUATUCA

nevertheless seized weapons and encouraged the men to defend the ramparts, the enemy could readily have forced an entrance. Thus state the *Commentaries*; but it seems as if five *cohorts* inside a camp were more than a match for two thousand horsemen outside. Where Cicero was is not stated; yet he had earned reputation last year by stanchly defending his camp. Aduatuca seemed to be a pitfall to Caesar.

But while the German horsemen were debating how to make good their capture, the foragers returned. These, in their turn, were unable to effect an entrance; for the whole camp was surrounded by the barbarians. Different counsels prevailed among them; the veterans urging one course, the new soldiers and camp-followers another. The foragers had apparently been sent out under several officers. No one seems to have had sole authority. The veterans, under command of C. Trebonius, a knight, took the only reasonable view of the case and resolved to cut their way through. Forming a compact column, a wedge or triangle (*cuneus*), by a bold push they reached the camp in good order and in safety, with the horse and camp-attendants. Another party, less well-led, had endeavoured to make a stand on an adjoining knoll; but on perceiving the success of the veterans, attempted to do the same thing. Of this party, however, a number were cut out and slain; for not only were the Germans on the lookout for such a manoeuvre, but the party presumably acted inexpertly, and passed over unfavourable ground. The entire matter shows demoralization and lack of management.

The camp having been regarrisoned, the Germans saw their chance of success gone, and withdrew, carrying their plunder beyond the Rhine. The forces in the camp were in a sorry state, and scarcely believed that Caesar was safe when his cavalry vanguard, under Volusenus, actually arrived. Caesar had returned with his work half done, because he had promised Cicero to do so, and had agreed to meet Labienus and Trebonius.

Having re-established affairs in the camp, he again set forth in pursuit of Ambiorix, this time accompanied by auxiliaries from all the neighbouring tribes, who scouted the country traversed by the army, and burned and ravaged to such an extent that those insurgents who escaped the sword would surely perish by hunger. But despite the greatest rewards offered for the capture of Ambiorix, this wily chief eluded every snare, though frequently nearly taken. With but four companions, it is said, he moved from one fort or hiding-place to another and escaped the closest pursuit.

Caesar next marched back to Durocortorum (Reims), the chief town of the Remi, the tribe which of all others, except the Ædui, was most faithful to and most highly esteemed by Rome. Here he held a council of the Gallic tribes, to decide upon the conspiracy of the Senones and Carnutes. Acco, the chief of the conspirators, was found guilty, together with a number of others. Acco was punished "accord-

Winter-Quarters, B. C. 53-52

ing to the custom of our ancestors" (*more majorum*), by being stood in a collar and beaten to death. Some of the conspirators fled, and to these all allies were forbidden to furnish fire and water.

Caesar now went into winter-quarters. Two legions were camped on the frontiers of the Treviri, two among the Lingones; the remaining six at Agendicum (Sens) in the land of the Senones. The legions were thus within better supporting distance of each other, in lieu of isolated, as they had been the year before. Corn having been provided in abundance and stored in safety, Caesar himself set out for Italy, feeling that his army was safe from insurrections for some months.

The operations of this year are characterized by the able and rapid dispositions and manoeuvres of Caesar against the equally subtle work of Ambiorix in northeast Gaul. The campaign was accompanied by thorough devastation of the country, but in this instance the devastation was not only not an unusual act, but it may perhaps be claimed to be the only means of subduing the tribes actually in revolt. Such measures have to be judged, even at that day, by the attendant circumstances. What on one occasion was a simple act of war, on another occasion might be an act of simple barbarity.

The one point of criticism in this year's operations is the carelessness of Cicero at Aduatuca, which Caesar felt called on gravely to rebuke. As good fortune would have it, no great evil came of it, but it might well have resulted in another Sabinus affair.

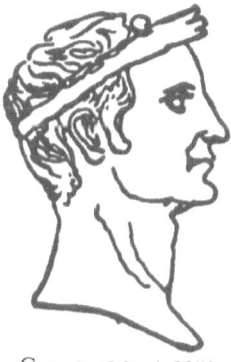

CAESAR, FROM A COIN

CHAPTER 15
Vercingetorix
Winter 53-52 B. C.

Gaul had apparently been reduced; Caesar could look back on a good six years' work. But Gaul was really ripe for a fresh revolt, for the Roman yoke was bitter. No one was habitually left by Caesar in supreme command while he was absent; the Gauls had free play. They rose under Vercingetorix, a man of remarkable ability and breadth, and before Caesar could rejoin his legions they had cut off his access to them. The outlook was desperate; so soon as Caesar reached the Province, he saw his dilemma. The province was threatened; but by activity he was able sufficiently to protect it. By a bold and difficult winter march across the Cebenna mountains with a few *cohorts*, Caesar attracted the attention of Vercingetorix, who, surprised at his audacity, advanced to meet him. Upon this, Caesar with a mere escort of horse pushed through the gap the enemy had opened, and by riding night and day kept well ahead of danger, rejoined his legions, and concentrated them at Agendicum in February. He had a critical war on his hands. Vercingetorix, finding that Caesar had eluded him, retraced his steps to the Liger. Caesar advanced from Agendicum south, taking Vellaunodunum and Genabum.

When Caesar reached Cisalpine Gaul, he heard of the intestine turmoils in Rome, of the murder of Clodius, and the report that all the youth had been ordered to take the military oath, or in other words to report for duty with the eagles. He therefore felt warranted in ordering a general draft in Cisalpine Gaul and the Province. His six years' campaign had borne good fruit. To all appearance Gaul had been subdued and her neighbours in Germany and Britain taught not to interfere with her internal economies. Rumours of these grave troubles in Roman politics had also reached Gaul, and though this country had been fully tranquillized, the quiet was but skin deep. No

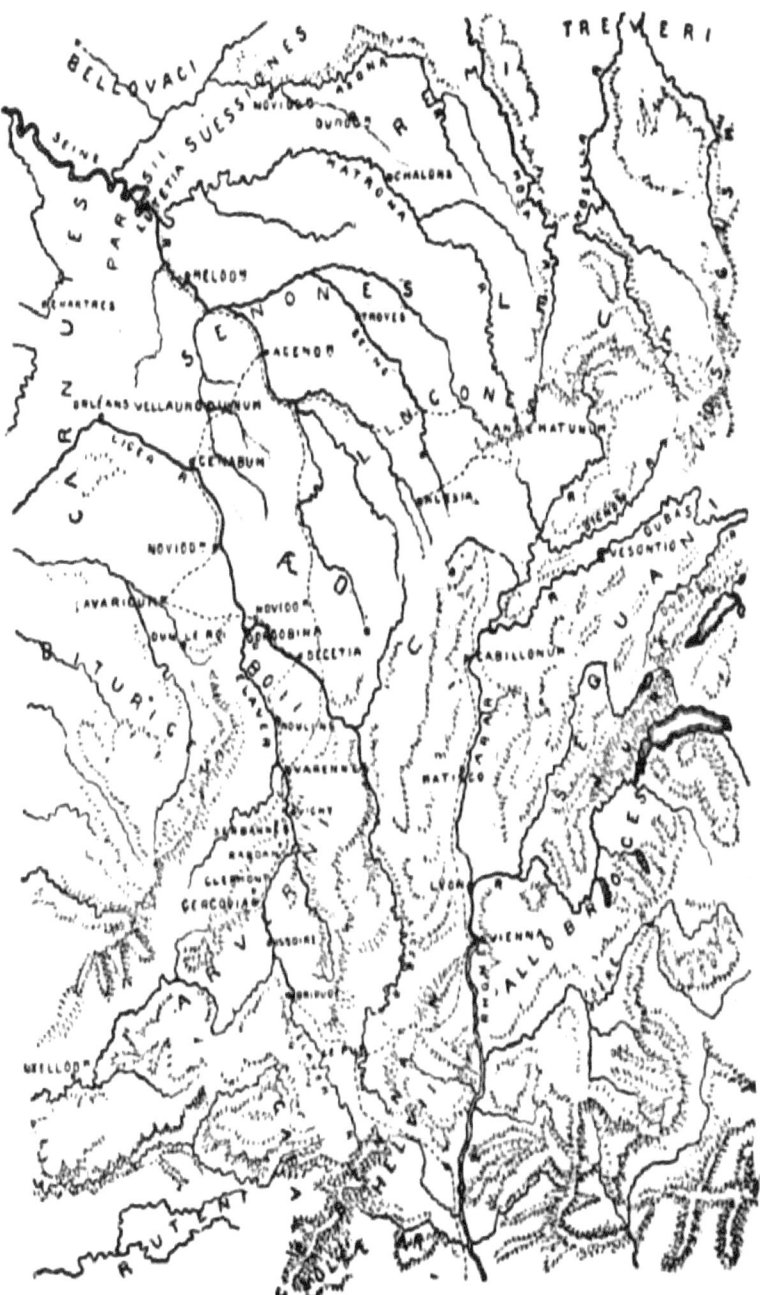

Central Gaul

sooner had Caesar's back been turned than the chiefs of the leading tribes began conspiring to rid their country of the burden of the Roman people. This was a favourable season, as Caesar, they thought, would be obliged to remain in Italy to protect his own interests in the home government; a necessity they deemed of far greater consequence to him than the allegiance of Gaul.

The conspirators met in secret and retired places; they discussed their grievances; they made especial complaint of the cruel death of Acco, and other leading Gauls; they foresaw the possibility of a similar fate befalling themselves; they denounced the devastation of their land; they bewailed the yoke put upon their country, and they bound themselves with a solemn oath to die, if need be, in freeing her. It was planned to attack, or at least blockade, the Roman camps before Caesar could return, and to try to cut him off from return by waylaying him on the road. This seemed all the more easy to accomplish because these chieftains knew that not one of the legions could move its camp without Caesar's personal orders,—it was not Caesar's custom to leave any special officer in full command,—and with the roads beset, Caesar could not himself reach the legions without an escorting army.

That there should be no one left in supreme command during Caesar's absence strikes us as a singularly weak method. Lack of positive rules of rank and command had more than once brought about disastrous results; but this custom, as well as the constant rotation in command among Roman officers, appears to have wrought less injury than might be expected. It worked, barely worked, in the Roman army; in no other army could such a system have worked at all.

The Carnutes, who had been most seriously struck by the death of Acco, were first under arms and agreed to begin the war, providing the other tribes would sustain them. An oath so to do was taken by all, and was pledged on their military standards in the most solemn manner. Accordingly, on the day set for the insurrection, under command of Cotuatus and Conetodunus, two desperate men, the Carnutes rendezvoused at Genabum (perhaps Orleans, but more likely Gien, to the east of Orleans) and massacred all the Romans, mostly traders, in the place. Among them was C. Fusius Cita, Caesar's commissary of this department.

The intelligence of this act travelled like lightning. It is said to have reached the Arverni (Auvergne), in other words, to have gone from Genabum to Gergovia, one hundred and sixty miles through the valleys of the Loire and Allier, from sunrise to the end of the first watch, nine a. m. The news was passed along by men stationed in towers on convenient hills, who gave out shouts of peculiar kinds, or as it is phrased "sonorous monosyllables." The habit of thus conveying intelligence continued in Gaul through the Middle Ages. Some remains of these towers still exist. If the wind was contrary, fire was employed in lieu of the voice. Similar' means have been used in many lands and ages. It is a natural thing to do. Signalling is very old; but alphabetical signalling is of quite recent origin.

Vercingetorix, a young, intelligent and powerful chief, born in Gergovia,—son of Celtillus the Arvernian who had been put to death for aspiring to the sovereignty of all Gaul,—excited the passions of his subjects and caused them to rise against their Roman tyrants. The older chiefs did not deem the movement opportune, for the Arverni had long been faithful allies of Rome. They caused Vercingetorix to be expelled from Gergovia, their chief fortress. But Vercingetorix was not to be so readily turned from his purpose. He called to his standard all the poor and desperate, and many of the young and ambitious; and in a short period of time grew so strong that he drove out all the other chiefs and established himself in Gergovia. Saluted as king, he won the ear of all the neighbouring tribes along the Liger to the sea, and even beyond that river,—Senones, Parisii, Pictones, Cadurci, Turones, Aulerci, Lemnovices,—and was chosen chief leader of the uprising. The Ædui declined to take part, and kept some of the tribes east of the Liger from joining in the insurrection.

Vercingetorix' army grew apace, though his discipline was so severe and cruel that he is said often to have forced recruits into his ranks from fear of death or mayhem. In one fashion or another, at all events, he assembled an army of vast numbers, which was especially excellent in cavalry. The infantry was not so good, but the horse was increased in numbers by mixing light troops with the squadrons.

Vercingetorix was undoubtedly a man of exceptional ability. His time, as it turned out, was inopportune, but this error can scarcely be attributed to want of judgment. At that moment, neither he nor any person could foresee how much more dangerous for the Romans and promising of success to his countrymen an uprising would be, if put off a few years, until Caesar was so deeply engaged in the Civil War that he could not personally come to Gaul. Fortunate indeed for Caesar, that so strong an adversary as Vercingetorix should not have delayed his action until after the final rupture with Pompey.

Vercingetorix opened his campaign by sending a force under the

Cadurcan Lucterius into the land of the Ruteni in southern Gaul, while he himself marched on the Bituriges south of the Liger, who had not joined his cause. The latter sent for aid to the Ædui, the ever faithful allies of Rome, who dispatched a force to their assistance. On arriving at the Liger, which is the boundary of the Ædui, this force heard, or the anti-Romans in it pretended to hear, that the Bituriges had treacherously planned to attack them; and, acting on this ground, returned home. The Bituriges then joined Vercingetorix.

Caesar heard of these things while in Italy. Pompey and he had again placed affairs in Rome on a basis satisfactory to both, and Caesar was enabled to leave. But so soon as he reached Cisalpine Gaul, perhaps at the Rhone, he perceived his dilemma. He was quite at a loss how to join his army. The Gallic chieftains had been shrewd in their plans. He could not send for the legions. He could get no messengers through to any one of his camps, nor indeed direct their movements. Isolated as they were, they might each be cut to pieces in detail if they attempted to move, and before they could concentrate. They had no special head on whom he could rely to do the wisest thing under the circumstances. Nor could he go to the legions, for he dare not trust himself to any one, the disaffection had become so general.

Meanwhile Lucterius had gained over the Ruteni and the Nitiobriges and Gabali, adjoining tribes, and was preparing to make a descent on Narbo, in the province near the coast. But Caesar was fertile in expedients. His restless nature recognized no impossibilities. Like all great soldiers he rose to the occasion, and gained in strength as the dangers thickened. He set out for Narbo, and reaching the place,—as he readily could, for the province was in no wise associated with the uprising,—he took the reins in hand.

Caesar's appearance restored confidence; he garrisoned Narbo, and by encouraging the populations nearby, raised a sufficient body of recruits to enable him to protect the border towns along the Tarnis River, adjoining the Ruteni, and those among the Volcae Arecomici and Tolosates. He thus made it impossible for Lucterius to invade the Province, for the front presented to him was too bold to promise lasting results.

Having secured the left flank of the province front, Caesar moved northward towards the Helvii, where he had meanwhile ordered to assemble a number of recruits from Italy and some forces from the province. He feared that Vercingetorix would move against his legions, and he planned to attract his attention away from them and towards himself. Something must be done to draw the Gallic leader near the

THE PROVINCE

province, where he could be neutralized. Caesar saw that he must undertake some daring operation to arrest the notice of Vercingetorix, if he would gain a chance to reach his army; and though the snow was six feet deep, he marched his troops with incredible labour and sufferings across the Cebenna mountains,—substantially up the Ardèche and down the Loire valleys by modern Aps, Aubenas, and St. Cirgues,—debouched into the territory of the Arverni towards Le Puy, and advanced to Brioude. He then sent his cavalry forward to cut a wide swath through the land to inspire dread and terror.

Dumfounded at seeing their land made the scene of war in lieu of the province, as well as at the sight of a fully equipped army emerging from mountains which not even an individual had ever before attempted to cross in winter, the Arverni cried aloud to Vercingetorix for aid. The latter left the Bituriges question to settle itself, and with his best troops moved by forced marches towards the Roman army. Caesar's diversion had lured Vercingetorix away from where he was

CAESAR'S MARCH TO HIS LEGIONS

most useful to his cause. Leaving the younger Brutus in command, with orders to use his cavalry in vigorous scouting and to keep restlessly on the move, Caesar himself hurried to Vienna on the Rhone; there, finding some cavalry which had been newly recruited, and had at his orders assembled in this town, he placed himself at their head, set out and marched day and night through the land of the Ædui to that of the Lingones, where two of his legions were wintering at Andaematunum (Langres). He had thrust aside a danger which menaced his entire scheme of conquest by a markedly fine diversion; he had, without a moment's hesitation, run a serious personal risk,—which, however, was unavoidable, and therefore advisable,—and had completely baffled the enemy. He was now safe. He had travelled so rapidly that he had kept ahead of the danger of discovery. From Andaematunum Caesar sent orders to the two legions among the Treviri to move towards him, so as again to gather his forces into one body. The other six had wintered at Agendicum, among the Senones. At this place he summarily rendezvoused all the legions. These exceedingly rapid and well conceived movements puzzled the Gauls as to his intentions, and forestalled any of the tribes engaged in the plot in an attack which they might otherwise have made on the legions during their concentration. Caesar reached Agendicum about the end of February. One cannot admire his conduct of this affair too highly.

Hearing that Caesar was thus concentrating, Vercingetorix moved back to the land of the Bituriges, and thence to Gergobina Bojorum (St. Parize le Chatel) at the confluence of the Liger and Elaver, which he determined to attack. This was the capital of the Boii, who had remained faithful to Rome. They had been settled there by Caesar after their defeat in the Helvetian campaign. It was a difficult task for Caesar to undertake a winter campaign, as the transportation of supplies was almost impossible; one can scarcely imagine how bad the few roads there were could be; but everything must be risked, lest the allied tribes should lose confidence in Rome, and, still more important, lose confidence in Caesar, which they would be sure to do if he allowed one of their chief towns to be taken. He concluded to rely largely on the good will of the Ædui to keep him supplied with corn.

Having got his forces well in hand, he left two legions and the baggage at Agendicum, and moved towards the Boii, hoping to keep them in allegiance by extending to them his protection. He sent forward messengers to encourage them to stout resistance and assure them of his speedy arrival. Coming on the second day after starting to Vellaunodunum (Triguères), he made arrangements to capture it, as he not only needed it for a storehouse, but could not leave it in the enemy's hands in his rear. In two days Caesar had drawn up his lines of contravallation, and the town, seeing plainly that resistance would be useless, capitulated, and gave up its arms and six hundred hostages. Leaving Trebonius to complete the surrender, Caesar marched

AGENDICUM TO AVARICUM

without delay on Genabum of the Carnutes. This, as above said, was probably modern Gien, though generally assumed to be Orleans. In pushing for Gergobina, which he aimed quickly to reach, it would be much out of Caesar's way and over a bad tract of country to march to Orleans, and as it was not essential to do so, he would not be likely at this moment to vary from his straight course. Moreover, Gien is a better location for an *oppidum*, being on a hill, while Orleans is on a slope. This town, Genabum, the Carnutes had not yet garrisoned, as they expected Caesar would be delayed a long time at Vellaunodunum, whereas he reached Genabum, much to the surprise of the inhabitants, in two days after Vellaunodunum had capitulated, when they had barely received news of the fact. He could scarcely have reached Orleans, hampered by his considerable trains, which is fifty miles as the crow flies, in this short time—another argument in favour of Gien. The population at midnight endeavoured to escape across the Liger, nearby, over which there was a bridge, but Caesar had already detailed two legions to observe the town; and the inhabitants, being much delayed at the bridge on account of its narrowness, were prevented from escaping and driven back into the place. Caesar entered the town and gave it up to pillage, as punishment for the recent murder of Romans within its walls. Thence he marched south on Noviodunum (Sancerre) and Avaricum of the Bituriges (Bourges).

GALLIC HORSEMAN
(FROM A TERRA-COTTA STATUETTE)

CHAPTER 16

Avaricum
Late Winter and Early Spring, 52 B. C.

Vercingetorix sought to interfere with Caesar's siege of Noviodunum, but to no effect. He conceived the idea that it was unwise to risk battle with the Romans; that more could be accomplished by a system of small-war. This was a remarkable plan of campaign for a barbarian. It is what gave Fabius his fame in the second Punic War. The Gauls burned their crops and towns to prevent Caesar from victualling his army. Avaricum alone in that section was spared. This town (Bourges) had but one approach. Here Caesar began siege works and built a mound. Vercingetorix tried to raise the siege by harassing the Roman army. He suffered much from the jealousies and dissensions of the allied tribes, but his ability and character sufficed to hold them together. The Gauls ably managed the siege. The wall, built up of logs, stones and earth, was strong and tough. Sallies were made with considerable success, still there was but one end possible; the place was taken and forty thousand souls perished. Caesar found on hand much corn. Labienus was sent from here against the Parisii. Vercingetorix, foreseeing Caesar's plans, sought to defend the line of the Elaver, but Caesar cleverly stole a passage, and marched on Gergovia.

Vercingetorix, on hearing of the havoc Caesar was playing with his allied towns, gave up the siege of Gergobina and moved forward to meet the Romans. Caesar had just completed the siege of Noviodunum. The inhabitants were in the act of delivering up hostages, horses and arms to the centurions, when the arrival of Vercingetorix' cavalry van-guard was seen in the distance. Encouraged by this apparent relief, a certain party of citizens again resorted to arms, shut the gates, manned the walls and refused to surrender. They were with difficulty suppressed, though the centurions receiving the surrender behaved with consummate skill. At the same time Caesar, by a smart attack of his cavalry, drove back the van of the Gauls with considerable loss. In the combat his native cavalry came near to being beaten, but a body of four hundred Germans newly recruited proved equal to their reputation, and by their vigorous and unusual tactics turned the tide.

Vercingetorix retired, and Caesar marched to Avaricum, the best fortified town of the Bituriges. He proposed to besiege it, in the belief that its capture would reduce all the region to obedience. The name Avaricum comes from the River Avara (Euse); Bourges is a relic of Bituriges.

Vercingetorix, who was by long odds the strongest opponent Caesar ever had in Gaul, was taught by the failures at Vellaunodunum, Genabum and Noviodunum, that he could not deal with Caesar in open warfare. He convoked an assembly of the tribes, and informed the chiefs that, in order to win success, he must undertake a system of small-war, so as, if possible, to cut the Romans off from rations and forage for their beasts, the want of which latter would render Caesar's cavalry more or less harmless. By self-sacrifice alone could they save Gaul from Roman oppression. They must burn and destroy their own farms and villages; everything not beyond capture from its defences or position must be made unavailable to the enemy. This course would oblige the Romans to send to a distance to gather supplies, and Vercingetorix could then fall upon their detachments and beat them in detail. So long as the legions could keep together, there was no Gallic courage or discipline which could cope with them.

This plan, however severely it fell on his own people, was full of wisdom in regard to the enemy. With a sufficiency of victual in his own rear, Vercingetorix proposed to starve out the Roman armies. As much credit is due to this barbarian chief for his masterly conception of the proper means of opposing Caesar's legions as was due to Fabius for the same method of meeting the victorious *phalanxes* of Hannibal. The plan was the more easy for the barbarians to carry out, as they scoured the country to a much greater extent than the soldiers of Caesar; were more familiar with its resources and topography, and had the population on their side.

Acting on the scheme thus devised for them by Vercingetorix, the Bituriges began to destroy all the towns and provisions which could possibly fall into the Roman possession. It was a hard lot, but they preferred this loss to the prospect of death themselves, and the sale of their wives and daughters into slavery—a certain fate, as they believed, if Caesar should now succeed in conquering the land. Twenty towns were burned in one day. Almost alone and after long debate, Avaricum was spared on account of its exceptional situation for defence, and a proper garrison was thrown into the town. And, at a distance of fifteen miles, Vercingetorix camped with his army in a spot defended by woods and marshes, probably near Dun-le-roy, at the confluence of the Taisseau and Auron, some eighteen miles southeast of Avaricum. The marshes have now dried up and the streams have been narrowed. He did not dare to interfere with the siege of Avaricum, but closely watched the operations of the Romans, faithfully scouted the neighbourhood, attacked their foraging parties whenever he could safely do so, and kept well posted in all their movements. He "received intelligence every hour in the day."

Avaricum, in the middle of an extended level stretch of country, was surrounded on north and east and west by marshy rivers, the modern Yèvres, Yèvrette and Auron, affluents of the Liger, and the marsh they produced. It had but one narrow approach on the southwest. This is now much wider than it used to be. The rivers of Bourges have gradually been canalled, a work which has broadened the strip of land, while constant accretions have raised the level of its slopes. The entire marsh

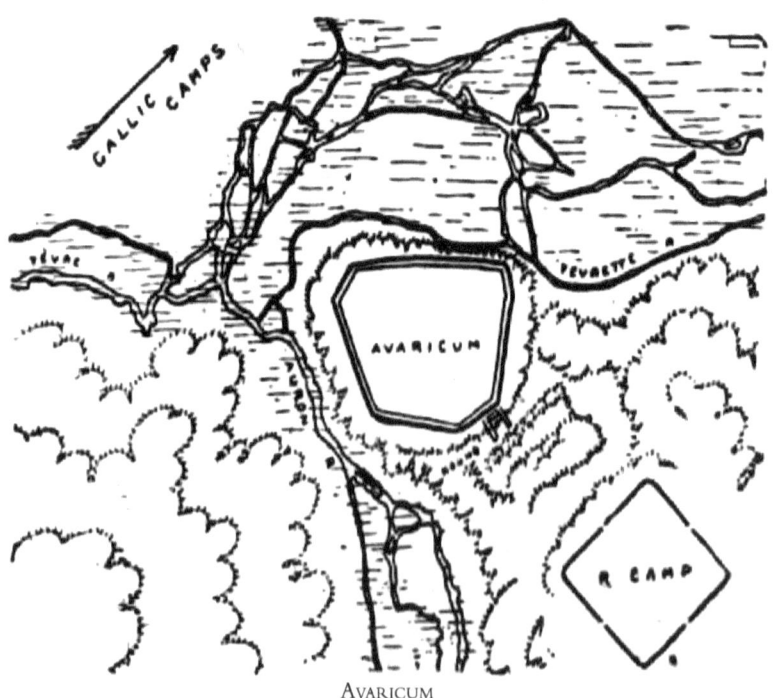

AVARICUM

has by the industry of generations been reclaimed, and rich fields and gardens now occupy its site. The plateau descends to these low-lying fields in a gentle grade. The general height of the plateau above the meadows is still what Caesar gives it, but its edges are less abrupt.

Avaricum had forty thousand souls. Caesar camped between the Auron and Yèvrette, on an eminence half a mile from the gates. The site of his camp is now, appropriately enough, occupied by a government gun-foundry and shop, and by other military establishments. Between the camp and town was a depression in the ground protecting the latter like a huge ditch. This has now been filled up to accommodate modern structures, though it can still be traced, if carefully sought. Caesar began the erection of a terrace, *vineae* and two towers. Owing to the marshes, a line of contravallation was neither feasible nor necessary. He must attack along the narrow approach, which was not over four hundred feet wide. The top of the wall of Avaricum was eighty feet higher than the floor of the ravine.

Vercingetorix carried out his small-war programme well. The Romans could not go far to forage without being attacked. Rations began to fail; the Ædui, growing lax in their fealty, were by no means prompt in furnishing corn; the Boii were poor; foraging was an altogether uncertain resource, now that the country was devastated. Still, the soldiers bore their deprivations well. Caesar not infrequently consulted the wishes of his army, as a matter of policy as well as precedent. Now, in his anxiety for the welfare of his legions, he went so far as to offer to raise the siege if the men felt that their hardships were too great; the answer came promptly, an emphatic "No." They would avenge the manes of their comrades at any cost. Thus rings with no uncertain sound the voice of all soldiers who recognize the great captain in their chief.

While the siege was progressing, and it was pressed with all vigour, Vercingetorix, from his camp to the south, approached near to Avaricum and camped on its northwest. He hoped for some chance to deal the Romans a blow. With his horse and the attendant light foot he soon after made his way to a place which the Roman foragers were wont to pass in going out on this daily duty, hoping to catch a large party of them in an ambush. Caesar fortunately learned of this attempt.

We do not hear much of the details of Caesar's scouting and spy system, but he was generally so well informed of what went on in the enemy's camp that we can but draw the conclusion that he had organized an effective "secret service" system.

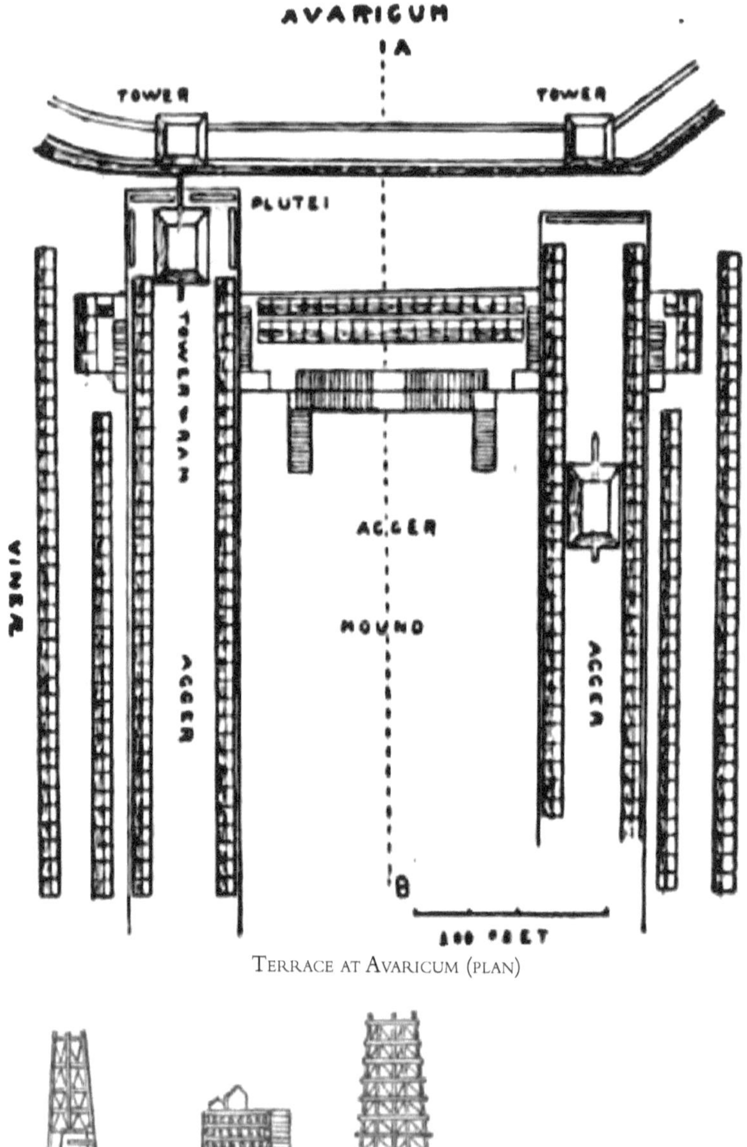

TERRACE AT AVARICUM (PLAN)

TERRACE AT AVARICUM (SECTION ON LINE A-6)

Caesar set out at midnight with the bulk of his force to checkmate the scheme of the barbarian leader by attacking his camp in his absence, where no person, he heard, was left in absolute command. On reaching the place he "ordered the baggage to be piled and the arms to be got ready," in other words, prepared for battle. Vercingetorix had placed his camp on a height surrounded by the Avaricum morass, where it was but fifty feet wide; had broken down the bridges leading to it, and occupied the few fords in force. On reconnoitring it, Caesar found the position so strong, that he sensibly declined an unequal combat from which nothing could be gained. The soldiers, not recognizing the dangers of the ground, demanded battle, but Caesar showed them that it would be too costly in life, and as he had already accomplished his aim in forestalling the ambush of Vercingetorix, it was not worth the doing. The army returned to the siege.

On the return to camp of Vercingetorix, the failure to bring the Romans to a fight on unequal terms, his having gone off with the cavalry just before Caesar appeared before the camp, and the general delay in affairs, raised a clamour against him among his fickle-minded Gallic allies, who accused him of treacherously playing into Caesar's hands. But this accusation and feeling Vercingetorix, by representing his case and prospects with great cleverness, managed to turn aside, and, indeed, change into so favourable a sentiment, that the Gauls determined to send ten thousand men to Avaricum, lest the Bituriges alone should reap all the glory of defeating Caesar. Still, the difference between the hearty cooperation of Caesar's legionaries, and the suspicious and jealous dissensions in the camp of Vercingetorix was marked, and made the chances run all the more in favour of the Romans. That Vercingetorix was able to hold these conflicting elements together redounds much to his credit.

The Gauls ably managed the defence of Avaricum. They opposed the Roman method of sieges with great ingenuity. The mural hooks and rams used by the Romans to pull and batter down the walls they would catch with a noose, and drag into the town. They undermined the Roman mound, at which work they were expert, as there were many iron and copper miners in the country; they raised towers as high as the Romans on the threatened side of their wall, and covered the woodwork with skins; they set the *vineae* on fire by nocturnal sallies; they made sorties every day, and impeded the work greatly by throwing sharp stakes, stones and hot pitch upon the besiegers. A civilized garrison could scarcely have done the defence greater justice.

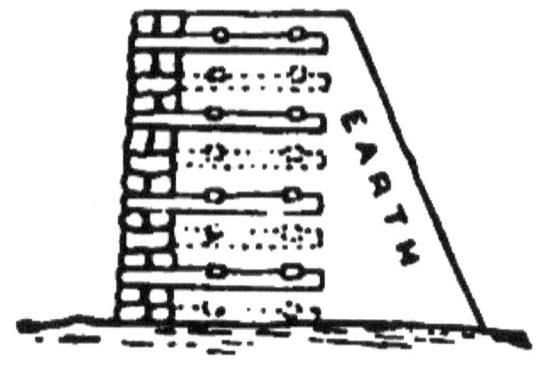

SECTION

PLAN OF ONE LAYER

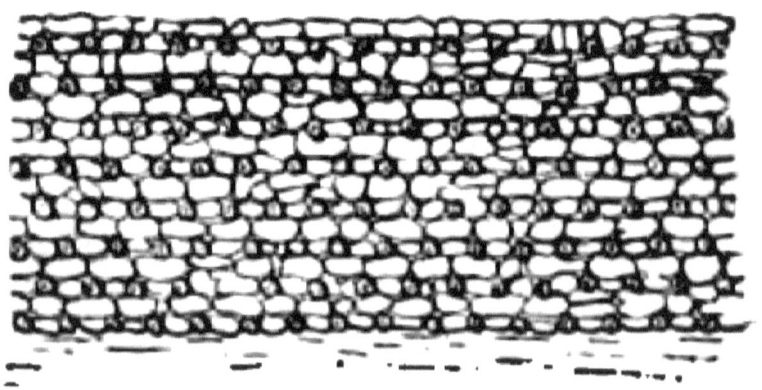

ELEVATION

GALLIC WALL

The Gallic wall, of heavy logs and stones, was peculiarly difficult to attack with battering-ram or fire. The logs were laid across the line of the wall, two feet apart, and held in place by heavy cross logs mortised together. These were packed with earth, and the ends of the logs at the outer side of the wall were held in place with the stones which made its facing. The stone protected the walls from fire; the ends of the logs would only char, and the logs and earth, from their greater elasticity, resisted the rams far better than stone alone could do. The wall had to be broken down piecemeal; it would not tumble together.

Still, the legions persevered, despite wet and cold, and in twenty-five days had raised a mound three hundred and thirty feet broad and eighty feet high. These figures are disputed by some critics, though given by the *Commentaries*. They are not exceptional, and the topography bears them out. When the mound had all but reached the enemy's walls, it began to sink. It had been undermined, and was, moreover, fired from the mine. This occurred at midnight, when Caesar happened to be making a tour of inspection, and at the same moment a vigorous sally from two gates on each side of the tower was made by the besieged. The Avaricans threw torches, pitch, dry wood and other inflammables on the towers and terrace. Two legions were generally on guard at night, and these were taken unawares. The fight lasted all night. The pent-houses were destroyed, and the Romans for a while had to march to and fro from the towers without cover. The besieged now saw a good chance of victory.

Caesar here mentions an occurrence which enables us to compare ancient with modern gallantry under fire:

"There happened in my own view a circumstance which, having appeared to be worthy of record, we thought it ought not to be omitted. A certain Gaul before the gate of the town, who was casting into the fire opposite the turret balls of tallow and fire which were passed along to him, was pierced with a dart on the right side and fell dead. One of those next him stepped over him as he lay, and discharged the same office; when the second man was slain in the same manner by a wound from a cross-bow, a third succeeded him, and a fourth succeeded the third; nor was this post left vacant by the besieged, until, the fire of the mound having been extinguished and the enemy repulsed in every direction, an end was put to the fighting."

It seems that three men or more were shot down at their post, and that the post was at once filled by fresh men. This is mentioned as an exceptional piece of courage. In our day we have seen many such. Entire colour-guards have not infrequently been shot down in battle; but there has never been a lack of men eager to take their places.

The sortie was, after a fierce struggle, beaten back. The Gallic soldiers in the city now formed a project of leaving the town by retiring across the marshes in its rear by night, and making for the camp of Vercingetorix; but the clamour of the women, who were to be left behind to the tender mercies of the besiegers, gave notice to the Romans of this evasion, and, for fear of being cut off, the garrison desisted.

Next day, a heavy rain coming on, the ramparts of the town were carelessly guarded. Caesar, perceiving this, quietly made his preparations, sharply advanced the towers and ordered the walls to be scaled, offering great rewards to those who first mounted them. The Romans broke from cover with exceptional energy, and assaulted in good form. The enemy, surprised and disconcerted, was driven in; but with admirable constancy drew up in the market-place in wedges (or close order), determined to resist to the end. And here no doubt they would have stubbornly fought; but when they saw the Romans moving along the walls so as to surround all who should be left in the city, the columns dissolved, and each man sought his individual safety in flight. Most fled to the northern extremity of the *oppidum*. Thus broken up, the Gauls lost head; and having thrown away their arms, the Romans had them at their mercy, and cut them down remorselessly, sparing neither age nor sex. What the infantry could not reach fell at the hands of the cavalry. Out of forty thousand men, women and children, barely eight hundred escaped across the marshes to Vercingetorix' camp. The Gallic chief received and distributed them among the several divisions of his army, lest in one body their sad tale should breed a mutiny.

Once again, Vercingetorix had a hard task in reconciling his fellow-citizens to this disaster; and nothing shows the native ability of this remarkable man better than the way in which, under the stress of misfortune, he kept his ascendancy over this fickle, unreasonable people. "As ill success weakens the authority of other generals, so on the contrary his dignity increased daily, though a loss had been sustained." Vercingetorix now advised the Gauls to imitate the Roman method and to fortify their camps. This counsel they followed and thenceforward continued to do. He also by skilful appeals to the neighbouring tribes succeeded in winning all over to his cause, and very shortly replaced the troops lost at Avaricum with a still larger force. Especially a fine body of cavalry came to him under Teutomatus, prince of the Nitiobriges. But though he would have been backed up by public

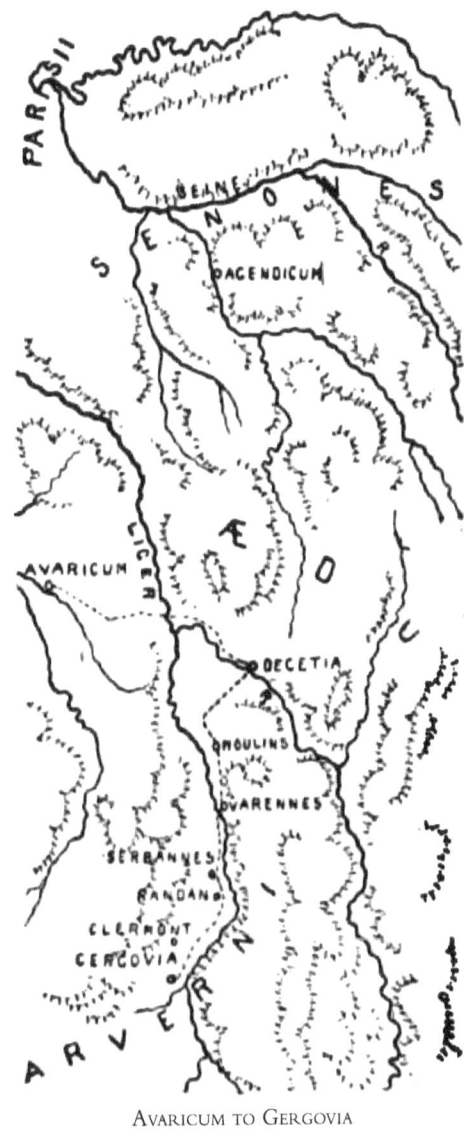

AVARICUM TO GERGOVIA

sentiment in an offensive policy, this barbarian chief refrained from an attack on Caesar's lines. He wisely kept to small-war.

Caesar found in Avaricum also a large supply of corn and provender, and gave his army a much needed, well-earned rest. The spring and the time for more active operations were at hand, when the Ædui sent urgent messages to Caesar praying him to come to their assistance, as there had arisen a serious division in the state, two parties respectively under Cotus and Convictolitavis, both of high lineage and much power, claiming the government, which was governed by an annual chief magistrate. Caesar was loath to leave operations against Vercingetorix, whom he now hoped either to drive from the forest retreats to which he had retired, or else to close in and trap. But Caesar could neither allow danger to lurk in his rear, nor temporize with the fealty of the Ædui. He therefore turned backward. It was through their land that his line of operations ran from his base, in the Province. If the Ædui were to waver in their allegiance, it would become a question of subsistence and not strategy. It was they kept his granary full of corn. They were indeed an intermediate base. Arrived among this people,—at Decetia (Decize) on the Liger,—Caesar sent for the senate of the Ædui to meet him, and not only decided the matter in dispute by making Cotus, who had but a minority at his back, resign, and by placing the government in the hands of Convictolitavis, whom the priests favoured; but he induced the Ædui to promise ten thousand infantry and all their horse for him to use in garrisons along his line of operations, to protect the trains of corn which they should forward him.

Having shelved this danger, Caesar sent Labienus with four legions, two from the army and the two left at Agendicum, against the Senones and Parisii (or Lutetii), who had been roused by Vercingetorix; while he, with the six remaining, marched on Gergovia in the land of the Arverni, proposing to besiege it. The Arverni, though they had long been faithful allies of Rome, were now the centre of the rebellion. The cavalry was divided between Labienus and Caesar. What Vercingetorix had been doing during Caesar's absence is not told us. It looks as if he had retired into the hills and woods of the Bituriges, and had been watching his opponent. On learning Caesar's direction, he guessed his objective and betook himself to the farther (left) bank of the Elaver (Allier), and occupied it before Caesar reached the right bank. This movement shows that Vercingetorix, too, had either the true instincts of the soldier, or else possessed an equally good corps of scouts and spies. His manoeuvre placed him athwart Caesar's path. He was intent on barring the Romans from approach to Gergovia, and he took care to break down all the bridges over the river. The Elaver is still a good-sized stream; it was then a mighty bulwark of his territory, and he must keep it intact at all hazards. This river was not then fordable except in the low-water season in autumn, and it was essential to Caesar to cross without delay—unless he was to acknowledge that Vercingetorix could force him to change his plans. He moved up the river, struck it near modern Moulins—from Decetia was an old Gaulish road which led to Moulins and was later made a Roman road—and sought a chance to cross. From day to day Vercingetorix moved exactly as far as the Romans moved, and camped opposite to them at night.

Caesar saw that he must resort to some stratagem to cross. Having camped one night at one of the broken bridges, most likely near Varennes, Caesar next morning sent forward only two thirds of the army and all the baggage, ordering it to march in six corps, and in such order as to appear to be the entire force of six legions. With two legions he remained behind in hiding in the woods well back of the river. Vercingetorix followed the moving column on the other side up the river. So soon as the enemy was out of the way, Caesar emerged from his hiding-place, and speedily rebuilt the bridge on the old piles which had been left standing, crossed to the left bank and entrenched a bridgehead; having done which he sent on and recalled the body which had marched ahead. This rejoined by stealing a march on Vercingetorix during the coming night. Vercingetorix, when he saw that he had been outwitted and knew that the whole Roman army had crossed, moved by forced marches on Gergovia, so as not to be brought to battle against his will.

This passage was skilfully accomplished. Caesar here earned as much credit for a clever strata-

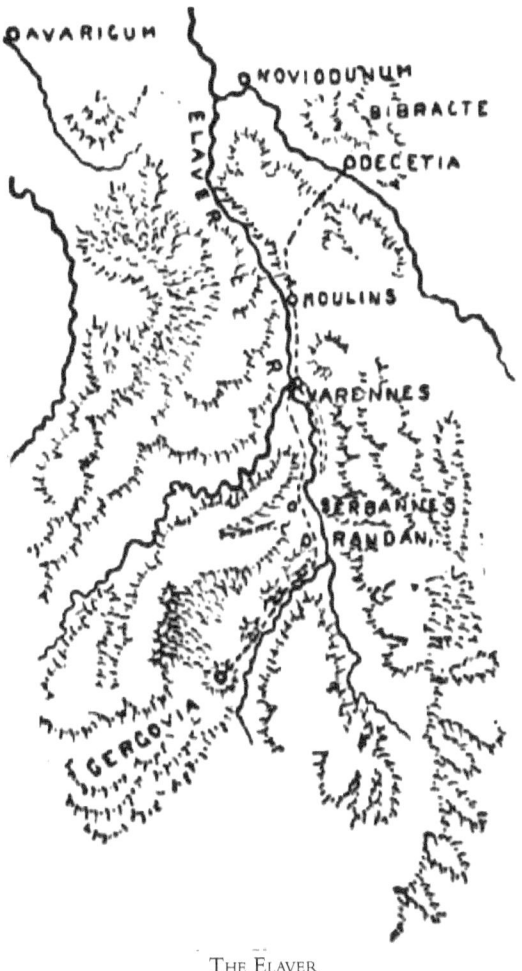

THE ELAVER

gem as Vercingetorix showed that he had been careless in scouting the river-banks. But we cannot too much praise the native ability of this barbarian chief, who without military education or example was able to do so much to oppose one of the greatest soldiers the world has ever seen. We cannot compare Caesar's operation at the Elaver to the passage of the Hydaspes by Alexander, or that of the Rhone by Hannibal. It was far from as distinguished an operation. But nevertheless it was skilful and well-conceived; and was so well executed as to deceive a very keen-eyed opponent.

CHAPTER 17

The Siege of Gergovia
Spring, 52 B. C.

The height of Gergovia stands twelve hundred feet above the plain, and has at the summit a plateau over a mile long. It could be attacked most easily from the south. Vercingetorix had drawn up his forces on this slope. So soon as the Romans arrived, cavalry skirmishes became common, but the Gallic infantry remained behind the defences. Caesar camped southeast of the town and later seized a hill on its south, entrenched a second camp, and joined the two camps by works. This cut the Gergovians off from the river, and made their water supply uncertain. The Ædui, Caesar's chief allies, had been giving him anxiety; rebellion now broke out in their army, which was on its way to join him. Caesar left Fabius in command at Gergovia, made a speedy march to the rear, brought the rebels to terms, and returned. In twenty-four hours, his column of four legions had marched fifty miles. After due consideration, Caesar determined to assault Gergovia. He laid his plans skilfully. Sending a force to make a demonstration against the west front, which the Gauls felt was not very strong, he drew all the Gallic troops to that quarter. He then suddenly threw forward his legions, which gallantly advanced and reached the very walls of the town. But they had not been furnished with scaling-ladders; few only mounted the top of the walls; the Gauls returned from the western front; Caesar was driven back with heavy loss. He essays to gloss over this defeat in the *Commentaries*, but the facts are plain. The Ædui now broke out into open revolt, and Caesar had to give over the siege. He had been roundly defeated.

In five days' march, the first one being short on account of the fatigue of the column which moved up the river and back, and the last one short because he reached Gergovia early in the day, Caesar arrived at the capital of the Arverni. The enemy opposed him only by a

GERGOVIA AND VICINITY

slight cavalry skirmish, and then retired to the upper slope of the very high hill on which the town was built, where, outside the wall of the *oppidum*, they camped.

The heights of Gergovia, four miles south of modern Clermont-Ferrand, stand boldly up twelve hundred feet above the plain. It has been rechristened its ancient name. At the top is a quadrangular plateau a mile long by over a third of a mile wide. On the north and east the slope was probably wooded; access to the plateau by a body of troops might have been difficult. The south slope is a succession of terraces rather wide and not over steep. These apparently were not wooded. On the west lie the heights of Risolles, whose top is only one hundred feet lower than Gergovia and is connected with it by a neck of land. Two other hills, Monts Rognon and Puy Giroux, flank the Risolles, and are north-west and southwest of Gergovia respectively. On the south, like a huge buttress, is the Roche Blanche, a long and narrow hill, with rocky face on the south and east, and easy slopes elsewhere, about five hundred feet below the plateau of Gergovia. The Auzon flows south of Gergovia, and falls into the Allier. On the northwest runs a small brook. On the east was a large shallow lake, now drained. On the south and southeast, Gergovia was thought to be most accessible to attack.

Caesar established his main camp on high and healthful ground south of the lake, perhaps one hundred feet above the plain. The Auzon ran behind his camp. It was certainly a task of some danger to attempt to take Gergovia by storm until Vercingetorix' army was disposed of, and Caesar must get together victual in abundance before he could blockade or besiege it.

Descriptions and pictures of Gergovia are somewhat misleading. One is apt to conceive of a rocky eminence with top palisaded by nature and practically inaccessible. The north slope is wont to be described as impossible to capture. It is not so. The slope is not steep, though it is long. The cultivation of many generations—it is now covered with rich fields and vineyards—may have softened the slopes, but it cannot have materially altered them. It is probable that in Caesar's day the slope was concealed by woods, and that he did not reconnoitre it thoroughly. But the position could have been surprised on the north far more easily than assaulted on the south. So far from being, as it is generally said to be, inexpugnable, the men who captured Lookout Mountain, or who charged with Pickett up Cemetery Ridge, would have laughed at the idea. But ancient warfare was different.

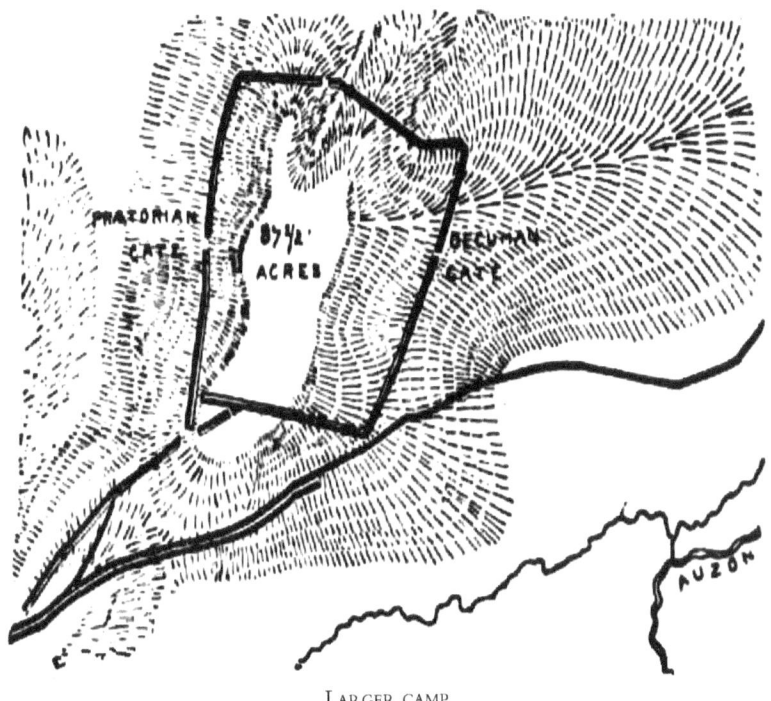

LARGER CAMP

The terraces of the southern slopes were no doubt more open, and it was on these terraces that Vercingetorix drew up his army, which was protected by a wall of heavy stones, six feet high, running along its front. Here Vercingetorix posted his allies, in order by tribes, in the most skilful manner, and daily exercised his troops—especially his cavalry mixed with light armed foot—in skirmishes with the Romans, so as to ascertain and improve their courage and discipline. These combats took place on the plains between Caesar's camp and the slopes of Gergovia; the barbarians debouching from the outlets of the south and east front of the *oppidum*.

Caesar soon discovered that a hill south of the town, and opposite the eminence on which was built Gergovia (Roche Blanche), was essential to the enemy. By its possession the Gauls were able to protect themselves in getting at their water, corn and forage, and here Vercingetorix had a small advanced post. He should have held it in heavier force. The hill in places was no doubt steeper in Caesar's day than it now is. Slides have since altered its slopes, but towards the plateau it could not have been steep. Caesar determined to capture this hill. By a carefully planned night attack he drove off the meagre garrison, and placing two legions in their stead, speedily entrenched a small camp upon it, and connected this hill with the main camp by a double trench, twelve feet wide, and a parapet, such that access from one to the other was secure. The two camps have been excavated. Their outlines are still distinct. This act of Caesar's cut the Gergovians off from their main supply of water, for the Auzon, to which they had been going by the glen road from the plateau, was not easily accessible from another place. They now had to rely on springs on the plateau, which still exist and are fed from the higher mountains to the west, and on the brook at the northwest of the town. On this side Caesar had made no demonstration.

Meanwhile the young Æduan nobles had been tampered with by the emissaries of Vercingetorix, who had contrived, by misrepresentations and gold, to abuse their minds about Caesar's intentions respecting their nation. Convictolitavis, even, whom Caesar had made chief of this

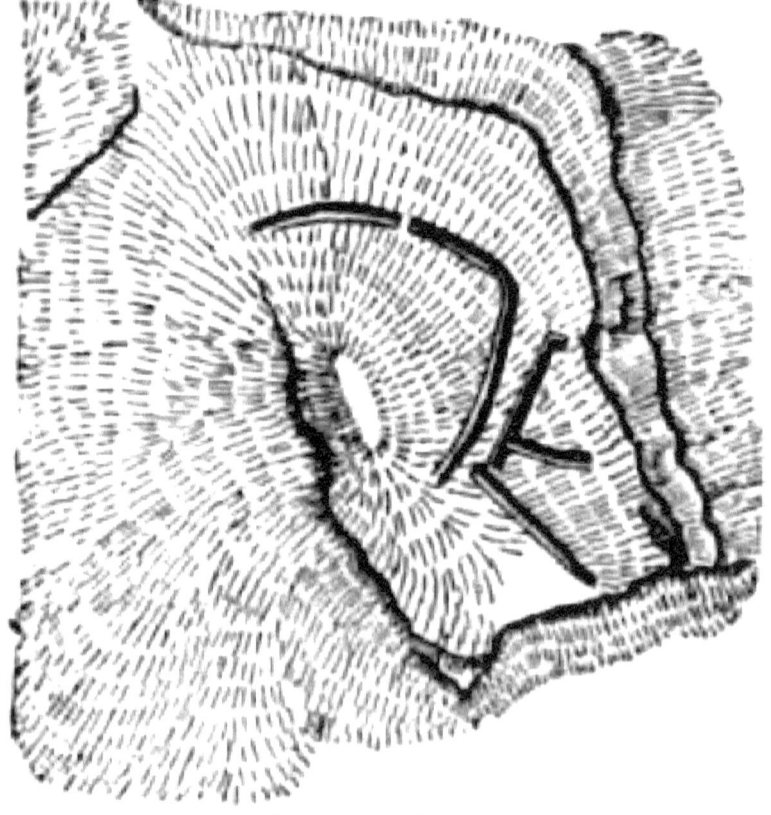

SMALL CAMP AT GERGOVIA.

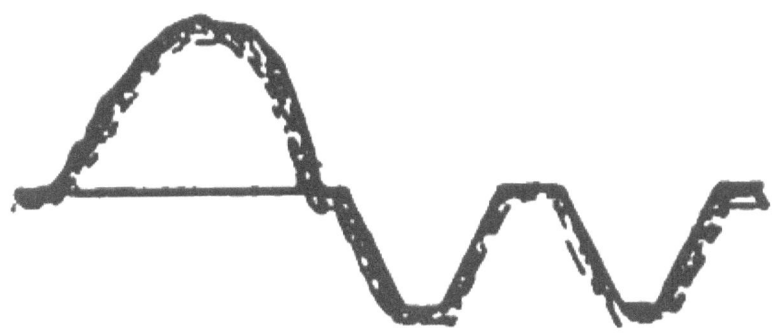
PROFILE OF DOUBLE TRENCH.

tribe, partook of this feeling, and ordered the ten thousand men who, it had been agreed, should guard Caesar's line of supplies, and who were just setting out with a large convoy, to march ostensibly to join Caesar, but really to make a junction with Vercingetorix. The leader of this body was Litavicus. On the way, he and his men first exhibited their treachery, perhaps near modern Serbannes, by massacring the Romans who accompanied the train. The plot was revealed to Caesar by Eporedorix, the Æduan noble, who was part of his *entourage*.

The matter was pressing. Caesar was between two fires. The danger was to the rations on which he relied. He delayed not a moment. Leaving Fabius in command at Gergovia, he hastened with four legions in light order, accompanied by all his cavalry, to the Æduan army, which was at Randan on the way to join Vercingetorix. Surrounding it, he speedily brought it to terms. He convinced the soldiers of the faithlessness of their leaders, all of whom had fled to Gergovia so soon as their real intentions had been discovered. Eporedorix and Viridomarus, both serving with Caesar, added their words to his; and their explanation and the conspirators' flight restored quiet in the Æduan army.

Caesar was, however, unable to reach the disaffected Æduan citizens at home. These, stirred up by sedition, fell to massacring the Romans in their midst, and incited many others to take up arms. The whole nation was in turmoil. Many, indeed, when they heard that Caesar had done no harm to the Æduan army for its treachery,—as he had not because he was obliged to temporize,—were desirous of returning to their allegiance; others were boldly for insurrection. In Bibracte, Convictolitavis murdered the Roman residents and plundered every Roman's property. All this made it essential that Caesar should return to quell this tumult, which threatened his very base. Vercingetorix had by his machinations attacked him in his weakest spot.

Many of the Æduans had acted with duplicity and faithlessness; when they were put in the wrong, they professed contrition and humbly craved forgiveness. Part had been really misguided. It was hard to distinguish the honest from the perfidious. A Fabian policy had to be resorted to. Caesar's military and political resources were taxed to the utmost. Though he had regained control of the Æduan army, the Æduan state was still capable of vast mischief.

During Caesar's absence to suppress the mutiny of the leaders of the Æduan army, Vercingetorix attacked the Roman camp; and owing to its large extent, the two legions left behind had much ado to defend the ramparts. Vercingetorix forced the fighting, and constantly sent on relays of fresh troops. Though the defences were strong, it was only with the aid of the engines and at great loss in men that the enemy could be held at bay. Fabius sent messengers to Caesar, who speeded his return, leaving the revolt in the Æduan territory—however dangerous—for the future.

Caesar's men made their long forced march with great alacrity. From the Gergovian camp to Randan, where Caesar met the Æduan army, is twenty-five miles. He heard of the plot "almost at midnight." He left the camp presumably at sunrise, say at four a. m., reached Randan at noon, spent six or seven hours in negotiations and consequent action, then gave "three hours of the night to his soldiers for repose," say seven to ten p. m. (the night watches began at six p. m.), and returned from Randan to the camp in six hours more, making twenty-four hours in all, during which his column covered fifty miles. Nor did they reach the camp any too soon to avert serious disaster. The two legions were well-nigh exhausted.

Some days after, a favourable opportunity occurred for attacking the enemy. Caesar gives us to understand that he had already determined to give up his attempt on Gergovia, owing partly to its difficulties, and especially to the Æduan *imbroglio*; but that he desired to make some demonstration, so as to retire with credit, and not allow Vercingetorix to accuse the legions of cowardice. He was not really besieging Gergovia. He was only observing it. Except that he was annoying the enemy, he had in no sense even blockaded him. Vercingetorix could have retired at any time.

This part of the *Commentaries* is plainly disingenuous. It may be true that Caesar felt that he would have to return to the Æduan territory before long, but the fact remains plain that he attacked the Gergovian stronghold in the full expectation that he could capture it out of hand, and that he was repulsed with a heavy loss. We have nothing but the *Commentaries*, with an occasional reference in other authors, added to the topography, on which to base our narrative; but, reading the *Commentaries* between the lines, and in the light of our other knowledge (as in the case of Hannibal, we must sometimes read Livy), and keeping the topography clearly in view, the fact of an assault in good faith and a bloody repulse is manifest.

Caesar had a keen eye. In the days when field-glasses were unknown, the eye, if naturally good, was trained, like those of our Indians, to a surprising degree of accuracy. He noticed from the Roche Blanche, where he had located his lesser camp, that the defences of the main plateau of the town, so far strongly beset, were quite disgarnished of troops. Deserters, "a great number of whom flocked to him daily," informed him that the top of one of the adjoining heights, the Risolles, marked 1 on the chart, was level, and communicated with the *oppidum* by a wooded and narrow neck (2); and that Vercingetorix had conceived some danger from that quarter. The north of the Gergovian height, it will be remembered, was not attempted by Caesar in any sense; but he had seized the Roche Blanche, and might seize the Risolles, and thus win a nearer, and to the Gauls more dangerous, access to the plateau. The gate (3) of the *oppidum*, and the road to it from the westerly height (1), has been dug out so as to show the lay of the land in Caesar's day. It varied but little from what it now is, except from a certain amount of natural debris, and gradual smoothing of the surface by generations of ploughing since. Should Caesar get possession of the Risolles height (1), he could do more towards cutting the enemy off from water and forage,—a fact which they cared not to face. What Caesar might do next was the unknown quantity of the Gallic problem. Vercingetorix had foreseen the danger, and had sent all his force to fortify this flanking height. Some authors pick out Mont Rognon or Puy Giroux as the object of Vercingetorix' solicitude; but for Caesar to take either of these would by no means compromise the Gergovians, both being beyond the range, and neither being connected with the plateau. Besides, the facts related show that the Gergovians were at work near at hand, at a place from which they could in a few minutes return to the *oppidum*.

Acting on this information, Caesar saw that here was an excellent opening for a general assault. He sent some *turmae* of cavalry at night round towards the height in question, to make a noisy demonstration on the west and south of it (6), and, to add to their number, he hel-

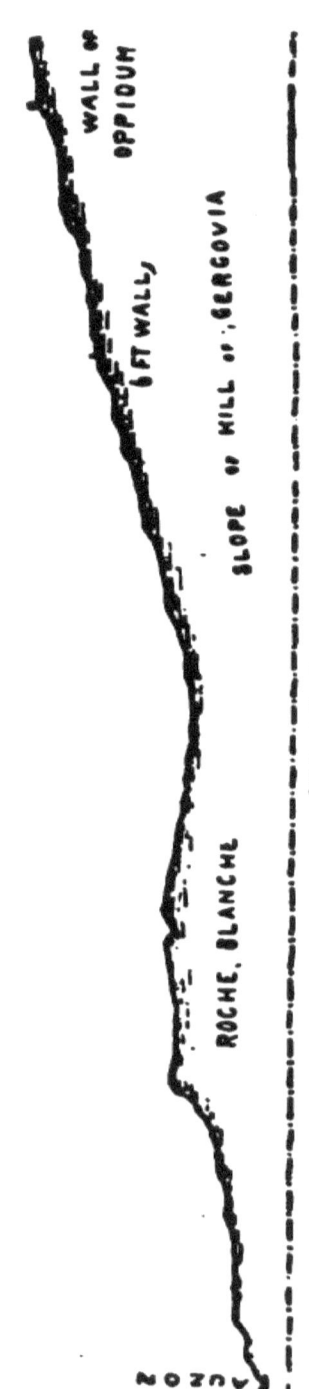

Profile of ground from lesser camp to Gergovia

Gergovia from Roche Blanche

meted many of his muleteers, and sent them at daylight on the same errand, instructing them by ranging about in the skirts of the woods to attract the attention of the Gauls, and lead them to believe that an attack was coming from that quarter. He also sent a legion in support, with orders to take post below Puy Giroux, and to pretend to be hiding in the hollows and woods as if preparing a surprise. This demonstration, seen from the *oppidum*, resulted, as Caesar anticipated, in the enemy withdrawing nearly all his force from the south front of the *oppidum*, and marching it over to the position (1) they thus deemed to be threatened. It was evident to them that Vercingetorix had been right in apprehending trouble from this quarter. They set to work to fortify its west front (a to b), and presumably the neck of land, for this was not precipitous enough to be its own defence. Caesar's capital feint had succeeded as it deserved to succeed. This Gergovia affair is one of the earliest where the terrain is so well explored as to give us a thorough insight into the manoeuvre. Barring the use of artillery, the whole operation closely resembles a modern assault, in its method of preparation and execution.

Thus much accomplished, Caesar, under cover of his feint, transferred the bulk of his force secretly and in small detachments from the greater to the lesser camp. The men marched behind the wall, as Polysenus says, crouching down so as not to be seen, and the ensigns, plumes and shields, which would have betrayed them, were covered so as not to attract attention to the manoeuvre. Then he gave out his instructions to his legates. The place, he said, could not be taken by assault, but only by surprise; the men were to be kept well in hand and not allowed to go beyond orders, either from zeal or hope of plunder, lest they should be taken in flank when in confused order; of which, to judge from Caesar's description, there was some danger, which would not otherwise appear. The Ædui were sent from the greater camp by another circuit on the right to attack in another place. This was probably on the southeast angle of the *oppidum* (4).

The town wall was twelve hundred paces distant from the foot of the mountain, as the crow flies. Irregularities in the ground made the access circuitous, and added to this distance at least a half. The road up the mountain now runs by the glen where lies Merdogne, and must always have done so. Midway up the ascent there was the stone wall six feet high, already mentioned. No defences or camps were below; but above the stone wall were the barbarians' camps very closely packed together.

The signal of attack was given. With a rush the *legionaries* debouched from the gates of the lesser camp, advanced the short mile up the hill (9 and 10), and, swarming over the wall, at once became possessors of the camp. The surprise was complete. So much was this the fact that the king of the Nitiobriges, Teutomatus, barely escaped half-clothed from his tent, where he was resting during the noontide.

At this point, and having made this gain, for some strange reason Caesar paused, and halted the Tenth legion, which he was with. This is one of the most inexplicable circumstances of his career. He states in his *Commentaries* that this much was all he intended to do. "Caesar, having accomplished the object which he had in view, ordered the signal to be sounded for retreat." But this is clearly an excuse framed after the event. It is probable that, from his position when the troops were swarming over the stone wall (it may have been the knoll marked 5 on the chart), he was better able to recognize the questionable nature of the task than from below, and decided to call off his men. It is not impossible that he purposed to hold this position and erect *vineae* and mounds; though, indeed, from what subsequently happened, it seems as if he might have been successful in a summary assault on the town, had he then and there pressed on. Writing afterwards, he says that "success depended on a surprise," and he had succeeded in surprising the enemy. Sounding the recall, he endeavoured to arrest the onset of the other legions; but though the *centurions* and *tribunes* did their utmost, the *legionaries*, with the flush of past victories and the hope of plunder, either would not or did not hear. There were accidents in the ground between Caesar and them to intercept the trumpet-blasts, but the legions at Thapsus broke away from Caesar, and perhaps they did so here. They pressed on till they reached the wall of the town, where they were stopped for want of means of escalading the rampart, which had not been provided—a curious lapse, if a surprise and assault was intended. So little defended were the walls, that the women were seen hanging over them and imploring for mercy, expecting no less than immediate capture or death, as at Avaricum. Some of the men did reach the top of the wall. L. Fabius, *centurion* of the Eighth legion, lifted by his soldiers, scaled it, and others followed. Had the legionaries been furnished with ladders, it seems as if one vigorous effort would have met with success. Even as it was, the fact that some managed to scale the wall shows that in the absence of the garrison the thing was feasible.

By this time the Gauls had heard of the Roman assault, and, preceded by the cavalry, came rushing back to the defence of the city. In a few moments the ground back of the wall was beset by defenders, and the women, who had been imploring mercy, now—as was their wont, with dishevelled hair and holding up their infants—bade their husbands defend them. The speedy return of the Gergovians proves that they could not have been so far away as Mont Rognon or Puy Giroux. The contest was now quite unequal, so much so that Caesar was constrained to send back to the camp for the *cohorts* left there on guard under T. Sextius, ordering them to take up a position at the foot of the hill, so as to threaten Vercingetorix' right (8), and to protect the retreat if it should have to be made, by attacking the Gauls in flank. He himself, with the Tenth legion, now advanced somewhat to the support of the other legions which had gone beyond the position where he had halted the Tenth, and awaited the issue, holding his men well in hand. The other legionaries were still fighting bravely, but against odds of position and numbers, the Gauls having been able to make a sortie on their flank. T. Sextius and the others who had climbed it were thrown from the wall; the centurion, M. Petronius, also of the Eighth, attempting to burst the gates, was killed in trying to save his men.

At this instant the Ædui emerged on the Roman right, and though they had their right shoulders bared,—as the Gallic allies of Caesar were in the habit of doing to distinguish them from the other barbarians,—the *legionaries* assumed that these were fresh troops of the enemy who had bared their shoulders as a stratagem, and at once began to retire somewhat confusedly. They had lost in killed, seven hundred men and forty-six *centurions*, but had illustrated Roman valour in every phase. The great loss in officers shows that these by no means lacked devotion.

The Tenth legion, by changes of position to suit the several cases, abundantly protected the retreat by threatening Vercingetorix' flank; the *cohorts* from the camp did their share, taking position on high ground to impose on Vercingetorix. by endangering his advance. So soon as they reached the plain, the legions all turned and faced the enemy. Vercingetorix, who had hoped to have them at his mercy and who had followed in pursuit, impressed by this bold front, decided not to risk an attack, but led back his forces into the town.

On the return to camp, Caesar took occasion to "censure the rashness" of the *legionaries* for not heeding the orders of their officers, while commending their valour; and showed them how nearly they had come to suffering a fatal defeat. As at Avaricum, said he, he had desired not to risk the lives of his men in a futile assault; and he bade them remember that he, their general, was the best judge of what it was wise to do, and that he required in his soldiers forbearance and self-command not less than valour and magnanimity. At the same time he encouraged them not to lose heart from one piece of bad luck, "nor attribute to the valour of the enemy what disadvantage of position had caused."

Caesar had, as he says, not obtained such success over the enemy as would enable him under its cover to retire from the siege with honour. He felt that he must do more. On the next day he led out his army into the plain and offered battle to Vercingetorix, which this chief declined, and hostilities were confined to a cavalry skirmish, in which the Romans proved the victors. The succeeding day Caesar did the like, having made all preparations to raise the siege. But as Vercingetorix would not accept his gage and descend into the level, Caesar began to withdraw in open daylight, in full view of the enemy. Vercingetorix did not pursue.

One cannot refrain from contrasting this assault on Gergovia with some of Alexander's,—as, *e. g.*, the Rock of Chorienes, or Aornus, or the city of the Malli. The energy of Hannibal, one of whose weak points was his conduct of sieges, in more than one instance—as at Saguntum—stands out in marked relief from the lack of vigour here exhibited by Caesar. And we have to judge Hannibal from the accounts of his enemies; Caesar, by his own statements.

Nor is this the only similar case. We shall see how he paused at Thapsus, until his men took matters into their own hands. At Munda he stopped at the brook which separated I him from Cnaeus Pompey. With all Caesar's consummate strategic courage, and a personal bearing above reproach, he was wont to lack the tremendous vitality in tactical initiative which we admire so heartily in other captains.

There are in other authors hints that this Gergovia affair is not accurately given by Caesar, but that a really serious defeat is explained away in a manner which would do justice to the report of a modern general. It is related by Servirus Maurus Honouratus that so marked was the defeat that Caesar was taken prisoner in the confusion, and only escaped by a lucky accident. Plutarch, indeed, says the Arverni had a sword captured from Caesar's person, either here or at the battle preceding the siege of Alesia. However apocryphal these statements may be, Caesar was clearly compelled to give up the siege for want of success in his assault. The Æduan question had, however, become so

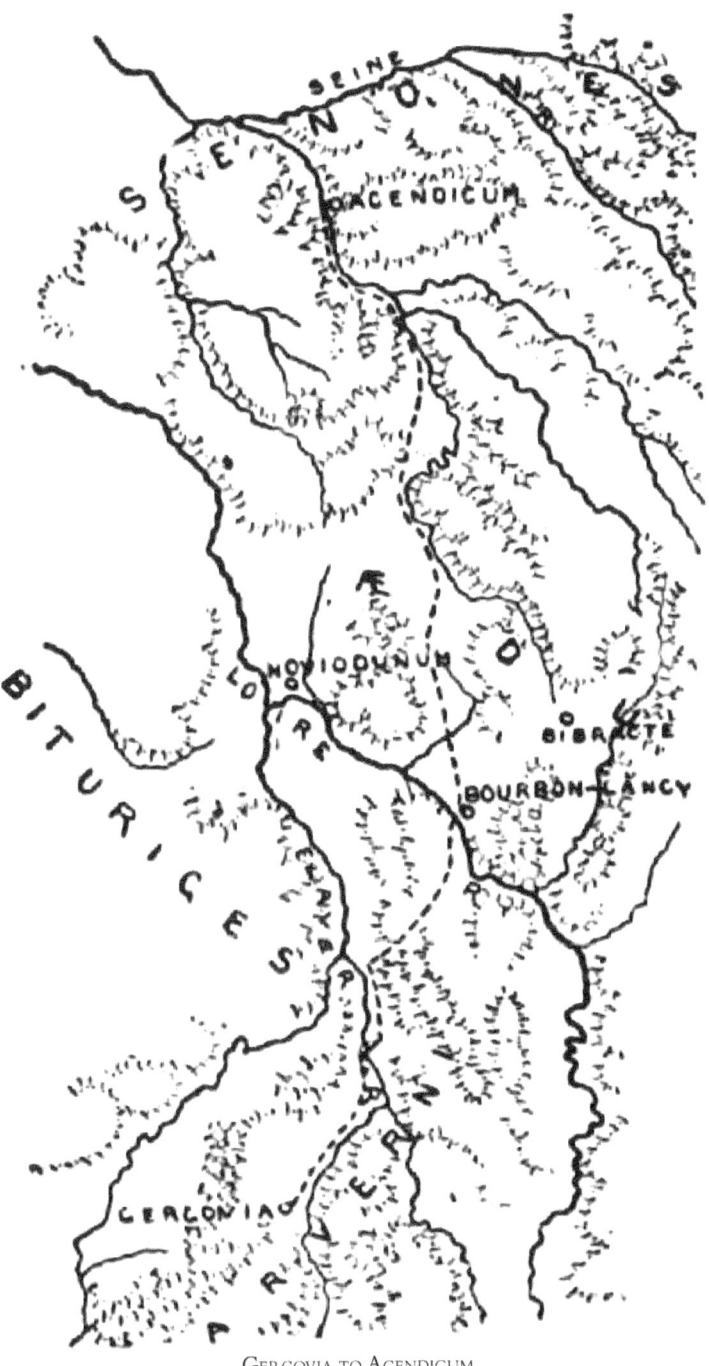

Gergovia to Agendicum

pressing that he was no doubt wise, for that reason alone, in retiring from Gergovia. That it was the only place he had failed to take in the Gallic war abundantly condones the failure. Caesar moved east, and on the third day after the assault he reached the Elaver, and repairing the bridge over the river, perhaps at Vichy, he retired to the right bank on the way to the territory of his former "kinsmen."

Caesar now deliberately took up the question of the Ædui, the treachery of many of whose prominent men was apparent, despite the manner in which he had honoured and protected them. The Æduan army, under Viridomarus and Eporedorix, probably disgusted at the late defeat, was leaving for home, and "Litivacus had set out with all the cavalry to raise the Ædui," but Caesar made no effort to retain them. He merely represented to them how he had found the Ædui at the mercy of their neighbours and had placed them in the highest position of any tribe in Gaul, and left them to draw the inference.

Caesar had collected a large amount of baggage, corn, horses and all his hostages in Noviodunum (Nevers), a town of the Ædui on the Liger. When the Æduan army came to this place, they found that the chief men of the state had sent to Vercingetorix to negotiate a peace, and that the Roman alliance had been thrown over. This act still more confirms the idea of a serious defeat at Gergovia. Not willing to neglect so favourable an opportunity for regaining their independence, Eporedorix and Viridomarus seized and massacred the garrison of Noviodunum and all its traders, divided the spoil, sent the hostages to Bibracte, drove off the reserve horses which Caesar had got from Italy and Spain for remounts, and burned the town, together with all the corn they could not carry away. They then placed troops at the fords of the Liger to prevent the Romans from crossing. They hoped to force Caesar by lack of provisions to retire to the Narbonese. They would then have Labienus, who was at Lutetia, at their mercy.

Learning of these things on the march from the Elaver towards the Liger, Caesar saw that he was in a very dangerous position. His enemies were in high spirits at his late defeat; he was surrounded by troops in revolt—the victorious Arverni were on his rear, the Ædui in his front holding the Liger, the Bituriges on his left. But he also saw that it would be a shameful as well as a perilous thing to allow himself to be driven back to the Province, for this would isolate Labienus. He proposed, come what might, to go to the bottom of the matter, join Labienus, and punish the traitors at their own threshold.

Here we have Caesar at his best. No one ever rose to the occasion more splendidly than this captain. The graver the danger, the bolder the front this great man presented to it. At times Caesar appeared to lack a certain spirit of enter-prise, in which Alexander and Napoleon excelled. But once put impending disaster before him, and no general ever proved himself more energetic, more able.

Caesar made speed to reach the Liger, and sought a ford. At modern Bourbon-Lancy there has always been one; it was on his direct road; and though this ford was not what he could have desired, it was the only one he could secure. He drove off the enemy and crossed, the *legionaries* being up to their armpits in water, but having the current broken for them by stationing cavalry obliquely in the water above them. On the other side he found corn—for the harvest was at hand—and cattle, and refreshed his troops. He then marched rapidly to the land of the Senones to join Labienus. It was still early in the year.

GALLIC HELMET

CHAPTER 18

Labienus' Campaign
Spring, 52 B. C.

Labienus bad been conducting a campaign against the Parisii. He reached Lutetia, but shortly heard of Caesar's failure before Gergovia. He was opposed by Camulogenus, an able man, and saw that he could not safely retire, as he ought to do, towards Caesar, without first imposing on the enemy. This he did in a bold and well-planned battle, and promptly retreated to Agendicum. The Æduan rebellion practically cut Caesar off from his lieutenant; and Vercingetorix was all the more active since Caesar's defeat at Gergovia. But by a bold march northward, Caesar made a junction with Labienus, and thus reunited his eleven legions in one body. His manifest policy was now to push for the province, from which he was cut off, re-establish his base securely, and again advance on the Gallic allies. He set out by the most promising route. Vercingetorix believed the moment to have come for a *coup de grace*. He gave up his policy of small-war, and intercepted Caesar on the way. But in the ensuing battle the Romans won, and Vercingetorix retired to Alesia, the last and main stronghold of the Gauls. This victory reopened Caesar's communications with the province, and he followed the Gauls to Alesia.

During Caesar's Gergovia campaign Labienus had marched on Lutetia of the Parisii with four legions, having left a suitable force of new recruits from Italy with his baggage and victuals at Agendicum. He marched down the left bank of the Icauna (Yonne) and the Sequana. A large army from the neighbouring states assembled to oppose him as soon as his arrival was known. The town of Lutetia occupied the island in the Seine where now stands Notre Dame de Paris. The chief command had been given to an aged but excellent soldier named Camulogenus. This officer, perceiving that Labienus

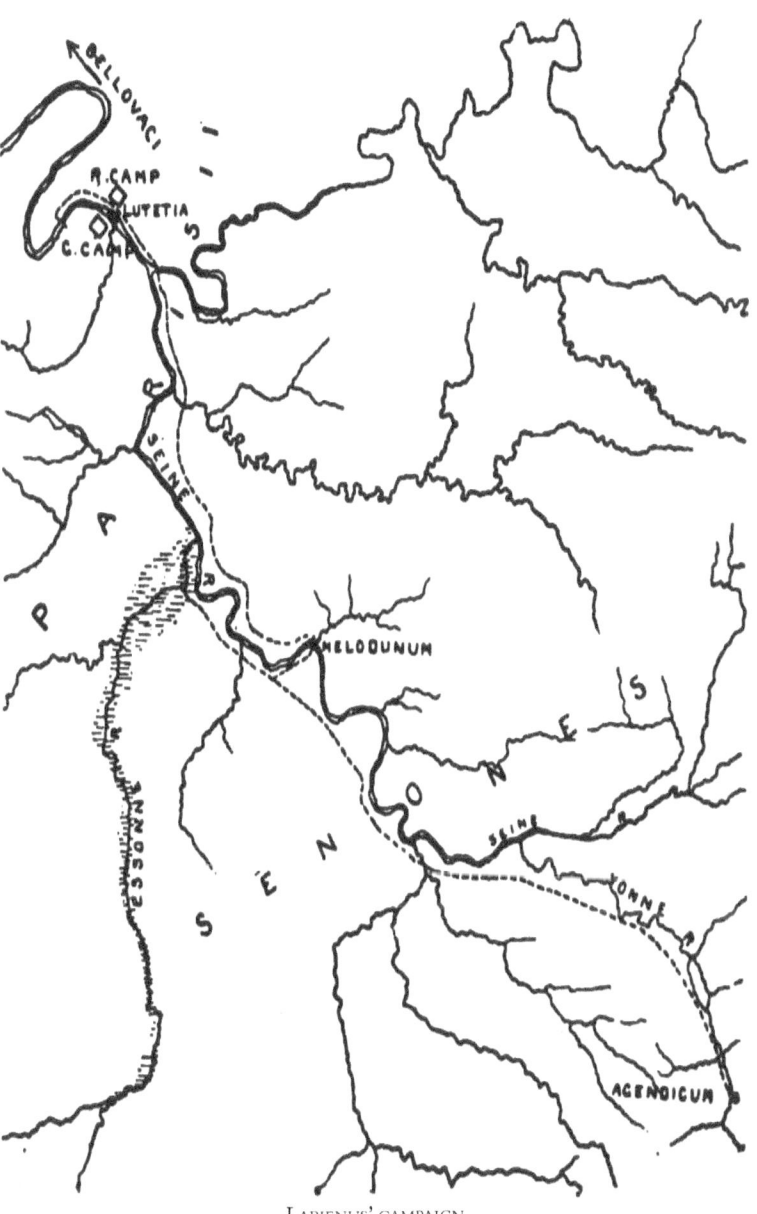

Labienus' Campaign

was marching along the left bank, camped and drew up his army near a neighbouring marsh. This was unquestionably where the Esonne flows into the Seine. It could not have been Le Marais, a part of Paris, as has been claimed. His position prevented the Romans from advancing. Labienus tried to make a road across the marsh by using hurdles and branches, a sort of corduroy-road, but failed in the attempt.

He then resorted to stratagem, and sought to steal a march on Camulogenus by a flank manoeuvre. He marched back at night by the way he came, along the left bank, on which he had so far been, to Melodunum (Melun), which was likewise on an island in the Seine. Here, by seizing boats, he crossed the left branch of the river to the island, captured the town and, having repaired the bridge which led to the right bank, moved down on the other side towards Lutetia. He reached the latter *oppidum* before Camulogenus, who did not at once see through Labienus' manoeuvre. But his delay was not long. He soon followed the Roman army. On his arrival he ordered Lutetia to be set on fire and its bridges to be destroyed. The two armies camped on either bank of the Sequana opposite the city.

Labienus now heard of Caesar's ill success at Gergovia, and the Gauls added to the story that his chief had been forced back to the province by hunger. The near-by Bellovaci, hearing of the revolt of the Ædui, assembled forces for war. Labienus was thus placed with this inimical tribe on one side, only separated from him by the Isara, and with the Sequana and the Parisii, on the other side. He was cut off from his depots at Agendicum, which was on the farther bank of the Sequana, and from the road to it leading up the left bank, the way he had advanced. He very properly thought it of no use to attempt to reduce the Parisii under these adverse conditions, but deemed that he had best retire towards his base and seek to preserve his army intact for Caesar. Single-handed, he could not suppress the insurrection.

In order to escape from his awkward situation, Labienus must recross to the left bank of the Sequana. To accomplish this in face of the army which was still on the other side and would oppose his passage, required ruse. To retrace his steps was to invite Camulogenus to oppose his crossing at Melodunum, and his boats would be hard to get so far up the river. A slow process would not accomplish his end. Labienus was a good soldier and a bold. He saw that it was safer to impose on the enemy by daring than to encourage him by a retreat, which would convey the idea of weakness. He called his lieutenants together

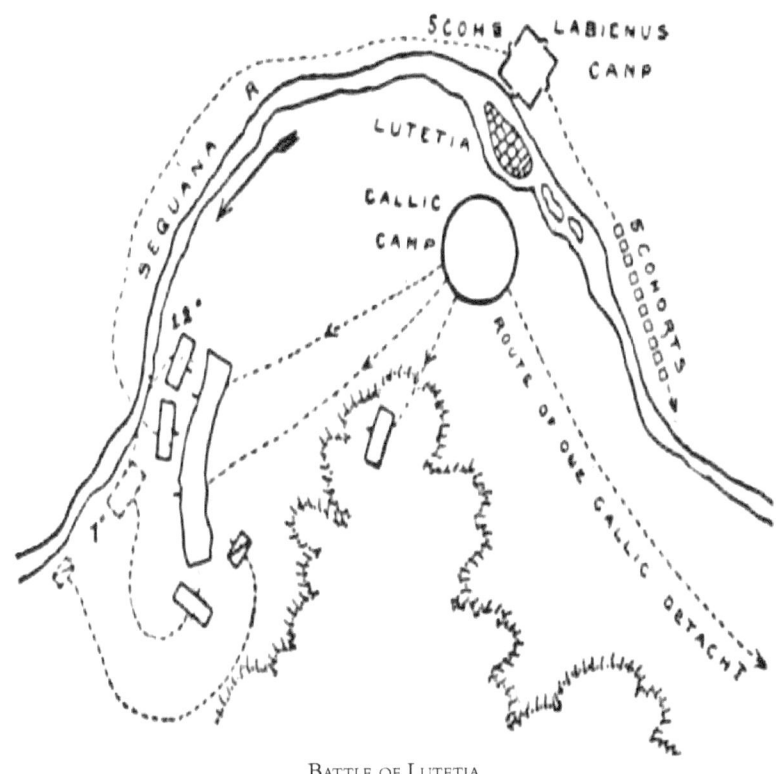

BATTLE OF LUTETIA

and impressed their task upon them. He placed the boats which he had brought from Melodunum under trusted Roman knights and ordered them quietly to fall down the river about four miles at an early hour of the night. He left a force of five steady *cohorts* in camp; the other five *cohorts* of the same legion he ordered up the river and sent some boats with them, instructing them to proceed in a noisy manner, to lead the enemy to suppose that he was marching that way. His other three legions he led downstream to the boats and crossed them unperceived under cover of a storm. This was probably near modern Point du Joir. The Gallic posts were sheltering themselves from the weather, and were easily dispersed.

Not knowing what Labienus was doing, but learning of these three parties, the enemy drew the inference that Labienus was trying to steal away in detachments, hoping that some might be saved by the sacrifice of the rest, and determined to capture all three. They broke up into three divisions, sending part up and part down the river, and leaving a part in camp. Camulogenus led the party which went down the river. By daylight the Romans were across, drew up in line and fell smartly upon the Gauls, who encountered them with equal boldness. The Seventh legion on the right at once routed the force opposed to it, but the Twelfth legion on the left, though it inflicted heavy loss on the barbarians, who were under the eye of their chief, was unable to break their ranks until the Seventh legion wheeled to the right and took them in flank and rear, and the cavalry rode them down. Even then the Gauls stood their ground until they were cut to pieces. The party in the camp, at the sound of battle, marched towards its chief, and took position on a hill (perhaps Vaugiraud). But they could not hold it. The cavalry cut down all who did not reach the woods. Camulogenus was killed. The detached forces of the enemy were next dispersed; and Labienus, having drawn in his own detachments, marched to Agendicum, where the baggage had been left. From here he moved towards Caesar.

This campaign proves Labienus to have been an able officer. His manoeuvring was excellent in every respect. It is a grievous pity that the latter part of his military career was clouded with ingratitude to his former chief. Under Caesar's control, Labienus did far better work than he later did when opposed to Caesar.

The revolt of the Ædui, the outbreak of which was an immediate consequence of the Gergovia defeat, gave a dangerous aspect to the war, for this people was all the more influential as having been long under Roman control. In order to terrify the neighbouring tribes into joining the war, they murdered the hostages Caesar had committed to their keeping, and threatened to do the like by those of such nations as did not join them. They were all the more determined now that they had broken loose. A council of all Gaul was summoned to Bibracte. All but the Remi, Lingones and Treviri came. Here the Ædui claimed the chief command; but it was given by universal choice to Vercingetorix, to whom, in consequence, the Æduan chiefs gave half-hearted support.

Vercingetorix exacted hostages from the allies, and ordered a general levy of cavalry, to the number of fifteen thousand, which he used as body-guard. Of infantry he already had an abundance. All Gaul had risen, save only the Remi and their clients, the Suessiones, Leuci and Lingones. It was the only occasion when the entire country was in arms. Vercingetorix proposed to continue his cunctatory policy of harassing the Romans and keeping them from obtaining corn; and advised the allies again to set fire to the crops and houses and thus to hamper Caesar, as they had done before. An Æduan and Segusian army of ten thousand foot and eight hundred horse under Eporedorix, he sent against the Allobroges; some of the Arvernian tribes and the Gabali he sent into the land of the Helvii, in the province, to devastate it; the Ruteni and Cadurci he sent against the Volcae Arecomici, hoping to tamper with some of the tribes in the Province. He tried to gain over the Allobroges by flattery and promises.

The only force in the Province to oppose this host consisted of twenty-two *cohorts* put in the field by the *legate* Lucius Caesar. The Helvii were defeated by the enemy and driven within walls, with loss of many of their leading men; but the Allobroges held their boundary, the line of the Rhone, by a multitude of posts.

Knowing how large the enemy's force of cavalry had grown to be, Caesar was obliged to send to Germany, to those tribes he had rendered tributary, to increase his own squadrons, as the peculiar warfare waged by the barbarians made this arm one on which at all times great reliance could be placed, and which sometimes was indispensable. In this effort he succeeded, and raised beyond the Rhine, in the states he had so far subdued, a most excellent though small body of cavalry, perhaps one thousand men, which he mixed with light troops. To add to its efficiency, as their horses were of poor quality, he dismounted the *tribunes*, knights and *evocati*, and gave their horses to the Germans. This was a radical measure, but Caesar never stopped halfway; nor was this the time to do so.

After crossing the Liger on his way from Gergovia, Caesar apparently directed his march due north to join Labienus, who, when he had defeated Camulogenus, had made his way towards his chief. Not far south of Agendicum, the captain and lieutenant met. The enemy's plan to divide the Romans had failed.

Caesar now had eleven legions, the First, Sixth, Seventh, Eighth, Ninth, Tenth, Eleventh, Twelfth, Thirteenth, Fourteenth and Fifteenth. The First was the one lent by Pompey. In 58 B. C. Caesar had six legions, the Seventh, Eighth, Ninth, Tenth, Eleventh, Twelfth. In 67 B. C. two new ones were raised, the Thirteenth and Fourteenth. In the winter of 55-54 B. C. he got five *cohorts* more. He lost at Aduatuca fifteen *cohorts*, a legion and a half, but in 63 B. C. he raised three more legions, *i. e.*, the new First, Fourteenth and the Fifteenth. Later the First and Fifteenth were lent to Pompey, and the Fifteenth became the Third. The legions were usually four to five thousand men strong. When reduced, they were so soon as possible recruited up to standard. When

Caesar raised new levies, they were not generally made into new legions, but were distributed among the old ones. These legions, during the Gallic War, were thus about fifty thousand strong. Caesar had also some twenty thousand Gallic, Cretan or Numidian light troops, and five thousand cavalry, of which one thousand were Germans; a total of seventy-five thousand men. This is an estimate, but it is not far from accurate. Later, in the Civil War, the legions were more depleted, the average being not much over three thousand men.

Having made his junction with Labienus, Caesar deemed it essential to direct his march as speedily as possible on his base. He could not move south, straight towards the province, because the Ædui lay between him and it, and they were in insurrection. He moved through the land of the Lingones to the east, and then heading south, purposed to make his way through the territory of the Sequani towards the province. He had a good storehouse and intermediate base, should he require it, at Vesontio. He followed the same route he had pursued when going to meet Ariovistus, and when moving from Vienna to Agendicum. He intended to march up the valley of the Vingeanne and cross the Arar, on his way to Vesontio. This is what the *Commentaries* mean by saying that he marched "through the confines of the Lingones into the country of the Sequani, in order that he might the more easily render aid to the province." Caesar's purpose in regaining the Province was not only to be able to protect this almost Roman territory; but, foreseeing that the uprising would probably be general, he preferred to base himself afresh on what was unquestionably safe place of retreat, and the only place from which he could be certain to obtain victual,— in other words, to make a fresh start for the conquest of Gaul.

Meanwhile, Vercingetorix, after driving Caesar from Gergovia, had concentrated his forces, some eighty thousand men, near Bibracte, and had moved up and encamped on the road he divined the Romans would pursue. He placed his army so as to bar Caesar's passage through the land of the Sequani. He camped at a fork in the roads in three divisions, each covering one of the paths Caesar might choose towards the Arar and Vesontio. Caesar marched to within ten miles of his enemy, ignorant of his presence. Vercingetorix' position on the modern heights of Sacquenay was very strong. The heights bulged out in three promontories, so to speak, on each one of which lay a third of Vercingetorix' army. The right flank of his army thus rested on the Vingeanne. The Badin brook was in its front.

That this is the field of battle seems to be proven by the *tumuli* of

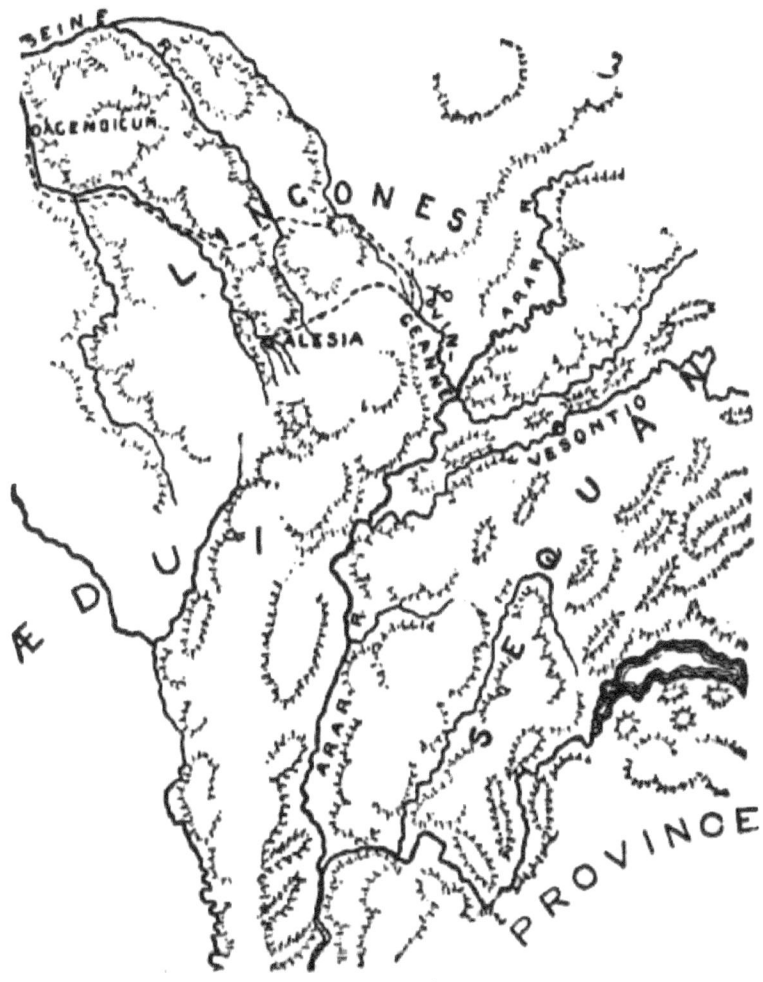

AGENDICUM TO ALESIA

the region, which contain skeletons identified from their ornaments as Gallic, and by the horseshoes, still occasionally dug up by the peasants. Moreover, it suits the distance from Alesia given by the *Commentaries*.

Calling a council of war, Vercingetorix declared to the chiefs that now was the moment forever to put down Roman tyranny, as even at that moment the enemy was flying to the Province. If he reached it, he would return with even larger forces; if destroyed without delay, which he could be if attacked on the march, no Roman would ever return. He especially encouraged his mounted troops, and the men of this body bound themselves by solemn oath to deprive of all his rights any soldier who did not ride twice through and through the Roman army.

While Vercingetorix was camping on the heights of Sacquenay, Caesar kept on his march up the Vingeanne, camping near Longeau. Next day, Vercingetorix moved his foot up to the Badin and sent out his cavalry to attack Caesar as he should debouch on the plain north of the brook. The Gallic cavalry was divided into three bodies. Of these one was to attack each flank of the Roman army and one the head of column. As Caesar reached the plain, he saw Vercingetorix' central division of cavalry opposite his own head of column. Shortly the other two columns appeared on its right and left. He was taken by surprise.

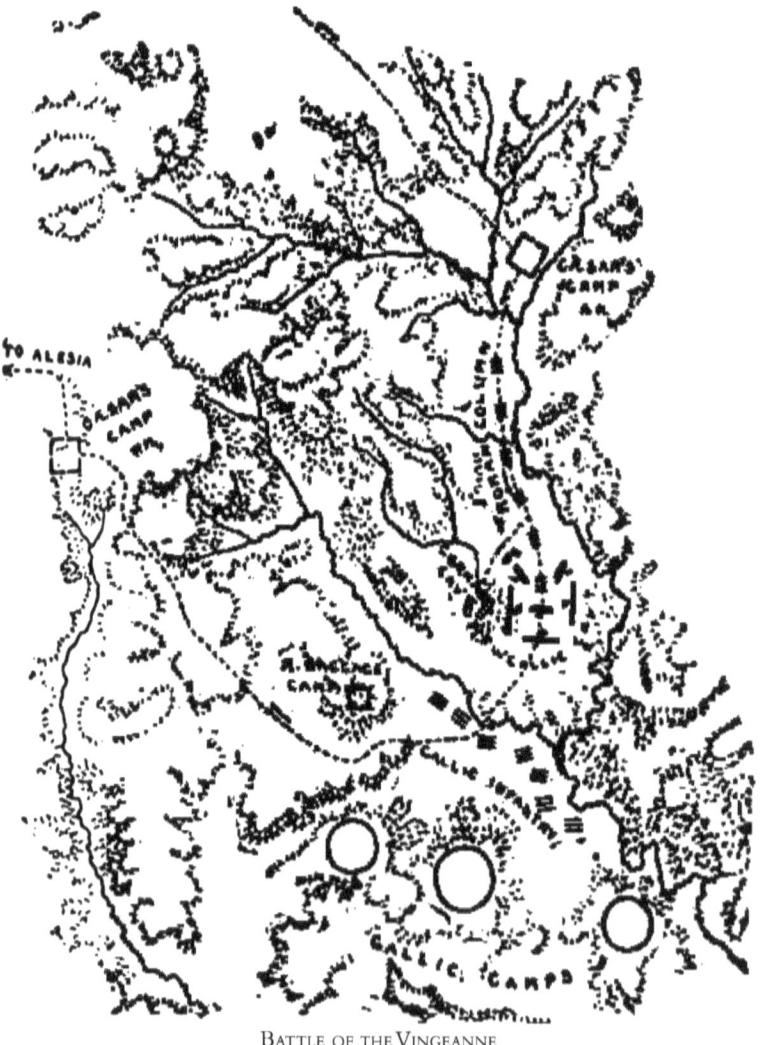

BATTLE OF THE VINGEANNE

Caesar had not anticipated this attack, but he was marching with care and with his troops well in hand. He met the attack by ordering out three bodies of his own cavalry. He called a halt, collected his baggage, and drew up the army in battle order, probably in three lines of legions,—a sort of square, for "the baggage was received within the ranks of the legions." Whenever the horse seemed hard pressed, Caesar supported it by an advance of infantry, and by making a sharp demonstration in that quarter, and thus kept up the courage of the fighting line. The affair was only a cavalry fight; Caesar's cavalry was supported by his foot, which was near at hand. Vercingetorix' foot was not put in at all. After considerable skirmishing, the German cavalry on Caesar's right got possession of the hill of Montsaugeon, drove the Gallic horse from it, and pursuing it to the infantry at the Badin, produced such demoralization as to weaken the other columns of the enemy's cavalry, which, thus taken in reverse, precipitately retired from the field. This retreat enabled Caesar's horse to kill many and capture more prisoners; among them Eporedorix and two other noted Æduan chiefs, Cotus commanding the cavalry, and Cavarillus commanding the foot.

This check was a serious blow to the prestige of Vercingetorix, and determined him to retire to Alesia (Mont Auxois) with his infantry and the baggage from his camp. Caesar followed up his advantage, parked his baggage on a hill nearby, and by pursuing the retreating Gauls, inflicted a loss of three thousand men on the enemy's rearguard. Vercingetorix was wise enough not to return to his camps on the hills of Sacquenay. Had he done so, Caesar could have cut him off from Alesia. But he risked his baggage to secure Alesia, which latter he did by moving at once by his left to the town. His baggage hurried thither by a parallel road farther to the south. Caesar, as it happened, made no effort to capture it.

Vercingetorix had been unwise in the last degree to give up his system of small-war. We do not know how much he was impelled to do this by the insistence of those who did not appreciate his Fabian policy. So long as he pursued this method, he might be more than a match for Caesar's army. A fighting machine can accomplish little unless it can fight, and meanwhile it must subsist. But Vercingetorix should have known that he could not meet the well-drilled *legionaries* in the open, especially when commanded by Caesar in person, and that Caesar's German horse, manoeuvred under his direction, would be more than a match for his own.

Caesar, in this movement, showed distinctly his great qualities.

Having drawn in the forces of Labienus, his one object was to reach the province, from which he was now cut off, drive from its borders the hosts of hostiles which were threatening it, and thence make a fresh start. He proposed that no obstacle should obstruct him in his march. Vercingetorix could not have attacked him at a less opportune moment. Nor when met by Vercingetorix, had Caesar any idea of fighting on the defensive. He at once undertook a sharp offensive. He sustained his cavalry handsomely, and by his able manoeuvres carried off a victory vastly more important in its moral effect than in its dimensions. For the affair itself was only a cavalry combat, and scarcely rose to the dignity of an engagement.

When Vercingetorix retired towards Alesia, the road to the province was thereby opened to Caesar. There was no more need for him to fray a path through the enemy's lines to his base. He could now rely on the fact that Vercingetorix would recall his outlying forces which were threatening the province, or that the *cohorts* there would be able to defend themselves. He decided not to continue his march to his base, but to march directly upon the enemy's army. There was no fear for his communications. He might at once pass over into a sharp offensive.

GALLIC SWORD

Chapter 19

The Siege of Alesia
Summer and Fall of 52 B. C.

The siege of Alesia was foreseen by both parties to be the final act in the struggle. Vercingetorix retired into the city with his army, eighty thousand strong; Caesar sat down before it with sixty thousand men, and began to draw his lines of contravallation. Meanwhile cavalry skirmishes were frequent. Vercingetorix had provisions for thirty days; he sent away his cavalry, and by them word to the allies that before that period was past he must be rescued or surrender. Caesar set to work on his defences. These were strongest at the western approaches, where there was a large plain. Aware that an army of relief would speedily come, lines of circumvallation were added. The works were singularly complete, and skilfully adapted to the ground. After about six weeks, an immense army of relief did, in fact, come up, numbering nearly a quarter of a million of men. This shortly attacked, and Vercingetorix from within lent his aid. But the attack was partial and did not succeed. A second attack had no better result. The Romans held their own. The failure of these two attacks did much to depress the Gauls.

On the day but one (*altera die*) after the battle of the Vingeanne, Caesar reached Alesia, and determined upon its siege. This siege is one of the most notable of antiquity, and shows Caesar's genius in high relief. The stronghold lay on an isolated hill (Mt. Auxois), or rather an elevated oval plateau, one and a quarter miles long east and west, by a half mile wide at the centre north and south, five hundred feet above the surrounding valleys, in the confluence of two of the small tributaries of the upper Sequana, the Lutosa (Ose) and Osera (Oserain) which bounded it on north and south. In front of the town to the west was a plain over three miles in length north and south—now called the Plaine des Laumes—bisected by the Oserain and a little brook.

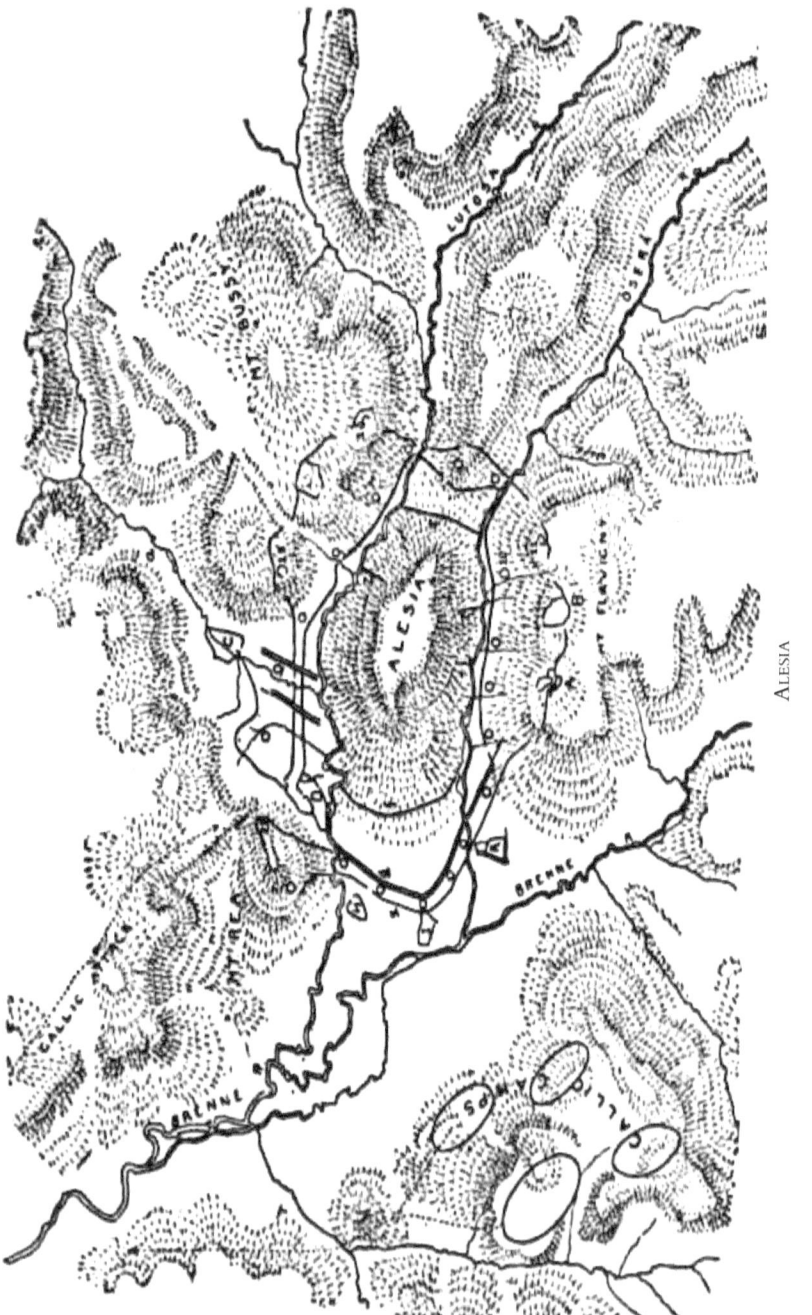

Alesia

Around the town on the three other sides, north, east and south, at the distance of a mile or so measured from the edges of the plateau, was a line of hills of about equal height as Mt. Auxois, separated each from the other by smoothly sloping valleys. There were springs on the plateau and many wells. The streams at the foot of the hill of Alesia were accessible by paths. The grade up the hill was easy, but at the top was a wall of rock interrupted at intervals, but on the whole steep and impracticable to assault.

It has been the habit of most authors to overrate the difficulties of the position at Alesia. It is a sort of pocket edition of Gergovia. While the slopes are unquestionably easier to-day than they were in Caesar's time, made so by the continuous labours of sixty generations of farmers, yet the ground itself can have changed comparatively little. This is abundantly demonstrated by the excavations of Caesar's lines; and though the position of Alesia, considered in the light of ancient warfare, was very strong, it was by no means inexpugnable. The place could readily be taken along the neck of land leading from the heights on the southeast, which was a sort of a natural siege-mound. Caesar's real difficulty lay in his knowledge of the fact that all Gaul would join hands in sending an army of relief before he could take the place by regular approaches.

The Roman army approached from the east, south of Mt. Bussy. The Gauls were encamped on the east of the town under the walls, with a trench and stone wall six feet high (z) as defence. This was their weak spot, and here they expected the struggle. They had prolonged their wall downhill to the streams on either hand; and because this wall could be readily taken in reverse, they had made a double crotchet at either end. On reconnoitring the place, Caesar deemed it inexpedient to attempt to carry it by storm, from the number of its defenders and especially in view of his recent failure at Gergovia; but that it might be starved out by a complete investment he believed. He no doubt appreciated the advantages of moving along the neck on the south-east; but having decided on a siege and not an assault, he threw his decision in favour of an approach from the west at the plain. He manifestly desired to shut in Vercingetorix, and he made his chief works where the position was weakest.

He had eleven legions, a scant fifty thousand men, five thousand Gallic and German horse, and perhaps ten thousand Gallic and other auxiliary foot. Vercingetorix is said to have had eighty thousand men. This has been doubted by many critics on account of the small size

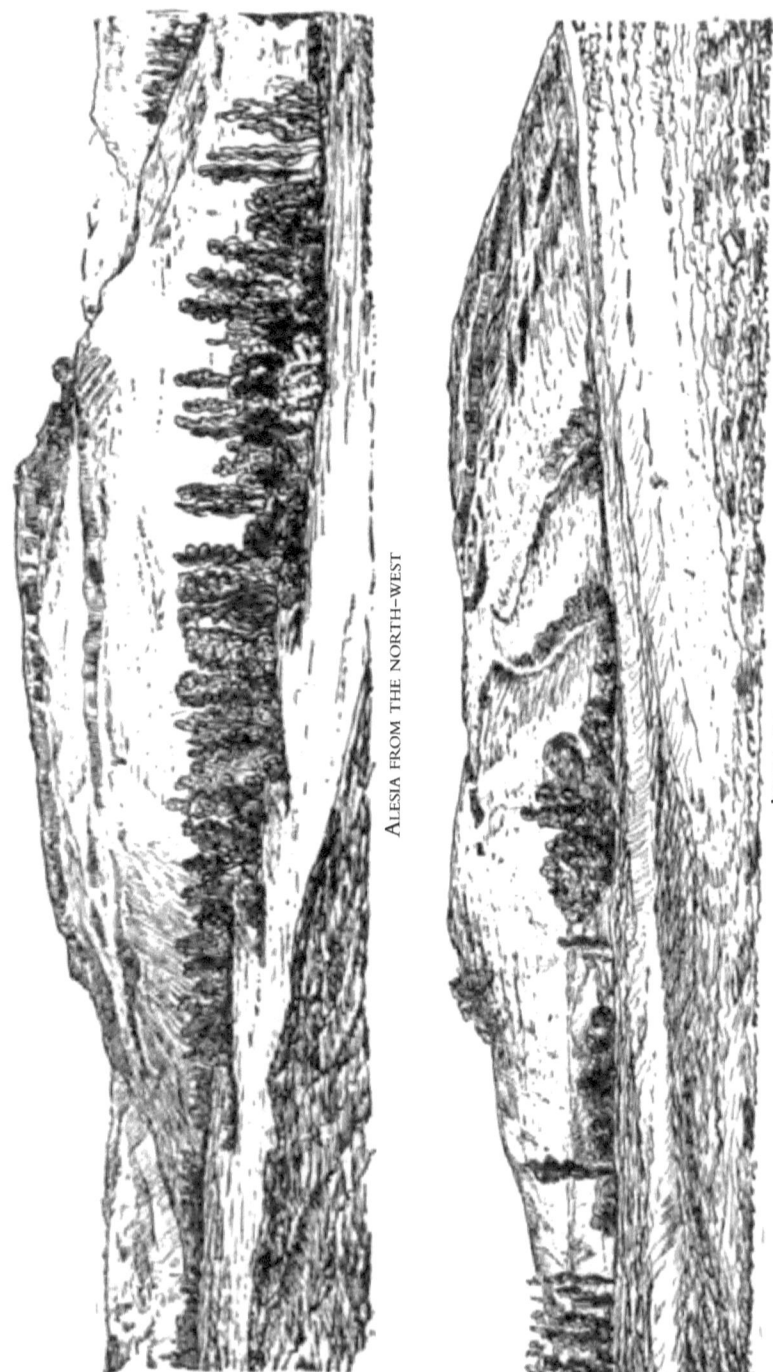

Alesia from the north-west

Alesia from the south

of the plateau and consequent lack of space to hold so large a body. But according to all the accounts, Caesar was undertaking with sixty to seventy thousand men to besiege eighty thousand. In all eras, a force less than twice that of the besieged has been considered too small to predicate success. But the question of number adds to or detracts little from the ability, boldness and far-reaching results of this noted siege. It is probable that Caesar had made up his mind that here was his last chance. Another failure would mean such encouragement of the Gauls as to prejudice his entire campaign. This must not be another Gergovia failure.

Caesar's first step was to seize all the hills on the north, east and south, place thereon suitable detachments, and determine where the lines of contravallation should run. The cavalry was established near the watercourses; the infantry on the hilltops. He then began along the slope of the hills, from point to point, the erection of entrenchments which were eleven miles in length. The camps were protected by twenty-three square and high earthwork redoubts near the foot of the slopes, and these were well guarded to prevent sallies, being held by day by small posts, at night by forces which bivouacked in them. The redoubts were as usual the first defences constructed, and were later joined by lines of earthworks.

There appear to have been four infantry camps, two (A and B) on the hilltop south of Alesia, one on the hill north-east (C), one on the hill northwest (D). The topography dictated the shape of these camps; the entrenchments commanded the ground in their front. The naturally weak side was made the stronger by art; the camp A, for instance, had three lines on the south front. It may have been Caesar's headquarters. The camp B was larger. The debouches of the camps were all towards Alesia. The ditches of D were excavated and found full of relics, coins and weapons, bones and helmets, collars and rings. Four cavalry camps, three in the big plain (H, I, K), one north of Alesia (G), have been found. Their ditches were less deep than those of the infantry camps. Of the twenty-three *castella*, five have been exhumed, 10, 11, 15, 18, 22. These are, no doubt, the stoutest ones that were made. The others were presumably mere block-houses, which have disappeared. The probable positions of the other eighteen are indicated by the topography.

The work on the lines had hardly been begun, when a cavalry action was brought about by Vercingetorix, who advanced into the open plain to the west. The fighting was obstinate. The Roman

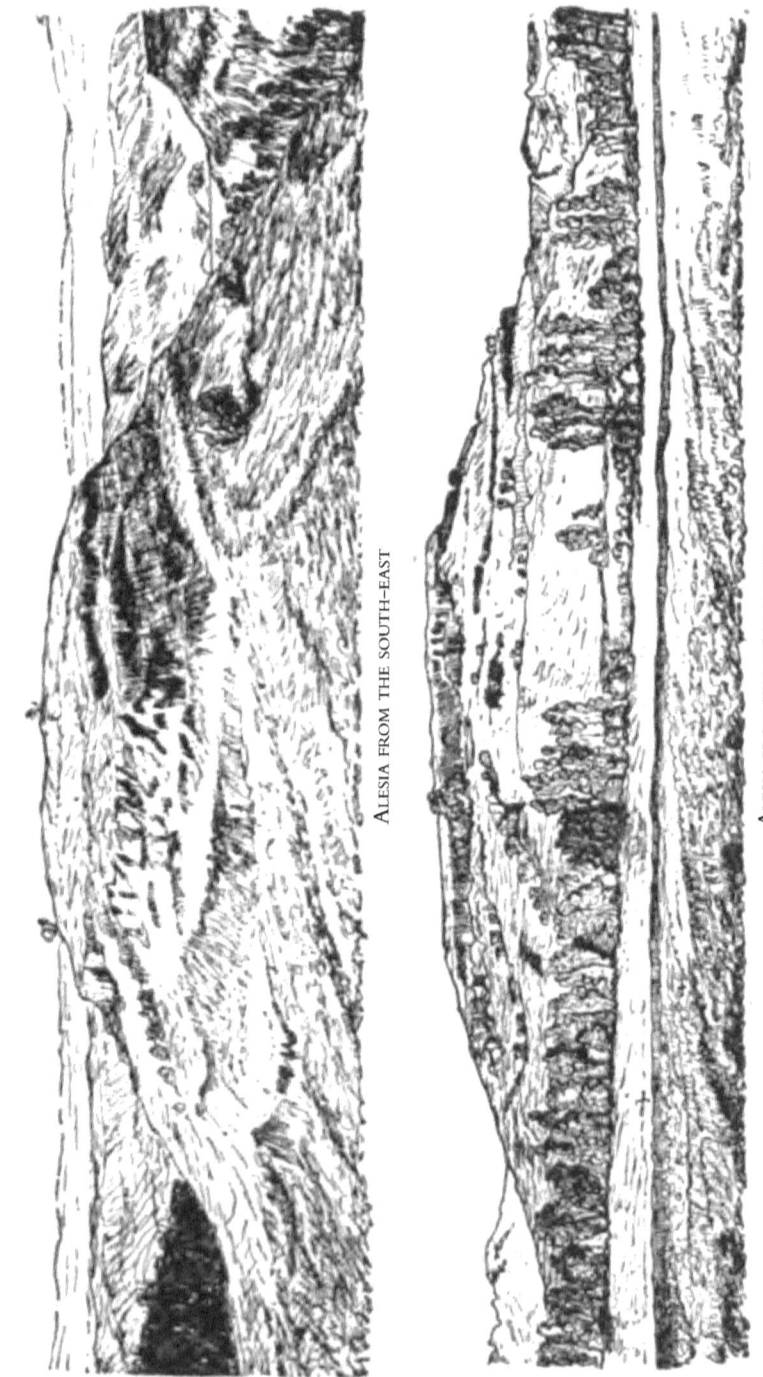

Alesia from the south-east

Alesia from the north-east

horse was at first unsuccessful. But the Roman infantry was ordered into line in front of the camps to forestall a sally from the town by its imposing front. Reanimated by the presence of the legions, which they had learned in the late battle could be relied on to sustain them heartily, the German horse took courage, redoubled the vigour of its charges, put the enemy's horse to flight, and pursued them to the gates of the entrenchments. Caesar advanced the infantry at the proper moment, and this demonstration increased the rout. The Gauls endeavoured to retire into the town, but Vercingetorix ordered the gates to be shut, so that the camp outside the city proper should not be left undefended. Many Gauls sought to climb the ditch and wall but failed. After inflicting a heavy loss on the enemy the Roman allied horse withdrew. It will be noted with curiosity how many of the engagements of the Gallic war were mere combats of cavalry. This arm did Caesar good service; and yet it was never used like the "Companions" or the Numidian horse.

Vercingetorix now saw that a siege was inevitable. Still he was not bold enough to cut his way out before it was too late. He feared again to encounter the *legionaries* in the open; but he had strong hopes that this siege might result like the one of Gergovia, and determined to abide by the result. The position was, if anything, stronger. He sent away his fifteen thousand cavalry one night in the second watch, before the lines of contravallation were completed, not only because he was unable to provide forage for them, but particularly because he desired these men to visit and arouse all the tribes to his aid. The squadrons escaped up the valleys of the two rivers. Vercingetorix sent word by them that he and his sixty-five thousand foot had beef and corn for thirty days, which, by good management, might be made to last a trifle longer, and that they must have succour before the expiration of that time, or else Alesia and the whole cause would fall together. He then withdrew all the forces to the plateau, and took into his own hands the distribution of rations. He divided the cattle, but kept the corn for regular issue. It remains a question as to whether sixty-five thousand men could actually crowd into the small limits of the place. The old city walls have in places been found. By close camping it might be done; and the barbarians were used to herding together in a very small space. Vercingetorix was now inclosed in a town whose well constructed walls rested on the edge of a cliff of stone which may have stood forty to sixty feet above the slope of the ground as it rises from the valley. This is the character, more or less marked, of all of the surrounding plateaux. Part of the slope and of the edge of the plateau was wooded or covered with bushes. Except from the neck of land on the east, nothing but hunger was apt to drive him out. He had a water-supply on the plateau. But his mouths were many. His main reliance was on the arrival of an army of relief.

Caesar went at the business of the siege in the most workmanlike manner despite its exceptional difficulties. The earth in some places was rocky and unsuited to entrenchments, and the land was, no doubt, rougher than it is today. As Vercingetorix could escape only by the plain or up one of the north ravines, Caesar devoted most of his attention to fortifying at these points. On the other sides the ground, was in itself a defence, and less was needed. While the men were at work they had constantly to be protected by out-lying guards of light troops against the sallies of the garrison, which were many and fierce.

Caesar's preparations were on a remarkable scale of magnitude. He dug a trench on the west side of the town twenty feet deep and wide, with perpendicular sides, to protect the building of his other works (f). This trench was four hundred feet in front of the main line of contravallation, at the foot of the slope at the west end of the *oppidum*, and stretched from one stream to the other. It both prevented sudden sallies and left the regular lines beyond the throw of javelins. The earth from the trench was piled up behind it. In front of the main line of works came two other trenches; first one trench (g) on low ground, fifteen feet wide and deep, which he located so as to be readily filled with water from the Osera. It now shows only eight or nine feet deep. Then back of it another equally big, dry trench on the same level. These ditches continued half a mile south of the Osera up the slope of the hill on the south. Thence the ditch was single. Back of these a rampart (*agger*) and wall (*vallum*) twelve feet high. The top of this wall

FACE OF WORK

had a parapet of hurdles (*lorica*) and battlements (*pinna*) and the top of the rampart was provided with stakes "like stags' horns," projecting outward and downward so as to hinder scalers, and was armed with towers eighty feet apart. When the length of the line is considered,—the front thus protected was over a mile and a half long,—this was indeed a fine piece of work. Caesar's *legionaries* handled the pick and spade as effectively as the *pilum* and *gladius*.

Performing all this work and foraging for corn at the same time made the duties severe on the men; and so long a line really needed more force than Caesar had at command. There were but three men per metre front; or if the men were all continuously on duty in three

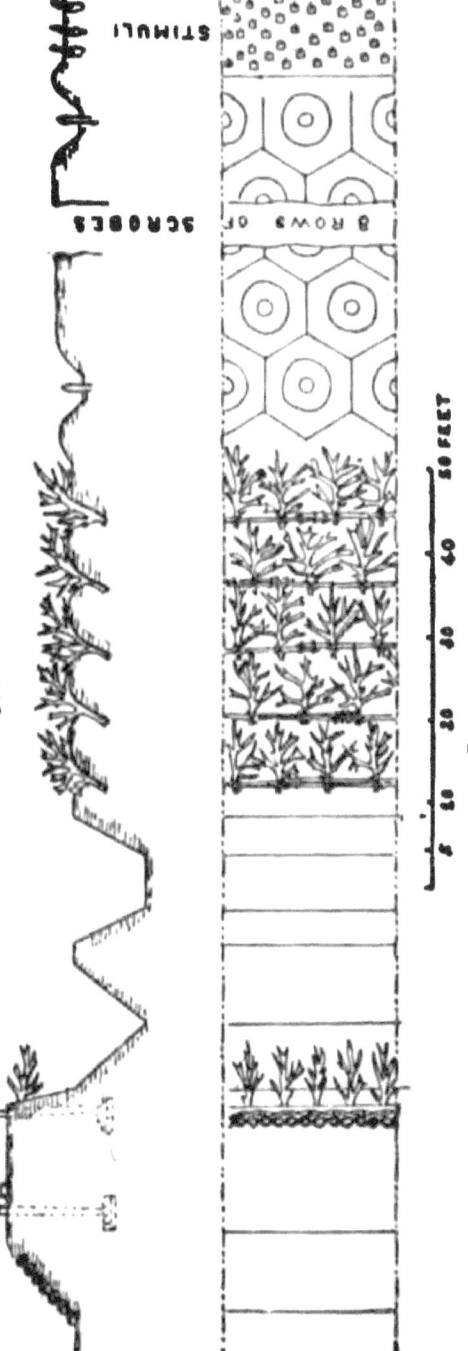

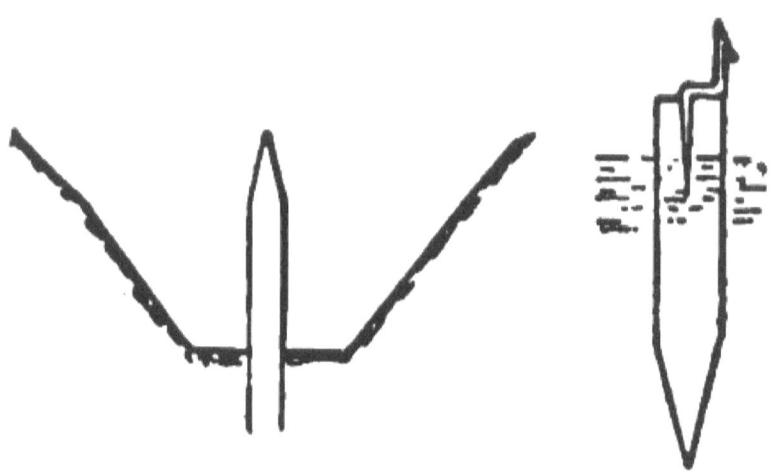

LILIA AND STIMULI

reliefs, there was but one man per metre front, and no reserves to draw on. The enemy made many assaults or demonstrations during the progress of the work, which added to the annoyance. For this reason Caesar deemed the defences not yet strong enough. He wanted to make them such that a small body of men could defend them, so that he could detach at need the bulk of his command to other points. The undertaking was one which demanded every possible aid from art, and he did not cease one instant from perfecting his lines. He devised several kinds of obstacles against sallies and drew up still another threefold line of entanglements. Five rows of slanting trenches, five feet deep, were dug, and sharpened branches like abatis sunk in the bottom. The men called these *cippi*. These five rows of *cippi* were close together, so that the abatis could be interlaced. Eight rows of conical pits (*scrobes*) three feet deep and three feet apart were placed checkerwise, each with a fire-hardened sharp stake as thick as one's thigh at the bottom, and the surface covered with osiers and twigs. These wolf-pits with stakes were nicknamed "lilies." Many of these *trous de loup* have been found. In front of these were sunk stakes close together, armed with iron hooks called *stimuli* (spurs), somewhat resembling huge fishing tackle. The fact that the Romans gave these devices new names looks as if they had not been previously used.

Outside this vast line of contravallation and two hundred yards back, Caesar drew another similar line of circumvallation (x) to provide defence against the Gauls who would certainly soon arrive to raise the siege. These latter works i covered an area of fourteen miles in circumference. The defences stopped at the perpendicular sides of the hills, and began again on the plateaux, as shown in the map. The line varied at places according to topography. Some authorities have attempted to cast a doubt on the accuracy of the extent of these lines; but the *Commentaries* give the figures as eleven and fourteen miles, and they have been completely verified by modern excavations. These have proved very fruitful. Caesar's entrenchments have been traced through their entire length, and many parts of the defences plainly shown. There is no reason, if the work of an ancient historian has come down to us intact, why, within the limits of his intelligence, his statements should not be as worthy of credit as those of an author of today. Caesar's works at Alesia are clearly as described in the *Commentaries*. They are no more wonderful than those of Vicksburg or of Petersburg. Unlimited numbers of men at work always accomplish wonders. To man these works facing both ways, Caesar had in three reliefs but two men per five metres front.

Caesar's defences, immense as were their dimensions, were completed in about forty days. Despite their hardships, the legionaries worked with the best of goodwill. Caesar said in later days that he could have overturned the heavens with such men. At Rome his friends were wont to say that scarcely a mortal man could imagine, none but a god execute such a work; his enemies, for once, were silenced.

It is probable that camp D had two legions. The size of the others leads one to place one legion in A, two in B, three in C, in all eight. The other three were in *castella*. The eleven-mile circuit was the line of the camps and redoubts.

Having completed this extraordinary task, each man was ordered to lay in provisions for thirty days, so as to reduce the danger due to foraging, and to provide against their being themselves blockaded by the army of relief.

Acting on the message of Vercingetorix sent out by his retiring cavalry, the Gauls immediately convened an assembly, probably at Bibracte, and decreed, from all the states, a levy, not a general but a specified levy, lest too large an army should be hard to ration,—two hundred and forty thousand foot, and eight thousand horse in all. The paper strength was two hundred and eighty-three thousand. Even those Gauls whom Caesar had best treated now caught the national infection, revolted and put their best efforts at the service of the cause. The Bellovaci alone declined to send their contingent, but sent two thousand men as an act of friendship. They proposed to be subject to no control. The chief command of this enormous army was given to Commius the Atrebatian, the man Caesar had sent to Britain, Vercasivelaunus the Arvernian, cousin to Vercingetorix, Viridomarus and Eporedorix the Æduan. How the latter escaped from imprisonment, for he was captured in the last battle, is not explained. A war council of members from each tribe was added to these chiefs. Full of confidence, as well it might be, for to barbarians strength resides solely in numbers, this huge army rendezvoused on Æduan soil, and marched to Alesia, imagining that the Romans could not, for a moment, withstand such a multitude, especially when sallies should also be made from within.

Not aware of the speedy arrival of this army, the besieged were already at a loss what to do. Six weeks had elapsed since Vercingetorix sent out his message, and he then had barely corn for thirty days. Starvation was at hand. It was proposed by Cirtognatus, an Arvernian, to eat the useless soldiers and inhabitants; but this yielded to a project to send them away. The whole population (Mandubii) was accordingly marched out; but the Romans declined to receive them even as slaves, and drove them back into the city.

Commius and the great army finally reached the Roman lines, and, camping on the heights southwest of the town, within a mile of Caesar's lines, led out their cavalry the very next day to the large plain, where it was supported by their infantry on the hills at their back. It covered the entire plain. Every movement could be distinctly seen from Alesia. Vercingetorix responded by marshalling his own army outside the city walls and making ready to sustain any assault by the relieving force. He had prepared great numbers of hurdles to fill up the trenches and cover the entanglements.

Vercingetorix' troops advanced. They had actually begun to fill up the first ditch, and the affair promised to develop into a general engagement of infantry. Posting his forces on the walls facing both to the city and towards the army of relief, Caesar opened the action by sending in his German and Gallic allied cavalry. The enemy had light troops mixed with their cavalry, to lend it steadiness. In a short while the battle waxed hot, the Gauls feeling confident of victory from mere force of numbers, and urging on their men by yells and shouts. The people of Alesia encouraged their friends by equal clamour. The action lasted from noon till sundown. Vercingetorix did not push on, nor did the army of relief put in its foot. The action does not appear to have gone beyond a combat of cavalry aided by slingers and bowmen. Finally, after the cavalry of Caesar had been all but defeated, the Germans, rallying in column for a final effort, drove in the Gauls despite their numbers, and broke them up. Once fairly routed, they could not recover themselves; Caesar's squadrons pursued them to camp, killing many of the archers who were supporting them, and who could not so speedily get away. The forces from Alesia retired dejected. There had been no organized attack upon the entrenchments. The prominent role played by the cavalry in all Caesar's wars shows that most of his battles were confined to a skirmishing contact. For pitched battle the legions alone were available. Caesar had no cavalry proper. The next day but one the army of relief again attacked, having, in the mean time, made a much greater number of hurdles, and provided themselves with scaling-ladders and wall-hooks. They selected midnight for the hour and delivered the assault suddenly at the westerly plain. Their shouts aroused Vercingetorix and the forces in the town, who at once sallied forth to lend assistance to their friends outside. The Gauls, as best they might in the darkness, filled up the pits and trenches with fascines and hurdles, covering their operation with a fire of sling-stones and arrows. The Romans were fully alive to the necessities of the occasion. Each man knew his place. They sent for troops from those redoubts which were least exposed, to resist the onset where it was hottest. The *legates* Trebonius and Antonius brought up reinforcements. The Romans replied to the Gallic fire with arrows, sling-stones, hand-hurled stones of about a pound weight, of which they had gathered a large supply, and pointed stakes kept on the walls in reserve. The military engines also came into play. In the dark, shields were almost useless. While the enemy's line was at a distance, the assault proved more harmful in loss to the Romans than when the barbarians neared the walls, for then many of them fell into the pits and trenches; this bred confusion and dismay; their aim grew wild, and their weapons inflicted little damage; the Romans, on the other hand, threw down their heavy siege *pila* from the entrenchments with deadly effect. Before long the vigour of the Gauls slackened. Finally, at daylight they conceived a fear of a demonstration on their uncovered right flank from the Roman lines on the hills south of the town, which, coupled to fatigue and loss of men, induced them to retire. Vercingetorix, from the town side, suffered equally from the entanglements. His men used up most of their time in filling the twenty-foot ditch, and did not get beyond it; and as daylight came on, seeing that the assault by the army of relief had failed, he also blew the signal to retire.

CHAPTER 20
The Battle of Alesia
Fall of 52 B. C.

The Gallic army of relief made a third and last assault on Caesar's lines, after careful preparation. They skilfully probed the weakest spot in the Roman line, which was at the northwest camp, and made a violent attack on it with a chosen body of sixty thousand men. At the same moment the cavalry made a demonstration at the western plain. The legions were put to it as never before to hold their own. Perceiving the attack by the army of relief, Vercingetorix moved against the lines from within. Caesar had an army equal to his own on either side of him, each delivering a desperate assault at the same moment, and with huge reserves in support. He himself was omnipresent and kept his men heartily to their work. The value of the defences was now apparent. The Gauls could nowhere penetrate the line, though attacks were made at several places, and came dangerously close to success. Finally, by a well-timed sortie with the sword and a simultaneous cavalry charge on their flank, the Gauls were driven back, and discouraged at their threefold defeat, the army of relief retired; Vercingetorix surrendered. The siege of Alesia practically sealed the doom of Gaul.

The Gauls had now been defeated in two assaults. These, indeed, had been partial ones, but want of success had begun to discourage the men. The leaders distinctly foresaw failure unless they could wrest a victory from the Romans in the next encounter. The Gallic character before the Christian era is universally described as illy adapted to bear the strain of continued disaster. Commius proposed to make one more strong effort to break through Caesar's lines, and the Gauls went to work systematically to discover the weakest part of the Roman walls. By inquiries of the country people they learned what were the troops and kinds of defences at each point.

On the northwest of the town was a hill which the engineers had not included in the circumvallation, on account of its area. They had been obliged to run the wall at its foot on comparatively low ground. Here was the camp D of two legions, under the legates Anstitius and Caninius. It was located on the steep slope of the hillside. Back of this point the Gallic chiefs decided to assemble sixty thousand men chosen from the tribes most noted for valour, and to attack on a given day at noon,—Vercasivelaunus being given the command of the assaulting party. This force was moved at night by a circuit of a dozen miles to near the spot selected and was concealed under cover of the hill on its north slope.

As noon approached, his men being well rested, fed and eager for the fray, Vercasivelaunus drew them up in order and marched rapidly against the Roman camp. There appear to have been some works on Mt. Rea; probably only an outpost. This body, at all events, was hustled out and the Gauls moved down the slope on camp D. At the same time, as agreed, the cavalry made a sharp demonstration upon the Roman defences fronting the plain, sustained by an advance of the foot. Vercingetorix, in the town, was not slow to perceive what his countrymen were about,—he was constantly and anxiously on the outlook for their assault,—and sallied forth with all his implements, movable pent-houses, ladders, mural hooks and other tools, of which he had prepared a large supply for such an occasion. His attack was delivered opposite Vercasivelaunus, somewhat to the left. Thus, while at the plain the cavalry demonstration caused Caesar no little anxiety, two infantry armies, each nearly equal to the entire Roman force, were again attacking his lines front and rear on the side where perhaps he was weakest. The Roman forces were widely distributed, and it was hard to say what other part of the line might be attempted. In fact, Caesar could scarcely expect that with some three hundred thousand men the Gauls within and without would put into action less than half their force.

The attack was sudden and severe. The Gauls, with every kind of expedient, pressed in on whatever part of the wall appeared most weak. They were evidently in earnest, and they fought as if they expected and meant to win. Their gallantry was consummate. Caesar had prepared several outlooks from which he could get a commanding view of the whole field. In one of these he stationed himself, probably near the south end of the twenty-foot trench, and dispatched troops from place to place, wherever they seemed to be

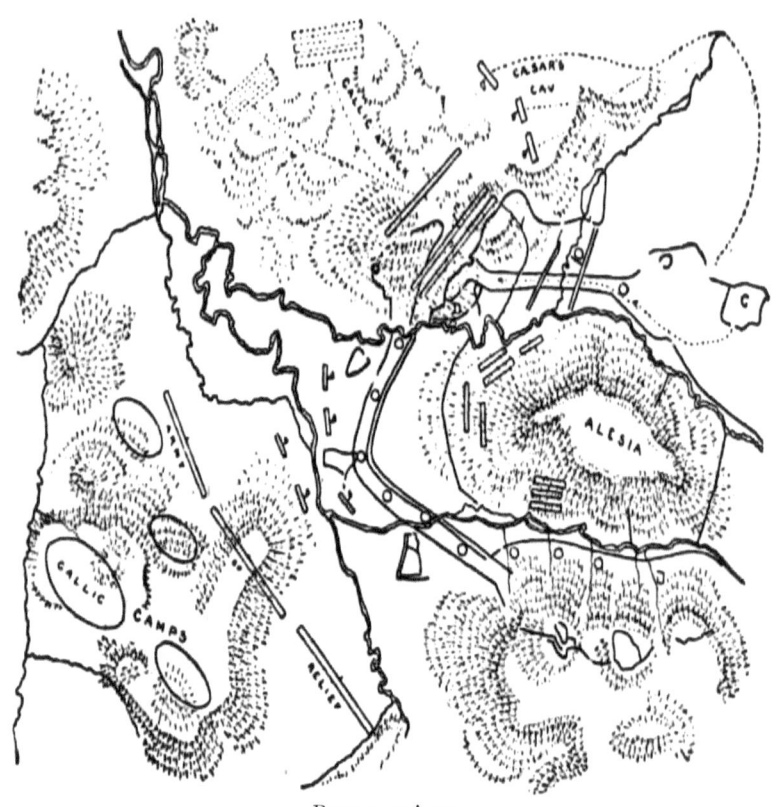

BATTLE OF ALESIA

most needed. Each party was nerved up to do its best. The Gauls evidently felt this to be their last chance of freeing themselves from the hated Roman yoke; the Romans understood that this battle, if gained, would be the term of their labours. Moreover, they recognized their certain fate if they did not win.

The brunt of the struggle came at the northwest camp, where, owing to the high ground above the Roman defences, missiles could be more effectively hurled by the barbarians, and *testudos* put to use. Here, too, were the most renowned warriors, while at the main lines the Gauls were, however numerous, of no marked fighting quality. The abundant force at the northwest camp enabled the enemy to relieve the weary with fresh men at frequent intervals, and to heap mounds up against the Roman wall, which put them on a par with the *legionaries*. After some hours of combat the Roman soldiers at this point had used up all their missiles.

Observing their distress, Caesar ordered Labienus with six *cohorts* from the northeast camp (C) to go to their relief, and if compelled to do so, to make a sally with the sword, while he himself repaired to the plain to encourage the troops. The Gauls under Vercingetorix, within, in despair of effecting a lodgement in the Roman lines at the point where they had been fighting, made a fresh attempt on a more precipitous but less guarded place, probably the foot of the south camp; and having brought engines and tools, which they used under cover of a storm of missiles, they succeeded in driving the defenders from the walls, in filling the ditches and tearing down the wattling cover of the palisades with mural hooks. To meet this new and threatening danger, Caesar dispatched Brutus with six *cohorts* to the point assailed, and as this did not appear to suffice, followed him up by Fabius with seven more. Even this did not turn the tide; he was at last personally obliged to hurry to this point in order to rehabilitate the battle, a matter which he succeeded in accomplishing after some time and with considerable effort.

As Labienus had been unable to hold the enemy in check at the northwest camp (D), Caesar sent a portion of his cavalry by a circuit outside the walls, to debouch from the north ravine, file up along the slope of the hills, and attack the enemy in the rear. He himself, so soon as the assault of Vercingetorix had been beaten off, taking four *cohorts* and some horse, rushed to the support of Labienus. The latter, meanwhile, had drawn a large number of *cohorts* from the redoubts which could best spare them. The bulk of the barbarians, happily for Caesar, remained inactive in reserve. His arrival—which all the *legionaries* could see, for he wore the imperator's robe, the purple *paludamentum*, over his armour—yielded the utmost encouragement to his men. They could always do wonders under the eye of Caesar. In their ardour they ceased the use of missiles and betook themselves to the sword.

At this moment the German cavalry, which Caesar had sent out, charged sharply in on the left rear of the Gauls, and raising a great shout the *legionaries* rushed upon them. Nothing could withstand their onset. Broken by its vigour, the enemy turned and fled, but only to be cut down by the cavalry. A number of the chiefs, among them Sedulius, prince of the Lemovices, were slain; others, principal among whom was Vercasivelaunus, were captured; and seventy-four standards were taken. The men under Vercingetorix, seeing their auxiliaries thus defeated, and Caesar ready to turn on them, withdrew from their attack and retired into Alesia, in the utmost dejection. The troops which had not been engaged caught the alarm and made haste to retreat;

retreat soon became rout. The flight of the Gauls from the battlefield was by no means arrested at their camp; the whole body of warriors began to seek safety wherever each could find it; had the cavalry been fresh, they could have been annihilated. As it was, a large number were cut down and the rest dispersed into the woods. Only after long wandering did they find their way to their respective states.

The stake having been nobly played and lost, Vercingetorix surrendered himself to his countrymen to be dealt with as they saw fit; and these at once sent ambassadors to Caesar. There was no alternative. Caesar disarmed the Gallic soldiers and ordered them to surrender their leaders.

"Vercingetorix, who was the chief spring of the war, putting his best armour on, and adorning his horse, rode out of the gates, and made a turn about Caesar as he was sitting, then quitting his horse, threw off his armour and remained quietly sitting at Caesar's feet until he was led away." (Plutarch.)

This gallant chieftain was kept for exhibition in Caesar's triumph, and immediate death thereafter, a thing which, whatever the precedent, is scarcely creditable to the Roman, for though an enemy, Vercingetorix was assuredly a hero. The Æduan and Arvernian prisoners were reserved to use in once more gaining over their respective tribes. Of all the other prisoners, Caesar gave one apiece to the soldiers as plunder. These were sold to the traders, of whom there were always plenty not far from a Roman camp. After a battle, they always appeared, ready to profit by the abundance of bargains.

The siege of Alesia exhibits the greatest art in Caesar and equal courage and endurance on the part of his troops. The inaction of the bulk of the barbarians in the last battle had been his salvation, as well as led to the loss of Gallic independence. Though there were, thereafter, isolated cases of insurrection, the country never again rose *en masse*. In a year Gaul was practically a Roman province. Her spirit of resistance had been finally crushed.

After this brilliant success, Caesar marched back to the land of the Ædui, and found no difficulty in recovering that state; and the Arverni made haste to bring in their submission and hostages. To both these tribes Caesar restored some twenty thousand prisoners. After his great victory he could well afford to make use of generosity in his treatment of the Gauls. He was then enabled to put his army into winter-quarters. Labienus, with the Seventh and Fifteenth legions and some cavalry, was placed among the Sequani with Rutilius as his lieutenant;

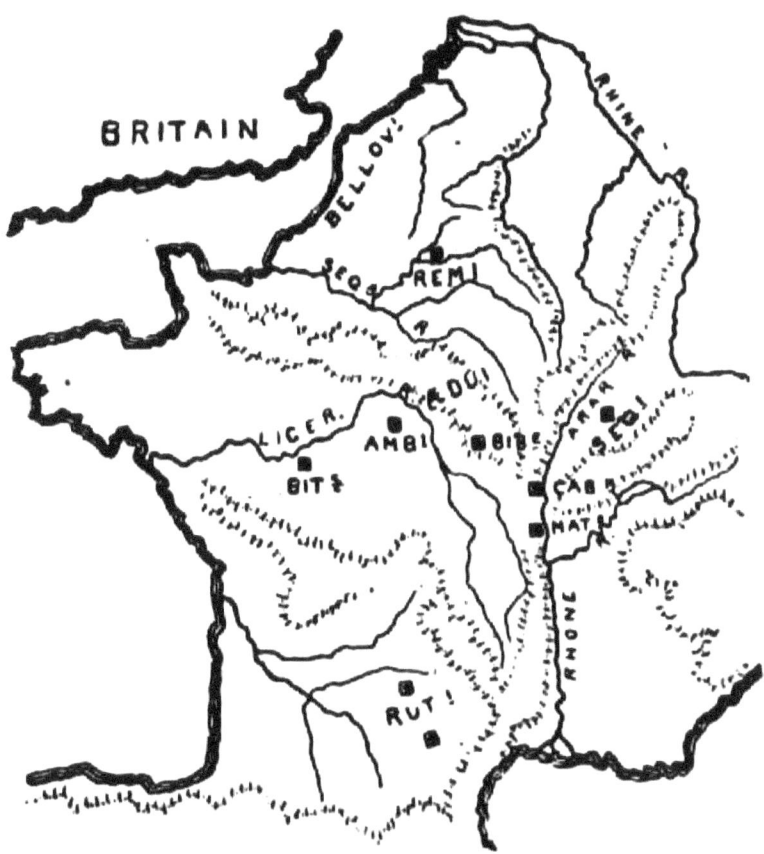

WINTER-QUARTERS, B. C. 52-51

Fabius with the Eighth, and Basilius with the Ninth, among the Remi to protect them against the Bellovaci; the legion of Antistius, the Eleventh, among the Ambivereti; that of Sextius, the Thirteenth, among the Bituriges; that of Caninius, the First, among the Ruteni; Cicero, with the Sixth at Matisco (Macon), and Sulpicius, with the Fourteenth, at Cabillonum (Chalons), charged with procuring corn along the Arar in the land of the Ædui. Caesar himself fixed his headquarters at Bibracte. The location of Antonius, with the Tenth and Twelfth, is not given. It was likely enough at headquarters. A *supplicatio* of twenty days was granted Caesar in Rome.

During none of the campaigns in Gaul did the tribes put so large a force into the field as on this occasion. Forty of the eighty-five tribes, in the course of a month, contributed a quarter of a million men which, added to the eighty thousand under Vercingetorix, made a grand total of three hundred and thirty thousand, almost five times as many as the Roman legions, light troops and allied cavalry together. The danger had been grave for Caesar. But his own genius, the stanchness of the Roman *legionaries* and especially the divided counsels of the barbarians, had saved him. The sixty thousand men who assaulted at the northwest camp at Alesia had been picked; the bulk of the barbarians on the west plain were of poor, stuff. But had even this force attacked from the western face, while Caesar was with difficulty driving back the front and rear assaults on the northern camp, and meeting Vercingetorix from within on the south, however good his lines, he must, it seems, have been overwhelmed. His own account of how hard pushed he was by the partial attack proves how near he came to a fatal outcome. Caesar's courage, the ambition and brilliant gallantry of his men, the loyalty of the allied and the splendid qualities of the German horse, added to good fortune, which smiled on him with even more constancy than it did on Alexander, yielded him the victory. And this victory led to results which were far reaching.

This seventh year is the most interesting as well as the most important of the entire war. It exhibits Caesar's power in engineering, in tactics, in strategy, in logistics. Let us recapitulate events, so as to group the superb list of achievements. Caesar's rapid appearance in the Province on hearing of the Gallic insurrection; his raising troops and crossing the Cebennae into the land of the Arverni, to forestall their invading the Province and deceive the enemy as to his intentions; his personal forced march thence through a network of dangers to the land of the Lingones, where he concentrated his legions on the rear of Vercingetorix, made a splendid and successful strategical opening, particularly as Vercingetorix flattered himself that he had cut Caesar off from his army, and had that army at his mercy. Following this concentration of his legions in the face of opposition came his march from Agendicum to Vellaunodunum, Genabum, Noviodiunun and Avaricum, and his rapid successive capture of these towns. Thence he marched up the Elaver, cleverly stole a passage of that river under the very eyes of Vercingetorix, and besieged Gergovia. Called away from the siege by the Æduan *imbroglio*, as he represents, or beaten back from his assault of it, as is the truth, which he could well afford to acknowledge, Caesar moved back over the Elaver through the land of the revolted Ædui and Senones, forcing the Liger and making his way to Agendicum, where he joined Labienus. Having recruited his forces, he retired through the land of the Lingones on his way to the

Province, beat in fair fight Vercingetorix, who stood across his path, and reopened his communications. Thence following the enemy to Alesia, Caesar finished the year by his wonderful siege and capture of this stronghold. These operations, alike splendid in conception and execution, make a string of military jewels hard to match.

Vercingetorix had proved a worthy antagonist. His plan to avoid open conflict with Caesar and to fight him by a Fabian policy is an extraordinary conception for a barbarian. Vercingetorix exhibited a true natural genius for arms. His mistake lay in not clinging to his original plan. So soon as he wavered in it, he lost. This was not his fault, but that of the political combination against him among his own people. Despite the capacity of Vercingetorix and the fact that the Gauls had more than five times Caesar's force, the genius of this great captain, added to Roman discipline and training, overcame the courage, but lack of unity, of the Gallic allies. Art versus mere strength—as always—could have but one ending.

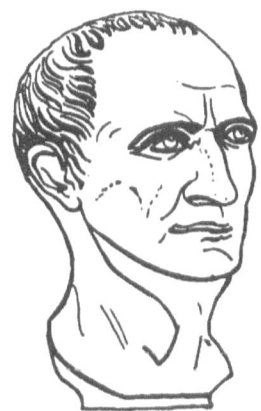

CAESAR, LATE IN GALLIC WAR

Chapter 21

The Bellovaci
January to April, 51 B. C.

The Gauls had learned that they were not equal to the Romans in whatever combination; but they saw that a number of isolated insurrections gave Caesar vastly more trouble than a single combined one. Several uprisings were therefore initiated; but Caesar did not delay an instant. He made a series of winter campaigns, and by taking them unawares, successively reduced the Bituriges and Carnutes. He then marched against the Bellovaci, who, with their allies, had rendezvoused in what is now the Forest of Compègne. Caesar found them strongly entrenched. He camped on an adjacent hill, making a ditch and his wall in two stories. After some skirmishing between the rival outposts and cavalry, the barbarians prepared to retire, fearing another Alesia. Caesar made ready to follow, but the Gauls detained him by a clever stratagem, and escaped. Seeking shortly to entrap him in an ambuscade, the barbarians were themselves surprised and defeated. Caesar then distributed his legions so as best to dope with the several insurrections, whose extent he could not yet gauge.

The rest which the Roman legions had fairly earned in the splendid campaign just ended was not destined to last long. The Gauls had been beaten, to be sure, but not all of them were subdued. Then as now they added to native gallantry the habit of not yielding until they had tried a number of ways to accomplish a desired end. They had tried the experiment of rising in one body and had been distinctly worsted; they had learned that they were, in whatever numbers, no match for Roman discipline, courage and intellect. But they had also learned that the most grievous blows they had inflicted on Caesar were those they had given by waging a judicious small-war in many localities at the same time. This system they determined once more to try. They were intelligent enough to understand that while Caesar could, no doubt, defeat them wherever he might be, he was unable to be everywhere at once. If the Gauls had all been willing to come within the scope of this plan, and if they had had another leader like Vercingetorix to carry through such a policy to the end, Caesar's conquest of Gaul might never have been completed. But fortune did not favour the Gauls in their brave struggle for liberty. It was destined, happily for them and for us, that they, too, should bear the Roman yoke.

Caesar was shortly informed of the consultations of the Gauls to this end, and determined to crush the uprising in the bud. While the leaders of the several tribes were still arguing and preparing, he went

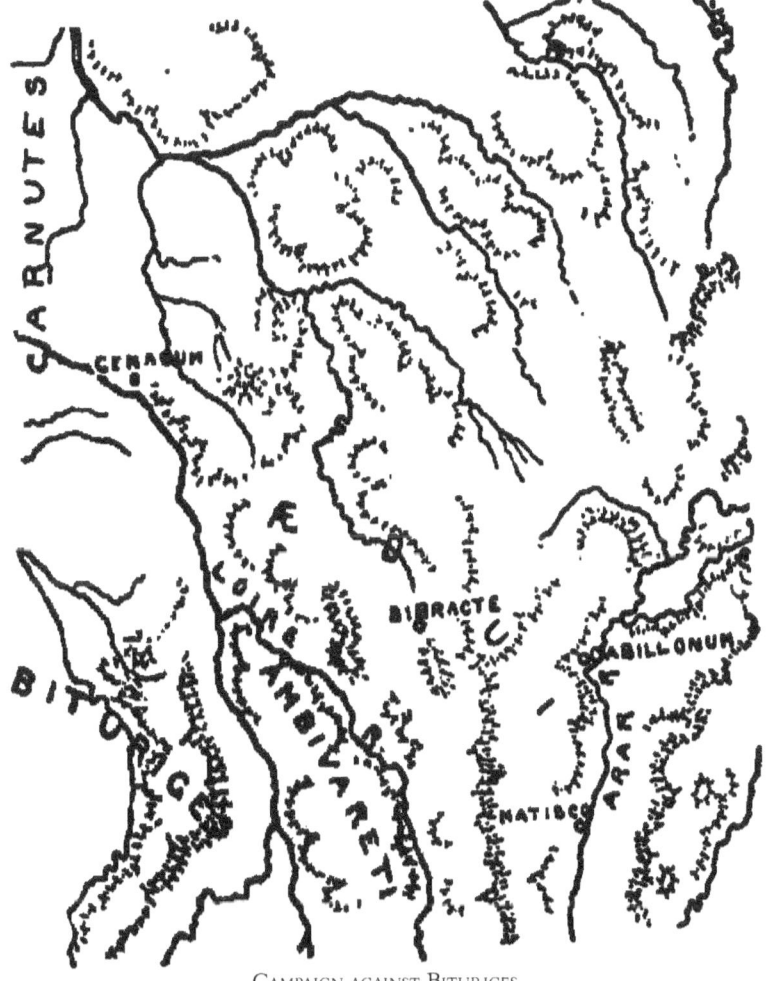

CAMPAIGN AGAINST BITURIGES

to work. Leaving Mark Antony in charge of headquarters at Bibracte, on the day before the *kalends* of January, he set out with a body of horse for the Thirteenth legion, which was wintering among the Bituriges on their boundary nearest the Ædui. Lest a single legion should not be sufficient to keep the enemy in control, he added to the Thirteenth the Eleventh legion, which was stationed among the Ambivareti nearby. Leaving two *cohorts* of each to guard the baggage and winter-quarters, he moved by forced marches upon the Bituriges and surprised them completely. He made many prisoners, but forbade plundering or burning, promising his men two hundred *sestertii* each, and every centurion two thousand *sestertii* in lieu thereof. He not only desired not to disaffect the population too seriously, but also to preserve the corn and forage for his own use. The burning stacks and farms would moreover serve to give warning of their danger to adjoining tribes, and it was Caesar's plan to attack and compel each tribe separately to bring in its submission.

The chiefs of the Bituriges endeavoured to escape, for their preparations were barely begun, but so hot was Caesar's pursuit of them wherever they fled, that, by heading them off, and capturing them one by one, he speedily broke up their combinations. Those of the population who desired to retain their allegiance to Rome he protected by taking from their midst the conspirators who were leading them astray. This policy of vigour flavoured with generosity forestalled a general uprising. The campaign had lasted but forty days. In its rapidity and success, it approaches some of Alexander's short operations against mountain tribes. The two legions went back to winter-quarters.

Eighteen days after Caesar had returned to Bibracte at the end of February, the Bituriges invoked his aid against the Carnutes who had begun war upon them. In order not to disappoint this tribe in its newly sworn allegiance, Caesar called in Cicero's Sixth legion from Cabillonum and Sulpicius' Fourteenth legion from Matisco, on the Arar, and marched to Genabum. From this place as a centre he conducted a partisan warfare against the Carnutes with his allied horse. This tribe made no pretence at resistance but dispersed into the country, where at this season they had much ado to get provisions, and finally fled to other tribes. The soldiers gathered much booty. Caesar had scarcely used his infantry. He preferred for the sake of his men not to undertake further active operations at this inclement season, and left the two legions in Genabum, where he could quarter them to advantage.

Caesar and Hannibal both disliked winter campaigns. Unlike Alexander, for whose exuberant physical and moral hardihood no season was too severe, they kept their troops in winter-quarters unless operations became imperative. But on this occasion Caesar sent out his cavalry detachments through the length and breadth of the land, and these, backed up by the presence of the legions, broke down all present opposition. He was fain to be content with so much at this season.

This task finished, he placed Trebonius in command of the two legions at Genabum, and left for the land of the Remi, who had appealed to him against the Bellovaci and neighbouring tribes; for these were preparing war upon them and the Suessiones, their clients, under the leadership of Correus the Bellovacian and the so long faithful Caninius the Atrebatian. The Remi were allies of Rome and had been stanch friends, who must be helped at any cost. Their early usefulness in the Belgian campaign will be remembered. Caesar hastened

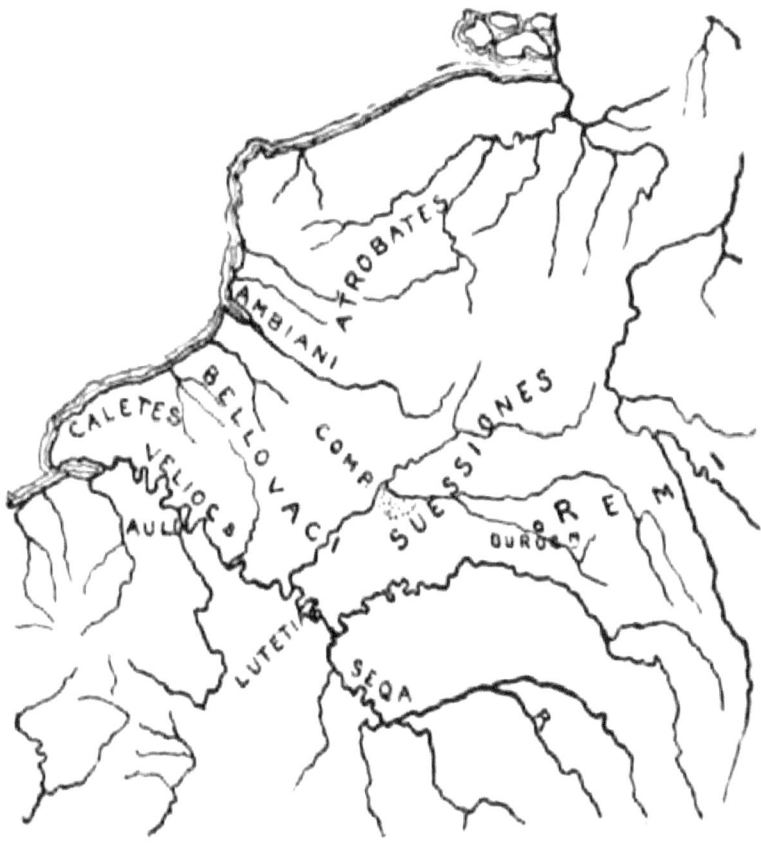

CAMPAIGN OF BELLOVACI

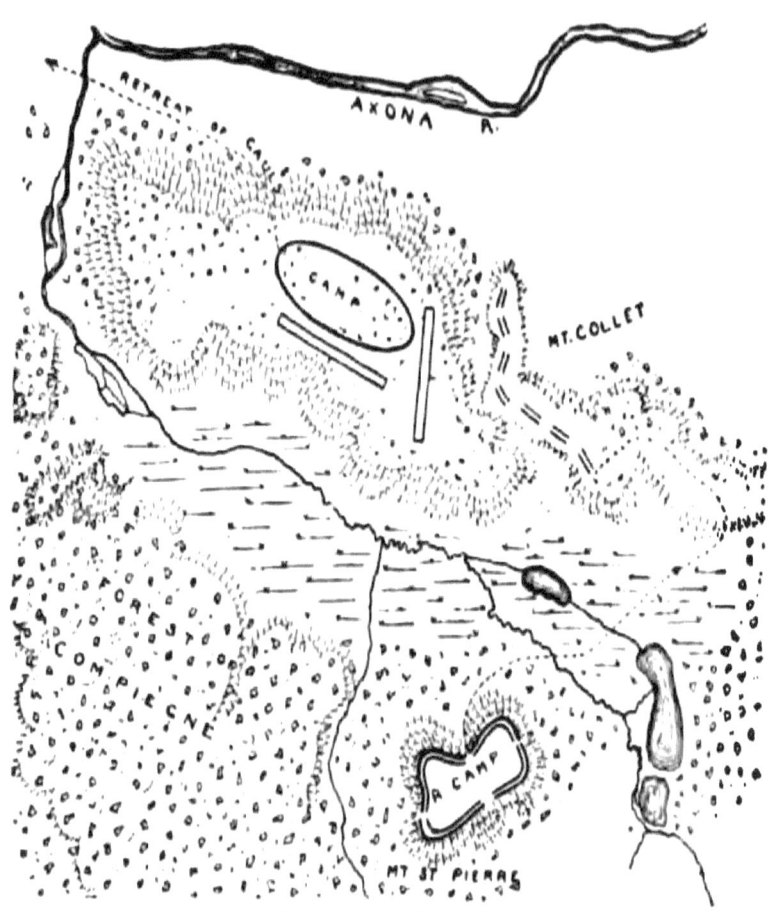

FIGHT AGAINST BELLOVACI

to Durocortorum with the Eleventh legion and one drawn from Labienus at Vesontio. The *Commentaries* say that the legion was drawn from Trebonius, but as this legate was later ordered to bring up both his from Genabum, it is probable that Labienus was meant. Caesar ordered Fabius to march to the land of the Suessiones with the two which, under his command, had been wintering among the Remi. By these details he endeavoured to give duty alternately to the legions. He, individually, ceased not from work.

Arrived in the territory of the Bellovaci, Caesar camped and sent his cavalry out to reconnoitre. He ascertained that all the able-bodied men of this and adjacent tribes (the Ambiani, Aulerci, Caletes, Veliocasses and Atrebates) had left their dwellings, were on a war footing, and camped on a hill surrounded by a morass—modern Mt. St. Marc in the Forest of Compiègne—with their baggage hidden in the depths of the forest farther away; that Correus was in general command, Commius being away to gather auxiliaries from the Germans on the Mosa; that they proposed to fight if Caesar had but three legions, but to remain in camp and harass him with small-war and cut off his forage, which was in any event hard to get, if he had more than three. "Caesar was convinced of the truth of this account by the concurring testimony of several prisoners."

This prudent resolution, so far as it applied to fighting only a small force, Caesar determined to encourage. Though he had four legions with him,—three veteran, the Seventh, Eighth and Ninth, and the Eleventh "composed of chosen young men of great hopes, who had served eight campaigns, but who, compared to the others, had not yet acquired any great reputation for experience or valour,"—he endeavoured to make the enemy believe he had only three. He therefore marched the Seventh, Eighth and Ninth by themselves in the van, and left the Eleventh to follow the train at a convenient distance. "By this disposition he formed his army almost into a square, and brought them within sight of the enemy sooner than was anticipated." He had given his officers full instructions as to his plans. There are fre-

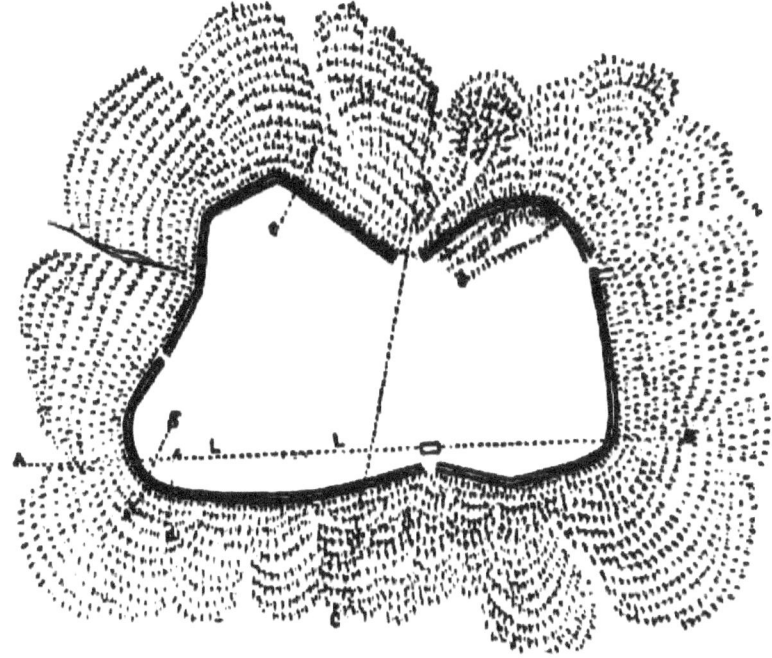

CAMP AT MT. ST. PIERRE

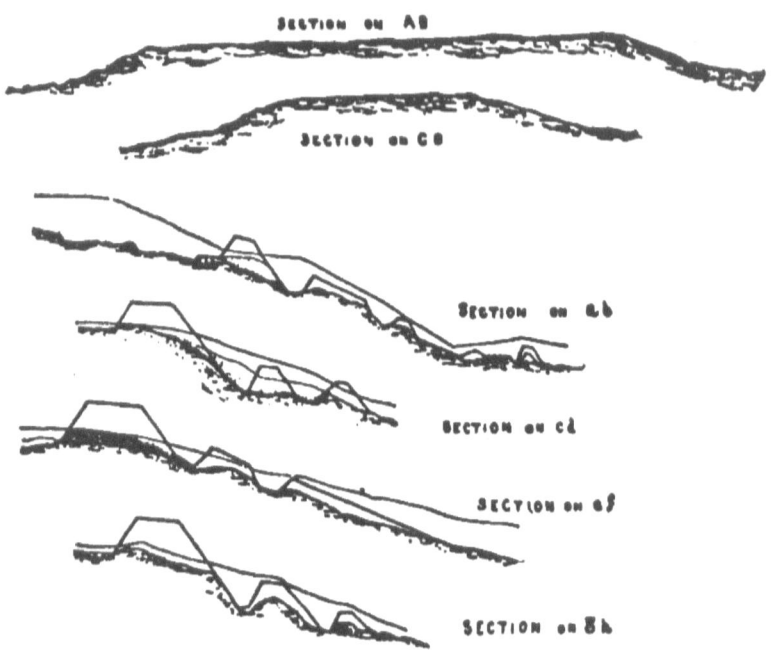

SECTION OF WALL AND DITCH

quent rather puzzling statements in the *Commentaries*. This was largely a wooded country, and how Caesar could move his column in anything like a square seems to us, who are familiar with the limitations of modern armies, highly singular. But infantry or cavalry, with no baggage except pack-mules, can, and on our Western plains does, get over ground which would be considered utterly impracticable for an army if hampered by artillery and trains. We may accept Caesar's statement as a broad description of his order of march, and not assume his square to have been an exact equivalent of our modern square.

On perceiving Caesar's approach, the enemy drew up in front of their camp, but declined to leave their advantageous position on the heights. Caesar saw that their number was much too great to attack without proper preparation, and went into camp on the other side of a deep valley,—on Mt. St. Pierre. His camp he fortified with a twelve-foot rampart, with roofed breastworks on it and down the slope two trenches fifteen feet wide, with, as he says, perpendicular sides and square bottom, though the excavations do not show them such. It was easy, when he later wrote about it, to forget the kind of trench he may have dug. He built several turrets three stories high, intercommunicating with galleries, all protected by hurdles. Two rows of men, one above the other, could fight on the ramparts. Those on the galleries could throw their darts farther, while the lower rank on the *vallum* would be protected by the platform against falling darts. The gates were flanked by heavy turrets. This camp would be secure when a part of the garrison had gone foraging; would make a safe magazine for stores; and Caesar hoped the enemy would suppose from all this preparation that he felt concerned for his safety and be induced to attack him in his entrenchments. This camp of Caesar's at Mt. St. Pierre has been exploited, and its contours and area and many of its details have been brought to light. These are interesting to show how the accentuation of the ground was put to use to facilitate the erection of defences. Caesar was fond of doing things in a novel way. Any new idea which occurred to him he was apt to carry out, to test its adaptability and usefulness.

There was constant skirmishing at a ford across the marsh, now a piece of low meadow land, which lay between the rival camps; either party crossing and engaging the other with alternate success. The Roman foragers were constantly attacked by the barbarians. Some successes thus obtained, and particularly the arrival of five hundred German horse, under Commius, greatly encouraged the barbarians.

Caesar deemed it wise to send back for more troops, as the Gauls were many and in a peculiarly strong situation, and as he deemed an investment the only safe means of attacking the barbarian stronghold. He ordered Trebonius to draw in the Thirteenth legion, which under Sextius was in the territory of the Bituriges, and with it and his own two, the Sixth and Fourteenth at Genabum, to join him by forced marches.

Meanwhile the barbarians were all the more encouraged by an ambuscade into which they led the Reman, Lingonian, and other allied horse, and during which a number were killed, including their chief. Caesar had drafted a considerable tale of mounted men from all the tribes which he had subdued. This was an easy and effectual way of insuring their good behaviour, for it took from among them their leading citizens,—in other words, those able to serve mounted,—and kept them under Caesar's own eye. It had its corresponding danger in keeping with the army a sometimes uncertain element; but under Caesar's immediate control the danger was minimized.

A few days after the above defeat, some of the German foot auxiliaries crossed the marsh, and in a hand-to-hand combat drove the enemy into and a few even beyond their camp. This defeat and the arrival of Trebonius frightened and disheartened the enemy as much as they had been before encouraged. Fearing another Alesia siege they prepared to leave, and sent forward by night their baggage and old people. As daylight overtook them during this operation, not daring openly to continue the retreat, they drew up part of their army in front of their camp to protect it and conceal the movement in retreat.

Caesar saw what the barbarians were doing. He bridged the morass in his front (there are still traces of this road), and making his way to a hill—Mt. Collet—overlooking the enemy, he drew up in line of battle. He did not wish to assault, nor was it worthwhile to follow the flying column, as owing to the River Axona on one side and the marsh on the other, he could not reach it except by exposing his flank. The enemy declined to leave their position. Caesar camped and fortified

THEATRE OF BELLOVACIAN CAMPAIGN

in that place and then remained in line of battle, the horses bridled ready for attack or pursuit, in case the enemy should divide in order to get away. The hill on which he lay had abrupt sides, and was separated from the Bellovacian position by a narrow valley in places but two hundred yards apart. The engines, it appears, could fire across it. This fire, which they were unable to return, galled the barbarians sensibly. Observing Caesar's intention, the Bellovaci resorted to the following clever stratagem. Piling bundles of straw, of which they used much to sit and lie upon, with hurdles and other inflammables in their front, at nightfall they set all this on fire. Under cover of the smoke they precipitately retired.

Caesar guessed as much, but advanced cautiously, naturally fearing some ambuscade. The horse could not easily advance through the line of fire. Thus the enemy was able to retreat in safety ten miles, where they took up another strong position on a hill fortified by nature. This is thought to have been Mont Ganelon, north of the confluence of the Aisne and Oise. It is only six miles from Mt. St. Marc as the crow flies, but a circuit may have been necessary to cross the rivers. It is not stated that Caesar followed them up. He probably kept to his camp and reconnoitred the vicinity to await a favourable chance of action. From their new camp the barbarians again engaged in their small-war by a number of lesser ambushes, doing much harm to the Roman foragers.

Learning soon after that Correus, the chief of the Bellovaci, had placed six thousand of his best foot and one thousand horse in an ambush where the Roman foragers were apt to go because there was considerable provision, Caesar himself accompanied these, and made his party somewhat larger than usual. His cavalry he mixed with light infantry and sustained by some *cohorts* of legionaries. The ground for the ambush was a plain about a mile in extent,—not far from Choisy au Bac,—surrounded by woods and the River Aisne. The enemy's force was led by Correus. At the proper moment Correus emerged from the woods and attacked the column of foragers, expecting entire victory. The ambush proved a failure, as the Romans were in force and fully prepared for it; the cavalry was quickly sustained by the bowmen, and after a severe combat of the van, in which the cavalry and light troops fought with commendable bravery, the legions arrived and hemmed in the barbarians. Correus tried to retire, but he was himself in the trap he had laid for the Romans, with the river closing him in. The Romans killed all but a very few, Correus among them, despite the latter's desperate resistance.

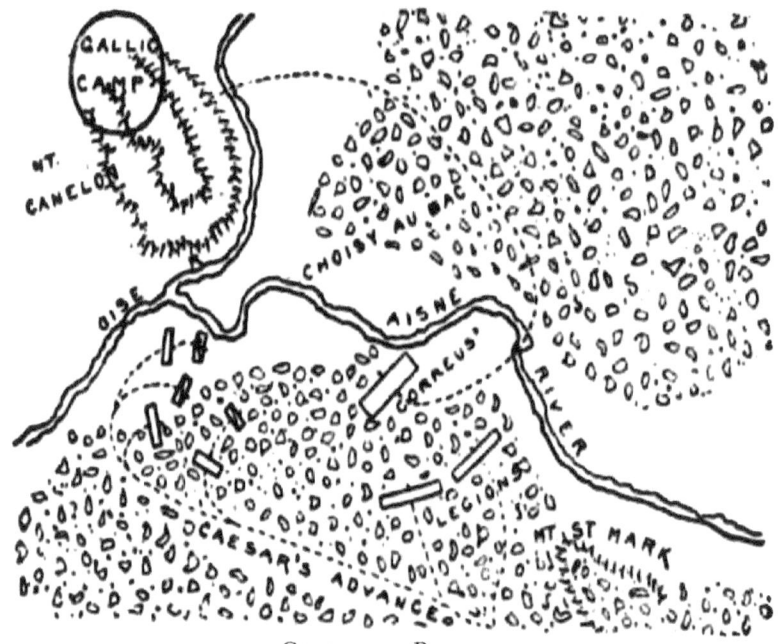

COMBAT WITH BELLOVACI

Caesar then marched sharply upon the camp of the main body, but the other chiefs, believing resistance useless, sued for peace. Commius the Atrebatian, who was the chief instigator of the revolt, fled to the Germans. Caesar gave the Bellovaci to understand that they themselves were the cause of all their own troubles, but pursued a liberal policy in dealing with them. He had become convinced that his system of extermination was politically unsound.

Caesar now saw that these nations were quite subjugated, but that many were endeavouring to get rid of the Roman dominion by emigration. To this he desired to put a stop. He distributed his army, the better to control the tribes. The *legate*, C. Caninius, had been previously sent south to the land of the Ruteni, with his two legions, the First and Tenth; but he found himself too weak to control the turbulent population on his route, and had stopped on the way, among the Pictones. To Caninius' assistance, Caesar now sent C. Fabius with twenty-five *cohorts*. He ordered the Fifteenth legion to Cisalpine Gaul to protect that province from inroads of mountain tribes, and smaller detachments (to one or other place where they were needed. He retained for his own disposition Mark Antony, now *quaestor*, and the Twelfth legion, together with Labienus and some of the other legions, and marched to the country of Ambiorix.

This chief had fled, but Caesar thoroughly devastated the Eburonian territory by fire, sword and rapine. This was the second time he had thus visited the land. It was an act which was entirely uncalled for, and as inexcusable as it was inhuman and unworthy of Caesar. The *Commentaries* give as a reason that Caesar desired to leave no territory for Ambiorix to return to which could afford him support, and to make the few remaining people hate this chief for the evils he had brought on them. But this is no valid excuse even for ancient days. Ambiorix was an enemy and had inflicted a heavy penalty on Sabinus and Cotta. Revenge against Ambiorix' person should not have been thus late carried forward upon his people. He had previously punished the Eburones with sufficient severity. Caesar shines most when he is magnanimous, least when he is cruel.

From the Euronean land Caesar sent Labienus with two legions to overawe the Treviri, who were much like the Germans, and never abode long in their allegiance.

It is rare that the *Commentaries* mention the legions by name or number. They cannot, therefore, always be followed with certainty. Subsequent mention often enables a legion to be identified, but not in every instance. Occasionally the *Commentaries* are manifestly in error. Whenever possible, the legions have been specified by number, but generally they have to be dealt with in gross. The rotation in command of the officers of the Roman army conflicts with the individuality of the legion. Only the Tenth, Caesar's favourite, and the one he was wont to have on the wing where he commanded, is specially prominent. This legion Caesar continually refers to.

CHAPTER 22

Uxellodunum
Spring of 51 B. C.

Caninius and Fabius, with four legions and a half, had pursued an army of freebooters heading for the province under Drappes and Lucterius, as far south as Uxellodunum, which these outlaws had seized. This *oppidum* was almost as difficult of access as Gergovia or Alesia. The barbarians having sent out a party to bring provisions to the place, the Romans managed to capture the entire convoy. Caninius and Fabius had the place invested when Caesar arrived. The enemy had enough corn, but relied for water on a stream flowing on the west of the place. Caesar cut off this supply by a system of outposts, and the Gauls were then confined to a spring on the hillside. Caesar set to work to cut this off also. He built a mound and tower from which he could direct missiles upon the water-carriers, and gradually undermined the spring, so as to tap and divert its flow. Uxellodunum then surrendered. Caesar spent the rest of the year in traversing Gaul from end to end to confirm the people in their allegiance, and to rectify the many abuses naturally arising from the war.

C. Caninius, meanwhile, hearing that Duracius, a friendly ally, was besieged in Limonum (Poitiers), a town of the Pictones, by Dumnacus, chief of the Andes, marched from his winter-quarters among the Ruteni with his two legions, the First and Tenth, to his assistance. Finding himself unable to cope with the barbarians, who were in large force, he camped nearby in a strong position. The barbarians attacked his camp but without success; they were driven back with loss. When it was reported, soon thereafter, that Caninius was to be reinforced by C. Fabius, whom Caesar had sent to his aid with twenty-five *cohorts*, the besiegers not only raised the siege

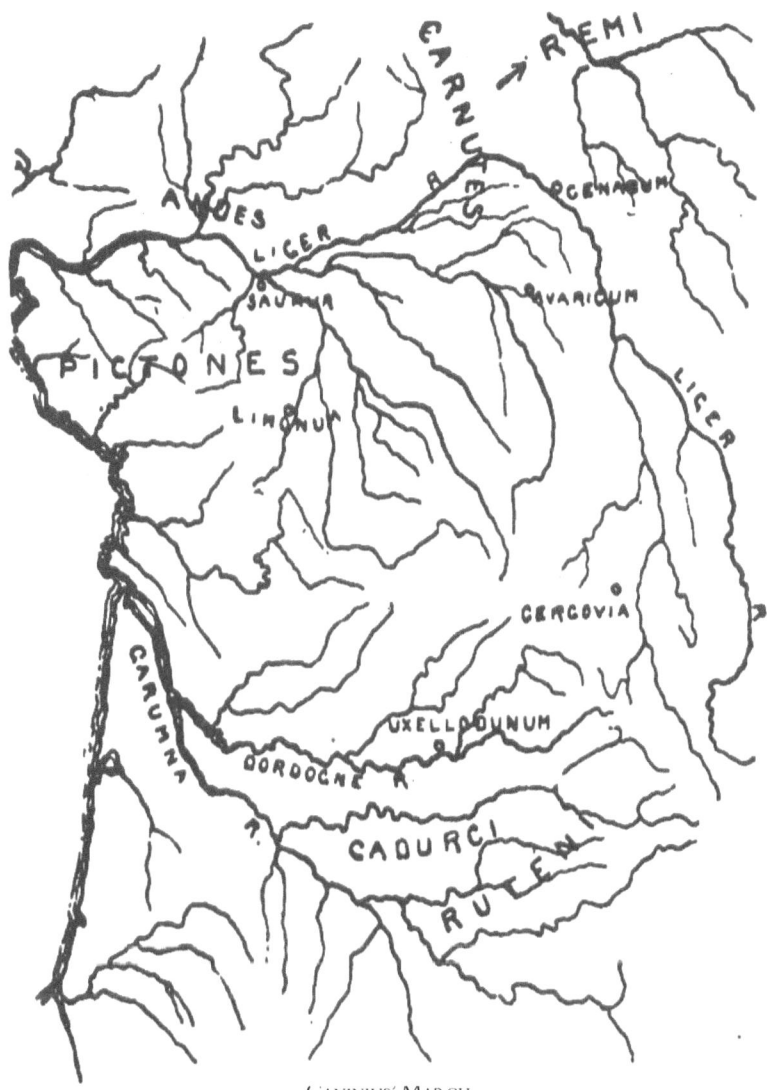

CANINIUS' MARCH

and decamped, but retired beyond the Liger. Fabius, coming from the north,—he had been among the Remi,—caught them on the march, harassed their rear with great loss at the bridge where now stands Saumur, and gained much booty. The next day, the horse in pursuit, having gone too far beyond the infantry for the purpose of bringing the fugitive army to a halt, engaged in a combat with the rear of the enemy, who turned upon them and, sustaining their cavalry with foot, pressed them hard. The legions arrived when the Ro-

Uxellodunum

man allied horse was all but exhausted, re-established matters, and put the enemy to rout with a loss of not far from twelve thousand men. Their entire baggage-train was captured.

The Andes having been disposed of and the land quieted by the destruction of all its warriors and warlike material, Caninius was called on to follow towards the province a body of some five thousand men, consisting of robbers, runaway slaves and other desperate characters, who under Drappes and Lucterius were moving thither. Fabius, with his twenty-five *cohorts*, marched to the land of the Carnutes, who had been engaged in the recent uprising, but with all the Armorican tribes between them and the ocean now brought in their submission. Dumnacus was obliged to flee to remotest Gaul.

Caninius followed Drappes and Lucterius, who, knowing that they could accomplish nothing in the Province against his legions, had stopped in the land of the Cadurci, and seized Uxellodunum (Puy d'Issolu), a, stronghold on very inaccessible rocks and hardly needing defences. It had been formerly a vassal town of Drappes. The location of Uxellodunum has been put on the Oltis (Lot), but late excavations have proved it to be modern Puy d'Issolu. Caninius followed the enemy, camped on three adjacent hills, and began to draw lines of contravallation to besiege the place.

The plateau of Uxellodunum covers some two hundred acres and is six hundred feet above the plain. It is north of the Duranius (Dordogne), between which and it lies a flat plain. On its west is a range of hills separated from it by a narrow valley, and on its northeast is a smaller plateau (Pech Demont) joined to it by a ravine. On these heights Caninius established his camps, which were on a level with the *oppidum*. On the west and south of the Uxellodunum plateau were perpendicular rocks one hundred and forty feet high. On the east was an easier slope. Of the three camps, 1 and 2 were not entrenched, as from the lay of the land it was not necessary, and there were few men in Uxellodunum; 3 was entrenched because it was accessible from the *oppidum*. The position of camps 1 and 2 is fixed upon from the topography. No remains have been found of their walls.

The barbarians, fearing another Alesia and determined not to be starved into surrender, sent out all but two thousand of their force to gather corn, of which they established a *dépôt* some ten miles away. Meanwhile the garrison simulated numbers by sundry attacks on Caninius' camps, and interrupted his work. Lucterius and Drappes proposed to gradually convey the provision to the *oppidum* in small

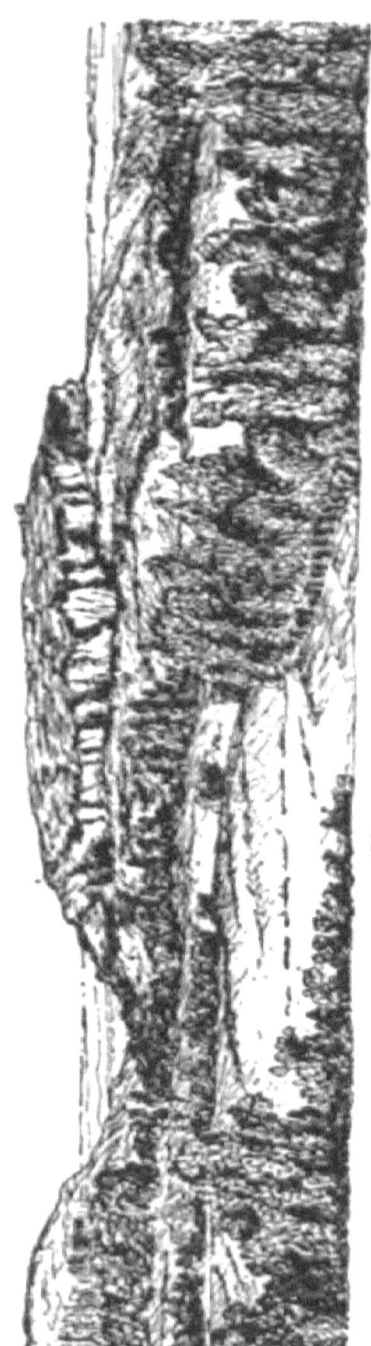

Uxellodunum from the South

Uxellodunum from the North

trains. But when Lucterius sought to carry some corn by night into the town on beasts of burden by a steep and wooded path, probably on the north side, passing camp 3 on the west, Caninius, notified by his outposts who had heard the sound of the moving convoy, fell upon and captured the whole train. Lucterius was cut off and could not rejoin Drappes, who, back in the supply-camp, knew nothing of the disaster but assumed his colleague to have reached the *oppidum*. Caninius then left one legion to guard his own camps and with the other and his cavalry he advanced on the enemy's supply-camp itself. This was on low ground, enabling Caninius to seize the hills around it and corral the whole party. Having well disposed his men, he fell on and destroyed the entire foraging force with the loss of but a few men wounded. Drappes was taken prisoner. Caninius then completed the lines around the town, and Fabius shortly joined him on completion of his work north of the Liger, thus giving him enough men to finish and man the lines. Fabius took one side of the town, Caninius the other.

Caesar had, meanwhile, left Mark Antony and fifteen *cohorts* in the territory of the Bellovaci to keep them in subjection, while he himself was making a tour of Gaul. He visited each region in turn, and by politic generosity and some necessary severity he won over each tribe. Among the Carnutes, he caused Guturvatus, said to have been the instigator of the late rebellion, to be brought to him and on the clamour of the soldiers executed *more majorum, i. e.*, beaten to death and decapitated. He did this, it is said, to save executing vengeance on the whole people.

Learning by letters from Caninius the situation at Uxellodunum, Cacsar put Q. Calenus in charge of the two legions which he had kept with himself, ordered him to follow by regular marches and, taking only the cavalry, moved rapidly to the aid of Caninius. This he did because it had now become essential speedily to stamp out all opposition; the natives well knew that his term in Gaul lasted but one summer more, and he feared they might argue that if they could hold out so much longer they would eventually get rid of the Romans. He therefore determined to make an example of this body of freebooters.

Caesar was wont to leave as little to his lieutenants and to do as much personally as he could. While abundantly busy with the political questions of Gaul and Italy, he yet deemed it wise never to allow a military operation to drag for want of his own supervision.

To this personal activity is traceable the remarkable success of his Gallic campaigns, which from beginning to end breathe of Caesar's genius, cool head, clear judgment, presence of mind, boldness and never-tiring energy.

On his arrival he found that the inhabitants of Uxellodunum had abundance of corn, and that, in order to accomplish his end, he must cut them off from water. This he could not easily do, for a stream (the Tourmente) flowed at the foot of the crags on the west side of the town, and through a narrow ravine, so that its waters could not be diverted. But, by disposing slingers, archers and engines in certain places in the ravine, Caesar rendered the operation of getting water so hazardous, that he finally confined the enemy to procuring it in one place.

This was between the town and the stream, where, near the walls, gushed out an ample spring (a). Caesar saw that he must also cut this off. He advanced *vineae* and a mound towards the place with great labour and constant skirmishing, in which a number of Romans were wounded. He also undertook to tap the sources of the spring by a subterranean passage which was run some distance in the rock towards it.

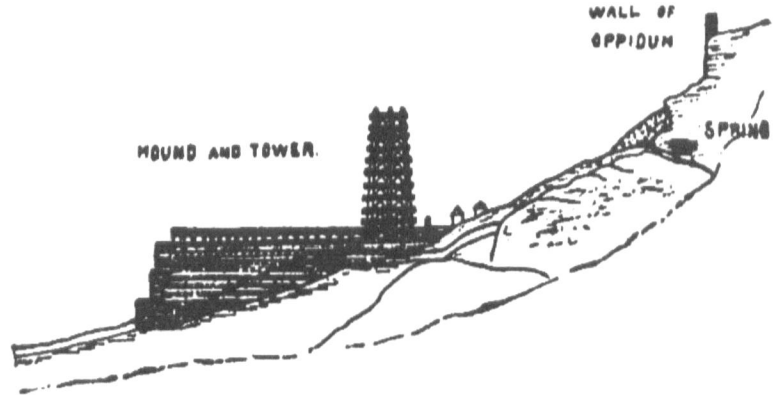

MOUND AND TOWER

This passage has been discovered, and some traces also of the mound and works. Finally, the outside works were advanced so near the spring that the Romans from the mound, which was sixty feet high and surmounted by a ten-storey turret, could cast their darts with marked effect upon any of the garrison who came for water; thus they succeeded in all but preventing its use. The tower was too far below the walls of the *oppidum* to attack the latter. Thus deprived of the spring, many people and all the cattle in the town died of thirst.

But the besieged, with the fury of despair, determined to make a supreme effort for their salvation. They accumulated an enormous amount of inflammable material,—tallow, pitch and tar,—and filling barrels, rolled them down upon the Roman works, at the same time making a desperate sortie in force against them. The patiently constructed works speedily caught fire. To beat back this sortie and at the same time to enable his men to handle the fire to advantage, Caesar ordered a feigned general attack from all sides at once, which being stoutly given, the barbarians withdrew quickly into their town, for they did not know which quarter was most in danger, and they feared that the Romans might enter the town. This enabled the legions to extinguish the flames and to gain a material amount of ground as well.

Some days after, the Roman mine reached the sources of the spring and diverted its flow. The barbarians, considering this to be an act of the gods and not of men, for they had deemed the spring unreachable, were compelled both by fear and by thirst to surrender. In pursuance of his determination above explained, Caesar cut off the hands of all those who had here borne arms. Both leaders had been previously captured and imprisoned. Drappes starved himself to death in prison to save himself from a worse fate.

Meanwhile Labienus, among the Treviri, had got the insurgent chiefs into his hands, and Caesar, seeing that his return thither would not be necessary, marched throughout Aquitania, where lie received the submission of all the tribes which Crassus had already partly brought under control. This occupied the summer. When the time arrived for going into winter-quarters, four legions (under Mark Antony, C. Trebonius, P. Vatinius and Q. Tullius) were left among the Belgae; two among the Ædui; two among the Turoni near the Carnutes to hold the seaside tribes in check; two among the Lemnovices near the Arverni. Caesar then personally went to the Province, where he attended to the duties of the state, returned to the legions among the Belgae, and wintered at Nemetocenna (Arras). There were no rebels left except a few bands of rovers, who could accomplish nothing unaided. But Caesar had to rest content with a merely nominal submission, in the north of Gaul. There was always a relic of war in that quarter. Commius, after some cavalry exchanges with Volusenus, turned freebooter. According to Frontinus, he retired to Britain. Only he and Ambiorix, of all the Gallic chieftains, survived.

Caesar now devoted his time to demonstrating to the Gallic tribes the advantages of the Roman alliance, as he had shown them the dangers of revolt.

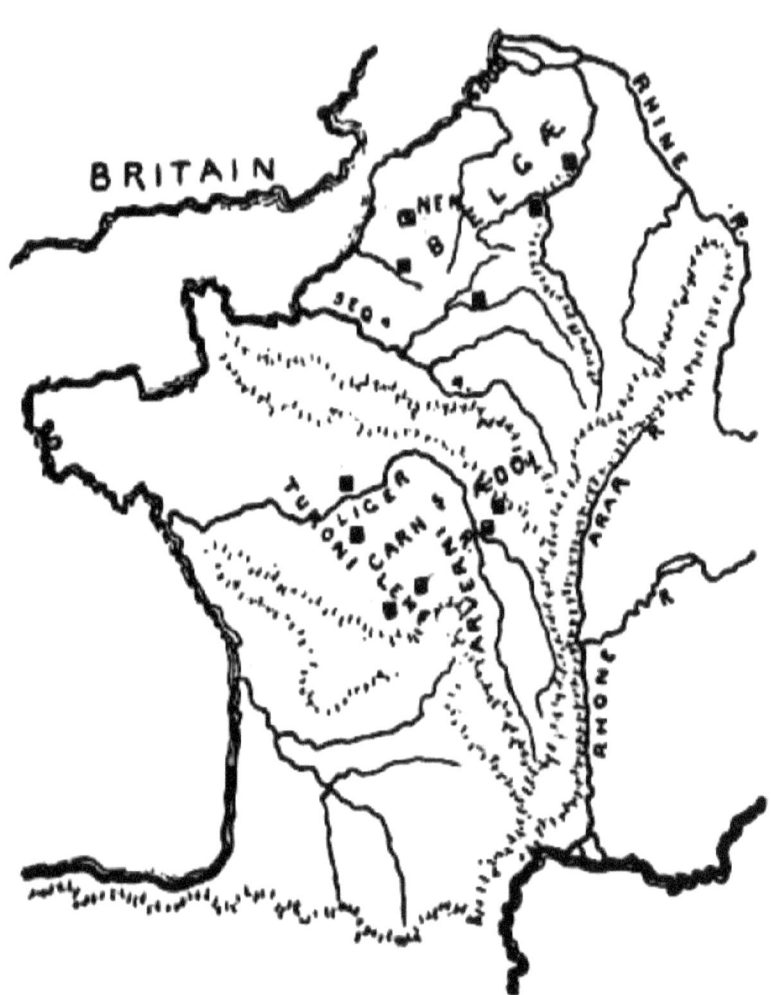

WINTER-QUARTERS, B. C. 51-50

"Caesar, whilst in winter-quarters in the country of the Belgae, made it his only business to keep the states in amity with him, and to give none either hopes of or pretext for revolt. For nothing was further from his wishes than to be under the necessity of engaging in another war at his departure; lest, when he was drawing his army out of the country, any war should be left unfinished, which the Gauls would cheerfully undertake when there was no immediate danger. Therefore, by treating the states with respect, making rich presents to the leading men, imposing no new burdens, and making the terms of their subjection lighter, he easily kept Gaul (already exhausted by so many unsuccessful battles) in obedience."

Thus Caesar spent the winter, and when the spring opened, he proceeded towards Italy, visiting all the towns by the way, and confirming them in their allegiance, as far as Cisalpine Gaul. He was received with the greatest honour and acclamations. He then returned to Nemetocenna, ordered his legions to the territory of the Treviri, and held there a grand review of his troops. Having settled the affairs of Gaul on a solid basis, Caesar journeyed to Ravenna to be near the events in Italy when his consulate should expire. He left Labienus in command, regarding whom, though warned that he was solicited by his enemies, he harboured no suspicion.

The Gallic campaigns are peculiarly interesting to the military student as showing how Caesar schooled himself and his legions. He began with but the ordinary military training, on a small basis of experience; he ended as a great general, with an experience which enabled him to rise to the most astounding height. His legions commenced green and untried; they ended as veterans equal to conquering the world. Each became so wedded to the other that mutual confidence and affection made the army commanded by Caesar irresistible.

It was impossible that during this period of schooling Caesar should not make mistakes,—grave ones. But all his mistakes bore fruit, and raised the qualities of both general and legions. One can see, step by step, how Caesar's successes and failures alike produced their effect; how his in-born ability came to the surface; how he impressed his own individuality on whatever he did; and how his intelligence led him to apply whatever he learned to his future conduct.

No praise is too high for the conduct or moral qualities of the army. From Caesar down, through every grade, all military virtues were pronounced. In organization and discipline, ability to do almost any work, endurance of danger and trial, toughness and courage, it was a model for the rest of Rome,—but a model unhappily not imitated. And not only his legionaries, but his auxiliary troops, were imbued with the same spirit,—all breathed not only devotion to Caesar, but reflected in a measure his own great qualities.

All this, however, was of a nature different from the high qualities of the legions of the Punic wars. These were wonderful in their devotion, discipline and effectiveness because the material in them was incomparable. Caesar's legions were equally wonderful, but it was because Caesar had fashioned and always commanded them. The discipline of the earlier legion depended largely on the men; that of Caesar's entirely on himself. As in the case of Napoleon, the discipline of

Caesar's legions was often terribly lax; but in that quality which may be called battle-discipline they were unsurpassed.

Caesar had in Gaul some opponents worthy even of him. Vercingetorix, Ariovistus, Casivelaunus were, each in his way, great leaders. That they were overcome by Caesar was but natural. Disciplined troops well led cannot but win against barbarians. The end could not be otherwise. And while the Gallic War does not show Caesar—as the Second Punic War did Hannibal—opposed to the strongest military machine in existence, it did show him opposed to generals and troops quite equal to most of those encountered by Alexander. The Gauls must not be underrated. Some of their operations and some of their fighting were of the highest order. They contended nobly for their independence. Defeat did not discourage them. Once put down, they again rose in rebellion so soon as the strong hand was removed. They were in no sense weak opponents, and while in all things Caesar's army was superior to theirs, yet in their motives and hearty cooperation they certainly were more commendable than Caesar in his mere love of conquest.

Gaul was conquered. Even though the master's grasp of the reins was soon relaxed, to reach for other and greater things, the subjected province rose not. There were small wars and rumours of wars, but these were so isolated and unimportant that the local governors could do them justice. In the remote corners of the new territory, the Pyrenees, the Scheldt, and the coast, some tribes were still *de facto* free. But time itself reduced these. Caesar's work had been thorough, and it was the work of civilization. Whatever fault can be found with his method, or indeed his abstract rights, that Gaul should be conquered was a historical necessity, and it is well that it fell to the lot of a man as broad, as thorough, as enlightened as Caesar.

GALLIC HORSEMAN
(FROM A TERRA-COTTA STATUETTE)

CHAPTER 23

Caesar's Method

The Gauls had been the terror of Rome for centuries. Whoever conquered them would be the national hero. Caesar understood this. His mission was to protect the province; he purposed to subdue Gaul. He worked for his own ends as much as for Rome, but he understood his problem thoroughly. He considered the strategic field of Gaul with a clear eye, and committed no errors in his general plan. It was natural that he should make early mistakes of detail, for Caesar had not been brought up as a soldier; and we find a hesitancy in his first campaigns which later he threw off. His line of advance from the province through central Gaul was in strict accord with the topographical values, and he studied the tribal instincts keenly. He educated himself as he went along, profiting by all his mistakes. His campaigns across the Rhine and to Britain were useless; they did not aid the general scheme. Caesar was energetic in obtaining information, ingenious in contending with new obstacles, intelligent in selecting his objective, careful of his base. He demanded severe exertions from his men, but rewarded them handsomely. He was much aided by fortune, but under trial was doubly energetic. In view of the fact that Caesar entered the Gallic campaign without experience in war, it was a marvellous success.

It has already been pointed out that Caesar, on being appointed governor of Gaul, had been vested with no right to do more than protect the exposed boundaries of the then province. All prefects had confined themselves to this role. The laws of nations in Caesar's day had already received some recognition; but right was no valid argument against might, and few rights were accorded to barbarian tribes by Rome in the last century before the Christian era, least of all to the redoubted Gauls, who had so often brought Rome to

Tribes of Gaul

the verge of ruin. Rome at that day was lawless. Every great man wrought for himself. Caesar had been brought up in a school which prompted him to bend all things to his ambition. He represented a great party; only by his personal success could his party succeed. War meant to him an army; an army was to him but a means of winning power. When he went to Gaul, Pompey was distinctly the leader of the triumvirate. With a man of Caesar's make-up, this could not last. Like his colleague, Caesar soon recognized that he must aim at the sole control of Rome if he would win any standing. Without war and conquest, he could gain neither the experience, fame nor influence requisite to this end. This was no unworthy ambition. Caesar could not be great with a lesser end in view, and the importance of his object was equalled by the splendour of his means. To deliver the republic forever from the Gauls was to make their conqueror the foremost of the Romans, as the Gauls had been the most dreaded of the foes of Rome. To subdue Gaul was a stepping-stone to certain and unapproached renown.

Caesar was fortunate. At the very inception of his charge of Gaul, the outbreak of the Helvetii opportunely occurred, and led, in its progress, to the current of events which ended in the conquest of the entire country. One thing after another, with Caesar's uniform good fortune, was sure to happen, to give him at least a pretence of right in extending his conquests. The Helvetian question solved, the Ædui called in his aid against the Germans under Ariovistus. In this, too, Caesar could assert that he was but protecting the allies of the province. The Romans always helped their allies when by so doing they could help themselves. Caesar worked on the like theory. Gaul publicly thanked the consul for freeing her from the Helvetii and the Germans; but Gaul did not then anticipate her own subjugation.

Caesar's next step requires more of his own plausible explanation. It is hard to justify his action in carrying the war among the Belgae, but he solves the enigma by reciting the danger to which the province would be subjected by any combination of tribes, even if not offensively meant. The same course of argument carried Caesar beyond the Rhine, and into Britain, and was the motive of all his other conquests. However unjustifiable this may have been,—and yet we see the same process of conquest going on in the nineteenth century,—Caesar's purpose was clear and definite, and he played his cards well. His course was consistent throughout; and he had the happy faculty in his public utterances of arguing the law to his side, of placing there the appearance of right. Whatever he undertook resulted in his favour, and, greatest accomplishment of all, he disciplined and hardened an army devoted to himself, by means of which he was able to make himself master of Rome.

All this is by no means to Caesar's discredit. He did but what other leading men had been doing in Rome for generations. The old-fashioned Roman patriotism had long since vanished. There was scarce another road to honour and power than the selfish one, scarce another means of safety for those who held high rank. Caesar cannot fairly be blamed for self-seeking; neither should he be held up as a model patriot. Judged by his own *Commentaries*, he never rose to the plane of a Washington, a Gustavus, a Hannibal.

PHYSICAL FEATURES OF GAUL

Ubi bene, ibi patria was a serviceable motto for him, so long as the good ran in his own favour. Rome needed a Caesar to shape the destiny to which she was manifestly drifting. It is well that such a man was at hand, and that he did his work with thoroughness; but though Caesar was as useful to the ancient world as Napoleon to modern Europe, it cannot be said that either worked on the instincts of elevated patriotism.

Whatever criticism may be passed upon Caesar in a political aspect, as a great captain he is almost beyond cavil. Barring such errors of vigilance and judgment as are of peculiar interest in showing certain characteristics as well as how Caesar educated himself to arms, his military conduct through this memorable series of campaigns is a fruitful study. His errors were more often in policy than in war. At times he could be generous, even magnanimous, to subjugated peoples. At times he was cruel beyond what any civilized conqueror has ever been, unnecessarily, unwisely cruel. The world had advanced since the days of Alexander, and while what is now known as the law of nations was not then a code, certain of its tenets had been established. But Caesar absolutely disregarded any such when they interfered with his own projects.

Statecraft counts for much in a great captain's work. Caesar's policy in Gaul was on the whole so harsh as scarcely to rate as policy at all. This is the civil aspect of the matter. From another point of view it was as masterly as the problem was difficult. Caesar had to conciliate some tribes while attacking other neighbouring and friendly tribes. He had to supply himself while destroying victual for the enemy. He had to elevate part of the people in order to suppress another part. He had to play one half of the population against the other half. He had a population of eight million Gauls to oppose his dozen legions. In no other way could he do his work. So far as this his military policy goes, his conduct was irreproachable.

Caesar's strategy was farsighted and sound. The province, when Gaul fell to his lot, as one of the *triumvirs*, was a sort of salient thrust forward into the midst of the country. West and north of its boundary, the Rhone, lived allied peoples; from the mountains on the east danger threatened from a number of restless tribes. The advantages of this salient position were by no means lost on Caesar, nor the power of concentrated action which it gave him. His first campaign, against the Helvetii, was intended to protect and resulted in protecting the right flank of the salient, an absolute essential to safety in advancing into north or northwest Gaul. From this point duly secured, northerly, the Rhine and the Jura and Vosegus mountains protected to a certain degree the right of an advancing army, provided the tribes on the left bank of the great river were not unfriendly; and it will be noticed that one of Caesar's early efforts was directed to making as many of these tribes as possible his firm friends by generous treatment and effective protection against their enemies. When he could not quickly accomplish his end by negotiation, lie resorted to drastic measures. In carrying out his scheme of conquest, Caesar advanced his salient along the Arar and the Mosa as far as the Sabis, and could then debouch from the watershed to the west of these rivers down the valleys of the Sequana and its tributaries, the Matrona and Axona, with perfect safety. And Caesar not only secured the friendship of the abutting tribes, but always kept several strongly fortified camps among them as an additional protection.

The flow of the Axona across his line of operations furnished Caesar an advanced base from which he could move against the Belgae. This line from his first base in the province to the secondary one on the Axona lay along the Arar and the Mosa. From Belgian territory, when once in his hands, Caesar could safely move even so far as Britain, provided he properly protected his rear and was careful that his victuals were accumulated or certain to be delivered by friendly tribes. Having subdued the Belgae, he could turn without danger to the southwest corner of Gaul, against Aquitania. Caesar thus exemplified in the fullest degree the advantage in grand strategy of central lines of operation. Neither Alexander nor Hannibal exhibited a clearer grasp of his strategical problem than Caesar. It is noticeable that the hardest part of Caesar's work was to establish this central salient by alliance or conquest of the tribes which abutted on it; his gravest danger when the Ædui, who guarded his line of operations, joined their revolting brethren. But this salient definitely gained, Caesar was able to reduce the operations of the war to the basis of single isolated campaigns. These, indeed, were difficult, but dangerous only when they threatened with intestine broils the military structure he had erected.

The several campaigns, from the cautious handling of the Helvetian question to the splendid management of the siege of Alesia, have each received comment in its proper place.

Caesar, as a Roman general, carried out the Roman idea of a conquest of the world by virtue of a constant offensive. In studying Caesar, one studies the Roman military status at its best, so far as generalship goes.; so far as concerns the soldier, all that was best in the burgess-militia of Rome had long ago disappeared. Caesar's legionary was a professional soldier in every sense. Caesar began the war by a defensive operation against the Helvetii; after that he always assumed the offensive, though in the *Commentaries* he frequently goes out of his way to convince his readers that he was the aggrieved party. If he ever resorted to the defensive it was but for a moment, shortly to resume the offensive and push it vigorously.

Like all generals who are careful of their men, Caesar preferred to campaign only in the season of good weather, and to lie in quarters in winter. But that he could conduct a winter campaign was more than once demonstrated. While in quarters he appears to have been fairly careful of good discipline and studious to keep his men busy. The panic at Vesontio was a good object-lesson, by which he profited. His teachableness was one of Caesar's admirable qualities.

Caesar was energetic in procuring information on which to form his plans. This was often both hard to get and unreliable when got, but he sought it intelligently. He constantly kept afoot some of his Gallic officers or horsemen; used spies from allied tribes or gained friends within the enemy's lines. Deserters were put to use and were handsomely rewarded. If information could not be otherwise procured, Caesar made reconnoissances in force. As such we may well treat Caesar's first expeditions against Germany and Britain. On no other ground can these be justified as military operations; and a reconnoissance in force should never risk the existence of army or commander,—as the first crossing to Britain did.

Caesar as a rule was numerically weaker than the enemy, but he was not so vastly overmatched as was Alexander, nor can the opposition to him be in any sense compared to what Hannibal encountered during his entire military life. Caesar was far stronger than his enemies in everything but numbers, especially in self-confidence and power of work. His *legionaries* would bear anything and could do anything. They were very Yankees for ingenuity. Caesar did not willingly mix the allies with his legions; he employed the native foot mostly as bowmen and slingers; his cavalry was uniformly native. He worked his army habitually well concentrated. If he divided his forces it was but for a short time, soon again to concentrate. This is an almost uniform test of military capacity. But Caesar sought to attack the enemy before the latter had concentrated, and generally made good use of such a chance. Nimbleness of movement stood in the stead of numbers. He understood how, as Napoleon phrases it, "*se multiplier par la vitesse.*"

Caesar's objective was always well chosen. It was either the most important strategic point, or more usually the army of the enemy. Thus in the campaign against the Belgae, he threw himself upon the Remi, who had not yet decided whether to join the confederacy, and by preventing their so doing at once made secure a secondary base. He chose the shortest road to march by. In 52 the enemy concentrated his forces between the Cebennae mountains and the upper Liger. Caesar's army lay between the Sequana and Matrona. He joined it, got his forces well in hand, and marched from Agendicum by way of Genabum straight on the enemy. In the division of his forces he was usually careful so to march as to be able again to make a junction of the bulk of his forces. In the campaign against the Veneti, while the army was divided into several parts, two of these, comprising six legions under himself and Titurius, were placed where they could easily be concentrated.

Caesar was careful of his base. This cannot be said to apply to the first British expedition, but in the second he left half of all his cavalry and three legions on the coast of Gaul as an intermediate base. In 52, in the general insurrection, the Province was his first base, with twenty-two *cohorts* under L. Caesar the *legate*. The second base was the land of the friendly Remi, and the line from the first to the second base lay along the Arar, through the land of the likewise friendly Sequani and Lingones, and was strengthened by Vesontio midway. In order to secure another line along the Liger, Caesar left Labienus with two (later reinforced to four) legions at Agendicum, well entrenched. Even these dispositions barely saved him. His leaving the fleet protected by an entrenched camp on the coast of Britain was a simpler instance of his care for his base, taught by unfortunate experience.

Caesar always sought to induce his enemy to divide his forces. In the war with the Belgae he sent the Ædui to attack the Bellovacian territory, thus easily detaching this powerful tribe from the confederacy. His diversions were well conceived and well timed. When he drew Vercingetorix down to meet him by crossing the Cebennae, and when, after so doing, he personally hurried to his legions, Caesar showed that he was a master of the art of blinding the enemy as to his real intentions. This was a device in the style of Hannibal.

Caesar was careful of his soldiers. But he called on them for the severest exertions at any time or under any circumstances. His logistics was good. He showed in Gaul more foresight in the matter of rations and magazines than in later campaigns. Protection of Gallic tribes was paid for by victual. He got rations from those neighbouring tribes whose alliance he had accepted. A beaten people was always mulcted in a given amount of corn. He was rarely in a strait for bread. Still he campaigned only when there was forage, if this was possible. A train of pack-animals accompanied his column, loaded with a supply in addition to what the men themselves carried.

Caesar speaks in his *Commentaries* of a threefold advantage of the Roman, or what Napoleon called the methodical system of conducting war, over that of any other nation, namely: the holding of decisive points, the entrenching of camps, and the breaking up of the enemy's communications. The capture of decisive points opened the campaign, and placed the troops where they were advantageously located for winning a victory; the Roman entrenched camp was a movable fortress which from its effect on the *morale* of the troops made victory more certain as well as neutralized defeat; by the breaking up of his communications the enemy was compelled to shift his ground, to fight under adverse circumstances, or surrender.

Decisive points were to be reached if possible through friendly or at least neutral territory. If they must be reached through the enemy's, then every step must be protected to secure his own communications. On Caesar's march from Agendicum to the Bituriges, he could not leave Vellaunodunum in his rear, but must capture it to keep open his communications with Labienus. Caesar describes a decisive point as one having many advantages, the most important being that of opening and holding an entrance into the enemy's country. In the march above instanced, such a point was Genabum where there was a bridge over the Liger. This bridge Caesar must have in order to approach Vercingetorix. In his campaign against the Belgae, so soon as he had crossed the Axona he was on the enemy's territory, and therefore his camp on the Axona was located at a decisive point. In moving on the Helvetii, after crossing the Rhone, Caesar entrenched in the angle of that river and the Arar, where he was among the friendly Ædui, and from here he could readily attack the enemy. This was a decisive point.

Whether Caesar laid much stress on secrecy in relation to his plans among his own men does not appear. In secrecy, even to his lieutenants, Hannibal was unapproached. Alexander, too, kept his own counsel, but rather as master than for military reasons. Hephaestion knew his every purpose. Caesar deemed great speed in executing his projects the equivalent of secrecy.

A captain must be largely gauged by the strength of his opponents. Caesar's in Gaul by no means lacked ability. Ariovistus was a man of exceptional strength, and Vercingetorix came near to being a genius. Both recognized the value of decisive points as well as Caesar,—though war to them was not a science, and what Caesar relied on against such men was not so much secrecy as the rapidity of his marches and the discipline of his legions.

The decisive point secured, a battle was sought or an attack on a town was made, or some operation was under-taken to bring the enemy to such action that he might be overwhelmed. Caesar preferred a battle in the open field because a victory so won was apt to result in many towns falling into his hands or in making their capture easier. But if the enemy constantly avoided it, he was compelled to forego a battle and to resort to a siege or a blockade. While it is true that Caesar sought battle, the fact that there were few pitched battles proper in the Gallic campaign shows how much stronger the legions were than any troops opposed to them. Defeat was often inflicted by Caesar's native cavalry alone.

When Caesar camped in the presence of the enemy in expectation of battle, he sought to lure him away from his camp so that should he win a victory, he might make the most of it by pursuit, without the enemy taking refuge within it and compelling an assault. With secret forced marches he approached the foe, camped a short march from him, and next day endeavoured to take him unawares. Thus he approached Ariovistus, thus the Usipetes and Tenchtheri. Sometimes Caesar would move nearer to the enemy the evening before he intended to bring on a battle, if there was some obstacle behind which he could easily camp unobserved, or he would do the same thing in case he needed more information before engaging. Occasionally he camped at a distance of two short marches.

In determining the locality of a camp, Caesar paid strict heed to his own communications and sought to prejudice the enemy's. At the outset he paid the more heed to his own. Later he showed more dash, more reliance on the enemy's inertia. When Ariovistus moved around his flank, Caesar at once took up a defensive and moved only a small body on Ariovistus' flank. In Britain Cassivellaunus moved on Caesar's communications. Vercingetorix cut Caesar's line at Gergovia by rousing the Ædui in his rear. There is sometimes a lack of strategic dash in

Caesar's movements in the Gallic campaign. We do not see him moving on the enemy's communications by the great turning movements he afterwards employed. He simply secured his own communications and fought. In besieging towns he disturbed enemy's communications after a fashion, but not by turning movements. This was caution bred of self-distrust which wore away before the Civil War.

When Caesar conquered in open fight, he pursued vigorously, as a rule with his cavalry, but not infrequently with the legions,—unless he had been very much exhausted. It was only the cavalry, however, which actually reached the enemy. No one ever pursued so remorselessly as Alexander, until Napoleon dawned upon the world and showed it how to utilize victories to the fullest. Caesar followed up the political chances keenly, and appearing after a victory in the very midst of his enemies had no difficulty in subjecting them and in forcing them to furnish victuals and transportation. He insisted on dictating what their government should be. After a victory, when danger was over, he divided his forces, the better to work on the moral nature of the people by a sudden display of his legions in many places at once.

The results of the summer's campaign having been gathered, Caesar went into such winter-quarters as best fostered what had been accomplished. He avoided loading the province with the care of the legions. His winter-quarters accustomed the newly subjected tribes to the army, to the Roman yoke and to furnishing regular supplies. After the victory over Ariovistus, winter-quarters were taken up in the east part of the land of the Sequani about Vesontio, where were rich supplies, with the province nearby; and at the same time Caesar was threatening the Belgae and keeping the Sequani well in hand. In 57 he took up winter-quarters on the lower Liger, when Crassus had already accustomed the Belgae to their masters. The Sequani needed rest from furnishing provisions, the Remi had been on Caesar's side, the Belgae were exhausted, and the Ædui and neighbours were friendly. Besides, Caesar wished to see what effect his eastern victories had had in the west, and whether it would still require force to subdue the western tribes. In 56 and 55 winter-quarters were taken with reference to the British expedition. In 54, after this expedition, he had winter-quarters near the coast, but spread over a large area because of the late bad harvest. In consequence of the terrible experience gained by distributing the legions too widely, in 63 and 52 they were kept close together; six were in Agendicum.

When Caesar had bad luck, his energy markedly grew. He particularly watched for and guarded against any loss of morale among his men. In such circumstances he could use his fluent tongue to the greatest advantage. He would convince his men that they were not beaten, turn to another field and by redoubled energy wrest victory out of failure. This he did after Gergovia. Caesar throughout his campaigns shows best after a backset. We shall meet notable instances of this in the Civil War.

It has been said that ancient differs so entirely from modern war that one can learn little from the great deeds of the captains antedating the Christian era. But what can be said of Caesar would be high praise for the best of the generals of modern times. When we read the old campaigns, not superficially but for their inmost meaning, they convey to us the same broad lessons which the most able captains since the Middle Ages have given us. An artist learns his technique in a modern studio; he gathers his inspiration from the old masters. So with war. In no better way can the characteristic quality essential to the soldier be developed than by the study of the work of the ancient captains; by searching earnestly for the reasons which led them to what they did. Every great general has confessed his debt to the soldiers of antiquity.

CHAPTER 24

Caesar's Army

Caesar's legionary was no longer a citizen-soldier, as in the Punic wars; he was a professional, or a mercenary. He served for a livelihood, not as a duty. The legion was no longer set up in three lines according to property rating; it was marshalled in two or three lines of *cohorts*, the *cohort* being a body of four to six hundred men, ranked according to military qualities, and ten *cohorts* went to the legion. The men retained substantially the old equipment; they occupied in line a space of but three feet front instead of five. The intervals between *cohorts* had sensibly decreased. The camp and camp-followers, musicians, standards and petty details of all kinds remained much as before. Light troops and cavalry were recruited from conquered tribes. Each legion had six tribunes who commanded it in turn under a legate. The general staff of the army had quartermasters, aides, engineers, *lictors*, scouts and a body-guard. The legionary's pay was about that of a day-labourer, but largesses and booty were bountiful. For defence, the legion or army formed square or circle. It readily ployed into column or deployed into line. The orders of march were accurately laid down and well observed. The average march was about fifteen miles. The train was less long than ours, there being neither artillery nor ammunition. For battle the army was drawn up on the slope of a hill; it still attacked, as had always been its habit. The legion of the Punic war was good because the men were good; Caesar's was effective because he was able.

The tactical formation of the early Roman army was described in the volume on Hannibal. Considerable changes in this tactical formation had taken place since the Punic wars; some were introduced by Marius, or by Caesar as a consequence of his campaigns. The Roman soldier as to arms, equipment and minor tactics, was to all intents and

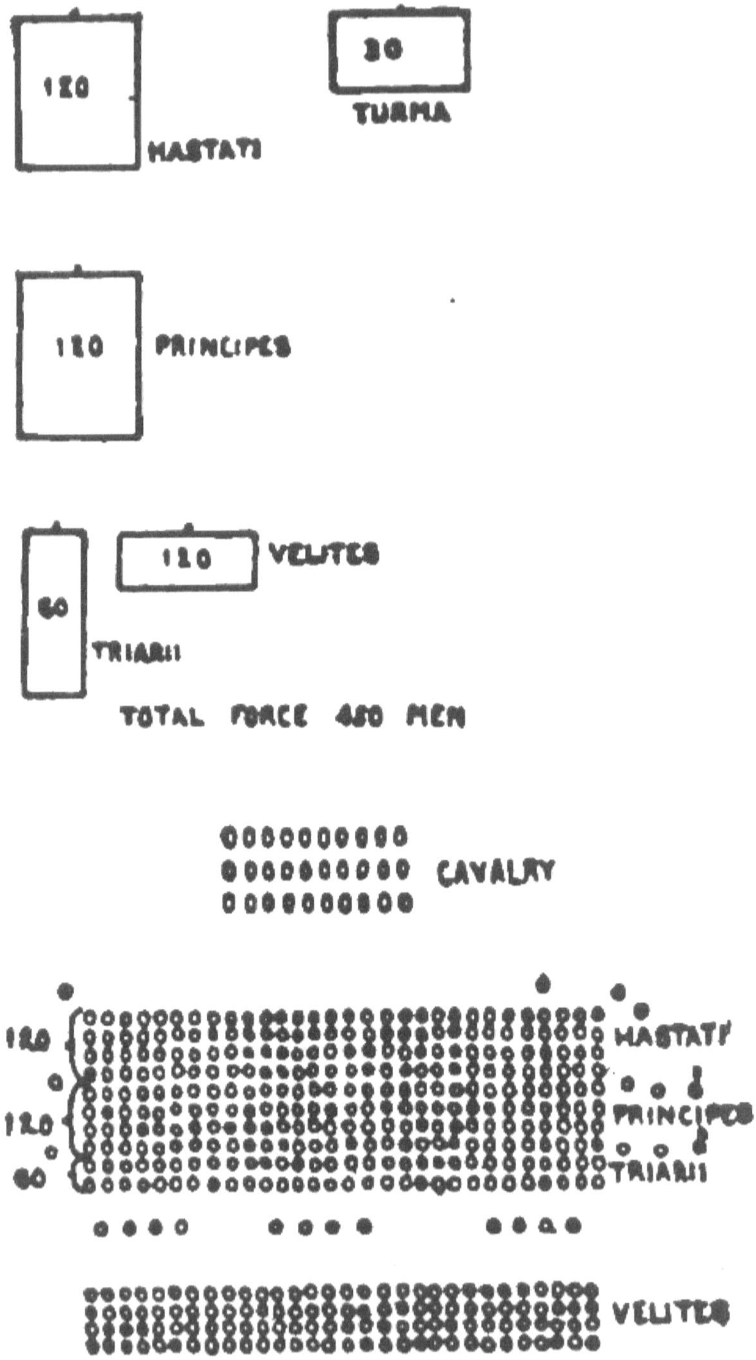

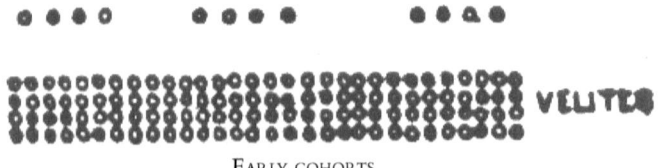

EARLY COHORTS

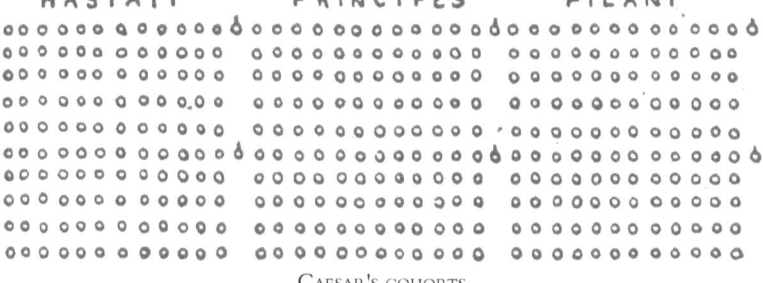
Caesar's cohorts

purposes the same as he had been in the time of Hannibal. He still wore helmet, *cuirass*, and greave on right leg; he still bore spear, shield and sword. But in character, quality and discipline, he was no longer the splendid citizen-soldier of that day. He was a professional if a Roman; a mercenary if a foreigner; and as such he was exactly what his commander made him. A similar change had obtained in the officers. The six *tribunes* of a legion were no longer appointed for their military qualifications or long service, but claimed their rank on the score of political or social standing, or of friendship for the chief.

The original smaller tactical unit of the Romans had been the century. It next became the maniple of two centuries. Later the three *maniples* of the *hastati, principes* and *triarii*, with some cavalry and *velites*, were merged into one body called a *cohort*. But the name alone remained. Under Caesar the *cohort* was no longer the ancient one, but a body the evolution of which has already been traced. It was divided only for the smaller details. It was practically the tactical unit of the legion, and all manoeuvres were by *cohorts*. The three-class formation of each *cohort* had entirely disappeared.

It seems odd, with all that has been written about Roman tactics and organization from Polybius to Vegetius and Onosander, that the exact structure of Caesar's legion, *cohort*, maniple and century cannot be given. The addition of a few words in some paragraphs would elucidate the difficulties we encounter in construing these authors. But, as the omission of the name of some single well-known spot by Polybius has given rise to endless discussion as to Hannibal's route across the Alps, so a certain lapse in explanation in all the Latin authors who treat of tactics has produced many different views as to the details of organization of Caesar's legion. Particularly Rüstow, Göler and Stoffel have discussed the matter *au fond*. But they disagree on many points.

The *maniples* of the *cohort*, according to Rüstow, stood beside each other; according to Göler still in rear of each other. It seems much more probable that they stood in line: the manoeuvres, of which we are given a more or less detailed account, can thus alone be readily understood. Göler's plan tends to make a deep file, whereas the tendency was to make the line of battle less rather than more deep as time wore on. If beside each other, the *maniples* would have come to stand from right to left: *pilani* (ancient *triarii*), *principes*, *hastati*, though these distinctions gradually disappeared.

The *cohort* which opposed Hannibal was formed of three *maniples* or companies, each maniple in two *centuries* or platoons, and the maniples standing in rear of each other with intervals between *hastati*, *principes*, *triarii*, and with cavalry and light troops conveniently disposed. The *cohort* with which Caesar conquered the world was a body of three *maniples*, each in two *centuries* (*ordines*) and the *maniples* standing side by side without intervals. The first *ordo* comprised the front five ranks of the *maniple*, the second *ordo* the rear five ranks. Or if the *cohort* was set up in eight ranks, there were four in each *century*.

The normal numerical force of Caesar's legions cannot be determined with the accuracy of the legions of the Punic wars. At times they had five or even six thousand men; at Pharsalus they had been reduced by service to an average of but twenty-seven hundred and fifty. Rüstow construes the various authorities to give the legion an average field strength of thirty-six hundred men; Göler puts it at forty-eight hundred. This latter is perhaps nearer the normal force, not often reached in time of war.

Ten *cohorts* composed the legion. If the *cohorts* had three hundred and sixty men, ten deep, there would be thirty-six men in each rank. If eight deep, which was not unlikely the usual case, and at Pharsalus probably so, there would be forty-five men in each rank. If these thirty-six men in close order for the march or parade or column of assault took up three feet each in breadth and six feet in depth and there was six feet between *maniples*, the size of a *cohort* would be one hundred and twenty feet front by sixty feet depth. If there were forty-five men in rank and eight in file, the size of a *cohort* would be, in close order, with say seven and a half feet between *maniples*, one hundred and fifty feet front by fifty feet depth.

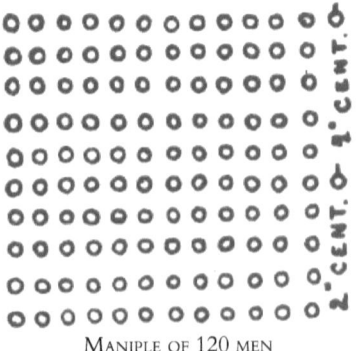

MANIPLE OF 120 MEN

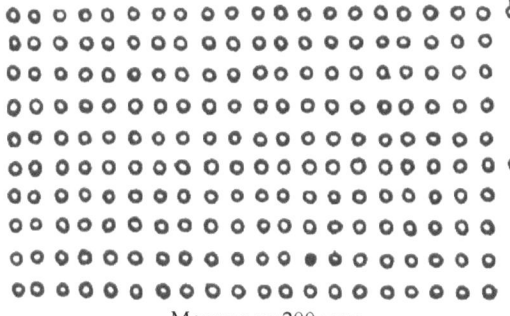

MANIPLE OF 200 MEN

But three feet front was not sufficient to enable the *legionary* to hurl his *pilum* or use his *gladius* to advantage. There was therefore an open order of battle. This was either taken by each odd-numbered man stepping three feet forward to gain arm-room, or more likely each rank deployed by a face to right or left from the centre and took distance as needed. This doubled the front of a *cohort*. On this latter supposition there must have been, in close order, intervals between *cohorts* equal to their front so as to provide for deployment; in open order—after deployment—there would be no intervals at all.

Taking the eight-deep formation, with close-order intervals equal to *cohort* front added, the *cohort* would occupy, in open or in close order, three hundred feet front by fifty depth. Taking the ten-deep formation, equally with intervals, it would occupy two hundred and forty feet front by sixty feet depth.

Rüstow makes calculations on the average strength of a legion in active service being thirty-six hundred men. At Ilerda, Caesar tells us that a certain ridge well identified today, was wide enough for three *cohorts* in line. The ridge, says Rüstow, measures three hundred and sixty feet in width which gives one hundred and twenty feet front to a *cohort*—as they stood without intervals. But the actual width of the ridge varies as it descends to the plain. This vitiates the calculation, though the deduction is not far from correct. We may fairly assume the average front of Caesar's *cohort* without intervals as one hundred and twenty to one hundred and fifty feet, and the *cohort* as commonly numbering not over three hundred and sixty men during his campaigns.

Each *maniple* had two *centurions*, a senior and a junior, and to each centurion there was a sub-*centurion*. These, like our company officers, all served on foot. The senior *centurion* of the *cohort* was its commander. While, like the non-commissioned officers of modern armies, the *centurions* could not rise in rank beyond their own grade, and while their duties were assimilated to these, they more nearly approached,

MULI MARIANI

in the extent of their command, our company officers than our sergeants. Their relative rank in the legion was well determined.

The music and standards of the *cohorts* and legions were much like those of the Punic wars. Each *maniple* had an ensign; each *cohort* an eagle. The baggage consisted of pack-train (*impedimenta*) and the soldier's own load (*sarcinae*), which Cicero says was sixty pounds in addition to his armour and weapons,—a possible maximum. Sutlers (*mercatores*) were the only persons accompanying the army who used carts. The tents were of skins, ten feet square. Each tent could accommodate ten men, of whom two would probably be on duty. Each centurion had a tent; the camp-followers must be sheltered; the higher officers had servants and more tents than the lesser. With tools for entrenching, tent-poles and pegs and the usual baggage carried, Rüstow estimates five hundred and twenty sumpter-mules for a field legion of thirty-six hundred men,—or one animal for every seven men. This was all there was to the pack-train, and is not far astray. Marius invented a forked stick or pole (*muli Mariani*) for convenience in carrying the *sarcinae*. The bundles of rations, clothing, etc., were tied to this, and it was borne on the shoulder. The ration for fifteen days, grain unground, weighed probably twenty-five pounds. The rest of the kit, armour, etc., much more than doubled this load. Cicero's estimate may be considered high.

The allied legions of old times had all disappeared. A legion no longer meant one Roman and one allied legion, or ten thousand men. It meant simply a body of ten *cohorts*. In place of the allied legions there was a larger force than theretofore of light troops armed like *legionaries*, but less heavily, and considerably more bowmen and slingers.

LEGION IN ONE LINE

The light troops had a leather jerkin but no armour, and carried the round shield (*parma*) instead of the cylindrical *scutum*. The bowmen and slingers wore no armour at all.

The six tribunes were divided into sets of two. Each set commanded the legion for—two months, the two *tribunes* alternating daily, after the odd Roman fashion, which only among them could work without destroying all idea of discipline. The four *tribunes* off duty acted much as quartermasters, commissaries or *aides de camp* do in modern times. All of them served mounted. To be sure that each legion should not suffer from the divided command, a legate was put in supreme supervisory control. Later Caesar put him in actual command, and under him the two tribunes on duty probably acted as chief of staff and adjutant gen-eral of a modern brigade.

The general staff of Caesar's army comprised:

Legates, assigned by the Senate to the consul, and deriving their authority from him. They were the general officers. Caesar had one for each of his legions. This was the first time their duty had been made definite.

Quaestors, who superintended the business of a province or of an

LIGHT-ARMED MAN   LEGIONARY READY FOR BATTLE.

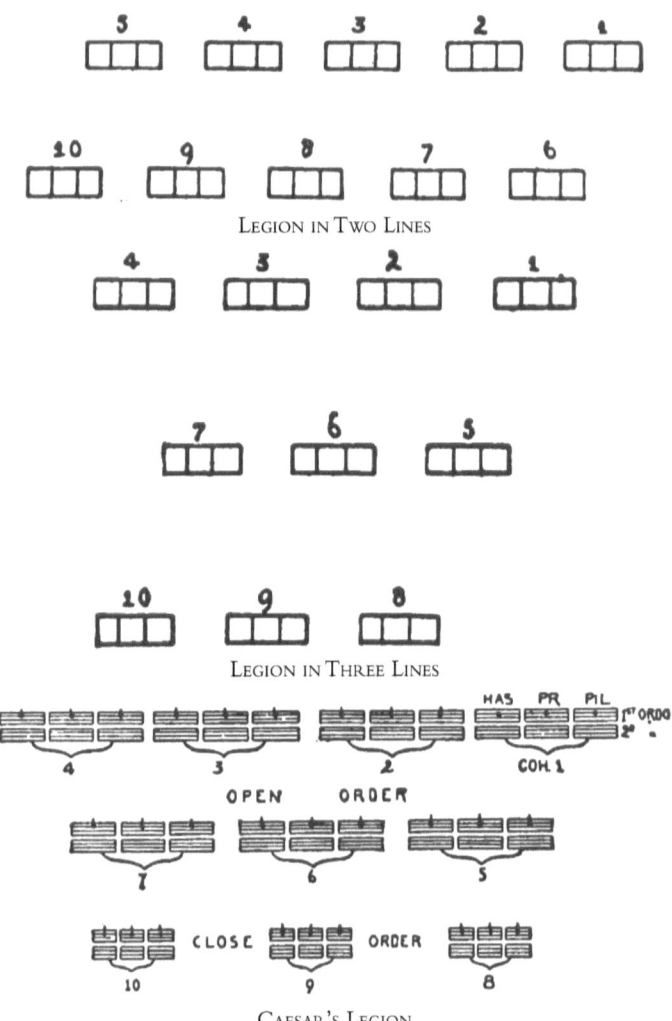

army. The *quaestor* was a sort of quartermaster-general.

Contubernales and *comites praetorii,* who were volunteer aides, or if numerous a sort of gentleman body-guard.

The *Cohors praetoria,* consisting of *lictors,* secretaries, marshals, spies, servants and orderlies.

Speculatores (scouts), who acted as vanguard and flankers on the march,—each legion had ten,—and who were generally sent out to reconnoitre. We must conclude that these had placed under them such details as the immediate circumstances called for.

The Body-guard, sometimes a small cavalry detachment, but principally *evocati*,—veterans past duty years who remained voluntarily in service. Though footmen, they had horses and servants, were highly honoured, served near the general, and were put into places of trust.

Fabri, or engineers, under a *praefectus fabrorum*, of whom mention has already been made. They were used to repair weapons, construct bridges, siege-mounds and towers, and generally do the engineering work of the army. Caesar had some very able engineers.

Antesignani, thought by some historians to have been a select body of a few men from each *cohort*, for service in delicate cases requiring skill and experience. They carried no baggage, and from them were often selected the *centurions*. But it is not improbable that the *antesignani* were actually what their name designates; that in each *maniple* they formed the first two ranks, to protect the ensign, which was carried in the second rank; and that they were thus a quarter or a fifth of the entire body. Some events, as at Ilerda, lead up to this belief.

The pay of Caesar's *legionaries* was two hundred and twenty-five *denarii* (forty dollars) a year. This was about the pay of a day-laborer. His rations and clothing were deducted from his pay, but booty and largesses greatly increased it. His ration is variously stated to have been from one to three pecks of wheat, or other grain, a month; which was probably supplemented by beef, and such vegetables and fruit as the foragers could find.

The offensive formation of the legion was in two, three or four lines (*acies duplex, triplex* or *quadruplex*). In two lines there were five *cohorts* in each, standing checkerwise. In three lines, which was usual, four *cohorts* were in the first and three in each of the others, also checkerwise. Intervals between *cohorts* in battle order are, by many commentators, said to have been equal to the *cohort* front; but though this was true of the era of the Punic wars, there is much room to doubt such intervals in Caesar's time. No doubt there was an interval, especially when the men stood in close order, that is, three feet apart; but the *quincuncial* formation, whose bodies and so remain in battle, had tended to disappear by gradual decrease of the intervals. What these actually were at this time we do not know. They may have been prescribed in the Drill Regulations, and used on parade; but it is probable that in action they were often reduced to a minimum. The best explanation of which the involved statements of the old authorities are capable seems to be the one already given, that in close (three-foot) order there were intervals between *cohorts* equal to *cohort* front; and in open or battle (six-foot) order, these intervals were quite filled up. As the third line was apt to be held in reserve and in close order, a legion in battle order would have the first two lines deployed,—*i. e.*, without intervals between *cohorts* and the third line ployed into close order with intervals equal to *cohort* front.

The lines were some one hundred and fifty feet apart, though this distance is also disputed. This would give, in an eight-rank formation, about four hundred and fifty feet depth and ten hundred and fifty feet front for a legion in three lines. The weight of such a legion was, therefore, very great, and still its mobility was well preserved. The phalanx of Alexander had twenty-eight men per metre of front line. The legion of the Second Punic War and Caesar's era had eleven men. The modern army has not far from seven.

An army of seven legions in three lines—twenty-five thousand men field strength—would take up somewhat less than a mile and a half of front.

```
   7              6           5           4           3           2           1
 ᓂᓂᓂᓂᓂᓂᓂᓂᓂᓂᓂᓂᓂᓂᓂᓂᓂᓂᓂᓂᓂ
 ᓂᓂᓂ   ᓂᓂᓂ   ᓂᓂᓂ   ᓂᓂᓂ   ᓂᓂᓂ   ᓂᓂᓂ   ᓂᓂᓂ
 ᓂᓂᓂ   ᓂᓂᓂ   ᓂᓂᓂ   ᓂᓂᓂ   ᓂᓂᓂ   ᓂᓂᓂ   ᓂᓂᓂ
```
SEVEN LEGIONS IN THREE LINES

The defensive formation of the legion was in one line (*acies simplex*), or in a square (*acies quadrata*), or a circle (*orbis*). The one line was usual for the defence of breastworks or of the camp,—depth being unnecessary, as reserves were kept for the protection of the gates and for sorties. The five front ranks were on the rampart without intervals, the five rear ones at the foot of the rampart. Sometimes only two ranks were on the rampart and the three other ranks of the *ordo* back of it in reserve, while the rear *ordo* of five ranks was similarly disposed at the left of the front *ordo*. The space allowed for the usual defensive line was six feet per man; or with only *ordo* depth and assuming that the *centurions* were not in line, two hundred and sixteen feet for the *maniple*, four hundred and thirty-two feet for the *cohort*, and forty-three hundred and twenty feet, four fifths of a mile, for the legion. A single line disposition was sometimes practiced to resist attacks in the field, but the *cohort* retained its front of about one hundred and twenty feet, and the intervals being closed, the legion had but twelve hundred feet front. How much of a circle the *orbis* was, we do not know. It was formed for defence in the field against overwhelming and surrounding forces. To resist such an attack, the *cohorts* drew up in what was the equivalent of our hollow square. Smaller bodies might form circular groups, using their shields and hurling their spears and occasionally falling to with the sword. Were not the hollow square also described we should be tempted to believe that the *orbis* was the same formation.

A legion in three lines could readily form square by leaving the first, second and third *cohorts* facing to the front; by facing the fifth and sixth to the right; the fourth and seventh to the left, and by facing the eighth, ninth and tenth to the rear. The term *orbis* may have come from the natural habit of flattening out the corners of such a square for easier defence. It is difficult to imagine the manoeuvre by which a legion ployed into anything approaching an actual circle and again deployed into line. It may have been an irregular half-square, half-circle, according to the accentuation of the ground or to the conditions demanding a defensive formation.

On rare occasions there was a quadruple line. The fourth was intended to protect a flank and might consist of some *cohorts* specially detailed and marshalled at an angle to the general line. Such was Caesar's disposition at Pharsalus.

The auxiliary troops were drilled to conform to the same methods. They had not the *cohort* formation, but they were utilized so as to sustain the legionary tactics, much as the *velites* of old had been. The bowmen and slingers were mere skirmishers having no definite tactical position.

In the cavalry, the *turma* of thirty-two enlisted men was the tactical unit. It rode in four ranks of eight front. It has been thought that the ranks were open so that the men stood checkerwise. There were three *decurions* to each *turma*, the senior being its chief. The *turma* must have been a body about forty feet square, reckoning crudely five feet front and ten feet depth per mounted man. Twelve *turmae* were an *ala* (wing) or regiment, which may have been formed in two (or three) lines, each say four hundred and forty (or two hundred and eighty) feet long, counting intervals equal to *turma*-front between *turmae*, which were more essential in the cavalry than the infantry. The cavalry was commanded by a *praefectus equitum*. In larger bodies, in which the cavalry often acted, we must guess at the formation. It no doubt, at this era, conformed much to the habits of the peoples furnishing the troops, modi-

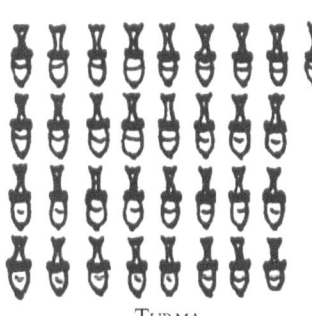

TURMA

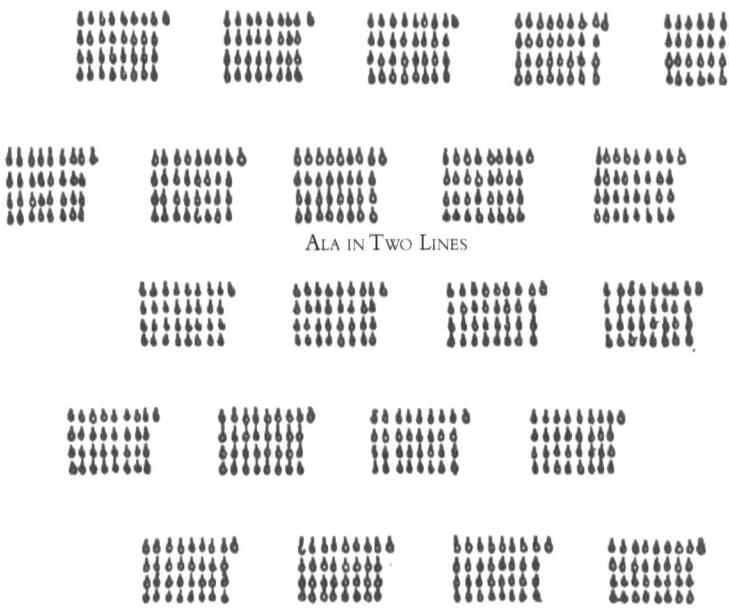

ALA IN TWO LINES

ALA IN THREE LINES

fied by Roman experience and the necessities of the army. Caesar had no Roman cavalry, properly speaking. It was all recruited among the Gauls or Germans.

The order of march (*agmen*) was quickly formed by facing the legion to the right or left, according as it was to move. The *cohorts* thus followed each other in order. If to the right, the maniples of each *cohort* would be *pilani, principes, hastati*; if to the left, the reverse. The depth of the file, on facing to the right or left, would be column front, *i. e.,* eight or ten men; and as the men could comfortably march in a breadth of three feet each, this front could be reduced to twenty-four or thirty feet by simply dressing on the front rank man; or by making each second *ordo* fall in behind its first, this could be again reduced to fifteen or twelve feet front. It was a "column of fives or fours." This was called marching in column of *maniples* (*manipulatim*). The legion in column of maniples could then file in any direction.

Or the legion could march in column of centuries (*centuriatim* or *ordinatim*) by the *maniple* on the right or left marching straight forward, followed in order by each succeeding *maniple*. In this order each *cohort* would march with its centuries in regular sequence: first *ordo* of *pilani*, second *ditto*; first *ordo* of *principes*, second ditto; first *ordo* of *hastati*, second *ditto*. In other words, the *centuries* (*ordines*) would successively

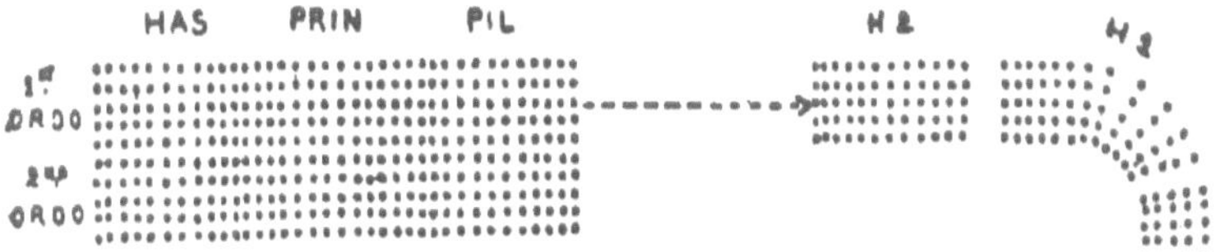

AGMEN MANIPNLATIM

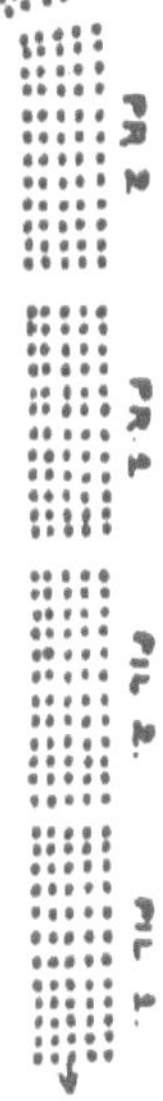

follow each other. This column would have a front of twelve men if the *cohort* had only field strength; but we can imagine it ployed into a "column of sixes." In its full width it was employed only in open country. Few roads would accommodate so wide a column.

Line was again quickly formed from column by converse means, just as it is today. Deployments were sometimes made by the left instead of the right, as, *e. g.*, when circumstances would expose the right flank, which, with the shield on the left arm, it will be remembered, was considered the weak or open side (*latus apertum*). Thus, in debouching from a defile, to deploy at its mouth, the column might issue left in front, and deploy to the right of the leading century or *cohort*. The open side would not be thus exposed.

The men could readily march each in a space of four feet from front to rear. A *cohort* of field strength (three hundred and sixty men) would thus take up, in length of column, if marching *centuriatim*, full front, one hundred and twenty feet; half front, two hundred and forty feet. If *manipulatim*, and the men kept their distance of three feet, as they could for short distances, it would be one hundred and eight feet long; if the column was extended so as to allow each man four feet, it would be one hundred and fifty-two feet long in full front, three hundred and four feet in half front. It scarcely seems probable that the column could be allowed to drag its length out so much beyond the space required by the line of battle. But marches then were governed by the condition of the roads as they are today, and it was, no doubt, difficult to keep the column closed up.

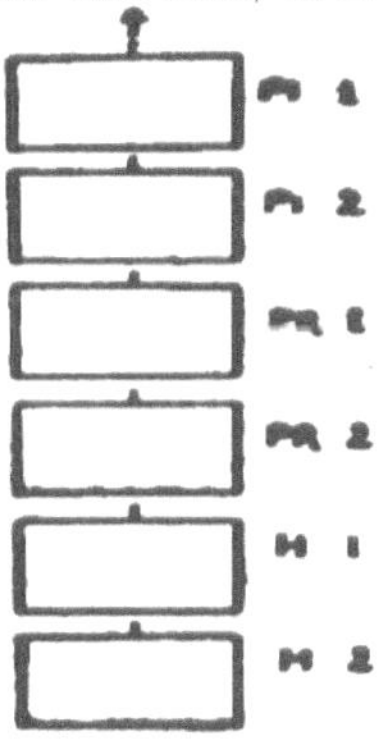

The legion could march in line (*acies instructa*); in column (*agmen pilatum*); in square (*agmen quadratum*). The march in line was only employed on the

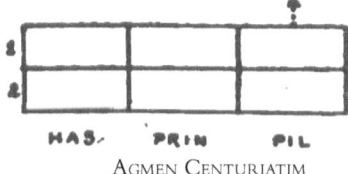

AGMEN CENTURIATIM

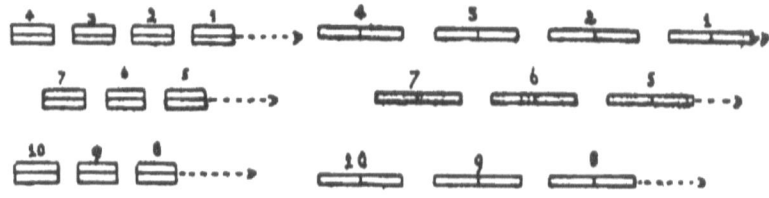

BY LINES TO THE RIGHT

battlefield and had the same advantages and disadvantages, saving the absence of artillery, as it has today. If the legion in three lines wished to take ground to the right, and still remain in line of battle, it could do so by facing the whole body to the right and marching the three columns so made as far as desired. By a halt and front the line of battle was again formed in three lines. This enabled a legion to change its position obliquely without great difficulty. If the line was on difficult ground it could advance by column of wings (*cornu*). The right wing would have *cohorts* 1, 5, 8; the centre would have cohorts 2, 6, 9; the left wing would have *cohorts* 4, 3, 7, 10. Each of these would march by the flank and file to the front, like our forward by the right of companies. On halting, each *cohort* would file to its proper place in line and dress forward on its right.

In marching in column the *cohorts* followed each other according to number (No. 1 to No. 10 from right to left). Thus marching *centuriatim* gave the legion, with an interval of twenty feet between *cohorts*, some fourteen hundred feet of length; if doubled up, twenty-six hundred feet.

The baggage-train of a legion Rüstow has estimated at five hundred and twenty pack-animals. In a breadth of forty feet eight animals could go abreast, which gave sixty-five ranks of them; or allowing ten feet for each, six hundred and fifty feet for the pack-train, or thirteen hundred feet if doubled on a road twenty feet wide. Thus the marching length of a legion of thirty-six hundred men, with its train, was not far from two thousand feet, or doubled, four thousand feet, say three quarters of a mile. If the legion was marching *manipulatim* in "column of fives," the *cohorts* would take up over three

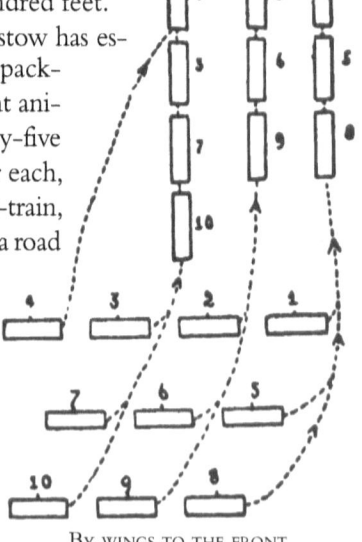

BY WINGS TO THE FRONT

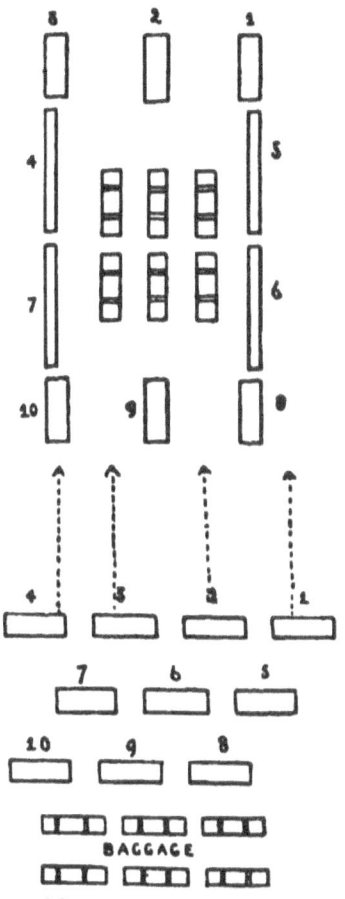

MARCH FORWARD IN SQUARE

thousand feet, and with baggage added would stretch out somewhat more; on a bad road, a full mile.

In presence of the enemy, or in line of battle, the troops were drilled to ploy into column or deploy back into line, to march by the right or left flank, to the front or rear, much as modern armies do. The drill-ground or battlefield manoeuvres of a legion were almost identical in principle and performance with our own, the variation relating mainly to the greater depth of the Roman lines, the difference in arms and the absence of artillery. The manoeuvres of one of our civil war brigades, in a line of battalion-columns doubled on the centre, would not be much unlike those of a legion.

The legion in presence of the enemy also marched, when the ground permitted, in a sort of square formed by a van and rear with baggage between, and heavy flanking columns on each side of the train. The square was quickly formed for the march from the legion in line. *Cohorts* 1, 2 and 3 kept straight on. *Cohorts* 5 and 6 formed column left in front so as to face outwardly when coming to a front. *Cohorts* 4 and 7 formed column right in front. *Cohorts* 8, 9 and 10 formed line to the rear, and then broke by the right of *cohorts* or *maniples* to the rear and marched behind the baggage. These last were then in such order as readily to form line to the rear and complete the square. The baggage was thus inclosed in the centre; its length might somewhat modify the formation of the marching square. We hear of the Roman army marching over what we know must have been very difficult ground in this formation. It is not to be presumed that accurate order was preserved when the ground was wooded or much cut up. Caesar is as perfectly exact in his use of terms to describe these manoeuvres as if writing a book of tactics. And the Roman "drill-regulations" had been established for generations and modified only as requirements from age to age dictated. Still there are many minor points which cannot be positively elucidated.

The cavalry wings of four hundred men marched by *turmae* forty feet wide, taking up, without baggage, nearly five hundred feet length of column. The train probably added half as much. The ranks of the *turmae* column were also doubled in narrow ways, just how is not known. They must often have been obliged to reduce front and thus lengthen the column. A body of four thousand horse, such as Caesar had in Gaul, with baggage, would take up, in simple column, nearly a mile and a half; doubled up, three miles.

All this was naturally subject to precisely the same difficulties which are encountered by every army in the field. And the more wooded and broken the territory the less accurately could the "tactics" be conformed to. In Gaul, no doubt, there was constant and great deviation from the regulations.

The day's march (*iter*) was reckoned from camp to camp. A day of rest was customary after every three or four marches. Each night, or whenever a stop was made, the camp was fortified. This entrenching practically took the place of our outpost system, besides being something else. The legions usually fought with their camp in their rear. If they came across the enemy on the march, they stopped, half the men fortified a camp, while the others protected them, placed the baggage in it and then fought,—provided, indeed, they could so long fend off the enemy. The ordinary day's march was from fifteen to eighteen miles, theoretically supposed to be done in five summer hours, nearly seven of ours, generally from early morning to noon, there being thus enough time left for camping.

The step (*gradus*) was two and one half Roman feet long; the route step one hundred to the minute; the quick step one hundred and twenty. This is about our own standard. The pace (*passus*) was two steps, from right heel to right heel. The Roman foot was nine tenths of ours.

The average Roman march was no greater than that of modern days. Some exceptional marches were remarkable. Caesar left Gergovia at daybreak to move on Litavicus, marched twenty-five Roman miles, struck him and brought him to reason the same day, marched back twenty-five miles, and the next day reached Gergovia before daybreak, the legions having rested three hours during the twenty-four, and six more having been consumed in watching the enemy under arms. The only superior to this march which can be quickly recalled is that of the Spartans to Marathon, one hundred and fifty miles in three days. Crassus marched to join Caesar, who was moving to the assistance of Cicero, and made from midnight to nine a. m. twenty-five Roman miles. In the Zeta raid, Caesar's legions marched thirty-six miles from before day-break to nightfall, capturing a town and fighting four hours in retreat on the way. We do not know just what periods of rest were allowed during the day's march. We rest usually ten minutes every hour. On occasion marches were made without baggage. It goes without saying that the Roman marches were subject to the same interruptions, difficulties and delays as our own. Muddy roads and freshets in rivers were as common in Gaul as in Mexico or Virginia.

A vanguard (*primum agmen*) was usual, and consisted of the

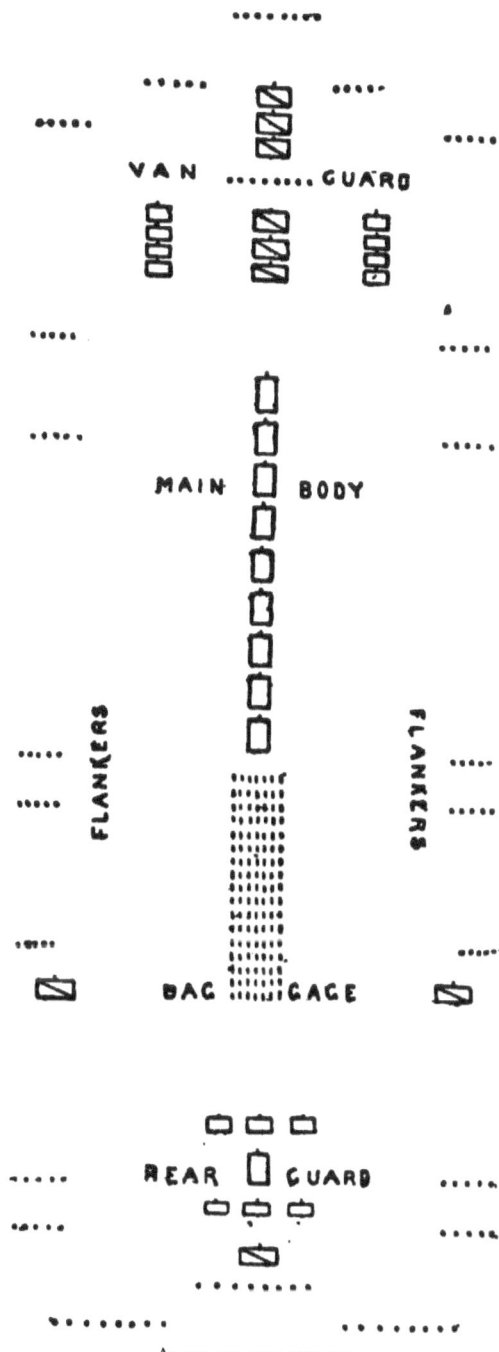

ARMY ON THE MARCH

bulk of the cavalry and light troops, scouts, staff-officers and camp men supported by some *cohorts* without baggage. The main body followed. A guard brought up the rear. The duty of the van was to attack and hold the enemy, if met, so as to enable the main body to form; to reconnoitre the front and advance flanks; to select and stake out a camp. The cavalry Caesar sometimes kept with the main body when he did not deem it reliable, or when one of the flanks had to be protected from danger of attack. Light troops alone were used as vanguard when the cavalry was on other duty.

The rearguard (*agmen extremum*) in marches towards the enemy had no duties except to keep order at the tail of the column and pick up stragglers.

The main body marched in simple column or in battle order by the flank, according as the enemy was far or near, or the land was friendly or inimical. An army of five legions, with baggage, eighteen to twenty thousand men, all told, took, in a forty-foot wide order, from two to two and a half miles of length, with ranks doubled twice as much. In practice, the column was much more strung out than this when the roads were not good.

Out of presence of the enemy, the train of each legion accompanied it for greater convenience; in his presence, the train was kept together in one body. When moving on the enemy, the bulk—say three quarters—of the main army was in front, then the train, then the remainder as baggage and rearguard.

In battle order the legions were not intended to march any distance. This order was used only in the immediate vicinity of the enemy. When Caesar moved against the Usipetes and Tenchtheri, each legion is supposed to have marched ployed into three columns at deploying distance. There were thus fifteen parallel columns for the five legions. The whole could at once deploy forward into line. The legionaries had their helmets on, their shields uncovered and their weapons ready; the baggage had been left in the camp.

We remember that on the march the legionary had his helmet hanging on his chest, his shield in a case, and his plumes, and other insignia of rank or corps, wrapped up. If suddenly attacked the men must lay down their baggage, prepare and put on their badges and get ready their weapons. At the River Sabis the Romans had to fight without this preparation.

The marches in retreat were conducted on reverse principles, with similar precautions. The baggage went with the vanguard, followed by the bulk of the army; then came a strong rearguard. The marches in squares were made through an enemy's territory, or in times of insurrection, or when the enemy was on every side. Sometimes the square was composed of the whole army; sometimes each legion marched in square. On every front of such a square, cavalry, bowmen and slingers were thrown out as skirmishers. The baggage was in the centre of the one large square, or that of the legion in the centre of each legionary square.

Flank marches were made in battle order, with baggage on the side opposite the enemy, or between the lines if there were more than one. Such marches were not usually made for any great distance. In the open field the legions so marching were protected by flankers. In a valley a stream might serve to protect the column. Caesar marched up the Elaver in battle order by the flank for several days.

The order of march was changed daily, to equalize the labour of the *legionaries*. Caesar's legions crossed rivers with ease, wading fords up to the waist, breast and even neck. They carried no ammunition; their armour and weapons could not be spoiled. Bridges took as a rule too long to build; Caesar preferred fords when available. If the river was deep and the current rapid, a line of cavalry was stationed above and below, the first in an oblique line to break the current, the last to catch men who were carried down. Fords were now and then passed in line of battle, as at the Thames.

Bridges were as quickly built as today. The absence of pontoon-trains was no apparent hindrance. They were built of boats picked up along the river, as often as on piles; whichever was at the moment handier. But once did Caesar in the Gallic War cross a river directly in the face of the enemy. This was the Thames. Bridgeheads usually protected both ends of a bridge.

Caesar kept to the uniform ancient habit of drawing up his legions for battle on the gentle slope of a hill, so that they might have the advantage of the descent for casting their *pila* as well as for the rush upon the enemy. The utmost reliance was put upon the initiative so as to make the first shock a telling one when possible. The legions were wont to await the advance of the enemy to within two hundred and fifty paces (if, indeed, he would advance), then at the common step to move upon him, and when within half this space to take the run (*cursus*). The distance was not great enough to wind the men, even in their heavy armour. The first two ranks held their spears aloft in readiness and hurled them at ten to twenty paces from the enemy. If the volley produced sufficient gaps, falling to with the sword the legionaries would penetrate into these and have the enemy at their mercy. In case the enemy was brave and determined, the legions often remained longer at javelin-casting distance and used their spears only, the rear ranks advancing through the front ranks to hurl their *pila* in their turn. The ten ranks could thus deliver five heavy volleys of javelins, having exhausted which, the first line of *cohorts* drew the sword or allowed the second line to advance in its turn. It sometimes occurred that the enemy *was* so rapid as to leave no time to hurl the *pila*, and the legionaries set to at once with the gladius. But this was rare. The light troops kept the fighting line supplied with javelins, collected from those hurled at it. Or again the two first lines, after casting their pila, would at once close in with the sword. When exhausted they would allow the next two ranks to come forward, hurl their *pila* and use the sword; and thus the ranks worked successively,—hours being often consumed in this array of duels between the individuals of each fighting line.

The old *legionary* always pushed his enemy with his bossed shield. He was so well armed and so expert that he could sometimes fight all day without receiving a wound. He was physically strong and could gradually force the enemy back in places by sheer pressure and thus make gaps into which he could penetrate with deadly effect. During battle, few *legionaries* were either killed or wounded,—but when one line broke, the other could cut it to pieces.

In case the enemy awaited the Roman advance, this was conducted in similar manner. The first ranks were sustained by the backward ones in such a manner that there was a never-ceasing motion in each *cohort* as those who still held their *pila* in their turn advanced to hurl them; yet there was no loss of formation, as the space occupied by each man gave ample room to advance and retire within the body of the *cohort*. The second and third lines remained at a suitable distance in the rear,—two hundred feet or more,—ready to support the front line by advancing into or through its intervals. The second line was ordered forward when the first line ceased to gain a perceptible advantage over the enemy. All the lines gradually came into action,—the third at the critical moment.

The legion in Caesar's time excelled because he was at its head. It was not without its disadvantages. The soldiery was brave and well disciplined, but the Roman army was not independent of terrain. The work of the skirmishers, slingers and bowmen, of the auxiliaries, and of the veteran *antesignani* did not always chime in with that of the legions. The two kinds of infantry would sometimes clash, owing to their different formation. The cavalry was often inefficient, and had to be strengthened by bodies of light infantry placed in the intervals of the *turmae*. This infantry, when the shock with the enemy's horse came, could inflict serious damage on it. It helped to steady the movements of the *turmae*, while protected at the same time from being run down by the enemy's cavalry. This mixing cavalry and foot is one of the most ancient of devices. In a modified form it has survived to our day. The Roman cavalry was serviceable, but at its very best it was not cavalry, such as were Alexander's companions or the squadrons of Seidlitz.

The real battle was fought out by the legions. In fact, the legions could be independent of any other troops. Cavalry could attack cavalry; it could cut up broken infantry; but unbroken *cohorts* could not be successfully attacked by cavalry except in flank. By a front attack, steady infantry could drive cavalry in every instance. During battle, cavalry was useful only against the enemy's squadrons. The cavalry and skirmishers were chiefly of use in outpost and reconnoitring duties and in pursuit. In actual battle, the cavalry was not much Employed. Since Alexander's day, it will be seen, cavalry had degenerated.

The *cohorts* were all-sufficient. When cavalry and light troops were not on hand, the legions found no difficulty in doing all the work themselves. Still they relied on the cavalry and light troops, if present, to protect their flanks while fighting. In case there was grave danger of a flank attack, especially on the right, a fourth line was more than once made by Caesar, the duty of which it was to stand near and defend the threatened quarter.

Habitually the line of *cohorts* in each legion was threefold as before detailed. This arrangement in an army of six legions in line would give twenty-four *cohorts* in the first line and eighteen *cohorts* in each of the others. The third was considered as a reserve not to go into action till ordered by the general. It was on occasion used to sustain the flanks of the legions, or threaten the enemy's. Its utility was shown at Bibracte and in the battle against Ariovistus. A curious feature of Caesar's formation, due probably to Marius, was that the oldest and best *cohorts* were placed in the front line, and the younger ones in the rear. This was the direct reverse of the principle which in the old legion had ranked the three class-lines as *hastati, principes, triarii*.

The cavalry was placed as occasion required. As a rule it was on the flanks. It might be posted in the rear, as was the case at Bibracte, because it was not deemed reliable, and in the battle against Ariovistus because the barbarians were protected in flank and rear by their wagons set up as defence, and cavalry against these was useless.

The light troops were only available as a curtain or as skirmishers. In battle they were harmful rather than of use. They do not appear to have been employed to open the action as uniformly as in earlier days, but rather in collateral duties. But they collected darts and kept the *legionaries* supplied with them.

The line had a centre (*acies media*), and right and left wing (*cornu dextrum, sinistrum*). The cavalry wings sometimes first advanced; then legion after legion under the legates in command. This was, as it were, an order of battle with the centre withdrawn. The oldest and most experienced legions were posted on the right and left. If there were no prevailing reasons to the contrary, Caesar preferred to attack with his right in advance, where, like Alexander, he was wont to take his stand. This resulted in a species of oblique order of battle. It was more the result of Caesar's predilection for personally leading off in action than a definite tactical oblique order, like that of Epaminondas, or as most perfectly exemplified by Frederick at Leuthen. On the signal being blown, the right *cohorts* at once advanced, those on their left successively following. It was not a tactical advance in echelon with heavily reinforced right flank, but a gradual rushing to battle of the *cohorts* from right to left. In a measure it had similar results. The best legions would naturally be stationed on the attacking wing.

The line of *cohorts* impinged upon the enemy only along part of its front when there were intervals between the *cohorts*; and the enemy might and sometimes did penetrate into these intervals, and take the *cohorts* on the sensitive right flank. But the second line was always on the watch for just this thing, and was ready to correct the evil by a vigorous onset. Caesar's probable formation, by which the *cohorts* deployed into a battle order without intervals, eliminated this danger. During the fighting contact there was not only a succession of smaller shocks by the several ranks of each *cohort*, but the first, second and third lines could deliver their heavier blows in succession, following each other as the tired lines got rest from the advance of those in rear. A hard-fought field was one of incessant motion.

The different acts of a battle might be stated as these. Before the action opened—unless it was precipitated—the general rode the lines and made a short address (*cohortatio*) to each of his legions, to rouse their martial ardour. He then went to the attacking flank and gave the trumpet signal, which was repeated down the line. The legions of the attacking flank advanced with their battle-cry and the legions on their right or left successively came on in a species of rough echelon. The legions of the first line were followed after a certain lapse of time, perhaps minutes, perhaps hours, by the second and third lines, the cavalry riding forward at the same time to protect the flank or attack the enemy's cavalry, or—when this was beaten—the flank of the infantry line. When the first line was exhausted, the lines in rear replaced them in places or along the whole front as ordered, and special bodies of troops were brought up to support decimated legions much as in our own days; moving forward through intervals when these existed, or allowing the broken lines in front to fall irregularly through intervals specially opened for the purpose. Victory being won, the cavalry pursued. Defeat ensuing, the legions withdrew to the fortified camp and re-formed there, the general holding back the enemy with his reserves or the legions least exhausted, and the cavalry. The battles of remote antiquity were very different; the battles of Alexander, Hannibal and Caesar bear more resemblance, in a general way, to our own.

Defensive battles were not fought unless the terrain was especially suitable. The flanks were then leaned on natural obstacles, and the front was protected by wolf-pits or other entanglements. If possible, the army backed on the camp, protected their flanks, and gave the enemy only one approach, in front and up a slope. The camp of Caesar on the Axona, where he invited an attack, was a good sample of this. If the barbarians had crossed the morass in his front, they must have broken ranks in so doing, and Caesar could have charged down on their *phalanx* with decisive effect, for his flanks were protected by ramparts. At Alesia, the fighting was defensive, coupled with sallies. But in the open field, the Roman strength lay in attack, or in inviting attack and in meeting it halfway.

ALSO FROM LEONAUR
AVAILABLE IN SOFTCOVER OR HARDCOVER WITH DUST JACKET

A HISTORY OF THE FRENCH & INDIAN WAR *by Arthur G. Bradley*—The Seven Years War as it was fought in the New World has always fascinated students of military history—here is the story of that confrontation.

WASHINGTON'S EARLY CAMPAIGNS *by James Hadden*—The French Post Expedition, Great Meadows and Braddock's Defeat—including Braddock's Orderly Books.

BOUQUET & THE OHIO INDIAN WAR *by Cyrus Cort & William Smith*—Two Accounts of the Campaigns of 1763-1764: Bouquet's Campaigns by Cyrus Cort & The History of Bouquet's Expeditions by William Smith.

NARRATIVES OF THE FRENCH & INDIAN WAR: 2 *by David Holden, Samuel Jenks, Lemuel Lyon, Mary Cochrane Rogers & Henry T. Blake*—Contains The Diary of Sergeant David Holden, Captain Samuel Jenks' Journal, The Journal of Lemuel Lyon, Journal of a French Officer at the Siege of Quebec, A Battle Fought on Snowshoes & The Battle of Lake George.

NARRATIVES OF THE FRENCH & INDIAN WAR *by Brown, Eastburn, Hawks & Putnam*—Ranger Brown's Narrative, The Adventures of Robert Eastburn, The Journal of Rufus Putnam—Provincial Infantry & Orderly Book and Journal of Major John Hawks on the Ticonderoga-Crown Point Campaign.

THE 7TH (QUEEN'S OWN) HUSSARS: Volume 1—1688-1792 *by C. R. B. Barrett*—As Dragoons During the Flanders Campaign, War of the Austrian Succession and the Seven Years War.

INDIA'S FREE LANCES *by H. G. Keene*—European Mercenary Commanders in Hindustan 1770-1820.

THE BENGAL EUROPEAN REGIMENT *by P. R. Innes*—An Elite Regiment of the Honourable East India Company 1756-1858.

MUSKET & TOMAHAWK *by Francis Parkman*—A Military History of the French & Indian War, 1753-1760.

THE BLACK WATCH AT TICONDEROGA *by Frederick B. Richards*—Campaigns in the French & Indian War.

QUEEN'S RANGERS *by Frederick B. Richards*—John Simcoe and his Rangers During the Revolutionary War for America.

AVAILABLE ONLINE AT **www.leonaur.com**
AND FROM ALL GOOD BOOK STORES

ALSO FROM LEONAUR
AVAILABLE IN SOFTCOVER OR HARDCOVER WITH DUST JACKET

JOURNALS OF ROBERT ROGERS OF THE RANGERS *by Robert Rogers*—The exploits of Rogers & the Rangers in his own words during 1755-1761 in the French & Indian War.

GALLOPING GUNS *by James Young*—The Experiences of an Officer of the Bengal Horse Artillery During the Second Maratha War 1804-1805.

GORDON *by Demetrius Charles Boulger*—The Career of Gordon of Khartoum.

THE BATTLE OF NEW ORLEANS *by Zachary F. Smith*—The final major engagement of the War of 1812.

THE TWO WARS OF MRS DUBERLY *by Frances Isabella Duberly*—An Intrepid Victorian Lady's Experience of the Crimea and Indian Mutiny.

WITH THE GUARDS' BRIGADE DURING THE BOER WAR *by Edward P. Lowry*—On Campaign from Bloemfontein to Koomati Poort and Back.

THE REBELLIOUS DUCHESS *by Paul F. S. Dermoncourt*—The Adventures of the Duchess of Berri and Her Attempt to Overthrow French Monarchy.

MEN OF THE MUTINY *by John Tulloch Nash & Henry Metcalfe*—Two Accounts of the Great Indian Mutiny of 1857: Fighting with the Bengal Yeomanry Cavalry & Private Metcalfe at Lucknow.

CAMPAIGN IN THE CRIMEA *by George Shuldham Peard*—The Recollections of an Officer of the 20th Regiment of Foot.

WITHIN SEBASTOPOL *by K. Hodasevich*—A Narrative of the Campaign in the Crimea, and of the Events of the Siege.

WITH THE CAVALRY TO AFGHANISTAN *by William Taylor*—The Experiences of a Trooper of H. M. 4th Light Dragoons During the First Afghan War.

THE CAWNPORE MAN *by Mowbray Thompson*—A First Hand Account of the Siege and Massacre During the Indian Mutiny By One of Four Survivors.

BRIGADE COMMANDER: AFGHANISTAN *by Henry Brooke*—The Journal of the Commander of the 2nd Infantry Brigade, Kandahar Field Force During the Second Afghan War.

BANCROFT OF THE BENGAL HORSE ARTILLERY *by N. W. Bancroft*—An Account of the First Sikh War 1845-1846.

AVAILABLE ONLINE AT **www.leonaur.com**
AND FROM ALL GOOD BOOK STORES

ALSO FROM LEONAUR
AVAILABLE IN SOFTCOVER OR HARDCOVER WITH DUST JACKET

AFGHANISTAN: THE BELEAGUERED BRIGADE *by G. R. Gleig*—An Account of Sale's Brigade During the First Afghan War.

IN THE RANKS OF THE C. I. V *by Erskine Childers*—With the City Imperial Volunteer Battery (Honourable Artillery Company) in the Second Boer War.

THE BENGAL NATIVE ARMY *by F. G. Cardew*—An Invaluable Reference Resource.

THE 7TH (QUEEN'S OWN) HUSSARS: Volume 4—1688-1914 *by C. R. B. Barrett*—Uniforms, Equipment, Weapons, Traditions, the Services of Notable Officers and Men & the Appendices to All Volumes—Volume 4: 1688-1914.

THE SWORD OF THE CROWN *by Eric W. Sheppard*—A History of the British Army to 1914.

THE 7TH (QUEEN'S OWN) HUSSARS: Volume 3—1818-1914 *by C. R. B. Barrett*—On Campaign During the Canadian Rebellion, the Indian Mutiny, the Sudan, Matabeleland, Mashonaland and the Boer War Volume 3: 1818-1914.

THE KHARTOUM CAMPAIGN *by Bennet Burleigh*—A Special Correspondent's View of the Reconquest of the Sudan by British and Egyptian Forces under Kitchener—1898.

EL PUCHERO *by Richard McSherry*—The Letters of a Surgeon of Volunteers During Scott's Campaign of the American-Mexican War 1847-1848.

RIFLEMAN SAHIB *by E. Maude*—The Recollections of an Officer of the Bombay Rifles During the Southern Mahratta Campaign, Second Sikh War, Persian Campaign and Indian Mutiny.

THE KING'S HUSSAR *by Edwin Mole*—The Recollections of a 14th (King's) Hussar During the Victorian Era.

JOHN COMPANY'S CAVALRYMAN *by William Johnson*—The Experiences of a British Soldier in the Crimea, the Persian Campaign and the Indian Mutiny.

COLENSO & DURNFORD'S ZULU WAR *by Frances E. Colenso & Edward Durnford*—The first and possibly the most important history of the Zulu War.

U. S. DRAGOON *by Samuel E. Chamberlain*—Experiences in the Mexican War 1846-48 and on the South Western Frontier.

AVAILABLE ONLINE AT **www.leonaur.com**
AND FROM ALL GOOD BOOK STORES

ALSO FROM LEONAUR
AVAILABLE IN SOFTCOVER OR HARDCOVER WITH DUST JACKET

THE 2ND MAORI WAR: 1860-1861 *by Robert Carey*—The Second Maori War, or First Taranaki War, one more bloody instalment of the conflicts between European settlers and the indigenous Maori people.

A JOURNAL OF THE SECOND SIKH WAR *by Daniel A. Sandford*—The Experiences of an Ensign of the 2nd Bengal European Regiment During the Campaign in the Punjab, India, 1848-49.

THE LIGHT INFANTRY OFFICER *by John H. Cooke*—The Experiences of an Officer of the 43rd Light Infantry in America During the War of 1812.

BUSHVELDT CARBINEERS *by George Witton*—The War Against the Boers in South Africa and the 'Breaker' Morant Incident.

LAKE'S CAMPAIGNS IN INDIA *by Hugh Pearse*—The Second Anglo Maratha War, 1803-1807.

BRITAIN IN AFGHANISTAN 1: THE FIRST AFGHAN WAR 1839-42 *by Archibald Forbes*—From invasion to destruction-a British military disaster.

BRITAIN IN AFGHANISTAN 2: THE SECOND AFGHAN WAR 1878-80 *by Archibald Forbes*—This is the history of the Second Afghan War-another episode of British military history typified by savagery, massacre, siege and battles.

UP AMONG THE PANDIES *by Vivian Dering Majendie*—Experiences of a British Officer on Campaign During the Indian Mutiny, 1857-1858.

MUTINY: 1857 *by James Humphries*—Authentic Voices from the Indian Mutiny-First Hand Accounts of Battles, Sieges and Personal Hardships.

BLOW THE BUGLE, DRAW THE SWORD *by W. H. G. Kingston*—The Wars, Campaigns, Regiments and Soldiers of the British & Indian Armies During the Victorian Era, 1839-1898.

WAR BEYOND THE DRAGON PAGODA *by Major J. J. Snodgrass*—A Personal Narrative of the First Anglo-Burmese War 1824 - 1826.

THE HERO OF ALIWAL *by James Humphries*—The Campaigns of Sir Harry Smith in India, 1843-1846, During the Gwalior War & the First Sikh War.

ALL FOR A SHILLING A DAY *by Donald F. Featherstone*—The story of H.M. 16th, the Queen's Lancers During the first Sikh War 1845-1846.

AVAILABLE ONLINE AT **www.leonaur.com**
AND FROM ALL GOOD BOOK STORES

ALSO FROM LEONAUR
AVAILABLE IN SOFTCOVER OR HARDCOVER WITH DUST JACKET

THE FALL OF THE MOGHUL EMPIRE OF HINDUSTAN *by H. G. Keene*—By the beginning of the nineteenth century, as British and Indian armies under Lake and Wellesley dominated the scene, a little over half a century of conflict brought the Moghul Empire to its knees.

LADY SALE'S AFGHANISTAN *by Florentia Sale*—An Indomitable Victorian Lady's Account of the Retreat from Kabul During the First Afghan War.

THE CAMPAIGN OF MAGENTA AND SOLFERINO 1859 *by Harold Carmichael Wylly*—The Decisive Conflict for the Unification of Italy.

FRENCH'S CAVALRY CAMPAIGN *by J. G. Maydon*—A Special Correspondent's View of British Army Mounted Troops During the Boer War.

CAVALRY AT WATERLOO *by Sir Evelyn Wood*—British Mounted Troops During the Campaign of 1815.

THE SUBALTERN *by George Robert Gleig*—The Experiences of an Officer of the 85th Light Infantry During the Peninsular War.

NAPOLEON AT BAY, 1814 *by F. Loraine Petre*—The Campaigns to the Fall of the First Empire.

NAPOLEON AND THE CAMPAIGN OF 1806 *by Colonel Vachée*—The Napoleonic Method of Organisation and Command to the Battles of Jena & Auerstädt.

THE COMPLETE ADVENTURES IN THE CONNAUGHT RANGERS *by William Grattan*—The 88th Regiment during the Napoleonic Wars by a Serving Officer.

BUGLER AND OFFICER OF THE RIFLES *by William Green & Harry Smith*—With the 95th (Rifles) during the Peninsular & Waterloo Campaigns of the Napoleonic Wars.

NAPOLEONIC WAR STORIES *by Sir Arthur Quiller-Couch*—Tales of soldiers, spies, battles & sieges from the Peninsular & Waterloo campaigns.

CAPTAIN OF THE 95TH (RIFLES) *by Jonathan Leach*—An officer of Wellington's sharpshooters during the Peninsular, South of France and Waterloo campaigns of the Napoleonic wars.

RIFLEMAN COSTELLO *by Edward Costello*—The adventures of a soldier of the 95th (Rifles) in the Peninsular & Waterloo Campaigns of the Napoleonic wars.

AVAILABLE ONLINE AT **www.leonaur.com**
AND FROM ALL GOOD BOOK STORES

ALSO FROM LEONAUR
AVAILABLE IN SOFTCOVER OR HARDCOVER WITH DUST JACKET

AT THEM WITH THE BAYONET by Donald F. Featherstone—The first Anglo-Sikh War 1845-1846.

STEPHEN CRANE'S BATTLES by Stephen Crane—Nine Decisive Battles Recounted by the Author of 'The Red Badge of Courage'.

THE GURKHA WAR by H. T. Prinsep—The Anglo-Nepalese Conflict in North East India 1814-1816.

FIRE & BLOOD by G. R. Gleig—The burning of Washington & the battle of New Orleans, 1814, through the eyes of a young British soldier.

SOUND ADVANCE! by Joseph Anderson—Experiences of an officer of HM 50th regiment in Australia, Burma & the Gwalior war.

THE CAMPAIGN OF THE INDUS by Thomas Holdsworth—Experiences of a British Officer of the 2nd (Queen's Royal) Regiment in the Campaign to Place Shah Shuja on the Throne of Afghanistan 1838 - 1840.

WITH THE MADRAS EUROPEAN REGIMENT IN BURMA by John Butler—The Experiences of an Officer of the Honourable East India Company's Army During the First Anglo-Burmese War 1824 - 1826.

IN ZULULAND WITH THE BRITISH ARMY by Charles L. Norris-Newman—The Anglo-Zulu war of 1879 through the first-hand experiences of a special correspondent.

BESIEGED IN LUCKNOW by Martin Richard Gubbins—The first Anglo-Sikh War 1845-1846.

A TIGER ON HORSEBACK by L. March Phillips—The Experiences of a Trooper & Officer of Rimington's Guides - The Tigers - during the Anglo-Boer war 1899 - 1902.

SEPOYS, SIEGE & STORM by Charles John Griffiths—The Experiences of a young officer of H.M.'s 61st Regiment at Ferozepore, Delhi ridge and at the fall of Delhi during the Indian mutiny 1857.

CAMPAIGNING IN ZULULAND by W. E. Montague—Experiences on campaign during the Zulu war of 1879 with the 94th Regiment.

THE STORY OF THE GUIDES by G.J. Younghusband—The Exploits of the Soldiers of the famous Indian Army Regiment from the northwest frontier 1847 - 1900.

AVAILABLE ONLINE AT **www.leonaur.com**
AND FROM ALL GOOD BOOK STORES

ALSO FROM LEONAUR
AVAILABLE IN SOFTCOVER OR HARDCOVER WITH DUST JACKET

ZULU:1879 *by D.C.F. Moodie & the Leonaur Editors*—The Anglo-Zulu War of 1879 from contemporary sources: First Hand Accounts, Interviews, Dispatches, Official Documents & Newspaper Reports.

THE RED DRAGOON *by W.J. Adams*—With the 7th Dragoon Guards in the Cape of Good Hope against the Boers & the Kaffir tribes during the 'war of the axe' 1843-48'.

THE RECOLLECTIONS OF SKINNER OF SKINNER'S HORSE *by James Skinner*—James Skinner and his 'Yellow Boys' Irregular cavalry in the wars of India between the British, Mahratta, Rajput, Mogul, Sikh & Pindarree Forces.

A CAVALRY OFFICER DURING THE SEPOY REVOLT *by A. R. D. Mackenzie*—Experiences with the 3rd Bengal Light Cavalry, the Guides and Sikh Irregular Cavalry from the outbreak to Delhi and Lucknow.

A NORFOLK SOLDIER IN THE FIRST SIKH WAR *by J W Baldwin*—Experiences of a private of H.M. 9th Regiment of Foot in the battles for the Punjab, India 1845-6.

TOMMY ATKINS' WAR STORIES: 14 FIRST HAND ACCOUNTS—Fourteen first hand accounts from the ranks of the British Army during Queen Victoria's Empire.

THE WATERLOO LETTERS *by H. T. Siborne*—Accounts of the Battle by British Officers for its Foremost Historian.

NEY: GENERAL OF CAVALRY VOLUME 1—1769-1799 *by Antoine Bulos*—The Early Career of a Marshal of the First Empire.

NEY: MARSHAL OF FRANCE VOLUME 2—1799-1805 *by Antoine Bulos*—The Early Career of a Marshal of the First Empire.

AIDE-DE-CAMP TO NAPOLEON *by Philippe-Paul de Ségur*—For anyone interested in the Napoleonic Wars this book, written by one who was intimate with the strategies and machinations of the Emperor, will be essential reading.

TWILIGHT OF EMPIRE *by Sir Thomas Ussher & Sir George Cockburn*—Two accounts of Napoleon's Journeys in Exile to Elba and St. Helena: Narrative of Events by Sir Thomas Ussher & Napoleon's Last Voyage: Extract of a diary by Sir George Cockburn.

PRIVATE WHEELER *by William Wheeler*—The letters of a soldier of the 51st Light Infantry during the Peninsular War & at Waterloo.

AVAILABLE ONLINE AT **www.leonaur.com**
AND FROM ALL GOOD BOOK STORES

ALSO FROM LEONAUR
AVAILABLE IN SOFTCOVER OR HARDCOVER WITH DUST JACKET

OFFICERS & GENTLEMEN *by Peter Hawker & William Graham*—Two Accounts of British Officers During the Peninsula War: Officer of Light Dragoons by Peter Hawker & Campaign in Portugal and Spain by William Graham.

THE WALCHEREN EXPEDITION *by Anonymous*—The Experiences of a British Officer of the 81st Regt. During the Campaign in the Low Countries of 1809.

LADIES OF WATERLOO *by Charlotte A. Eaton, Magdalene de Lancey & Juana Smith*—The Experiences of Three Women During the Campaign of 1815: Waterloo Days by Charlotte A. Eaton, A Week at Waterloo by Magdalene de Lancey & Juana's Story by Juana Smith.

JOURNAL OF AN OFFICER IN THE KING'S GERMAN LEGION *by John Frederick Hering*—Recollections of Campaigning During the Napoleonic Wars.

JOURNAL OF AN ARMY SURGEON IN THE PENINSULAR WAR *by Charles Boutflower*—The Recollections of a British Army Medical Man on Campaign During the Napoleonic Wars.

ON CAMPAIGN WITH MOORE AND WELLINGTON *by Anthony Hamilton*—The Experiences of a Soldier of the 43rd Regiment During the Peninsular War.

THE ROAD TO AUSTERLITZ *by R. G. Burton*—Napoleon's Campaign of 1805.

SOLDIERS OF NAPOLEON *by A. J. Doisy De Villargennes & Arthur Chuquet*—The Experiences of the Men of the French First Empire: Under the Eagles by A. J. Doisy De Villargennes & Voices of 1812 by Arthur Chuquet.

INVASION OF FRANCE, 1814 *by F. W. O. Maycock*—The Final Battles of the Napoleonic First Empire.

LEIPZIG—A CONFLICT OF TITANS *by Frederic Shoberl*—A Personal Experience of the 'Battle of the Nations' During the Napoleonic Wars, October 14th-19th, 1813.

SLASHERS *by Charles Cadell*—The Campaigns of the 28th Regiment of Foot During the Napoleonic Wars by a Serving Officer.

BATTLE IMPERIAL *by Charles William Vane*—The Campaigns in Germany & France for the Defeat of Napoleon 1813-1814.

SWIFT & BOLD *by Gibbes Rigaud*—The 60th Rifles During the Peninsula War.

AVAILABLE ONLINE AT **www.leonaur.com**
AND FROM ALL GOOD BOOK STORES

ALSO FROM LEONAUR
AVAILABLE IN SOFTCOVER OR HARDCOVER WITH DUST JACKET

ADVENTURES OF A YOUNG RIFLEMAN by *Johann Christian Maempel*—The Experiences of a Saxon in the French & British Armies During the Napoleonic Wars.

THE HUSSAR by *Norbert Landsheit & G. R. Gleig*—A German Cavalryman in British Service Throughout the Napoleonic Wars.

RECOLLECTIONS OF THE PENINSULA by *Moyle Sherer*—An Officer of the 34th Regiment of Foot—'The Cumberland Gentlemen'—on Campaign Against Napoleon's French Army in Spain.

MARINE OF REVOLUTION & CONSULATE by *Moreau de Jonnès*—The Recollections of a French Soldier of the Revolutionary Wars 1791-1804.

GENTLEMEN IN RED by *John Dobbs & Robert Knowles*—Two Accounts of British Infantry Officers During the Peninsular War Recollections of an Old 52nd Man by John Dobbs An Officer of Fusiliers by Robert Knowles.

CORPORAL BROWN'S CAMPAIGNS IN THE LOW COUNTRIES by *Robert Brown*—Recollections of a Coldstream Guard in the Early Campaigns Against Revolutionary France 1793-1795.

THE 7TH (QUEENS OWN) HUSSARS: Volume 2—1793-1815 by *C. R. B. Barrett*—During the Campaigns in the Low Countries & the Peninsula and Waterloo Campaigns of the Napoleonic Wars. Volume 2: 1793-1815.

THE MARENGO CAMPAIGN 1800 by *Herbert H. Sargent*—The Victory that Completed the Austrian Defeat in Italy.

DONALDSON OF THE 94TH—SCOTS BRIGADE by *Joseph Donaldson*—The Recollections of a Soldier During the Peninsula & South of France Campaigns of the Napoleonic Wars.

A CONSCRIPT FOR EMPIRE by *Philippe as told to Johann Christian Maempel*—The Experiences of a Young German Conscript During the Napoleonic Wars.

JOURNAL OF THE CAMPAIGN OF 1815 by *Alexander Cavalié Mercer*—The Experiences of an Officer of the Royal Horse Artillery During the Waterloo Campaign.

NAPOLEON'S CAMPAIGNS IN POLAND 1806-7 by *Robert Wilson*—The campaign in Poland from the Russian side of the conflict.

AVAILABLE ONLINE AT **www.leonaur.com**
AND FROM ALL GOOD BOOK STORES

ALSO FROM LEONAUR
AVAILABLE IN SOFTCOVER OR HARDCOVER WITH DUST JACKET

OMPTEDA OF THE KING'S GERMAN LEGION by *Christian von Ompteda*—A Hanoverian Officer on Campaign Against Napoleon.

LIEUTENANT SIMMONS OF THE 95TH (RIFLES) *by George Simmons*—Recollections of the Peninsula, South of France & Waterloo Campaigns of the Napoleonic Wars.

A HORSEMAN FOR THE EMPEROR *by Jean Baptiste Gazzola*—A Cavalryman of Napoleon's Army on Campaign Throughout the Napoleonic Wars.

SERGEANT LAWRENCE *by William Lawrence*—With the 40th Regt. of Foot in South America, the Peninsular War & at Waterloo.

CAMPAIGNS WITH THE FIELD TRAIN *by Richard D. Henegan*—Experiences of a British Officer During the Peninsula and Waterloo Campaigns of the Napoleonic Wars.

CAVALRY SURGEON *by S. D. Broughton*—On Campaign Against Napoleon in the Peninsula & South of France During the Napoleonic Wars 1812-1814.

MEN OF THE RIFLES *by Thomas Knight, Henry Curling & Jonathan Leach*—The Reminiscences of Thomas Knight of the 95th (Rifles) by Thomas Knight, Henry Curling's Anecdotes by Henry Curling & The Field Services of the Rifle Brigade from its Formation to Waterloo by Jonathan Leach.

THE ULM CAMPAIGN 1805 *by F. N. Maude*—Napoleon and the Defeat of the Austrian Army During the 'War of the Third Coalition'.

SOLDIERING WITH THE 'DIVISION' *by Thomas Garrety*—The Military Experiences of an Infantryman of the 43rd Regiment During the Napoleonic Wars.

SERGEANT MORRIS OF THE 73RD FOOT *by Thomas Morris*—The Experiences of a British Infantryman During the Napoleonic Wars-Including Campaigns in Germany and at Waterloo.

A VOICE FROM WATERLOO *by Edward Cotton*—The Personal Experiences of a British Cavalryman Who Became a Battlefield Guide and Authority on the Campaign of 1815.

NAPOLEON AND HIS MARSHALS *by J. T. Headley*—The Men of the First Empire.

AVAILABLE ONLINE AT **www.leonaur.com**
AND FROM ALL GOOD BOOK STORES

ALSO FROM LEONAUR
AVAILABLE IN SOFTCOVER OR HARDCOVER WITH DUST JACKET

COLBORNE: A SINGULAR TALENT FOR WAR *by John Colborne*—The Napoleonic Wars Career of One of Wellington's Most Highly Valued Officers in Egypt, Holland, Italy, the Peninsula and at Waterloo.

NAPOLEON'S RUSSIAN CAMPAIGN *by Philippe Henri de Segur*—The Invasion, Battles and Retreat by an Aide-de-Camp on the Emperor's Staff.

WITH THE LIGHT DIVISION *by John H. Cooke*—The Experiences of an Officer of the 43rd Light Infantry in the Peninsula and South of France During the Napoleonic Wars.

WELLINGTON AND THE PYRENEES CAMPAIGN VOLUME I: FROM VITORIA TO THE BIDASSOA *by F. C. Beatson*—The final phase of the campaign in the Iberian Peninsula.

WELLINGTON AND THE INVASION OF FRANCE VOLUME II: THE BIDASSOA TO THE BATTLE OF THE NIVELLE *by F. C. Beatson*—The final phase of the campaign in the Iberian Peninsula.

WELLINGTON AND THE FALL OF FRANCE VOLUME III: THE GAVES AND THE BATTLE OF ORTHEZ *by F. C. Beatson*—The final phase of the campaign in the Iberian Peninsula.

NAPOLEON'S IMPERIAL GUARD: FROM MARENGO TO WATERLOO *by J. T. Headley*—The story of Napoleon's Imperial Guard and the men who commanded them.

BATTLES & SIEGES OF THE PENINSULAR WAR *by W. H. Fitchett*—Corunna, Busaco, Albuera, Ciudad Rodrigo, Badajos, Salamanca, San Sebastian & Others.

SERGEANT GUILLEMARD: THE MAN WHO SHOT NELSON? *by Robert Guillemard*—A Soldier of the Infantry of the French Army of Napoleon on Campaign Throughout Europe.

WITH THE GUARDS ACROSS THE PYRENEES *by Robert Batty*—The Experiences of a British Officer of Wellington's Army During the Battles for the Fall of Napoleonic France, 1813 .

A STAFF OFFICER IN THE PENINSULA *by E. W. Buckham*—An Officer of the British Staff Corps Cavalry During the Peninsula Campaign of the Napoleonic Wars.

THE LEIPZIG CAMPAIGN: 1813—NAPOLEON AND THE "BATTLE OF THE NATIONS" *by F. N. Maude*—Colonel Maude's analysis of Napoleon's campaign of 1813 around Leipzig.

AVAILABLE ONLINE AT **www.leonaur.com**
AND FROM ALL GOOD BOOK STORES

ALSO FROM LEONAUR
AVAILABLE IN SOFTCOVER OR HARDCOVER WITH DUST JACKET

BUGEAUD: A PACK WITH A BATON *by Thomas Robert Bugeaud*—The Early Campaigns of a Soldier of Napoleon's Army Who Would Become a Marshal of France.

WATERLOO RECOLLECTIONS *by Frederick Llewellyn*—Rare First Hand Accounts, Letters, Reports and Retellings from the Campaign of 1815.

SERGEANT NICOL *by Daniel Nicol*—The Experiences of a Gordon Highlander During the Napoleonic Wars in Egypt, the Peninsula and France.

THE JENA CAMPAIGN: 1806 *by F. N. Maude*—The Twin Battles of Jena & Auerstadt Between Napoleon's French and the Prussian Army.

PRIVATE O'NEIL *by Charles O'Neil*—The recollections of an Irish Rogue of H. M. 28th Regt.—The Slashers—during the Peninsula & Waterloo campaigns of the Napoleonic war.

ROYAL HIGHLANDER *by James Anton*—A soldier of H.M 42nd (Royal) Highlanders during the Peninsular, South of France & Waterloo Campaigns of the Napoleonic Wars.

CAPTAIN BLAZE *by Elzéar Blaze*—Life in Napoleons Army.

LEJEUNE VOLUME 1 *by Louis-François Lejeune*—The Napoleonic Wars through the Experiences of an Officer on Berthier's Staff.

LEJEUNE VOLUME 2 *by Louis-François Lejeune*—The Napoleonic Wars through the Experiences of an Officer on Berthier's Staff.

CAPTAIN COIGNET *by Jean-Roch Coignet*—A Soldier of Napoleon's Imperial Guard from the Italian Campaign to Russia and Waterloo.

FUSILIER COOPER *by John S. Cooper*—Experiences in the 7th (Royal) Fusiliers During the Peninsular Campaign of the Napoleonic Wars and the American Campaign to New Orleans.

FIGHTING NAPOLEON'S EMPIRE *by Joseph Anderson*—The Campaigns of a British Infantryman in Italy, Egypt, the Peninsular & the West Indies During the Napoleonic Wars.

CHASSEUR BARRES *by Jean-Baptiste Barres*—The experiences of a French Infantryman of the Imperial Guard at Austerlitz, Jena, Eylau, Friedland, in the Peninsular, Lutzen, Bautzen, Zinnwald and Hanau during the Napoleonic Wars.

AVAILABLE ONLINE AT **www.leonaur.com**
AND FROM ALL GOOD BOOK STORES

ALSO FROM LEONAUR
AVAILABLE IN SOFTCOVER OR HARDCOVER WITH DUST JACKET

CAPTAIN COIGNET by *Jean-Roch Coignet*—A Soldier of Napoleon's Imperial Guard from the Italian Campaign to Russia and Waterloo.

HUSSAR ROCCA by *Albert Jean Michel de Rocca*—A French cavalry officer's experiences of the Napoleonic Wars and his views on the Peninsular Campaigns against the Spanish, British And Guerilla Armies.

MARINES TO 95TH (RIFLES) by *Thomas Fernyhough*—The military experiences of Robert Fernyhough during the Napoleonic Wars.

LIGHT BOB by *Robert Blakeney*—The experiences of a young officer in H.M 28th & 36th regiments of the British Infantry during the Peninsular Campaign of the Napoleonic Wars 1804 - 1814.

WITH WELLINGTON'S LIGHT CAVALRY by *William Tomkinson*—The Experiences of an officer of the 16th Light Dragoons in the Peninsular and Waterloo campaigns of the Napoleonic Wars.

SERGEANT BOURGOGNE by *Adrien Bourgogne*—With Napoleon's Imperial Guard in the Russian Campaign and on the Retreat from Moscow 1812 - 13.

SURTEES OF THE 95TH (RIFLES) by *William Surtees*—A Soldier of the 95th (Rifles) in the Peninsular campaign of the Napoleonic Wars.

SWORDS OF HONOUR by *Henry Newbolt & Stanley L. Wood*—The Careers of Six Outstanding Officers from the Napoleonic Wars, the Wars for India and the American Civil War.

ENSIGN BELL IN THE PENINSULAR WAR by *George Bell*—The Experiences of a young British Soldier of the 34th Regiment 'The Cumberland Gentlemen' in the Napoleonic wars.

HUSSAR IN WINTER by *Alexander Gordon*—A British Cavalry Officer during the retreat to Corunna in the Peninsular campaign of the Napoleonic Wars.

THE COMPLEAT RIFLEMAN HARRIS by *Benjamin Harris as told to and transcribed by Captain Henry Curling, 52nd Regt. of Foot*—The adventures of a soldier of the 95th (Rifles) during the Peninsular Campaign of the Napoleonic Wars.

THE ADVENTURES OF A LIGHT DRAGOON by *George Farmer & G.R. Gleig*—A cavalryman during the Peninsular & Waterloo Campaigns, in captivity & at the siege of Bhurtpore, India.

AVAILABLE ONLINE AT **www.leonaur.com**
AND FROM ALL GOOD BOOK STORES

ALSO FROM LEONAUR
AVAILABLE IN SOFTCOVER OR HARDCOVER WITH DUST JACKET

THE LIFE OF THE REAL BRIGADIER GERARD VOLUME 1—THE YOUNG HUSSAR 1782-1807 *by Jean-Baptiste De Marbot*—A French Cavalryman Of the Napoleonic Wars at Marengo, Austerlitz, Jena, Eylau & Friedland.

THE LIFE OF THE REAL BRIGADIER GERARD VOLUME 2—IMPERIAL AIDE-DE-CAMP 1807-1811 *by Jean-Baptiste De Marbot*—A French Cavalryman of the Napoleonic Wars at Saragossa, Landshut, Eckmuhl, Ratisbon, Aspern-Essling, Wagram, Busaco & Torres Vedras.

THE LIFE OF THE REAL BRIGADIER GERARD VOLUME 3—COLONEL OF CHASSEURS 1811-1815 *by Jean-Baptiste De Marbot*—A French Cavalryman in the retreat from Moscow, Lutzen, Bautzen, Katzbach, Leipzig, Hanau & Waterloo.

THE INDIAN WAR OF 1864 *by Eugene Ware*—The Experiences of a Young Officer of the 7th Iowa Cavalry on the Western Frontier During the Civil War.

THE MARCH OF DESTINY *by Charles E. Young & V. Devinny*—Dangers of the Trail in 1865 by Charles E. Young & The Story of a Pioneer by V. Devinny, two Accounts of Early Emigrants to Colorado.

CROSSING THE PLAINS *by William Audley Maxwell*—A First Hand Narrative of the Early Pioneer Trail to California in 1857.

CHIEF OF SCOUTS *by William F. Drannan*—A Pilot to Emigrant and Government Trains, Across the Plains of the Western Frontier.

THIRTY-ONE YEARS ON THE PLAINS AND IN THE MOUNTAINS *by William F. Drannan*—William Drannan was born to be a pioneer, hunter, trapper and wagon train guide during the momentous days of the Great American West.

THE INDIAN WARS VOLUNTEER *by William Thompson*—Recollections of the Conflict Against the Snakes, Shoshone, Bannocks, Modocs and Other Native Tribes of the American North West.

THE 4TH TENNESSEE CAVALRY *by George B. Guild*—The Services of Smith's Regiment of Confederate Cavalry by One of its Officers.

COLONEL WORTHINGTON'S SHILOH *by T. Worthington*—The Tennessee Campaign, 1862, by an Officer of the Ohio Volunteers.

FOUR YEARS IN THE SADDLE *by W. L. Curry*—The History of the First Regiment Ohio Volunteer Cavalry in the American Civil War.

AVAILABLE ONLINE AT **www.leonaur.com**
AND FROM ALL GOOD BOOK STORES

ALSO FROM LEONAUR
AVAILABLE IN SOFTCOVER OR HARDCOVER WITH DUST JACKET

LIFE IN THE ARMY OF NORTHERN VIRGINIA by Carlton McCarthy—The Observations of a Confederate Artilleryman of Cutshaw's Battalion During the American Civil War 1861-1865.

HISTORY OF THE CAVALRY OF THE ARMY OF THE POTOMAC by Charles D. Rhodes—Including Pope's Army of Virginia and the Cavalry Operations in West Virginia During the American Civil War.

CAMP-FIRE AND COTTON-FIELD by Thomas W. Knox—A New York Herald Correspondent's View of the American Civil War.

SERGEANT STILLWELL by Leander Stillwell —The Experiences of a Union Army Soldier of the 61st Illinois Infantry During the American Civil War.

STONEWALL'S CANNONEER by Edward A. Moore—Experiences with the Rockbridge Artillery, Confederate Army of Northern Virginia, During the American Civil War.

THE SIXTH CORPS by George Stevens—The Army of the Potomac, Union Army, During the American Civil War.

THE RAILROAD RAIDERS by William Pittenger—An Ohio Volunteers Recollections of the Andrews Raid to Disrupt the Confederate Railroad in Georgia During the American Civil War.

CITIZEN SOLDIER by John Beatty—An Account of the American Civil War by a Union Infantry Officer of Ohio Volunteers Who Became a Brigadier General.

COX: PERSONAL RECOLLECTIONS OF THE CIVIL WAR--VOLUME 1 by Jacob Dolson Cox—West Virginia, Kanawha Valley, Gauley Bridge, Cotton Mountain, South Mountain, Antietam, the Morgan Raid & the East Tennessee Campaign.

COX: PERSONAL RECOLLECTIONS OF THE CIVIL WAR--VOLUME 2 by Jacob Dolson Cox—Siege of Knoxville, East Tennessee, Atlanta Campaign, the Nashville Campaign & the North Carolina Campaign.

KERSHAW'S BRIGADE VOLUME 1 by D. Augustus Dickert—Manassas, Seven Pines, Sharpsburg (Antietam), Fredricksburg, Chancellorsville, Gettysburg, Chickamauga, Chattanooga, Fort Sanders & Bean Station.

KERSHAW'S BRIGADE VOLUME 2 by D. Augustus Dickert—At the wilderness, Cold Harbour, Petersburg, The Shenandoah Valley and Cedar Creek..

AVAILABLE ONLINE AT **www.leonaur.com**
AND FROM ALL GOOD BOOK STORES

ALSO FROM LEONAUR
AVAILABLE IN SOFTCOVER OR HARDCOVER WITH DUST JACKET

THE RELUCTANT REBEL by William G. Stevenson—A young Kentuckian's experiences in the Confederate Infantry & Cavalry during the American Civil War..

BOOTS AND SADDLES by Elizabeth B. Custer—The experiences of General Custer's Wife on the Western Plains.

FANNIE BEERS' CIVIL WAR by Fannie A. Beers—A Confederate Lady's Experiences of Nursing During the Campaigns & Battles of the American Civil War.

LADY SALE'S AFGHANISTAN by Florentia Sale—An Indomitable Victorian Lady's Account of the Retreat from Kabul During the First Afghan War.

THE TWO WARS OF MRS DUBERLY by Frances Isabella Duberly—An Intrepid Victorian Lady's Experience of the Crimea and Indian Mutiny.

THE REBELLIOUS DUCHESS by Paul F. S. Dermoncourt—The Adventures of the Duchess of Berri and Her Attempt to Overthrow French Monarchy.

LADIES OF WATERLOO by Charlotte A. Eaton, Magdalene de Lancey & Juana Smith—The Experiences of Three Women During the Campaign of 1815: Waterloo Days by Charlotte A. Eaton, A Week at Waterloo by Magdalene de Lancey & Juana's Story by Juana Smith.

TWO YEARS BEFORE THE MAST by Richard Henry Dana. Jr.—The account of one young man's experiences serving on board a sailing brig—the Penelope—bound for California, between the years 1834-36.

A SAILOR OF KING GEORGE by Frederick Hoffman—From Midshipman to Captain—Recollections of War at Sea in the Napoleonic Age 1793-1815.

LORDS OF THE SEA by A. T. Mahan—Great Captains of the Royal Navy During the Age of Sail.

COGGESHALL'S VOYAGES: VOLUME 1 by George Coggeshall—The Recollections of an American Schooner Captain.

COGGESHALL'S VOYAGES: VOLUME 2 by George Coggeshall—The Recollections of an American Schooner Captain.

TWILIGHT OF EMPIRE by Sir Thomas Ussher & Sir George Cockburn—Two accounts of Napoleon's Journeys in Exile to Elba and St. Helena: Narrative of Events by Sir Thomas Ussher & Napoleon's Last Voyage: Extract of a diary by Sir George Cockburn.

AVAILABLE ONLINE AT **www.leonaur.com**
AND FROM ALL GOOD BOOK STORES

ALSO FROM LEONAUR
AVAILABLE IN SOFTCOVER OR HARDCOVER WITH DUST JACKET

ESCAPE FROM THE FRENCH *by Edward Boys*—A Young Royal Navy Midshipman's Adventures During the Napoleonic War.

THE VOYAGE OF H.M.S. PANDORA *by Edward Edwards R. N. & George Hamilton, edited by Basil Thomson*—In Pursuit of the Mutineers of the Bounty in the South Seas—1790-1791.

MEDUSA *by J. B. Henry Savigny and Alexander Correard and Charlotte-Adélaïde Dard*—Narrative of a Voyage to Senegal in 1816 & The Sufferings of the Picard Family After the Shipwreck of the Medusa.

THE SEA WAR OF 1812 VOLUME 1 *by A. T. Mahan*—A History of the Maritime Conflict.

THE SEA WAR OF 1812 VOLUME 2 *by A. T. Mahan*—A History of the Maritime Conflict.

WETHERELL OF H. M. S. HUSSAR *by John Wetherell*—The Recollections of an Ordinary Seaman of the Royal Navy During the Napoleonic Wars.

THE NAVAL BRIGADE IN NATAL *by C. R. N. Burne*—With the Guns of H. M. S. Terrible & H. M. S. Tartar during the Boer War 1899-1900.

THE VOYAGE OF H. M. S. BOUNTY *by William Bligh*—The True Story of an 18th Century Voyage of Exploration and Mutiny.

SHIPWRECK! *by William Gilly*—The Royal Navy's Disasters at Sea 1793-1849.

KING'S CUTTERS AND SMUGGLERS: 1700-1855 *by E. Keble Chatterton*—A unique period of maritime history-from the beginning of the eighteenth to the middle of the nineteenth century when British seamen risked all to smuggle valuable goods from wool to tea and spirits from and to the Continent.

CONFEDERATE BLOCKADE RUNNER *by John Wilkinson*—The Personal Recollections of an Officer of the Confederate Navy.

NAVAL BATTLES OF THE NAPOLEONIC WARS *by W. H. Fitchett*—Cape St. Vincent, the Nile, Cadiz, Copenhagen, Trafalgar & Others.

PRISONERS OF THE RED DESERT *by R. S. Gwatkin-Williams*—The Adventures of the Crew of the Tara During the First World War.

U-BOAT WAR 1914-1918 *by James B. Connolly/Karl von Schenk*—Two Contrasting Accounts from Both Sides of the Conflict at Sea During the Great War.

AVAILABLE ONLINE AT **www.leonaur.com**
AND FROM ALL GOOD BOOK STORES

ALSO FROM LEONAUR
AVAILABLE IN SOFTCOVER OR HARDCOVER WITH DUST JACKET

IRON TIMES WITH THE GUARDS *by An O. E. (G. P. A. Fildes)*—The Experiences of an Officer of the Coldstream Guards on the Western Front During the First World War.

THE GREAT WAR IN THE MIDDLE EAST: 1 *by W. T. Massey*—The Desert Campaigns & How Jerusalem Was Won---two classic accounts in one volume.

THE GREAT WAR IN THE MIDDLE EAST: 2 *by W. T. Massey*—Allenby's Final Triumph.

SMITH-DORRIEN *by Horace Smith-Dorrien*—Isandlwhana to the Great War.

1914 *by Sir John French*—The Early Campaigns of the Great War by the British Commander.

GRENADIER *by E. R. M. Fryer*—The Recollections of an Officer of the Grenadier Guards throughout the Great War on the Western Front.

BATTLE, CAPTURE & ESCAPE *by George Pearson*—The Experiences of a Canadian Light Infantryman During the Great War.

DIGGERS AT WAR *by R. Hugh Knyvett & G. P. Cuttriss*—"Over There" With the Australians by R. Hugh Knyvett and Over the Top With the Third Australian Division by G. P. Cuttriss. Accounts of Australians During the Great War in the Middle East, at Gallipoli and on the Western Front.

HEAVY FIGHTING BEFORE US *by George Brenton Laurie*—The Letters of an Officer of the Royal Irish Rifles on the Western Front During the Great War.

THE CAMELIERS *by Oliver Hogue*—A Classic Account of the Australians of the Imperial Camel Corps During the First World War in the Middle East.

RED DUST *by Donald Black*—A Classic Account of Australian Light Horsemen in Palestine During the First World War.

THE LEAN, BROWN MEN *by Angus Buchanan*—Experiences in East Africa During the Great War with the 25th Royal Fusiliers—the Legion of Frontiersmen.

THE NIGERIAN REGIMENT IN EAST AFRICA *by W. D. Downes*—On Campaign During the Great War 1916-1918.

THE 'DIE-HARDS' IN SIBERIA *by John Ward*—With the Middlesex Regiment Against the Bolsheviks 1918-19.

AVAILABLE ONLINE AT **www.leonaur.com**
AND FROM ALL GOOD BOOK STORES

ALSO FROM LEONAUR
AVAILABLE IN SOFTCOVER OR HARDCOVER WITH DUST JACKET

FARAWAY CAMPAIGN *by F. James*—Experiences of an Indian Army Cavalry Officer in Persia & Russia During the Great War.

REVOLT IN THE DESERT *by T. E. Lawrence*—An account of the experiences of one remarkable British officer's war from his own perspective.

MACHINE-GUN SQUADRON *by A. M. G.*—The 20th Machine Gunners from British Yeomanry Regiments in the Middle East Campaign of the First World War.

A GUNNER'S CRUSADE *by Antony Bluett*—The Campaign in the Desert, Palestine & Syria as Experienced by the Honourable Artillery Company During the Great War .

DESPATCH RIDER *by W. H. L. Watson*—The Experiences of a British Army Motorcycle Despatch Rider During the Opening Battles of the Great War in Europe.

TIGERS ALONG THE TIGRIS *by E. J. Thompson*—The Leicestershire Regiment in Mesopotamia During the First World War.

HEARTS & DRAGONS *by Charles R. M. F. Crutwell*—The 4th Royal Berkshire Regiment in France and Italy During the Great War, 1914-1918.

INFANTRY BRIGADE: 1914 *by John Ward*—The Diary of a Commander of the 15th Infantry Brigade, 5th Division, British Army, During the Retreat from Mons.

DOING OUR 'BIT' *by Ian Hay*—Two Classic Accounts of the Men of Kitchener's 'New Army' During the Great War including *The First 100,000* & *All In It*.

AN EYE IN THE STORM *by Arthur Ruhl*—An American War Correspondent's Experiences of the First World War from the Western Front to Gallipoli-and Beyond.

STAND & FALL *by Joe Cassells*—With the Middlesex Regiment Against the Bolsheviks 1918-19.

RIFLEMAN MACGILL'S WAR *by Patrick MacGill*—A Soldier of the London Irish During the Great War in Europe including *The Amateur Army*, *The Red Horizon* & *The Great Push*.

WITH THE GUNS *by C. A. Rose & Hugh Dalton*—Two First Hand Accounts of British Gunners at War in Europe During World War 1- Three Years in France with the Guns and With the British Guns in Italy.

THE BUSH WAR DOCTOR *by Robert V. Dolbey*—The Experiences of a British Army Doctor During the East African Campaign of the First World War.

AVAILABLE ONLINE AT **www.leonaur.com**
AND FROM ALL GOOD BOOK STORES

www.ingramcontent.com/pod-product-compliance
Lightning Source LLC
Chambersburg PA
CBHW030228170426
43201CB00006B/147